THE PRINCESS DES URSINS

Giraudon

THE PRINCESS DES URSINS

From a portrait by Largillière, reproduced by kind permission of the Duchesse de la Trémoïlle.

THE
PRINCESS DES URSINS

By
MAUD CRUTTWELL

London & Toronto
J. M. DENT AND SONS LTD.
NEW YORK: E. P. DUTTON & CO.

All rights reserved

FIRST PUBLISHED IN 1927

TO
THE PRINCESS MÉDIHA D'ÉGYPTE

INTRODUCTION

"It is a loss eternally to be regretted," writes Saint-Simon of the Princess des Ursins, "that this woman, illustrious among the most illustrious of her time, has left no memoir of her life, which would have been equally curious, agreeable and instructive." [1]

Saint-Simon does his best to compensate us for the lack in his own *Mémoires*, and a great part of our knowledge of her is obtained from them. His personal intimacy and the keen interest with which he follows her career make his writings concerning her invaluable, but he is too capricious and biased to be reliable. At the beginning of their friendship he paints her with a brush so overloaded with flowery praise as almost to swamp her personality, while after her rupture with his patron, the Duc d'Orléans, she becomes all that is diabolic and detestable. Nevertheless, prejudiced as he is, a better idea of the woman, if not of the politician, is obtained from him than from her more modern biographers.

Of these the most important are François Combes and A. Geffroy, but in the study by the former the numerous errors and unauthenticated statements render it more dangerous than useful, while that of Geffroy, though reliable as far as it goes, is little more than a series of notes to the documents discovered and published by him.

Of necessity then in studying the life of the Princess we have to go to the source itself, and this source is a mass of correspondence prolix and often insignificant, and for the

[1] Saint-Simon, v. 514, appendix vi.

most part ill-arranged and unindexed. Two works, however, in the mass of letters and memoirs, of futile pamphlets and notices, stand out like rocks for the student's salvation, the recently published and still incomplete *Mémoires de Saint-Simon*, edited by A. de Boislisle, with its numerous notes and documents,[1] and the collection of letters entitled *Madame des Ursins* published in 1902 by the Duc de la Trémoïlle, chief of the house of which her own was a younger branch. These have been selected and arranged with so much skill that they form in themselves the best existing biography—I had almost written autobiography —of the Princess.

My first idea was to write as far as possible on the same lines, that is to say, to extract all that is of interest concerning her private life and public career from the documents and contemporary literature, and without comment or criticism of my own to bind them together and let them speak for themselves. Unfortunately, such a system is possible only during the fifteen years of her public life, when both documents and notices are voluminous enough. Yet the fact that her first fifty-eight years and the last seven of her old age are veiled in almost complete obscurity which, with the exception of Geffroy, no one has tried to penetrate, and the psychological interest of the few existing notices of these epochs, induced me to include them also in my biography. It is at this later period when, brutally expelled from public life, she lived in enforced

[1] All extracts from the *Mémoires de Saint-Simon* are from the edition of A. de Boislisle in "Les Grands Ecrivains de la France," not yet completed. The Duc de Saint-Simon was accustomed from his early youth to jot down notes for these *Mémoires* which he was preparing in secret, but it was not till 1729, when he had retired more or less from the Court, that he devoted himself to their arrangement, aided by the *Journal* of the Marquis de Dangeau, the manuscript of which had been lent him in that year.

retirement, that one would naturally expect her to have been engaged on her Memoirs, but her nature was too energetic to dwell on the past, and up to the end of her long life she employed herself on a reduced scale in the same way as in her days of glory, with the affairs of kings and the intrigues of a court, though the King was without a throne and the Court but the miniature imitation of James Stuart the Pretender in Rome.

The life of the Princess des Ursins is as full of extraordinary episodes, her character as harmonious and complete, her rise to power as marvellous and her fall as dramatic and tragic as the most imaginative novelist could conceive. The woman whose personal charm twice seduced Louis XIV. and who retained it up to her death at eighty; who governed Spain during fourteen years with the most absolute power and almost succeeded at the age of seventy-four in marrying its sovereign, aged thirty-two; who held her own against the despotic tyranny of the arch-egoist Louis XIV.; whose political acumen saved Spain from the clutches of France and Austria and established the present dynasty on the throne in independence, is a heroine worthy of a more skilful pen than mine, and I can claim for my work only that it is honest and complete, that nothing of interest concerning her has been omitted, and that no statement has been made without the support of documentary evidence.

MAUD CRUTTWELL.

PARIS, 1927.

CONTENTS

PART I

CHAP.		PAGE
	INTRODUCTION	vii
I.	PRINCESSE DE CHALAIS	3
II.	EARLY AMBITIONS	10
III.	DUCHESS OF BRACCIANO	17
IV.	ROME AND PARIS (1675–95)	24
V.	PRINCESS DES URSINS	34
VI.	ACCESSION OF PHILIPPE D'ANJOU TO THE THRONE OF SPAIN (1700)	44
VII.	INSTRUCTIONS OF LOUIS XIV. TO HIS GRANDSON (1700)	49
VIII.	CAMARERA MAYOR (1701)	52
IX.	ROYAL PUPPETS (1701)	63
X.	THE MARRIAGE (1701)	71
XI.	FIRST INCIDENTS OF THE WAR	82
XII.	THE ART OF REIGNING (1702)	88
XIII.	PHILIPPE V. IN ITALY (1702)	99
XIV.	STRUGGLES FOR THE MASTERY (1703)	109
XV.	THE QUARRELS CONTINUE (1703)	120
XVI.	THE ANNOTATED LETTER (1703)	128
XVII.	FIRST DISGRACE OF THE PRINCESS (1704)	139
XVIII.	THE DUC DE GRAMONT (1704)	147
XIX.	TRIUMPH OF THE PRINCESS (1704–5)	155
XX.	VISIONS OF A CROWN (1705)	165
XXI.	TREACHERY OF PHILIPPE V. (1705)	169
XXII.	RETURN OF THE PRINCESS (1705)	177

PART II

I.	IN DEFENCE OF A MONARCHY (1705)	185
II.	THE FLIGHT TO BURGOS (1706)	191
III.	BIRTH OF THE PRINCE OF THE ASTURIAS (1707)	199
IV.	THE DUC D'ORLÉANS (1707)	204

CHAP.		PAGE
V.	Second Campaign of the Duc d'Orléans (1708)	210
VI.	Conspiracy of Philippe d'Orléans (1709)	217
VII.	Dictatress of Spain (1709)	222
VIII.	Intrigues to force the Princess to Retire (1709)	230
IX.	The Princess remains (1710)	242
X.	The Duc de Vendôme in Spain (1710)	248
XI.	Signs of Peace (1711)	259
XII.	The Sovereignty (1711)	264
XIII.	Deaths of Louis' Heirs (1712)	273
XIV.	Peace without Honour (1713)	284
XV.	Death of the Queen (1714)	292
XVI.	Alleged Sequestration of the King (1714)	295
XVII.	The Peace of Rastadt (1714)	305
XVIII.	Alberoni (1714)	310
XIX.	D'Aubigny the Faithless (1714)	322
XX.	Elisabeth Farnese (1714)	327
XXI.	Disgrace of the Princess (1714)	341
XXII.	Expulsion (1715)	356
XXIII.	Hopes and Fears (1715)	365
XXIV.	Disgrace at Versailles (1715)	377
XXV.	Upheavals in Madrid (1715)	386
XXVI.	Farewell to France (1715)	390
XXVII.	Death of Louis XIV. (1715)	396
XXVIII.	Lex Talionis (1715–21)	402
XXIX.	"I have fought a Good Fight, I have finished my Course" (1716–22)	408
	Bibliography	422
	Table of Events	424
	Index	435

LIST OF ILLUSTRATIONS

THE PRINCESS DES URSINS . . . . *Frontispiece*
From a portrait by Largillière, reproduced by kind permission of the Duchesse de la Trémoïlle.

PHILIPPE V. . . . . *facing page* 62
From a portrait by Rigaud in the Musée du Louvre.

LOUIS XIV. . . . . ,, 186
From a portrait by Rigaud in the Musée du Louvre.

LOUIS DE BOURBON, DUC DE VENDÔME . . ,, 249
From a contemporary engraving.

MADAME DE MAINTENON . . . . . ,, 306
From a portrait by Mignard in the Musée du Louvre.

MADAME, DUCHESSE D'ORLÉANS, PRINCESSE PALATINE . . . . ,, 377
From a portrait by Largillière in the Musée de Chantilly.

THE PRINCESS DES URSINS
PART I

PART I

CHAPTER I

PRINCESSE DE CHALAIS

MARIE-ANNE DE LA TRÉMOÏLLE is the name of the illustrious woman foremost among the politicians of her day, twice nearly crowned queen, better known as the Princess des Ursins. Practically dictatress of Spain during the first part of the reign of the miserable weakling placed by Louis XIV. as his viceroy on the throne, during the long war of Spanish Succession in which she played so prominent a part, she succeeded singlehanded and in the teeth of all Europe in wresting it from the clutches of Austria, and in defiance of Louis himself in preserving it from French domination. History records no such brilliant example of feminine courage and capability, yet she is known but little to the general public even in France, and in our own country hardly at all.

Even the date of her birth is doubtful, some placing it as early as 1636, others at 1642. The latter is the date accepted in this book as the most probable. It is sufficiently marvellous, even so, that a woman whose youth and early maturity had been passed in relative obscurity should suddenly leap to the supreme place she occupied in European politics at the age of sixty. Yet this must perforce be accepted, as well as the fact that fifteen years later she was still in possession, not only of her extraordinary mental faculties and physical energy, but also of the irresistible charm and seduction which had twice turned the head of Louis himself.

Nothing in her ancestry accounts for her remarkable personality and genius. On her father's side she belonged to all that was noblest in France, it is true, but of no exceptional brilliance. The Dukes of La Trémoïlle, of which her own family was a younger branch, were Counts of Poitou at the date of the Norman Conquest and allied by marriage with the Kings of France. Her father, Louis de la Trémoïlle, Marquis de Noirmoutier, had been rewarded for his military services with the title of duke, but *à brevet* only, that is to say, not hereditary. On her mother's side she belonged to the middle classes, for the marquis had married the daughter of Jean Aubry, a wealthy lawyer, distinguished in his profession since he was president of the Chambres des Comptes, but "not born," in the cant phraseology of the day.

She was one of nine children, but two only besides herself are of any importance in our history. The eldest son, exiled at the same time as her husband for taking part in a duel, died fighting in Portugal in 1667, and the title—marquis only—was inherited by his brother Antoine-François, several years her senior. As the latter played an important part in the later history of the Princess, a few words concerning him will not be out of place.

Here is his portrait, traced by the vivacious pen of the Duc de Saint-Simon:

> He was one of the handsomest and best-made men of his day, very intelligent, agreeable and gay, solid and of equal value in society and business. Thus he made his way, his brilliance and talents causing him to be sought out by the best company of the court. But the small-pox, which attacked him as he was on his way to join the court at Chambord and blinded him in both eyes, arrested at eighteen years at its commencement a life so full of promise. In his despair he shut himself up for many years, unwilling to be seen by anyone, soothing his grief with continual reading; and as there was nothing to dissipate his thoughts he never forgot anything, and unconsciously modelled himself on all he read. The Comte de Fiesque, friend of his youth, finally went to live with him, and tormented him so much that he forced him to tolerate some company, and with one and another he soon saw many people, and his house became the centre of all that was best and choicest, on account of his agreeable conversation, his reliable qualities, and the solidity and excellence of his counsels. His mind was straightforward and just, and he had a great facility of imagination and speech. Fashion is everything. It became the mode to be received by him, and without quitting his own house he had friends very important by rank and position, and took part in an infinity of affairs. Without posing as important he became so actually, and his house a tribunal whose approval counted and where it was flattering to be admitted. The marvel is that, although poor, he built himself a charming house in Paris at the end of the Rue de

Grenelle, of which he himself arranged the distribution and proportions even to the mirrors, cornices and chimney-pieces, and chose by touch the stuffs for the furniture.[1]

The Noirmoutier family had never been rich, and on emerging from his isolation, and resuming his place in society, the marquis sought wealth in a wife. But, poor and blind, it was not so easy to find an heiress in his own class, so he decided to take one from that below him, to whom his name would be some compensation. Thus in 1688 he married the rich widow of a lawyer, Madame Brémond, daughter of another lawyer—La Grange-Trianon, President of the Court of Appeal, who died a year later, leaving him all her fortune.

He remained a widower till 1700, when he married another heiress, again the daughter of a lawyer—Duret de Chevry. This year marks the beginning of his sister's brilliant career, and she (in the words of Saint-Simon) "cried out against the *mésalliance* as though her own mother, as well as her two grandmothers, had not been daughters of lawyers."[2] The marriage, however, turned out well and his new wife exceedingly devoted. Besides being blind, the marquis suffered from a malady of the stomach which prevented his taking any other nourishment than milk, which rendered him so weak that he could never move from his chair. His wife nursed him devotedly through all his illnesses, and loved him so sincerely that she died of grief a few days after his death. We shall meet this admirable brother several times in the course of our history. Always a good friend and wise counsellor to his sister, he was one of the few who remained faithful in her adversity. The benefits were reciprocal, for in spite of her anger at his *mésalliance* she procured him the title of duke with the full honours of heredity, so that her "unborn" sister-in-law had eventually her *tabouret* at Versailles.

Another brother, the Abbé Joseph-Emmanuel de la Trémoïlle, who also figures, though less honourably, in her life, was of a very different type. Of him Saint-Simon writes: "A little hunchback, very ugly, very debauched, who could never learn to do anything conformable to his profession, which he had chosen only to repair his poverty

---

[1] Saint-Simon, vii. 65 and 389, and xiii. 63.
[2] Ibid., xiii. 65.

by its benefices. He had intelligence, an agreeable wit, and was a pleasant companion, but had no sort of solidity and thought only of pleasure." [1] Of his frivolity and foolish insults to his sister at the beginning of her career, and ingratitude towards her at the close, we shall speak in place. She gauged him at his worth, and had for him neither esteem nor affection. Nevertheless, for her own aggrandisement, rather than his benefit, and in spite of the Pope's reluctance, she had him raised to the dignity of cardinal—a despicable figure, but prosperous, up to the last.

Of her three sisters one only appears in her history— Louise-Angélique, her junior by seven years. She was a child of her epoch, gay, frivolous and self-indulgent, with beautiful eyes, great charm, and a talent for poetry. At the beginning of her career, when she herself was the wife of one of the greatest nobles in Italy, the Princess married her to the Duke Lanti delle Rovere, and the two sisters took the lead in the fashionable Roman world and counted half the College of Cardinals among their lovers. She died before the Princess's advent to power, but the latter befriended her two children, sent for them to Spain, heaped titles upon them, and married them both brilliantly.

Another sister, Yolande-Julie, married in 1675 her cousin the Marquis de Royan, son of the Duc de la Trémoïlle, and died in 1693, leaving a daughter whom the Princess also befriended and married well. Always good to her relatives, in her days of power she raised them all to high rank and loaded them with titles and wealth, and with the exception of the Abbé all responded by affectionate devotion. But it is time to dismiss them into the background, from whence they will emerge from time to time, and make way for the brilliant figure of the Princess herself.

In 1659, at the age of seventeen, she married Adrien-Blaise de Talleyrand, Prince de Chalais, of whom little is known. According to Saint-Simon (who despised everyone below the rank of duke and peer of France) he was "without rank or distinction whatever," but he belonged nevertheless to the ancient family of Talleyrand-Perigord, sovereign counts from the beginning of the twelfth century.

The only notice we have of her during her early married life in Paris seems to show that her native air was not

[1] Saint-Simon, xiii. 68.

PRINCESSE DE CHALAIS

stimulating to her latent genius, and that she differed in no way from other young girls of rank and beauty.

This notice, which recurs *ad nauseam* in all books concerning her great rival Madame de Maintenon, is found in the *Souvenirs* of that lady's niece, Madame de Caylus. Madame de Maintenon, then Madame Scarron, had, as is well known, an ardent admirer and would-be lover in the Maréchal d'Albret and was constantly at his house, where the Princess was also a frequent guest.

> I have heard Madame de Chalais say, in talking to Madame de Maintenon [writes Madame de Caylus], that she was very impatient because the Maréchal and other important personages had always so many things to say to her in secret, while she, the Princess, was left with the young people as though she were incapable of serious talk. Madame de Maintenon confessed to me with the same frankness that she herself was no less bored by these confidences which Madame des Ursins envied her, and would often have liked to be thought less serious that she might amuse herself, and not be forced to listen to the complaints and projects of the courtiers.[1]

An interesting glimpse enough: these two women destined to play such important parts in European history, rivals already, the Princess with all the prestige of her high rank and beauty neglected for the wife of Scarron, a mere hanger-on in the house, poor and socially unimportant, yet already singled out and deferred to.

In 1663 her husband, together with her brother, the Marquis de Noirmoutier, was disgraced for taking part in a duel, four against four, very notorious in its day, the result of a quarrel which took place at Versailles, in which the Marquis d'Antin was killed. Louis, who detested duelling and repressed it rigorously, was furious, and condemned all the survivors to the Bastille. The Marquis de Noirmoutier, though badly wounded, managed to escape to Portugal, where he died four years later fighting against Spain. The Prince de Chalais fled to Spain, where, strangely enough, he took service on the opposite side and fought against the Portuguese.

Was it fear for her own safety, husband and brother

---

[1] Caylus, *Souvenirs*, ed. Raunié (Paris, 1881), p. 18. Madame de Maintenon also refers to it in a letter to the Princess. See Bossange, *Lettres inédites de Madame de Maintenon et la Princesse des Ursins* (Paris, 1826), ii. 380; letter of 29 April, 1713.

being both compromised, or was it conjugal virtue, or perhaps love, which made the Princess, at the age of twenty-one, abandon home and country to follow her husband into exile? Whatever the motive, the act brought its reward, and was the first step on the ladder which led to her future triumphs, for while her husband was earning laurels in Portugal, she in Madrid was laying the basis of her incredible success, winning by her grace and charm the friendship of all that was most important at the Spanish Court.

For if in Paris she had been obscure and neglected, she was by no means so in Madrid, where at once she took a foremost place at Court, in high favour with the two most influential personages of the kingdom, no less than the Queen-Regent herself, sister of the Emperor Leopold of Germany and mother of Charles II., then in his minority, and her Prime Minister and favourite the Austrian Jesuit Nidhardt.

Seven years were thus spent basking in royal favour, but we are without further news concerning her, and the next notice we have is that she and her husband had left Spain for Italy.[1] It would be idle to speculate as to the reason for this abandonment of a court where she had been so well received. Disgrace it was not, since she retained the Queen's favour. All that is known is that in 1670 they were established in Rome, that the Prince left his wife there in order to seek service at the Court of Venice, and that he was taken ill before he arrived, and died at Mestre.

Saint-Simon gives the following account of these events, unsupported, however, by any documentary evidence:

In Spain they were not happy and went to Italy, and while undecided what to do, curiosity attracted them to Rome, where they remained for some time in search of a post. The

[1] La Beaumelle, among the many fraudulent documents he attributes to Madame de Maintenon, gives a letter to a certain Madame de Chanteloup under the date 28 April, 1666, supposed to have been written after the death of Scarron, at the moment of her deepest financial misery, in which the following words occur: "Madame de Chalais has offered me her protection but without meaning it (*du bout des lèvres*). Madame de Lyonne told me, 'I will see—I will speak—,' in the same tone in which she would have said the contrary. Everyone offers me help and no one gives it" (La Beaumelle, *Lettres de Madame de Mainienon*, ed. Rollin (1752), i. 33). Lavallée, while condemning the letter as false, omits to state in proof that at this date Madame de Chalais was in Spain.

service of Venice seemed better than nothing. Chalais wished to engage himself, and died on the way thither at the village of Mestre, near Venice, in 1670. It was strange news for his wife, who had remained in Rome and had made many friends there.[1]

She took his death so much to heart, say her biographers, that she retired to a convent and for a long while refused to go into the world. That she retired to a convent is true, but is neither a proof of austerity nor extreme grief, since it was the custom for ladies of rank travelling alone, in default of palace-hotels, to lodge in a convent. It will be seen later that, when leading the gayest, most worldly life, flirting with all the Sacred College and otherwise amusing herself, she was still in a convent, and when, after her second marriage, she visited Paris, she frequently stayed in the Convent of the Holy Sacrament at Montmartre, a retreat so little austere that, in the words of Saint-Simon, "she received there her friends and all the court."

Not that I would insinuate that she did not mourn her husband with decent and genuine grief, but a series of interesting documents prove that, during the first years of her widowhood, her energies were engaged more profitably than in bewailing the inevitable.

Madame de Sévigné wrote to her daughter on 20 April, 1672, as follows:

Madame de Chalais is mad. They think her so here in Paris. What an idea to go about Italy like a *princesse infortunée* instead of coming back to Paris and living peaceably with her mother, who adores her.[2]

Far from being mad, the Princess was at that time most sanely occupied with a very important affair—no less than to obtain from the Emperor of Germany the title and treatment of Princess of the Empire, a fact omitted by all the biographers but of much importance in the study of her life and character. Of so much importance indeed as to demand a chapter to itself.

[1] Saint-Simon, v. 495, appendix vi. The accounts vary, some saying that she had preceded her husband to Rome and that he died on the journey from Spain to join her.
[2] *Lettres de Madame de Sévigné* (Paris, 1852), iii. 26.

CHAPTER II

EARLY AMBITIONS

THE key to the character of the Princess des Ursins, the dominant force which explains all her achievements, all her failures and her final ruin, was an innate and apparently irresistible ambition, a craving for self-aggrandisement so violent as to force her, otherwise prudent and reasonable, to commit the most rash and imprudent acts, which but for the recognition of this as an obsession, almost a mania, would be entirely unaccountable.

At this commencement of her career it forced her to take a treasonable step which, had it succeeded, might have changed the whole aspect of European affairs, and it is a question whether, with so prodigious a weight in the balance, the War of Succession would not have ended in favour of Austria and Europe been spared fifteen years of bloodshed and misery. On such threads hang the fate of nations.

So strange, however, does it appear that the woman who spent twenty-five years in the service of Louis XIV., and fifteen in that of Philippe V. of Spain, should have been thus eager to sell herself to their worst enemy, that it needs the support of the most irrefutable documents to be credited.

Although in her defence it may be said that her husband and brother had been treated with unjust severity, exiled for an act which only royal prejudice could construe into a crime, yet it would seem that puerile vengeance had little or no place in the mind of the Princess, so teeming, even at this early age, with high ambitions as to exclude all lesser vices. It will be remarked also that from beginning to end of her career she showed a rare indifference to that deceptive form of egoism known as patriotism. She was cosmopolitan in the largest sense of the word. Her fatherland was the country which best remunerated her services, and she placed no sort of value on her birthright, which,

EARLY AMBITIONS

considering her epoch and ancient lineage, is curious, to say the least. But apologies are futile and the Princess herself would have disdained them. The fact remains that to satisfy her ambitions she was ready to repudiate her country, eager to devote all her wits and energy to the service of its arch-enemy the Emperor, if he would but consent to reward her with the rank she coveted—a rank modest enough when compared to her later aspirations.

Here is the story of her first struggle for a diadem, and its failure:

Nidhardt, confessor and favourite of the Queen-Regent of Spain,[1] was made Prime Minister in 1666, but his arrogance and incompetence stung the grandees to such a pitch of fury that to avoid a revolution she was forced to dismiss him, and in 1669 had sent him into honourable exile in Rome as ambassador at the Papal Court. On the arrival there a year later of the Princesse de Chalais they had renewed their relations, probably of an amorous nature, and to such a point of senility (he was then sixty-six) did she reduce him that he had the audacity to claim for her from the Emperor of Germany, without any sort of adequate reason, the title and treatment of Princess of the Empire.

Now the Queen-Regent, his own sister, had already demanded this dignity for her favourite and been refused, but it would be to mistake the Princess's character to suppose that she was discouraged. On the contrary, rebuffs seem but to have stimulated her energies, and on this occasion she set all machinery in motion to achieve her end.

Her first step had been to interest the Spanish Ambassador at the Court of Vienna in her claim, and to this end she had already dispatched certain agents to plead her cause, but this apparently having failed, she persuaded Nidhardt to intercede in her favour, which he did in the following letter, dated 23 September, 1673:

> Madame la Princesse de Chalais, wife of the Prince de Chalais, French gentleman who has very well served His Majesty in the war with Portugal, desires to obtain the title of Princess of the Empire. To this end the Queen our Sovereign has written to His Imperial Majesty to recommend her. This

[1] He received the cardinal's hat only in 1672.

lady, besides the motives already alleged by herself which her agent has exposed to Your Excellency, has much merit in addition to the great attachment she bears to the Crown and the fact that she desires to live under no other protection than that of this very august House. I wish to serve her in all that can be agreeable to her and beg Your Excellency to assist her demand in taking all suitable steps with His Majesty the Emperor and his Ministers.[1]

To which the Ambassador, not being in love with the Princess and apparently rather horrified at her audacity, replied with no great encouragement:

I will try to serve the Princesse de Chalais in her request for the title of Princess of the Empire, and I shall solicit it all the more strongly that Your Eminence tells me how much you desire it, but . . . I do not hide from Your Eminence, knowing the importance of the request, that I doubt if it will be accorded.[2]

This rebuff only stimulated the Princess to fresh activities and decided her to call up her reserve forces and attack at headquarters.

Three cardinals besides Nidhardt were pressed into her service to plead for her with the Emperor himself and expose the reasons why he should thus honour her, as we learn from a letter written later by the Cardinal d'Estrées. Who they were may be guessed without difficulty. First the Cardinal de Bouillon, himself Prince of the Empire and although nominally in Louis' service, paying treacherously his court to the Emperor Leopold; the Cardinal Porto-Carrero, the most important of the Spanish statesmen, and lastly the Cardinal d'Estrées himself, brother and coadjutor of the Duc d'Estrées, then French Ambassador at the Papal Court, all of them, if report be true, her lovers.

What they wrote is not forthcoming, but the letter of Nidhardt has survived and is worth quoting in part as a curiosity.

HOLY, IMPERIAL AND ROYAL MAJESTY,—The Queen my Sovereign has been kind enough to write to Your Imperial Majesty in favour of Doña Marianne de la Trémoïlle, Princesse de Chalais . . . lending thus her Royal services to her great desire to obtain that Your Majesty in His Imperial and Royal

[1] De Courcy, *L'Espagne après la paix d'Utrecht* (Paris. 1891), 26.
[2] Ibid., op. cit., 27; letter of 10 October, 1673.

EARLY AMBITIONS

Greatness would do her the honour to accord her the title and treatment of Princess of the Empire, and this in consideration of the good services rendered by her husband the Prince de Chalais to the Crown of His Catholic Majesty [1] during the war with Portugal, and because of her great personal merits, to which those of her blood are not inferior, that of La Trémoïlle being among the most illustrious and ancient in the Kingdom of France. . . . I consider very justly the uselessness of my humble prayers when the Sovereign supplications of the Queen intervene . . . and may therefore dispense with them, but at the same time, *knowing that other Cardinals are writing to Your Imperial Majesty to make known to Him the great qualities of the Princess*, I cannot renounce the merit I hope to gain in exposing to your Majesty . . . that this lady, for the motives I have just named, as well as for her affection, zeal and inclination for your very august House, deserves that Your Majesty confer on her this honour. . . . I can attest to Your Imperial Majesty the truth of all I say, given the knowledge I have of her since the time she has been residing here in a convent, and I add that I esteem it useful to the Royal Service of Your Imperial Majesty that this favour be accorded her. For besides . . . the personal merits of the Princess it will be very agreeable to the Queen my Sovereign who wishes her the greatest welfare. . . . And I, placing myself at the Imperial and Royal feet of Your Imperial Majesty, beg you with the greatest veneration *to accord to this lady* and at the same time to myself, *the honour of being employed in the Royal Service of Your Imperial Majesty*.[2]

What the result of this combined attack might have been we have no means of judging, for the outbreak of hostilities between France and Germany put a stop to further negotiations and she received a peremptory order from the Ambassador to cease all relations with Nidhardt and the other Spanish cardinals. This order, however, she flatly refused to obey, declaring publicly that she would not fail in gratitude towards the Queen-Regent who had treated herself and her husband with so much kindness, and that besides these obligations "she would always be both by taste and inclination a Spaniard."[3]

Whether Louis' order was a protest against her treasonable manœuvres or merely a general warning usual at the declaration of war is uncertain, but that the affair was

[1] The King of Spain.
[2] De Courcy, *L'Espagne après la paix d'Utrecht* (Paris, 1891), 26. The italics are my own.
[3] Ibid., 30.

commented on and disapproved at Versailles is known by a letter written thirty years later by one of her bitterest enemies, Louville, of whom more than enough will be heard in place, who cited it among her many crimes. "The hatred of Madame des Ursins for the French and all that belongs to France is notorious," he wrote in 1703; "when I was in Rome little else was spoken of. While she was there she always flattered the Spanish even when we were at war with them, and during that time was preparing honours for herself at the Court of Vienna." [1]

Far from bringing her any punishment, however, it seems to have served her ambitions, for the Sacred College came again to the rescue in the person of Cardinal d'Estrées, at this time one of her most ardent admirers. It may be, as Saint-Simon says, that, struck by her ability and intelligence, he was sincerely anxious to secure her services for France, but it seems more likely that, foiled in her hopes for advancement in Austria, the Princess had herself turned her thoughts to the French Court and had cajoled him as she had Nidhardt to plead her cause. At any rate, plead her cause he did and with such warmth that she at once obtained the position she coveted, namely to employ her beauty and intelligence in the service of the King of France with a pension of ten thousand francs a year. In other words, she was appointed secret agent of Versailles with the mission to win over the Spanish subjects in Italy to vote for the Bourbon succession to the Throne of Spain.

"She had recourse in Rome," writes Saint-Simon, "to the Cardinals d'Estrées and de Bouillon, who first began to notice her out of respect for her name and country, but soon after for more sentimental reasons." [2]

Michelet, venomous and epigrammatic as usual, accuses her of "trailing about Rome, aged mistress of cardinals, of d'Estrées and Bouillon, *galante* at sixty." [3]

Galante at sixty and even at seventy she remained, but when she was "trailing about Rome" with cardinals at her heels she was little over thirty. At the age of sixty she had had more than enough of them and was bent on much higher game.

But it is time to give a description of this woman endowed

[1] Saint-Simon, vi. 513, appendix vii.
[2] Ibid., v. 103.
[3] Michelet, *Histoire de France*, xiii. 170 (Paris, 1896).

EARLY AMBITIONS

with so many extraordinary gifts that among them her beauty though great was thrown in the shade. All her contemporaries are unanimous in their verdict that her irresistible attraction lay in her intelligence, her eloquence and her personal charm and distinction. Unfortunately the few portraits of her which exist are poor and mannered and give little idea of her personality.[1]

But if painted portraits are lacking, the description of her by Saint-Simon is so vivid as almost to compensate for their absence. Thirty-three years her junior, Saint-Simon was in his youth among her most ardent admirers and she may be said to fill in his *Mémoires* the rôle of heroine, so often does she appear and reappear in defiance of tautology and chronological sequence, and although as sycophant of her enemy the Duc d'Orléans he thought fit later to attack, calumniate and even betray her, his early notices are full of praise and appreciation. Here are extracts from his long and famous descriptions:

> She was tall rather than short, dark, with blue eyes, which said without ceasing all that she pleased; with a perfect figure, a beautiful neck, and a face which, without beauty, was charming. An air extremely noble, something majestic in all her bearing, and a grace so natural and constant, even in the smallest and most indifferent things, that I have never seen any other approach her either in body or intelligence, of which she had an infinity and of all kinds. Flattering, caressing, insinuating, measured, desirous of pleasing, and with a charm impossible to resist when she wished to be seductive; with a grand manner, which nevertheless attracted instead of repelling; a conversation delicious, inexhaustible, and very amusing besides, because of all she had seen and known of men and countries; a voice and enunciation extremely agreeable and an air of sweetness. She had also read much and was given to much reflection. Very courteous, but with great distinction, and above all very careful not to obtrude herself except with dignity and discretion. . . . The person in the world most fit for intrigues. . . . Very ambitious, but with ambitions vast

[1] In the possession of the Duchesse de la Trémoïlle is a life-sized portrait painted in her youth. (*See* frontispiece.) Another belongs to the Prince de Bauffrement-Courtenay, and a chalk drawing to the Duke of Alva in Madrid. A poor mannered engraving forms the frontispiece to vol. i. of the Duc de la Trémoïlle's collection of her letters, and another, equally poor, to vol. xxvii. of Dalloye's edition of the *Mémoires de Saint-Simon*. As far as I know these are the only existing portraits of her, a fact which says much for her lack of vanity.

and far above those of her sex and of the ordinary ambitions of men. With her, to exist and to rule were synonymous. She had besides, without letting it be seen, the most subtle mind in the world. . . . *Galanterie* and obstinacy as to her appearance were her chief weaknesses and dominated everything even in her old age, resulting in unsuitable clothes and finery. . . . At bottom haughty and proud, making straight for her ends without troubling herself much as to the means, but honest when it was possible. By nature kind and obliging but wanting nothing by halves, and that her friends should be hers unreservedly. Thus she was an ardent and excellent friend, of a friendship which neither time nor absence could weaken, and consequently a cruel and implacable enemy, pursuing her hatred even to Hell. . . . In all her words an eloquence simple and natural . . . so that she said all she chose as she chose and never the slightest hint of what she did not choose. Very reserved about herself and reliable about her friends, with an agreeable gaiety which had nothing indecorous. An extreme decency in all externals . . . with an equable temper which always and in everything left her mistress of herself. Such was this celebrated woman, who has so long and so publicly governed the Court and Monarchy of Spain and who has made such a stir in the world in her reign and in her fall.[1]

Elsewhere he writes:

She was in all her ways grace personified; a nobility, a courtesy, a restraint in this courtesy and a discernment which charmed still more; a language special to herself but natural and spontaneous; an involuntary eloquence which moved one, and above all an irresistible fascination, infinite intelligence, an intelligence superior enough to inspire others and keep in the background, and a rare talent for adapting herself to others. All about her was flowers and perfume, all attracted one naturally to her, and she had still more graces of mind than of body. . . .

But so many enchanting charms were not without their opposite sides. She was not always inflexible to *galanterie*. She was accused of being not always truthful, nor without artifice when she judged it necessary, and when she was on a wider stage she revealed a limitless ambition to which nothing was sacred. As she lived, so she died; accompanied and always sustained by the greatest courage in all the states and trials of her life. . . .[2]

[1] Saint-Simon, ix. 97, etc.
[2] Ibid., v. 496, appendix vi.

CHAPTER III

DUCHESS OF BRACCIANO

THREE men of rank and authority almost royal are connected inseparably with the name and success of the Princess des Ursins—three great princes of the Church, who, seduced by her charm, aided her in her upward climb to the supreme place she occupied as dictatress of Spain—the Cardinals de Bouillon, d'Estrées and Porto-Carrero.

To us, dazzled by her brilliance, to whom she appears a gigantic statue holding aloft the torch which kept Europe ablaze with a fifteen years' war, it is difficult to realise what she must have appeared at the outset of her career to these statesmen, a mere Princesse de Chalais, living in a convent, poor and of little importance except for her rare charm and intelligence. The possibility of her developing into a rival much less a superior, could never have entered the arrogant minds of these magnificent ecclesiastics.

For in those days cardinals counted for something. They maintained a state equal to that of sovereign princes and swept their silken robes over the Vatican marbles with the conscious pride of a peacock. And the Cardinals d'Estrées and de Bouillon were not only spiritual princes very close to the Throne of Saint Peter, but were among the highest and most powerful of the nobles of France.

César d'Estrées, of whom so much will be heard in the course of this history, was nephew to la belle Gabrielle, mistress of Henri IV., and brother to the Maréchal d'Estrées, at this date Ambassador at the Papal Court.

Rich, handsome and successful, Fortune had loaded him with her best gifts, and a glance at his noble arrogant face in contemporary portraits is enough to show that this arrogance was justified and that the following description of him by Saint-Simon was not exaggerated:

> He was the best and most nobly made in body, mind and face of all men in the world . . . with an air obliging but majestic, of great height, with a physiognomy which promised great intelligence and kept its word. A superior mind and

delicate wit, an erudition rare, vast and profound, exact, clear and precise. . . . Naturally eloquent and with much grace and facility of speech . . . extremely noble, disinterested, magnificent and generous, with much honour and probity, great sagacity, great penetration, good and just discernment, though often too fiery in his acts. . . . Always gay but often absent-minded. He knew how to hate but knew better how to love. . . . So many great and amiable qualities made him generally loved and respected. His knowledge and intelligence, his firmness and freedom, the sharpness of his expressions when it pleased him, a wit delicate and sometimes biting, caused people to fear and defer to him.[1]

Born in 1628, at the time of his infatuation for the Princess he was forty-five years old and at the height of his favour with Louis XIV. He had been sent to Rome, where his brother was ambassador, with the special mission to further his interests in the succession to the throne of Spain, which was then preoccupying all Europe. And since the history of the Princess des Ursins is inseparably connected with this succession, a few words on the subject cannot be omitted.

Charles II. of Spain, last of the elder branch of the House of Austria, son of Philippe IV. and the Queen-Regent already mentioned, was at this date a child of twelve,[2] but so sickly that his death at any moment had to be reckoned with.

The right of succession would fall naturally to the children of his two half-sisters, one married to Louis XIV., the other to the Emperor Leopold of Germany. On her marriage with the King of France the former had been forced to renounce her rights, but only on condition of the payment of her dowry, half a million of gold crowns. This Spain had hitherto been incapable of doing and Louis, insatiable of conquest and already dreaming of uniting all the crowns of Europe on his head, employed all means fair and foul—chiefly the latter—to assert his claim and coerce Charles into signing a testament in his favour.

Leopold of Germany had without doubt a better claim, since his wife had not renounced her right of succession, and he also on his side was working by means of his sister the Queen-Regent to influence the half-imbecile King, and all Europe headed by England was on the watch, ready,

---
[1] Saint-Simon, xxv. 171, etc.   [2] Born 1661.

when the crisis arrived, to throw in her weight with the weaker of the two claimants in order to maintain that balance of power supposed to be so necessary to the well-being of the nations, but which has caused more bloodshed than if all the crowns of the planet were piled on one head.

Now Madame de Chalais, having failed in her intrigue to become Princess of the Empire, in which case no doubt she would have worked for the Austrian succession, turned her attention to Louis and his claim and gave such value to the fact of her popularity with the Spanish, her knowledge of their tongue and her intimacy with their Prime Minister Porto-Carrero, that she persuaded d'Estrées he could have no better colleague than herself in his mission, and that she was admirably equipped to seduce the Neapolitan, Sicilian and Milanese nobles, then under Spanish rule, to give their suffrages to a Bourbon prince, and d'Estrées, under her charm and perhaps recognising the value of her collaboration, recommended her, as has been said, with so much enthusiasm that Louis at once accepted her.

Her other protector of this date, to whom she was equally indebted for this first success in her career, Emmanuel-Théodose de la Tour d'Auvergne, Cardinal de Bouillon, Sous-Doyen of the College of Cardinals and Grand Almoner of France, was of a very different type to the handsome d'Estrées. He was a year younger than the Princess and at this time her fervent admirer, though if the rumour be true that his tastes were not for her sex, his admiration may have been confined only to her intelligence. Like herself he was a supreme egoist, proud and ambitious, with no other thought or aim than his own aggrandisement, and his leanings towards Austria and the Emperor eventually brought about his ruin.

His personal appearance is thus described by Saint-Simon:

He was very thin and brown, of middle height and well made. His face would have nothing remarkable if his eyes had been like other people's, but besides that they were very near his nose, they looked one at the other as though they would have liked to meet. This squinting, which was continual, was frightful and gave him a hideous expression. He wore grey coats lined with red, with wrought gold buttons set with fine diamonds, and was never dressed like other people, always inventing something to make himself remarked. He was intelligent but confused, had little learning but very much the air and manners of the world, frank, cordial and generally polite, but all this was mixed with such an air of superiority that even his politeness was wounding. . . . His extravagance was continual and prodigious in everything, his ostentation most elaborate. . . . His morals were infamous. . . . It might be said of him that he could only be surpassed in pride by Lucifer—to whom he sacrificed everything as to his unique Deity.[1]

The Princesse de Chalais, poor and relatively insignificant, could certainly by her charm and knowledge of their tongue and country do much to seduce the Italian and Spanish nobles, subjects of Charles II.; but married to a man of high rank and position she could do more. So thought the two cardinals her lovers, or so she inspired them to think, and two years after her appointment—in 1675—a fine opportunity offering itself, the three arranged a veritable trap into which fell the man of the highest rank in Rome.

Flavio degli Orsini, Duke of Bracciano and San Gemini, Prince of Nerola, Count of Anguillara, Marquis della Penna, Spanish Grandee of the First Class, First Laic of Rome, Prince of the Soglio,[2] Prince of the Empire, etc., was chief of a house which had given queens to France, Naples and Poland, and numbered six popes, thirty cardinals, and a canonised saint among his ancestors. His wife had just died, leaving him without children. She was of the Ludovici, who were staunch adherents of Austria and violently opposed to the Bourbon succession, so that at her death there was great rejoicing among the French and a rush to secure the widower, who was allied to the Montmorency and had been before his marriage favourable to France.

This was the grand opportunity for which the Princess and her protectors had been on the watch and they seized it with admirable promptness and ability—a little too hastily, indeed, as the event proved.

Geffroy, the most reliable of the Princess's biographers, discovered among the archives of the Odescalchi family

[1] Saint-Simon, xxvi. 151.
[2] The Princes of the Soglio were, with the exception of the Orsini and Colonna, exclusively nephews of the reigning Popes. Their duty was to stand one on either side of the Pope's throne, or " Soglio," in official ceremonies.

in Rome, a memoir addressed towards the end of 1674 by the Duc and Cardinal d'Estrées in their capacity of ambassadors to the Marquis de Pomponne, then Foreign Minister, giving an account of this plot. From this it appears that the Princess, having lost one of her brothers, all Rome, headed by her two friends the cardinals, went to the convent where she was living to offer their condolences. The Duke of Bracciano, too great a personage, or too lazy, to go himself, sent his secretary, a certain Prior Gismondi, secretly in the pay of the cardinals, who, on his return, professed himself so dazzled by her charms, "by the majestic grace of her face and the elegance of her incomparable manners," that the Duke's curiosity was excited, and he hurried off at once to see this phenomenon.

She received him with all the grace and charm of manner for which she was celebrated, using her irresistible eyes and tongue to such good effect that he was immediately entrapped and, in the words of the memoir, "knew not which most to admire: the extent of her learning, the comprehensiveness of her intelligence, the keenness of her wit, the activity of her mind, or her penetrating wisdom "—all which qualities it would seem he himself lacked.[1]

D'Estrées and Bouillon, seeing him thus entrapped (*tonnelé*, snared like a partridge, is the word employed by Saint-Simon), added fuel to the flames so skilfully kindled by expatiating on her beauty, her great respectability, her high rank, her warm and generous heart, her conjugal virtues and austere widowhood, pointing out what an admirable duchess she would make, and promising in their official capacity that, though a dowry was lacking, she would bring to her husband the favour of the King of France, together with the Order of the Saint-Esprit.

Thus was the good Duke snared. Intelligence, all are agreed, was not his strong point, and the marriage took place in March 1675 at the French Embassy under the ægis of the Ambassador and with all possible magnificence at the cost of the King of France. The Princess was thirty-three, her husband twenty years older, but no matter. The marriage was of the highest advantage to her since it gave her the rank and position she coveted, of importance enough also to the French monarchy for Louis to write her an autograph letter of congratulation, with another to the

[1] Geffroy, *La Princesse des Ursins*, pp. viii, etc.

Duke, conferring on him the Order of the Holy Ghost, together with a pension of ten thousand francs—not a penny of which was naturally ever paid.

However, with all its apparent brilliance, the Princess soon discovered that this was superficial, for in spite of his great name, endless titles and large territories the Duke was in reality no better than a pauper, and it is doubtful whether, had she been aware of his actual position, she would have consented to share his poverty. His debts were immense and his pockets absolutely empty, for several years before he had been declared bankrupt, forced to sell most of his patrimony and hand over the proceeds to the Pope, who paid his creditors all that was available, reserving for the Duke himself an annuity so small that it was barely enough to keep up the dignity of his rank. At the date of his marriage he still owed over eight hundred thousand crowns and had not an inch of property which was not mortgaged.

Personally, too, he seems to have been no great prize, for he is described as stupid, lazy and insignificant, which defects, added to his poverty, must have been terribly trying to a woman of a character so exactly opposed, and since patience was not one of her virtues it is probable that their domestic life was a stormy one.

However, she was not one to throw away such advantages as could be extracted, and during the first two years (1675–7) they appear to have lived together and supported each other with more or less philosophy, the Princess turning to the best account the name she had bought so dearly.

All Rome was at her feet. The huge palace in the Piazza Navone [1] was not large enough to contain the crowds which flocked to her receptions. She had the official position of "First Princess of Rome," and her *salons* were the centre not only of *le monde où l'on s'amuse*, but of that where kingdoms are made and unmade, the headquarters of French political intrigue.

Madame de Bracciano [writes Saint-Simon] displayed all her wit and charm in Rome and soon made of the Palazzo Orsini a kind of Court where all that was greatest and noblest both of men and women assembled. It was the fashion to go

---

[1] Now Palazzo Braschi, near the statue of Patroclus of the Pasquinades. Hence the Princess often dated her letters "Palazzo Pasquin."

and to be on a footing of distinction to be received there. The husband [he adds significantly] counted for little.[1]

This is the first tableau in the series of triumphs which make up the life of the Princess des Ursins. A lover of splendour and pomp as she was, it may be supposed that no sort of display was lacking, that the vast *salons* were dazzling with gold and mirrors, that the furniture was gilt and gorgeous, the tapestries magnificent and she herself resplendent in jewelled silks and velvets, nucleus of the brilliant throng among whom the handsome d'Estrées and sinister Bouillon watched with complacency the triumph of their *protégée*.

[1] Saint-Simon, v. 105.

CHAPTER IV

ROME AND PARIS (1675-95)

UNFORTUNATELY, these days of triumph in Rome did not last long, for the next thing we hear is that she had abandoned her husband and mission and was living in Paris. "The couple did not always agree, and without open rupture were sometimes very glad to separate," writes Saint-Simon.[1] So glad, indeed, that before another year was over they spent more time apart than together, the separation becoming presently so complete that on one occasion the Duchess remained absent more than eight years.

But it was not in her character to parade her domestic griefs in public, and to this day the cause and extent of their rupture remain a mystery. Whether the poverty and stupidity of her husband irritated her to the point when contact becomes impossible, or whether the Duke himself objected to her numerous lovers and political intrigues, is uncertain. The latter seems most probable, for in 1677 she, then in Paris, made overtures towards a reconciliation and wrote to a certain agent of hers in Rome, Béraud by name, to feel the ground for her return. This is known by the answer of this Béraud, dated 1677, in which he writes that "permission to return to her husband would probably be refused."[2]

For twenty-three years she supported this disastrous semi-conjugal life, returning now and again to Rome, but living for the most part in Paris, and with the exception of a few fragmentary notices these years are veiled in almost complete obscurity. In February 1677 she was lodging in the Convent of the Holy Sacrament at Montmartre, living the gayest of lives. The notorious Grand Duchess of Tuscany, Marguerite-Louise d'Orléans, who declared that she would rather live in Hell than with her husband, had also taken refuge in this convent, of which her aunt was

[1] Saint-Simon, v. 105.
[2] Geffroy, xix. The document is in the Lanti archives now in the Capitol, Rome.

abbess, and the two semi-widows saw much of each other and became fast friends. Three years later, in 1680, the Duchess of Bracciano was accorded the *Tabouret*, the *Pour*, and the *Honours of the Louvre*.

The *Tabouret* was the right, reserved for duchesses only, to be seated in the Royal presence on a stool or *tabouret*, chairs being sacred to the Royal family and an arm-chair to Jupiter Olympus alone. Ordinary mortals, marquises, barons and the like, might stand till they dropped, a fact which accounts for the popularity of the card-tables at this date, for even Louis, high-priest of etiquette, could hardly exact that his unfortunate guests should remain standing till the small hours while staking their millions. The *Tabouret* awarded to the Duchess of Bracciano was what was called the *Tabouret de grâce* only, reserved for foreign princes.

The *Pour* consisted in the right (very highly prized) to have chalked over the door of the apartment allotted to a guest in the Royal châteaux "*pour Madame la Duchesse*," etc., instead of merely "*Madame la Duchesse*," a distinction reserved for princes of the blood, cardinals and foreign princes. The *Honours of the Louvre* included the treatment of *cousin*, that is to say that when the King wrote to them he began, *My cousin*, and the right for their coaches to enter the courtyard of the Royal palaces and châteaux instead of remaining outside the gates.

In 1682, with the help of Cardinal d'Estrées, she married her younger sister, Louise-Angélique, to the Duke Antonio Lanti delle Rovere, of the family of the Popes Sixtus IV. and Julius II. The marriage took place in Rome by proxy on 11 November, but both sisters remained in France till the following February when they returned to Rome together, which seems to show that some sort of reconciliation had been patched up between her and her husband. From other notices it would seem that they remained together for the next three years, during which she and her sister took the lead in the social life of Rome, amusing themselves with the College of Cardinals and holding a kind of little Court where they reigned supreme.

It would appear that the Duchess Lanti was as *galante* as her sister, and indulged besides in other excesses of which the Princess was never guilty, but which were very much the fashion at Court. She seems to have had a brilliant success in the gay world of Rome, to the point even of eclipsing her sister and robbing her of her lovers, Cardinal d'Estrées among them, a defection to which the Princess's subsequent enmity has been attributed.

The following extract from the *Mémoires* of the Marquis de Coulanges, cousin of Madame de Sévigné and a noted rhymester of his day, gives an idea of the popularity of the Duchess Lanti and in the dearth of more important notices is worth quoting.

He was travelling in Italy in the autumn of 1689 and describes his visit to Rome and the way in which he spent his time there.

Another palace, which was an agreeable resource for passing the evenings, was that of the Duchess Lanti, sister of the Duchess of Bracciano and of the Abbé de Noirmoutier [Abbé de la Trémoïlle], who had come with us to Rome. The Duke Lanti her husband, in the interest of France and thinking to merit the Order of the Saint-Esprit. . . . gave us, with a liberality truly French, the *entrée* of his house either for conversation or for play while awaiting the supper-hour. Thus we never missed going there towards the close of the day, and this became such a habit that at our return from our promenades, our outriders, without waiting for orders, used to cry to the coachman: "To Madame Lanti!"

As a supplement to this notice he composed the following verses, foolish enough, but which give the atmosphere of the epoch :

> Quand la nuit est venue
> Tout retentit du cri,
> " Da Madama Lanti! "
> Qui donc est Madama Lanti ?
> Ecoute-moi, je m'en vais vous le dire.
> Digne d'un empire
> Elle regne ici.
> Tous ses aieux etaient gens d'importance,
> Son cœur répond à sa grande naissance.
> L'Hymen au bord du Tibre
> A conduit ses pas.
> Voulez-vous être libre ?
> Ne la voyez pas.
> Plus on la trouve aimable
> Plus elle est redoubtable.
> Défendez-vous des feux
> Qui partent de ses yeux.[1]

[1] Coulanges, *Mémoires* (Paris, 1820), p. 194.

It is to her correspondence with the Duchess Lanti that we owe the partial lifting of the veil which obscures the Princess's early life. The letters were written from Rome during the stay of the former at her husband's villa at Bagnaia near Viterbo, and their chief interest is that they show that for some part at least of 1685, which she is supposed to have spent entirely in Paris, she was living with her husband in Rome.[1]

The first contains a mention of the notorious d'Aubigny —invariably called "the faithful," but whom the documents prove to have been quite the reverse—who played so important a part in her later life. Nominally her secretary (for the cataract in her eyes, from which she suffered all her life and which ended in almost total blindness, already prevented her writing), he was probably even at this date her lover. It will be seen to what high honours she raised him during her triumph in Spain: Equerry to the Queen, Councillor to the King, Envoy Extraordinary to the Court of Versailles, where he was received with all honour, and ending his days, after witnessing with indifference the ruin of his benefactress, in the magnificent château she had built for herself as the seat of her sovereignty.

In another letter she reproves her sister for her indulgence in the pleasures of the table, and alludes to the infidelity of Cardinal d'Estrées with an irony which betrays more than a touch of bitterness :

Monsieur le Cardinal d'Estrées did me the honour to see me expressly to entertain me with your charms and the effect they produced on him. . . . I do not doubt that you responded to all his attentions, if you were not too sleepy or if the fumes of the meats and wines, which you take it seems in great quantity, did not make you too heavy to be able to reply to the vivacities which His Eminence writes you in verse and prose. If you could avoid abandoning yourself entirely to your leaning for this kind of pleasure you would do well, it seems to me. You would have

[1] They were discovered by Geffroy among the archives of the Lanti family and published in 1859 (*Lettres inédites de la Princesse des Ursins*). Geffroy gave too little importance to this collection of letters, which has now been transferred to the Capitoline Library, publishing only a few of those to her sister. Madame Saint-René Taillandier, whose clever work, *La Princesse des Ursins*, appeared only after my own was in the hands of the printers, has extracted from them many interesting notes from her letters to her husband, but without citations or references. It is to be hoped they will some day be reproduced entire.

a fine opportunity to exercise the rare talent for poetry with which Nature has endowed you, and it would be a charming thing if you wrote a letter in verse, comic or heroic, to the Cardinal. I think, however, you would succeed better in the former, above all after having drunk five or six bumpers of the wine of Canapine which you swallow with so much facility. The rumour goes that your gluttony has not pleased all your lovers.[1]

In June 1687 she had to leave Rome hurriedly to escape the painful results of another financial catastrophe of her husband.

Here are extracts from a letter by a certain Claude Estiennot, dated 29 June, 1687, from which we learn that the Duke's creditors had made a fresh onslaught on what remained of his property. " The Camera," he writes, " has placed in the Pope's hands Bracciano and all it contains; has dismissed all the Duke's servants, installed others and seized even the corn and oats. This conduct has made a great noise here. The Duchess left yesterday. . . . She is extremely regretted, not only by the French but by many Italians, and everyone pities her for being forced to undertake so long and painful a journey in so severe a season." [2]

In a preceding letter dated 17 June he writes that the Cardinal d'Estrées had offered to pay the Pope twelve thousand crowns and guarantee another fifty thousand to save the situation, but had been refused, " which makes one think," he adds, " that it is the Duke's attachment to France which has procured him this annoyance." [3]

For Innocent XI. was not friendly to France and disapproved strongly of Louis' efforts to dominate Europe, and so freely did he express his sentiments that in the following year a violent quarrel broke out, with the result that he threatened to excommunicate all who had intercourse with the French in Rome. As the Duke of Bracciano was entirely at his mercy, all his property being in his hands, he had no choice but to obey, and treated the French Ambassador with such insolence that in August he received orders to remove the Fleurs-de-lys from over his door, which so enraged him that he sent back the Order of the Saint-Esprit he had received on his marriage. It was the first time in the history of the Order that such an insult had been

[1] Geffroy, 2; letter of 1685.   [2] Ibid., 7, note 1.   [3] Ibid., 7.

offered, and the King's fury can be imagined. He sent word to his ambassador to heap all possible indignity upon him and cut off his pension of ten thousand crowns, which, like most of the Royal pensions, had never been paid.

As for the Duchess her situation was embarrassing, for not only the satisfaction of her ambitions but her material existence depended on Louis. Besides this, her husband's behaviour made her position exceedingly difficult at Versailles, where she had been so well received. She had reason to regret a marriage which had brought her little but money difficulties and misfortune.

However, Louis acted *en grand seigneur* and, so far from venting his anger on her, pitied her and gave orders that the unpaid pension allowed to her husband should be transferred to her, and her name figures several times in the *Journal* of Dangeau and elsewhere as being among his guests at Versailles, Marly and Fontainebleau, and also at the Court of James II. of England at Saint-Germain, where she was in high favour.[1]

She remained in France till 1695, following the Court in its eternal peregrinations from one Royal château to another, but though amusing herself she did not lose sight of her money affairs, and was employing all the means at her command to obtain a pension out of the wreckage of her husband's fortune. On 17 September, 1690, she writes in the greatest indignation to one of the Papal officials to complain of the way she was treated. Innocent XI. had died the preceding year and the new Pope, Alexander VII., seems to have acted with less rigour towards her husband, and had even allowed the use of the Palazzo Orsini and a pension of six thousand crowns to himself and his brother the Prince of Vicovare. Her complaint was that in this arrangement no mention of herself had been made and

[1] The Marquis de Dangeau (born 1638, died 1720) for thirty-six years had the habit of noting down each day all the principal events of the Court. After his death the manuscript was lent to the Duc de Saint-Simon, who made use of it in his own *Mémoires* and added numerous notes which were published with the *Journal* for the first time in 1854. Nevertheless, though he owed to it all that is reliable in his *Mémoires*, he condemned it as " thin, dry, restrained and cautious, a repulsive mixture of insipidity, base vanity, dryness as to facts and prodigality of the most servile flattery." " One must be a Dangeau," he writes, " to have written it, that is to say, a mind below mediocrity, very futile, very incapable in every respect, knowing no other gods than the King and Madame de Maintenon."

that the Cardinals d'Estrées and de Bouillon, whom she had deputed to look after her interests, had completely failed her.[1] But her complaints were received with indifference, and in despair at their slackness she decided to abandon her gay life in Paris and go herself to Rome.

The necessary passports and Royal permission were obtained, but whether she made use of them is uncertain. If so she did not remain long, for six months later (May 1691) we find her name among the guests invited to a *collation magnifique* given by Louis in a pavilion belonging to the Princesse de Conti, his daughter by the Duchesse de la Vallière, called "le Desert" at Versailles, at which all the Court was present.[2] In any case her presence did not have the desired effect, for a year later her affairs were still *in statu quo*, and she wrote to her brother the Abbé de la Trémoïlle attacking him bitterly for neglecting her interests.[3]

She seems indeed at this time to have been on the verge of beggary, and according to her biographers it was this which made her solicit the post of *dame d'honneur* to the King's bastard, Mademoiselle de Blois, on the occasion of her marriage with the Duc de Chartres, later Duc d'Orléans and Regent of France,[4] "a strange post for the wife of the first Prince in Rome," as Saint-Simon remarks. And a strange mysterious affair it turned out, for having coveted the post so eagerly that, according to Madame de Maintenon, she had helped her to arrange the marriage solely to obtain it, for some reason which never transpired she suddenly changed her mind and refused it, thereby bitterly offending Louis and bringing on herself temporary exile from the Court.

> It still remains a problem [writes Saint-Simon] whether she intrigued for or whether she refused this place, so strange for her, but whether she intrigued for it and Madame de Maintenon did not wish it, or whether she refused it and the King was stung, and Madame de Maintenon very glad to foment his anger in order to get rid of her, it is certain that she was no more on the same footing at Court as before and that she felt it so bitterly that she retired little by little and almost ceased to go at all.[5]

---

[1] Geffroy, 12 ; letter to the Auditor of the Ruota of 17 Sept. 1690.
[2] Dangeau, ii. 81.
[3] Geffroy, 18 ; letter of 15 Sept. 1692.
[4] The marriage took place in February 1692.
[5] Saint-Simon, v. 497, appendix vi.

The Princess herself explained the matter by saying that she had asked the Duke, her husband, for permission and that he had refused, which is improbable for two reasons—first, that had she feared his refusal she would have found out before applying for the post, and next that, separated as she was, his permission was unnecessary.[1] A letter from Madame de Maintenon herself, written to the Duchesse de Ventadour, then *dame d'honneur* to the Princess Palatine, mother of the Duc de Chartres, deepens the mystery. "Madame de Braquiane" (so she spells her name) "arranged the marriage of the Duc de Chartres in order to be *dame d'honneur*. She and I began the intrigue when we were at Fontainebleau, and now we see that she does not wish to be *dame d'honneur*. Do not such things open one's eyes?"[2]

Open one's eyes to what?

The interest of the affair lies in its connection with the almost incredible scandal that at this time the Duchess of Bracciano was doing her utmost to supplant Madame de Maintenon in the favour of Louis XIV. and had succeeded nearly enough to terrify that lady into plotting her ruin.[3]

Saint-Simon, very *au courant* of Court scandals, throughout his *Mémoires* never wearies of insinuating that the cause of all her disgraces as well as her triumphs was the bitter jealousy of Madame de Maintenon—"who feared her graces of mind and body," and lived in perpetual terror of the attraction she undeniably had for the King. He hints that she encouraged her nomination to the post of Camarera Mayor as well as her subsequent return to Spain, not at all from good will or any political reason, but simply to keep her at a distance from Versailles.

One thing is clear in this otherwise hazy matter—that if the ambitious Duchess of Bracciano took the trouble to

---

[1] Jean de Préhac, spy in the service of the War Minister Chamillart, wrote to him from Pau where he had interviewed the Princess after her first disgrace : " She wanted to be *dame d'honneur* to Madame la Duchesse de Chartres, but a delay of three weeks which she demanded to write to her husband about it, spoiled everything " (Saint-Simon, xii. 544 ; letter of 19 July, 1704).

[2] Lavallée, *Corréspondance général de Madame de Maintenon*, iii. 323. The letter is undated but docketed as of February 1642.

[3] The exact date of Louis' marriage with Madame de Maintenon is uncertain, but it was before June 1684, probably in the autumn of 1683.

intrigue for a post so beneath her rank as that of *dame d'honneur* to the Duchesse de Chartres, it was in order to satisfy some higher ambition, and who knows but what that ambition was actually to supplant Madame de Maintenon. Louis adored his daughter, and the opportunities of seeing him in comparative privacy would be frequent to one in constant attendance. In that atmosphere of intrigue who knows what tales were carried to Madame de Maintenon of the King's infidelity, causing her to employ all her efforts that her rival should be exiled from his Court.

However, her disgrace was neither so sudden nor so complete as Saint-Simon makes out, for two months after the marriage—April 1692—she was again at Versailles, preparing to accompany Louis to Marly the following day, the invitations to Marly being *dans l'intimité* and accorded only to the King's special friends. In June also she was staying at Saint-Germain to assist at the confinement of the ex-Queen of England, Mary of Modena, together with half the princes and princesses of the blood.[1]

But retire from the Court she eventually did, and in consequence of the mysterious affair, as the following words, written a year later by her secretary, d'Aubigny, to the Duchess Lanti, prove: "Your sister," he wrote, "has quitted the Court and lives altogether in Paris. The affair of the post has done her very much harm. For the rest, she is always beautiful and amiable. She is very handsomely lodged near La Charité and is ordering furniture. She has with her Mademoiselle de Cosnac." And later: "Madame la Duchesse wants to marry Mademoiselle de Cosnac and to have Mademoiselle de Royan to live with her."[2]

Now Mademoiselle de Cosnac, great-niece of the Archbishop of Aix, who was cousin-german of her first husband, the Prince de Chalais, and Mademoiselle de Royan, daughter of her dead sister, were both great heiresses, very much sought after by the young nobles of the Court.

"I have with me Mademoiselle de Cosnac," she wrote herself to her sister in Rome. "She is not strong, but has a very sweet temper. She is dying to accompany me to Rome . . . but as she is a great heiress I do not know if they would consent to her making this journey. She receives

---
[1] Geffroy, 15 and 16; letters to the Duchess Lanti of 23 April and 7 June, 1692.
[2] Ibid., 25; letters of 2 March and 15 Sept. 1693.

five hundred pistoles a year for her clothes, enough, as you may imagine, wherewith to dress respectably." [1]

Thus, driven from her husband's house, excluded from the Court, with characteristic energy she at once proceeds to make another life for herself, hires a fine house, furnishes it magnificently, and takes to live with her (and probably pay for all) two young and pretty heiresses, the surest bait to attract the gay world she could not live without. In default of Versailles, Marly and Fontainebleau the Duchess of Bracciano found means to create without expense a brilliant little Court of her own.

"Madame de Bracciano gives little dances which end at ten o'clock in the evening," writes Saint-Simon. "One finds there all the marriageable heiresses." [2]

The young Duke, himself at this time in search of a wife, was among her most assiduous courtiers and evidently, boy as he was, one of the many victims of her charms. "The Duchess of Bracciano," he writes, "has been for some time in Paris, far from husband and Rome. She lived quite near me and was a friend of my mother whom she saw often. Her wit, her grace and manner, enchanted me. She received me kindly and I hardly stirred from her house. She had living with her, Mademoiselle de Cosnac, her relative, and Mademoiselle de Royan, daughter of her sister. She was dying to give me Mademoiselle de Royan and often spoke to me of marriage, and to my mother also, to see if we should say something she could take up. It would have been a noble and rich marriage, but I was alone and needed a father-in-law and a family on whom I could lean." [3]

It is not often that boys of eighteen have so much prudence and worldly wisdom, but the Duc de Saint-Simon, despite his literary genius, had all the insignificant—what have been called the ignominious—virtues.

[1] Geffroy, 22 ; letter of 12 Jan. 1693.
[2] Saint-Simon, ii. 261, note 1.   [3] Ibid., ii. 288.

CHAPTER V

PRINCESS DES URSINS

THE tranquil life the Duchess had made for herself with her two nieces in Paris did not last long, for in 1695 she had again to make the long and tedious journey to Rome to look after her money affairs. Innocent XII. had succeeded Alexander VII. and would seem, even more than his predecessor, to have relaxed the Papal hold on her husband's property, since he had the right to dispose of it for his own benefit in spite of the crowd of creditors. For while she was taking the waters at Vichy the bad news reached her that he had sold the Duchy and title of Bracciano to Don Livio Odescalchi, and without any reference to herself had adopted him as his heir.

This Don Livio, nephew of Innocent XI., was her *bête noire* —" This dishonest fellow, with the ridiculous face, for whom I have always had the same antipathy, regarding him as a horror of nature! " she wrote of him, and certainly to her he was a cruel and malignant foe, probably because, as an ally of Austria, he had objected to the marriage. One of the richest of the Roman nobles, his collections of pictures and other works of art were celebrated all over Europe. He bought at her death that of Queen Cristina of Sweden, which included the famous " Leda " of Correggio, now in Berlin. It would seem, however, that in other matters he was avarice personified. He was created Duke of Ceri in 1680, Prince of the Empire and Grandee of Spain in 1690, and posed as candidate for the throne of Poland in 1697. For the moment his ambitions were confined to the Duchy of Bracciano and the cardinal's hat, and his desire to be adopted by the Duke was to obtain the hereditary post of Prince of the Soglio after his death.

On hearing the extraordinary news of this adoption the Princess left her cure unfinished and, without losing a moment, hurried off to Rome to prevent it. On 20 December she wrote from her palazzo in the Piazza Navone to the Comte de Maurepas, Secretary of State :

I have been received by all Rome with great demonstrations of joy. I found Monsieur le Duc de Brachane and Monsieur le Prince de Vicovare his brother [1] in bad health, but very embittered against each other and of very different opinions as to the means of putting some order in the affairs of the House. Don Livio is protected by Monsieur de Brachane and the Duke of Gravina by Monsieur de Vicovare. Each desires to have me on his side, but up to now I have maintained a neutrality which I thought necessary in order to get to know better the real state of affairs and which side to take. . . . I act only at the advice of the Cardinal de Janson,[2] who shows me all possible kindness. He is coming to-morrow with many other Cardinals to hear a rehearsal in my house of what is to be sung on Christmas Eve before the Pope. All the singers and musicians of His Holiness will be there. . . .[3]

So she combined business with pleasure.

Strange as it may seem during the life of her husband, she at once began a lawsuit against Don Livio for having extorted the adoption and inheritance. This is proved by a letter, half-serious, half-jesting, to Maurepas in which she writes as follows:

All your kindness towards me merits that I should tell you myself that I have won my great lawsuit against Don Livio. You know that this filthy prince (*crasseux de prince*) wished in spite of myself to be my son and inherit later the honours and properties of this House in virtue of the adoption made in his favour by the Prince des Ursins. The Court esteems him too ugly to figure at the Soglio with the representatives of Crowned Heads, and has decided that what remains of this House will belong more suitably to another. I pray you to rejoice with me over this happy decision, for I am enchanted not to have this ugly child, and I can assure you that I shall one day enjoy very great wealth if I survive Monsieur le Prince des Ursins.[4]

It will be remarked that she uses for the first time this title as the result of his sale of the Duchy of Bracciano and that it was the Duke himself and not the Duchess, as all the biographers affirm, who adopted the name of his House, Orsini, or as it was frenchified—des Ursins.

Neither is it a fact that the Princess was in Paris when the news of his last illness reached her, and hurried back to his side, where a death-bed reconciliation took place,

---
[1] Lelio degli Orsini, Prince of Nerola and Vicovare. He died unmarried the following year.
[2] Then French Ambassador.
[3] Trémoïlle, *Madame des Ursins*, i. 5.
[4] *Cabinet Historique*, xi. 307; letter of 10 March, 1697.

arranged by the Cardinal de Bouillon. Six letters written from Rome prove that for three years she did not leave that city for a length of time sufficient for a stay in Paris. One of 9 April, 1696, to Pomponne, Secretary of State, another of 9 October to the Maréchale de Noailles of the same year, that of 10 March, 1697, to Maurepas above quoted, and another of 18 August, 1697, one to Pomponne of 15 October, 1697, and finally one to the Duchess of Burgundy of 30 December to congratulate her on her marriage which took place on 7 December, and which she claimed the merit of having helped.[1] In April 1698 her husband died. From these dates it will be seen that it was materially impossible that she should have made the long journey to and from Paris, and it may, therefore, be concluded that during the three years preceding his death she was living, preoccupied with her lawsuits, but otherwise not unpeaceably, with her husband in the Palazzo Orsini in Rome.

Her letter to Louis, announcing his death, is worth quoting in part:

"SIRE,—The goodness which Your Majesty has shown me on all occasions, gives me the liberty to tell you that Monsieur le Prince des Ursins is dead after seven days' illness, and that he confirmed by a codicil before dying the treaty and testament he had made in my favour.

Although I have succeeded by my efforts since I returned to Rome in procuring that more than seven hundred thousand francs have been paid to this House . . . and that the Congregation renounced making an inventory of the furniture of the palace . . . I had nevertheless to fear that the Duke of Gravina and Don Livio Odescalchi would find means by their credit to do me this ill turn, but the protection with which Your Majesty honours me and the obliging way in which the Cardinal de Bouillon has given it effect in this encounter, have rendered all their efforts useless, and the Pope has done me the justice to order that this inventory be made in my name.[2]

Her praise of the Cardinal was premature, and in the very next letter we find her complaining bitterly of his "malignity," and declaring that, "from the day he entered Rome up to now I have always equally had reason to be displeased with him."[3]

---

[1] All these letters are to be found in the Duc de la Trémoïlle's collection, *Madame des Ursins*, vol. i. 3–11.
[2] Trémoïlle, i. 10.
[3] Ibid., i. 14; letter to Torcy of 17 Aug. 1698.

We have now arrived at the first of the many celebrated quarrels for which the Princess was renowned, quarrels which seem to a certain extent to have been systematic, the deliberate throwing down of the ladders by which she had attained her ambitions. Born to dominate, the idea of gratitude was insupportable to her authoritative nature, and Bouillon, one may be sure, was not one to allow his protection to be forgotten. To this, rather than to the foolish inadequate reasons adduced by both adversaries, must be attributed this first quarrel at least.

Bouillon, with his sinister squint, had, as we know, been twenty-four years earlier among her admirers, and it was he who, together with Cardinal d'Estrées, had procured her her post and pension in the service of Versailles. What then had occurred to change their friendship to a hatred so violent that all their friends were dragged into the quarrel?

"He hates me because he knows me to be friends with the Cardinals d'Estrées and Janson," the Princess herself explained to Torcy, and in a letter to Maurepas she writes more fully: "You would be surprised if I told you the way the Cardinal de Bouillon behaves to me, but such complaints would be useless, and I must not hope that anything will make him change, since my conduct up to now has not been able to destroy the resolution with which apparently he left France—to do me all the harm he could. In an explanation which I desired to have with him he confessed that he had no other cause of complaint against me than that I had friends who were not his." [1]

The reasons the Cardinal himself gave are even more trivial, unless, indeed, we are to suppose that the quarrel was of an amorous nature, which, considering the mature age of both, is improbable. Here is the narrative of the Duke of Berwick, natural son of James II. (of whom much will be heard later), who was a friend of both the belligerents, and at the time of the quarrel a guest of the Cardinal [2]:

I made a voyage in Italy for my pleasure [he writes in his *Mémoires*] and went to Rome where I was the guest of the

[1] *Cabinet Historique*, xi. 311; letter to the Comte de Maurepas of 23 June, 1698.
[2] James Fitzjames, son of James II. and Arabella Churchill; born 1671. Forced by the Revolution to retire to France with James II., he took service in the French army and was made Marshal of France in 1706.

Cardinal de Bouillon, who was there looking after French affairs. The Duchess of Bracciano, who has since taken the name of Princess des Ursins, was also at that time in Rome, and I went to see her every day, having known her in France. She had a mortal quarrel with the Cardinal, the origin of which I will tell in a few words, to show how often the gravest quarrels arise from trifles. The Duke of Bracciano being dead, the Cardinal, who was a great friend of the Princess, went to see her at once, in order to prevent the lawyers from setting their seals on her property, for in Rome it is one of the privileges of Cardinals that the agents of the law may not enter a house in which they are. Madame de Bracciano ordered a grand dinner to be served for him in her antechamber, but he would not eat it because he had counted on eating with her at her bedside. She did her best to show him that, her husband's body being still in the house, it would be very unconventional, but he considered himself insulted and returned fasting to his palace. A few days after, Madame de Bracciano wished to drape her palace with violet, as she claimed was the right of the House of Orsini. The Cardinal, vexed at what had happened, opposed it with all his might, maintaining that it was a distinction reserved only for Cardinals. The matter was decided in favour of Madame de Bracciano and since then, not only have they not met but each has sought to do the other the greatest harm possible. The Duchess moved heaven and earth to injure him, and he gave her only too much occasion by his conduct in the matter of the Archbishop of Cambrai (Fenélon), whom he defended publicly, although he had been sent to Rome solely to solicit his condemnation.[1]

The Cardinal, whose excessive arrogance had already cost him five years of exile from the Court,[2] had been pardoned by Louis and permitted to return, and had even been honoured with a special mission to the Pope in connection with Fenélon's *Maximes des Saints*, which had incurred his disapproval. His instructions had been to persuade the Pope to condemn the book, but finding him at that time rather inclined to favour it, and considering that the interests of a prince of the Church lay rather with the Pope

[1] Duc de Berwick *Mémoires*, i. 159.
[2] In 1685 he had refused to officiate at the marriage of the Duc de Bourbon because etiquette forbade his sitting at the royal table during the banquet. For this he was disgraced and exiled to one of his estates for five years. Madame de Maintenon in a letter to her brother, dated 27 Sept. 1685, wrote: "The Cardinal de Bouillon is dismissed for several reasons. . . . He wanted to be on an equality with the princes of the blood. He is little pitied in his disgrace because he is little esteemed" (Lavallée, *Corréspondance général de Madame de Maintenon*, ii. 409; letter to d'Aubigny of 5 Aug. 1685).

than the King of France, he publicly announced his own approval, which so enraged Louis that he ordered him to leave Rome and again condemned him to exile at one of his abbeys.

In open revolt he refused on the plea that the doyen of the College of Cardinals, Cibo, was dying, and that as he was next in succession it would be an insult to the Pope. It was at this critical moment that the quarrel between him and the Princess broke out. Already enraged against him for having, as she said, neglected her interests, she seized the opportunity of his disgrace to fan the flames by all kinds of accusations trivial and serious, cleverly chosen to rub Louis on the weak point of his vanity. For example, she relates how, at a supper given by himself at the Embassy, while all his guests were enthusiastically toasting the King of France, he maintained a surly silence, and when rallied on this, merely shrugged his shoulders and muttered, "Ah, yes—he plays the guitar well." This was a trump-card and Louis' fury at this lack of respect on the part of his Ambassador can be imagined.

She accused him also of morals and manners ill-suited to his functions. He drove himself about the campagna, she recounted, and even paid visits of ceremony, accompanied by his mistress, in a light chaise with four running footmen, which she condemned as "entirely unsuitable to an ecclesiastic who has the honour to represent his Sovereign." Worse than all, he and his mistress were suspected of cheating at cards and robbing "a young milord" of considerable sums of money.[1]

The energy she expends in abuse and complaints of her quondam lover is amazing. Immensely long violent letters —it is true she only dictated them—filled with the minutest details of his crimes and follies, follow each other in quick succession for nearly a year, letters addressed, not to Louis himself, to whom naturally she dared not write so freely, but to all those whom she knew would repeat their contents to him: to the Maréchal de Noailles and his wife, both very intimate with Madame de Maintenon; to the ministers Torcy and Pomponne, whose duty it was to keep him informed of his Ambassador's behaviour; to everybody in fact whom she thought likely to increase his anger against him.

[1] Trémoïlle, i. 26; letter to the Maréchale de Noailles of 11 Nov. 1698.

She accused him of contempt for France, of speaking slightingly of Louis himself, of neglecting French interests, of coldness and inaccessibility towards his compatriots, of leanings towards Austria, protecting the German Ambassador, etc. "A more unpatriotic Frenchman or a Minister less attached to his Master's interest never existed," she wrote. And, indeed, if all her accusations are true, it is surprising that the Pope himself did not deprive him of his cardinal's hat. "The Duchess of Bracciano," wrote the Duke of Berwick, "has had a larger share than anyone else in exciting the Court against him."

However, the Cardinal proved himself more than her match. His letters and official despatches were fully as violent as her own, and in petty spite and malice he outdid her.

The quarrel continued to rage with increasing fury till everyone in Rome was drawn into it and forced to take sides whether they would or no. Don Livio Odescalchi profited by it to make another onslaught on her rights of inheritance and the Cardinal stirred up her brother the Abbé, who was devoted to him, to provoke and insult her. This young fellow had hurried to Rome on her marriage in order to profit by her position. She had been kind to him and had even tried to persuade the Pope to name him Cardinal, but he would hear of nothing higher than Auditor of the Ruota, one of the clerical tribunes, for the Abbé's vices were notorious. Seeing that no more was to be extorted from her, he neglected her and, attributing his failure to her lack of zeal, was only too delighted to throw himself on the side of her enemy. He abused her, avoided her, slighted her publicly and excited his servants to assault hers in the street. However, he learnt to his cost that she was not one to be attacked with impunity, for she retaliated by accusing him to the Pope of sodomy, and not only was he deprived of his appointment, but had to fly for his life.[1]

Longer and more bitter grew her complaints and abuse of the Cardinal, and so preoccupied was she with her quarrel that even the death of her sister the Duchess Lanti, which took place at the time, failed to extract more than a passing regret.[2] Incidentally, however, in these long letters,

[1] Dangeau, xviii. 212; addition of Saint-Simon.
[2] The Duchess Lanti had gone to Paris to consult the doctors for

breathing fire and fury, we get a few glimpses of the life she was leading in Rome, a life brilliant and pompous in spite of debts and poverty. She had had the French Fleurs-de-lys again set up over the door of her palace, and gave a magnificent reception in honour of the event. More than twenty thousand persons in the piazza, waiting since daybreak for a *fête* which began only at ten o'clock at night, all listening in breathless silence to harangues in praise of the King of France. " A silence so great," she wrote, " that its like has never been." So important an event was it that the Prince of Monaco, who had replaced Bouillon as Ambassador, described it at great length in his dispatches to Louis, telling him how " all Rome was in the Piazza Navone," and how the Pope had lent his best musicians to sing a "*grande pièce*" which the Princess had had composed in honour of his sacred self.[1]

The Prince of Monaco, on his arrival, had at once shown himself friendly and helpful, and through his good offices even Bouillon became less malignant. He had persuaded Don Livio to make her an advantageous offer for her rights of succession, in particular for that of the Soglio, of which she was now proprietor. So eagerly did he covet this post that he was ready to pay one hundred thousand crowns and a pension for life if she would consent to cede it to him. As a French subject dealing with the enemy, before she could accept this tempting offer she had to obtain the consent of Louis XIV. and this he peremptorily refused. Whereupon the new Ambassador came again to the rescue and pleaded her cause with so much warmth that a compromise was arranged, and an armistice eventually concluded between these bitter foes.[2] " Don Livio," she wrote to Torcy, " pays me an assiduous court which I tolerate, and even

a cancer and died in November 1698, leaving there one of her children, for whose journey back to Rome Louis paid two thousand crowns. In his *Journal* under the date 15 Nov., Dangeau notes: " The Duchess Lanti, sister of Monsieur de Noirmoutier and the Duchess of Bracciano, who is now called Princess des Ursins, is in Paris at the last extremity. She came from Rome to be cured of a cancer and the remedies she has taken have ended by killing her " (Dangeau, vi. 460). And again under the date 25 Nov. 1698 : " The Duchess Lanti died in Paris after a long and cruel malady " (Dangeau, vi. 465).

[1] Geffroy, 41 ; letter of 4 Aug. 1699.

[2] Trémoïlle, i. 53 ; letters of the Prince de Monaco to Louis XIV. of 4 Aug. 1699, and the King's answer of 29 Oct.

permit him to go to sleep in my presence according to his laudable custom." [1]

On 4 September she wrote to the Princess Palatine:

I have already concluded several important lawsuits, and Don Livio Odescalchi, who wished to appropriate what is left of this House by an adoption which he extorted, has renounced his pretensions and asked my pardon for the forgeries he produced against me since the death of the Prince des Ursins. This enemy, formidable to a stranger like me for the great number of his creatures, whom his uncle Innocent XI. had placed in the tribunals of Rome, is not the person who has caused me most difficulties. The Cardinal de Bouillon, vexed that I had in France friends who were not his own, since two years has done all he could to ruin me with the King my Master.[2]

The property she inherited was enormous, but all the revenues went to the creditors. For example, in the Abruzzi she was nominal owner of the principality of Amatrice, " with more than twenty thousand vassals," about which she was in litigation with the Cardinal dei Medici who had seized it illegally,[3] one of the many costly lawsuits which drained the little money she possessed.

However, in spite of poverty her life in Rome was on a scale of magnificence almost regal; necessary, she contended, for the success of her mission. Four gentlemen of noble birth —two Italian, two French—six pages, also noble, almoners and secretaries, countless females of duties unspecified, " *mes filles*," she calls them, twelve lackeys in gorgeous gold-embroidered liveries, an army of underlings, *femmes-de-chambre*, valets, hair-dressers, grooms, coachmen and all the retinue necessary to the maintenance of a huge palace and a gilt coach drawn by six horses.

And to pay for all this pomp? " You will have difficulty in believing," she wrote to the Maréchale de Noailles, " that my revenues consist only of seventeen thousand francs, including the pension allowed me by the King." And, business-like, she proceeds to give the details.

From the Orsini property absolutely nothing but the furniture of the palace: for the small amount of ready money she had succeeded in saving from the creditors goes in annuities to the Duke's poor relations and old servants,

---

[1] Trémoïlle, i. 55; letter to Torcy of 7 Dec. 1699.
[2] Geffroy, 450; letter of 4 Sept. 1699.
[3] Trémoïlle, i. 61; letter to Torcy of 29 Jan. 1699.

PRINCESS DES URSINS 43

in paying his debts, her own numerous lawsuits and the administration of the properties. From her own House of Noirmoutier and that of her first husband the Prince de Chalais she receives eleven thousand, which with the King's ten thousand ought to bring her income up to twenty-one thousand, but the loss on the exchange reduces it to seventeen. "Sordid poverty, little suitable to the First Princess of Rome," she remarks bitterly. And she hints that her expenses are more to Louis' profit than her own since her mission necessitates keeping open house and a certain state in order to win over the Spanish subjects to his cause. "Mine is the only French house open, not only to the French but to everyone," she boasts. "The days that I do not give to business I receive every evening about a hundred persons of every nationality."[1] All which preludes the demand that the Maréchale will support her request for an increase of pension by transferring to herself that of one of the cardinals recently deceased.

A modest request enough considering the services she was rendering. "My house up to now," she wrote to Louis himself, "has been the most frequented in Rome and all the French who come here should do me the justice to say that it does honour to the nation. Few Neapolitans of rank come to Rome who do not seek my acquaintance and become my friends."[2]

The answer to this request is not forthcoming and presently quarrels, lawsuits, income and position as First Princess of Rome faded into insignificance before a new ambition which surged into her mind; visions of a post so high as to satisfy even her aspirations, so high, indeed, that she dared not even hint it to the Maréchale, but with a skill and tact which proved her fitness for it, schemed and intrigued so ably that it seemed to fall unasked into her hand.

[1] Geffroy, 76, etc.; letter to the Maréchale de Noailles of 15 June, 1700.
[2] Trémoïlle, i. 59; letter to Louis XIV. of 14 June, 1700.

CHAPTER VI

ACCESSION OF PHILIPPE D'ANJOU TO THE THRONE OF SPAIN (1700)

WE have now arrived at the epoch when the veil which has hitherto allowed but fitful and hazy glimpses of our heroine is raised for good and she emerges on the stage of European politics before the garish light which beats on thrones.

A *protagoniste* no longer young, twice a widow, battered and bruised by passions and struggles, who makes her bow to the public at the mature age of fifty-eight. And what a public! Kings, popes and emperors hang on her words. Prime ministers and state secretaries are her pupils in diplomacy. Her quarrels and *coups d'états*, her scandals and intrigues keep all Europe on the alert. Ambassadors are recalled and disgraced at her frown and the College of Cardinals furnishes her with willing slaves to be utilised and thrown aside when done with.

Her real history begins only at the accession of Philippe d'Anjou, grandson of Louis XIV., to the throne of Spain, and we must leave her for a moment to speak of that important event.

Charles II. of Spain was on his death-bed. Feeble-minded as a boy he had grown ever more imbecile, until now, at the close of his life, he had become completely insane, an easy prey to the intrigues of which his throne was the object, miserable victim on one side of the machinations of Louis XIV., claiming it for one of his grandsons, on the other, of the Emperor Leopold insisting on the rights of his second son the Archduke Charles.

Louis' first open move had been to strengthen his claim and thwart the influence of the Queen-Regent by a marriage with his niece, Marie-Louise d'Orléans. She died, however, in 1689, poisoned, it was said, by the partisans of Austria, and a year later Leopold in his turn married him to his wife's sister, Marie-Anne of Bavaria-Neubourg, Princess Palatine. As it was no secret that he was incapable of having children, these marriages had no other object than

ACCESSION OF PHILIPPE D'ANJOU 45

to influence him to sign away his kingdom in favour of one of the claimants, and the European Powers, aware that war was inevitable, kept their armies in readiness to support the Emperor's claims.

For there was no longer any hesitation as to the side they intended to take in the coming tussle. Louis' ambitions had been a source of alarm ever since his first invasion of Flanders and his fortification of the frontier towns had set the seal on their apprehensions. His intrigues in Italy and the cruel pressure put by his agents on the imbecile King had excited universal reprobation, and they were prepared to throw themselves on the side of Austria all the more readily that the possession of Spain would make him practically master of Europe, for at that date not only Lombardy, the Two Sicilies and the Netherlands were under Spanish rule, but part of America and the Indies with their immense wealth and commercial advantages. Added to this, instead of trying to disarm them by prudence and conciliation he had adopted an air of arrogance and exuberance as though he were already the conqueror.

Whether he would have succeeded in his latest imprudence of annexing the vast Spanish empire without the aid of the Princess des Ursins is open to doubt. The Queen of Spain was a formidable power with her intelligence and the facilities offered by her position of perpetually torturing the dying King in his last moments, and had she not been opposed by one more terrible still, since to his victim's superstition he had the power of torturing not only here but hereafter, it is probable that the testament which set all Europe ablaze would never have been signed.

This sinister personage, who played with so much cruelty on his morbid fears, menacing him with eternal fire if he refused his signature to a will in favour of a Bourbon heir, was no other than the Cardinal Porto-Carrero, and the ignoble coercion of which he was guilty at this important crisis was undoubtedly due to the influence if not the direct order of the Princess, for whom his early passion had degenerated into a senile infatuation.

Louis-Emmanuel Boccanera, Cardinal Porto-Carrero, Regent of Spain during the King's incapacity, Archbishop of Toledo and in that capacity Primate of Spain, Chancellor of Castile and First Grandee, was at this time a man of seventy. He was said to be the richest of the Spanish nobles, and to this and his high ecclesiastical rank, rather than to any personal power, merit or intelligence, was due the great influence he formerly had, for at this date both faculties and influence were on the wane, and sinister as he appeared to the demented King, to the rest of humanity he seemed now little more than a weak and foolish old man.

Here is his portrait in the words of Saint-Simon :

> Tall, with white hair, rather fat and with a cheerful expression, a venerable mien and noble and majestic bearing. Honest, courteous, frank, with much probity, grandeur and nobility, with justice and common sense but very mediocre intelligence and capacity. Very opinionated and obstinate, a fairly good politician, an excellent friend, an implacable enemy, wanting to meddle with everything and govern everybody.[1]

Jealous and envious of any authority in the hands of his own countrymen he preferred to admit foreigners to the Government, and had for this reason always been in favour of the French succession. He had been extremely useful to the Princess in the fulfilment of her mission in Rome, and her success in winning over so many of the Spanish subjects in Italy was due in a great measure to him. He was her tool and she made full use of him, and by this final act of obedience to her will he threw open the door through which she passed to her full triumph, winning at one stroke the favour of the King of France and the high place she filled in the monarchy of Spain. It will be seen later how she rewarded him.

On receipt of the news that his dearest wish was fulfilled and the twenty-three crowns of the Spanish monarchy left to his grandson, Louis lost for the moment his habitual autocratic reserve. Usually, he decided the gravest political questions in the solitude of his private cabinet and on issuing thence had already made up his mind without any show of consulting his ministers. But this question of the Spanish succession was too fraught with danger to be borne entirely on his own shoulders, shoulders already beginning to be bowed with age, for Louis was well aware that his acceptance of the inheritance would excite not only Austria but the whole of Europe against him, and that in sending his grandson to mount the throne of Spain he was certainly sending him to peril and probably to his death. Thus there was

[1] Saint-Simon, vii. 256.

ACCESSION OF PHILIPPE D'ANJOU

a stir in the palace of Versailles and a secret council was summoned in haste to the apartment of Madame de Maintenon.

Madame de Maintenon, apparently indifferent, but in reality supremely interested, was seated as usual in her *niche* by the chimney-piece.[1] At the head of the table Louis, stately and serious, presided. Around it were the Dauphin, the Chancellor, the Duc de Beauvillier and the Marquis de Torcy. Louis' face, arranged for the circumstance, for Louis was always on parade, wore a determined expression, and all read in his attitude that his mind was already made up to accept the will.

However, the danger was too formidable for conscientious advisers to be merely complacent, and all three of the ministers gave their voice against; Torcy as Secretary for Foreign Affairs being particularly opposed. Louis remained silent, too well versed in statecraft not to know he was right.. But the Dauphin, usually "encased in fat and apathy," lost for once his indifference, and red with anger, declared violently that the throne of Spain belonged to him of right, but that since his position forbade his ascending it himself, nothing in the world should deprive his son of the inheritance. Still Louis remained silent and thoughtful. As for Madame de Maintenon she might as well not have been in the room for all sign she gave of her presence.

Suddenly Louis turned to her. "And you, Madame," he asked, "what is your opinion?"

Madame de Maintenon, by inclination and principle, warmest partisan of peace, and well aware of the European conflagration the acceptance would ignite, but aware also that her despot's decision was irrevocable and that her own position was not as solid as it seemed, was probably quaking at the choice she was forced to make between her God and her King. So she remained silent.

"Madame! I asked your opinion," Louis repeated sternly.

All eyes were fixed upon her, the ministers with hope, the Dauphin, who never liked her, with anger, Louis with

[1] Madame de Maintenon, grown old and rheumatic and unable to support the icy draughts between window and door which Louis loved and inflicted on everybody, had invented a kind of high wooden pew lined with red damask, of which she had one in each room she frequented in the different palaces.

menace. Poor Madame de Maintenon, so unjustly envied and maligned! Uncrowned Queen of France she might be, but her life as Louis' wife was not enviable. Forced now against her better judgment and religious convictions to obey, she faltered tremulously, "My opinion is that the testament be accepted." And she sighed as she leant back in the obscurity of her *niche*, for she probably foresaw already the downfall of the monarchy.

The next day, 16 November, 1700, Louis, rising early, sent for the Spanish Ambassador to his cabinet which the young Duc d'Anjou had already entered by a private door. "Here is your King!" he said, with his grand air, as the Ambassador presented himself in the doorway. The Ambassador fell on his knees, and immediately at a sign from Louis, the incomparable comedian, all the doors were thrown wide and the crowd of courtiers, awaiting the signal, entered. "Gentlemen, here is the King of Spain!" Louis again proclaimed with appropriate arm-gesture. "His birth called him to the Crown, the late King, also, in his testament. All the nation has desired and begged me urgently for it. It is the order of Heaven which I gladly obey." Then turning to his grandson he added: "Be a good Spaniard, that is your first duty, but never forget that you are born French." With which enigmatic words he closed the scene and the Spanish Ambassador again threw himself on his knees, and with clasped hands raised to Heaven cried out the memorable words (attributed to so many different personages): "The Pyrenees have ceased to exist!"

So the curtain dropped on the prologue to the fifteen years' War of Spanish Succession.

CHAPTER VII

INSTRUCTIONS OF LOUIS XIV. TO HIS GRANDSON (1700)

It will not be out of place to insert at this point the famous instructions composed by Louis for his grandson, and presented to him at the moment of his departure for Spain on 5 December, 1700, curious mixture as they are of worldliness and piety :

I. Omit none of your duties, above all towards God.

II. Preserve yourself in the purity in which you have been brought up.

III. Cause God to be honoured everywhere where you have power. Procure His glory, by yourself giving the example. It is one of the greatest benefits that kings can bestow.

IV. Declare yourself on every occasion for Virtue opposed to Vice.

V. Never tie yourself to anyone.

VI. Love your wife, live well with her, pray God for one that is suitable. I do not think you should take an Austrian.

VII. Love the Spaniards and all your subjects attached to your Crown and person. Do not give preference to those who flatter you most. Esteem those who, for a good purpose, risk your displeasure, for they are your true friends.

VIII. Make the welfare of your subjects and to this end make no war except when you are forced and after you have well weighed and considered the reasons in your Council.

IX. Try to restore your finances. Watch over the Indies and over your fleet. Consider your commerce. Live in close union with France, nothing being so good for our two powers as this union which makes them invincible.

X. If you are forced to go to war, put yourself at the head of your armies.

XI. Think of re-establishing your troops everywhere and begin by those of Flanders.

XII. Never abandon business for pleasure but draw up for yourself a kind of programme which gives you hours of freedom and amusement.

XIII. No amusements are more innocent than hunting and building châteaux, provided you do not thereby incur too great expense.

XIV. Give the greatest attention to business when you are consulted. Listen much at the beginning without making any decision.

XV. When you have more knowledge remember that it is for you to decide, but however much experience you may have, listen always to all the advice and reasonings of your Council before deciding.

XVI. Do all in your power to study the people of most importance so as to make use of them at the right time.

XVII. Do your best that your viceroys and governors shall be always Spaniards.

XVIII. Treat everyone well, never say disagreeable things to anyone but distinguish people of quality and merit.

XIX. Show gratitude to the late King and all those who helped to choose you as his successor.

XX. Have great confidence in Cardinal Porto-Carrero and show him how much you appreciate his conduct.

XXI. I think you should do something considerable for the Ambassador who has had the happiness to first salute you in the quality of subject.

XXII. Do not forget Bedmar who has merit and is capable of serving you.[1]

XXIII. Have entire confidence in the Duc d'Harcourt. He is a clever and honest man and will give you none but disinterested counsel.[2]

XXIV. Keep all the French in order.

XXV. Treat your servants well but do not allow them too much familiarity and still less credit. Make use of them when they behave well, dismiss them at the least fault they commit and never take their part against the Spanish.

XXVI. Have no more dealings with the Queen-Dowager than such as are strictly necessary. Arrange that she quits Madrid but see that she does not leave Spain. Wherever she is, observe her behaviour and prevent her from interfering in any affairs. Be suspicious of those who have much to do with her.

XXVII. Love always your relatives. Remember the pain they had in parting from you. Keep up relations with them in large and small matters. Ask us for all you need and desire

---

[1] The Marquis of Bedmar, Spanish general much liked by Louis; later Viceroy of Sicily.

[2] French Ambassador at Madrid on Philippe's accession.

which you cannot obtain in Spain and we will do the like with you.

XXVIII. Never forget that you are French and what may happen to you. When you shall have assured the succession of Spain by children, visit your kingdoms. Go to Naples and Sicily, pass through Milan and come to Flanders, it will be an occasion for us to see each other. Meanwhile visit Catalonia, Aragon and other places.

XXIX Throw money to the people when you arrive in Spain and, above all, on entering Madrid.

XXX. Do not appear shocked at the strange figures you will find. Do not mock them. Each country has its special customs and you will soon grow accustomed to that which at first may appear the most astonishing.

XXXI. Avoid as much as possible to bestow favours on those who pay to obtain them. Give them freely and at the right moment and do not accept gifts except they be very trifling. If sometimes you cannot avoid receiving them, give something more considerable to the donors after a few days.

XXXII. Keep a coffer for your private affairs of which you only have the key.

XXXIII. I end by one of the most important counsels I can give you. Do not let yourself be governed. Be the Master. Never have a favourite nor a Prime Minister. Listen to and consult your Council but decide for yourself. God, who has made you King, will give you the necessary light as long as your intentions are good.[1]

[1] *Mémoires de Louis XIV.* (Paris, 1806), ii. 173.

CHAPTER VIII

CAMARERA MAYOR (1701)

PHILIPPE D'ANJOU, a youth of seventeen, left Versailles for his kingdom on 5 December, 1700, and arrived in Madrid the middle of the following February. Louis and all his Court accompanied him as far as Sceaux and both kings wept as they bade each other farewell. They were never to meet again.

His brothers, the Dukes of Burgundy and Berry, rode with him to the Spanish frontier and then turned back, leaving him entirely alone, and, for sole friend, guide and comforter, the man least suited to be either, the Marquis de Louville, his tutor and gentleman of the bedchamber.

The boy was terribly depressed, for he loved his family, his brothers especially, and he had left everything he cared for to go into exile among a people who, in their sombre superstition and melancholy, were the very reverse of his own frivolous countrymen.

Brought up in the gayest Court of Europe, accustomed to the perpetual fêtes which made up its life, he was homesick and miserable. He missed the incessant movement of the Court, the hunting-parties and open-air life of Versailles and Marly, the helter-skelter drives in the forest, the balls and comedies, the companionship of his brothers and his gay little sister-in-law the Duchess of Burgundy, and would gladly have renounced the crown for which he had sacrificed all he held dear.

However, he was welcomed with enthusiasm by his new subjects, but in a manner which only increased his misery, for after the fashion of the country they showed their joy by burning heretics and slaying bulls in his honour. Bullfights and *autos-da-fé* greeted his arrival in every town from the moment he crossed the frontier till he reached Madrid, and the sight of blood and smell and crackle of burnt flesh sickened him so much that, finally, he refused to assist. This was his first offence in the eyes of his subjects; the second was that God was visibly unfavourable, and showed His displeasure by a premonitory omen.

The road to Madrid was lined with the coaches—five thousand of them—of the nobles who had driven out to welcome him, and when all this cavalcade reached the city the crowd was so dense that sixty citizens were crushed to death, and as the day happened to be Friday, those in favour of Austria began to look askance, boding no good from the advent of the foreigner.

Spain, at the time of Philippe's accession, was in a state of complete decadence. "A country without army, justice or police, and absolutely without liberty," Louville described it: "a veritable oligarchy composed of people united by pride, divided by ambition, and sunk in sloth. A palace silent and filled with intrigue, a clergy too rich and too dependent on Rome. A formidable Inquisition always at war, externally with the Pope, internally with the people, and thousands of monks—each Order, often each convent, opposed to and at open warfare with the rest."[1] And again: "The grandees are contemptuous and contemptible. They have nothing except pride, poverty, laziness and the pox. They have no education and no sort of knowledge."[2]

The people, incredibly idle or disdaining to work, left whole provinces of fertile ground uncultivated. There was no commerce, no industry, and consequently no money. Even at Court the poverty was sordid, and Louville wrote to Torcy that there was not a sou to buy napkins nor put new doors to the cellars, that the palace servants were in rags and had to beg for alms, and that on his arrival Philippe had not a penny to put in his pocket.[3]

His depression grew so great that soon after his accession he declared that, happen what might, he would renounce the crown and return to France, and Louville, aware of the peculiarities of his temperament, wrote to Louis that if he did not speedily marry his grandson he would either die or go mad.

Naturally, from the moment that the crown was accepted, there had been talk of a suitable wife, and all the princesses

---

[1] Louville, *Mémoires secrets sur l'établissement de la Maison de Bourbon en Espagne*, i. 68. The *Mémoires* were not written by Louville himself but compiled from his correspondence by Comte Scipion du Roure.
[2] Saint-Simon, xi. 532; letter to Chamillart of 23 Aug. 1703.
[3] Louville, i. 162; letter to Torcy of 19 April, 1701.

of Europe were passed in review. In his testament the late King, or rather his advisers, had wisely expressed the desire that the future Queen should be a Hapsbourg in order to unite the rival houses. The Pope was strongly in favour of an Austrian alliance, and so were the majority of the Spanish. But Louis preferred the prospect of war to sharing his newly acquired province with his enemy, and since the centre of the pro-Austrian party was in Rome, the Princess des Ursins was again employed to reconcile them to an alliance which should strengthen French influence.

The wife chosen by Louis was the sister of the Duchess of Burgundy, Marie-Louise-Gabrielle, second daughter of Victor-Amédée II., Duke of Savoy, whose alliance at this time had special value on account of the position of his territory. Her blood was more than half French, for her mother was daughter of Philippe d'Orléans, Louis' brother, and Henrietta of England, daughter of Charles II., and her grandmother was also a French princess.

On account of these alliances it might be supposed that the Duke was entirely Francophile, but he had suffered so much from Louis' arrogance and exactions that all his sympathies were with his enemy and, egoistic as Louis himself, he had adopted since the outbreak of the war the policy of allying himself to whichever of the rivals was uppermost for the moment. Louis, less tyrannic now that he needed his services, hoped that this fresh alliance might strengthen an allegiance obviously wavering, but it will be seen that the Duke of Savoy was perfectly indifferent to family ties and, bent on obtaining the title of King, was ready to sacrifice both his daughters to satisfy this ambition.

The Princess, in her journeys to and from France, had seen much of the little Court of Turin, was liked by the Duchess and Dowager Duchess and esteemed by the Duke himself, since she had been instrumental in the marriage of his eldest daughter, and her opinion being asked as to the suitability of the younger as a wife for Philippe V., she declared unhesitatingly that nothing could be better.

The marriage, therefore, was decided, but not without bitter opposition on the part of Austria and Spain. Indignation ran high in the papal states, where nearly all were in favour of an Austrian archduchess, but the Princess succeeded in winning over the most important of the objectors with so much tact and skill that Versailles was enthusiastic

CAMARERA MAYOR

in her praise, and Torcy himself wrote that he "lowered his flag before her and would like to become her pupil in diplomacy."[1]

After this second success it is not surprising that she should think of claiming a reward higher than a mere increase of pension, and even before the date of the marriage was fixed she sent in her demand that she might be appointed to accompany the young Princess from Turin to Madrid. Humbly she asked, and with a persistence and eagerness which the post in itself did not warrant to a woman of her rank, but behind it she had in view another so important that she did not dare hint it even to her old friend the Maréchale de Noailles.

It was to this old friend that she now appealed to intercede in her favour at Versailles, and as at the commencement of her career the Maréchale served as intermediary between her and Madame de Maintenon, thus playing an important part in her success, she in her turn must be presented with due ceremony.

Marie-Françoise de Bournonville, Duchesse de Noailles, had, thanks to the great name and credit of her husband the Maréchal, a high position at Court, much influence and constant access to Louis and Madame de Maintenon, in spite of the fact that she was liked by neither.[2] She had no less than twenty-one children, nine of them daughters, and having produced this astonishing family, lived to the ripe old age of ninety-three. But this is to forestall. At this time she was one of the closest and most solid of the Princess's friends and helped her with never-failing kindness, and it was to her that the Princess now turned to obtain the appointment she coveted.

The great affair of which I want to speak to you [she had written as early as 27 December] regards the marriage of the King of Spain with the Princess of Savoy and my great wish, in case it takes place, and since a *dame titrée*[3] is necessary to accompany this young Princess, I beg you to suggest me for the post before the King casts his eyes elsewhere. I may say that I am better fitted for it than anybody else by reason of the great number of friends I have in the country and the advantage I possess of being grandee of Spain.[4] Besides this I

---

[1] Geffroy, 15. [2] Saint-Simon, xxviii. 245.
[3] No one below the rank of duchess was *titré* at the Court of Versailles.
[4] She was grandee of Spain as wife of the Duke of Bracciano.

speak Spanish and am moreover sure that the choice would please all the nation, by whom I can boast of having been always loved and esteemed.

My plan would be to go as far as Madrid, to remain there as long as the King pleased and return to the Court to render an account to His Majesty of my journey. If it were merely a question of accompanying the Queen to the frontier I should not think of the post, for what makes me chiefly desire it—after the King's service which comes first—is that I want to settle at the Spanish Court some important affairs I have in Naples. I should be very glad also to see my friends there and among others the Cardinal Porto-Carrero, with whom I could try to arrange marriages for a dozen of your daughters. You must know that I rely on him in Spain almost as solidly as I do on you in France. The friendship he has for me goes so far that he sends me gifts of all that is rarest in his country, and only a week ago I received one charming and magnificent enough to be offered to a queen. Judge by this if I could not make rain or sunshine at that Court and if it is too much vanity that I offer my services.[1]

A modest request enough from a person of her rank and social importance to play the *gouvernante* to the child-Queen on her journey from Turin to Spain, to accompany her to Madrid and then retire into the background. But she had no intention once there of leaving and the post she actually coveted was the reverse of modest, of such importance, indeed, that with all her high rank and qualifications she knew it to be out of her reach except through intrigue, for the post to which she aspired was no less than that of Camarera Mayor, First Lady of the Palace, an appointment to which only Spanish ladies of the very highest rank could aspire and hitherto absolutely inaccessible to a foreigner.

The Camarera Mayor indeed had influence in the palace second only to that of the King and Queen, to whom she came next in rank. Her coach followed directly after theirs in State ceremonies. Her liveries were the same. Her apartment was in communication with that of the Queen. The ladies of the palace—all grandees of the highest rank—were under her control, chosen by her and dismissed if necessary. She arranged audiences, admitted or rejected applicants, assisted at the Queen's toilet and served her and the King at table. It was a post extremely fatiguing, as she soon found out, but of unlimited opportunities for ambitions of the highest order, and in the present case, con-

[1] Trémoïlle, i. 69; letter of 27 Dec. 1700.

sidering the Queen's youth and the influence such perpetual contact must bring, of an importance second only to that of the King himself.

The Camarera Mayor [writes Saint-Simon] unites the functions of superintendent, *dame d'honneur* and lady of the bedchamber. She is always a grandee of Spain, a widow, generally old, and of the highest rank. She lodges in the palace, presents persons of quality to the Queen, enters her apartments at all hours and shares the command of them with the Mayordomo Mayor. . . . She looks after the clothes and personal expenses of the Queen, whom she may never quit but must follow her wherever she goes. She has the first right to ride in the Queen's coach when the King is not with her, and she is served even in her own house by the inferior officers of the Royal chamber and can dispose of much of the Royal provisions. . . . She serves the King and Queen when they eat in the Queen's apartment, and the Queen when the King does not eat with her, and kneels on one knee when she presents the wine or basin for washing.[1]

Elsewhere he writes:

The Camarera Mayor is always a grandee of Spain, a widow and with great experience of the Court. . . . Those are generally chosen who have much virtue, reason, intelligence and modesty. She has her apartment adjoining that of the Queen. It is she who puts on her chemise and indoor clothing and she continues to dress her, aided by the ladies of the palace on service, and the *caméristes* bring and give all that Her Majesty puts on, taking care that all is in order and very clean. She assists at the Queen's toilet as well as her breakfast. She lays the cloth with the Mayordomo Mayor and stands facing Her Majesty to carve and serve the meats, changing the plates at dinner and supper, and afterwards she assists at the Queen's undressing until she gets into bed.[2]

It will be seen that the duties of this high priestess of the Court were no sinecure, and in our own democratic postwar days it would be difficult to find a maid-of-all-work to undertake work so unceasing and laborious.

Louis and his Foreign Minister, the Marquis de Torcy,[3] broken-in to intrigues—and it must be owned that the Princess's letter was fairly transparent—divined at once her true object in demanding the relatively unimportant

[1] Saint-Simon, viii. 173.
[2] Ibid., viii. 518, appendix xi.
[3] The Marquis de Torcy was nephew of the great Colbert and at this time Secretary of State for Foreign Affairs.

post of accompanying the Queen to Spain, and their answer was far from encouraging. The Spanish were a jealous, susceptible people, not too well pleased to have a French Prince to reign over them, and capable of open revolt at the appearance side by side with their new sovereign of a Frenchwoman known to be in the service of Louis XIV. But in view of the services she had rendered, Louis was unwilling openly to refuse, and shifted the responsibility from his own shoulders to those of the Duke of Savoy, declaring in answer to her petition that the appointment rested with him.

But the Princess was not easily discouraged, and aware that it was untrue, yet unable to give the lie to the King of France, she lost not a moment in bombarding the Court of Savoy—the Duke and the two Duchesses—with fresh entreaties. From them she received nothing but replies politely vague. Finally, she attacked no less a person than Philippe himself through his minister Porto-Carrero, who wrote her the truth, that no one but Louis had the smallest voice in the matter.[1]

This letter was all she needed, and she immediately sent it to the Maréchale de Noailles with fresh prayers and arguments, imploring her intercession with Madame de Maintenon, and bribing her with promises to recommend to Porto-Carrero's good graces her son the Comte d'Ayen, then setting out to win his laurels in Madrid.[2]

So great, however, was Louis' objection that, notwithstanding the mediation of Porto-Carrero and the Duc d'Harcourt, his Ambassador at Madrid, he continued to hesitate, until finally the one person capable of moving him was persuaded to intervene. On 16 April, nearly three months after the Princess's first appeal, Madame de Maintenon wrote to the Duc d'Harcourt as follows:

As I give my opinion on matters concerning ladies more readily than on others, I propose that it shall be Madame de Bracciano who brings the Princess of Savoy to you. She is a woman of intelligence, gentle and polite, with a knowledge of foreigners, who has always represented well and made herself liked everywhere. She is grandee of Spain, without husband

---

[1] Trémoïlle, i. 74; letter of Porto-Carrero to the Princess des Ursins of 3 March, 1701.

[2] Ibid., i. 75, etc.; letters to the Maréchale de Noailles of 29 March and 26 April, 1701.

or children, and thus without embarrassing pretensions. I say all this to you without design or special interest, but simply because I think her more suitable for your purpose than any other woman here.[1]

What was the reason of this friendly intervention? It is generally stated that Madame de Maintenon, having taken Spain under her special protection, was desirous of governing it through a reliable and able viceroy. Saint-Simon, giving voice to the whispers of Versailles, decides otherwise. According to him, she dispatched the Princess to Spain in order to put the Pyrenees between her and Louis, terrified of the attraction she undoubtedly had for him, in constant fear of being ousted from her nest as she had ousted her protectress Madame de Montespan. " Madame de Maintenon was easily persuaded," he writes, " because she would for ever be rid of her." [2]

It is possible that Saint-Simon was right. So much has been written of the friendship of these two women, of Madame de Maintenon's admiration for and reliance on her " lieutenant in Spain," that it has grown to be a popular tradition, and their names have become inseparably linked in the category of ideal friendships.

The truth is that friendship never existed between them. Fate threw them across each other's path as opponents rather than allies. Up to now their positions were so different that their personal relations had been of the slightest, the Princess hardly daring to approach the wife of Louis XIV. except through the Maréchale de Noailles, for, although her marriage was never openly acknowledged, she received from his family all the deference due to his wife, and held at Court a position inferior only to his own. Feared and flattered by all the Royal family, even the Dauphin, who disliked her, her influence with Louis was so great that she could make or mar with a smile or a frown. Friendship at this date between her and the Princess could not exist, but rivals they already were for the affections of their sovereign. Only later, when the Princess had achieved for herself in Spain a position almost analogous to that of her protectress in France, did they meet on more equal ground,

---

[1] Lavallée, *Correspondance de Madame de Maintenon*, iv. 423 ; letter of 16 April, 1701.
[2] Saint-Simon, v. 499, appendix vi.

and by that time their rivalry had developed to open hostility.

Whatever the cause of Madame de Maintenon's intervention, the Princess was the gainer by it. Four days after her letter Torcy wrote officially to d'Harcourt to announce the appointment and at the same time to prepare him for that of Camarera Mayor.

> His Majesty will appoint the Duchess of Bracciano to conduct the new Queen from the frontier of the kingdom on the side of Savoy to that of Spain. . . . During the journey she will perform the functions of Camarera Mayor, and the King of Spain must name no other. Should difficulties arise later, either on the part of the Spaniards or for any other reason, the time she will have remained with the Princess during this long journey will always have been useful. . . . The King is convinced that no one is more capable than she of acquitting herself well in this post.[1]

A week later Louis himself wrote to Blécourt, temporarily replacing the Duc d'Harcourt during a severe illness (which eventually forced him to resign the embassy):

> My view has always been, when I chose the Princess des Ursins to conduct the Queen of Spain, that she should afterwards remain in Madrid in quality of Camarera Mayor. I am persuaded that it is also the intention of the King my grandson, and as she will not be given this title during the journey it is very necessary to prevent that the post be filled by another. It must remain vacant during the journey of the Queen of Spain, and the Princess des Ursins, having completed the function of conductress, will then be appointed by the Catholic King [2] to remain near the Queen his wife.[3]

Finally, on 7 July, Torcy wrote to the Comte de Marsin, the new Ambassador:

> As the King of Spain is of a gentle, yielding disposition it will be easy for the Queen his wife to acquire a strong influence over his mind. Consequently it would be dangerous to place near her people whose intentions are open to suspicion. The choice of Camarera Mayor or *dame d'honneur* is very important, and His Majesty thinks that the post cannot be better filled than by the Princess des Ursins. The late Duke her husband, head of the House of Orsini, was grandee of Spain. She has

---

[1] Saint-Simon, ix. 384, appendix ix.; letter from Torcy to the Duc d'Harcourt of 20 April, 1701.
[2] The official title of the Kings of Spain was *Sa Majesté Catholique*, as that of the Kings of France was *Sa Majesté Très-Chrétienne*.
[3] Trémoïlle, i. 81; instructions to Blécourt of 28 June, 1701.

spent part of her life in foreign countries. She knows the customs of Spain, and adding to these advantages a great deal of intelligence and courtliness, she seems more capable than anyone else to instruct a young Princess in the art of governing a Court with dignity. She will not be regarded as a stranger in Spain, and yet she will be sufficiently so not to take part in the intrigues and cabals of the Court of Madrid. The Catholic King should write to her to beg her to conduct the Princess of Savoy to Spain, but it is not sufficient that she make the journey only, the intention of the King being that she remain there after this function . . . and as the Princess des Ursins will not accompany the Queen in the capacity of Camarera Mayor, but only to conduct her, the charge must not be filled during this interval.[1]

A few days later he wrote to Porto-Carrero that it was uncertain whether she would consent to remain in Madrid, but to be hoped that she would, " no one being more capable than she of acquitting herself well in such a post." [2]

Thus, so skilfully had she played her cards that not only had she gained the post she coveted and dared not ask for, but was begged as a favour to accept it.

She received the news of her success informally the beginning of May, and at once began her preparations for the journey—none too soon since the wedding was fixed for August. On 20 June the Spanish Ambassador arrived at her palace and handed her with great ceremony the official brevet of her appointment, accompanied by an autograph letter from Philippe himself. Her first act, now that she was in his service, was to set up over her door the Royal Spanish arms side by side with the Fleurs-de-lys of France.

I do not think there exists in the world a woman so busy as I [she wrote in high spirits to the Maréchale a week later]. I do not know if it is too vain to tell you, but I see no one who does not applaud the honour the King has done me. . . . Everyone comes to congratulate me, and the Pope himself sent a prelate to tell me of his infinite joy and assure me that he would look after my affairs during my absence. The Spaniards regard the choice as very advantageous to their country.

She wishes, she continues, to make her appearance in Madrid with some magnificence to do honour to her position.

---

[1] Trémoïlle, i. 82 ; letter of 7 July, 1701.
[2] Ibid., i. 83 ; letter of 13 July, 1701.

THE PRINCESS DES URSINS

Her household, already, as we have seen, of some importance, has to be increased, two or three more nobles added to her four gentlemen, eight pages instead of six, and a dozen more lackeys. New liveries must be provided, for the Spanish Court is in mourning (for Philippe d'Orléans, Louis' brother), and hers, which are embroidered with gold, may not be worn there and must, for economy's sake, be used up on the journey. On her arrival she will order new liveries even more magnificent, entirely of silk. Her gold coach drawn by six horses she will take with her for use when the mourning is over, and meanwhile has ordered another equally splendid but more sober. As for women—necessary evils she considers them—she will have as few as possible, one lady companion only as indispensable, but no Italians, for " they are too intriguing and bold and have not sufficiently good manners." This lady companion must naturally have her own servants—a valet and *femme-de-chambre*—and no doubt, though she omits to mention them, she herself would be accompanied by a regiment of *femmes-de-chambre*, hairdressers and other officials of the elaborate toilet for which she was celebrated. And all this splendour was to be paid for out of the thirty thousand francs allowed her by Louis for the expenses of her journey, for she is decided to ask no more. " I am a pauper (*Je suis gueuse*), but I am proud all the same," she ends her letter.[1]

[1] Geffroy, 109 ; letter of 28 June, 1701.

PHILIPPE V.
From a portrait by Rigaud in the Musée du Louvre.

CHAPTER IX

ROYAL PUPPETS (1701)

WE must leave the Princess busy with her preparations, and see who and what are the boy and girl she has elected to be her future masters—or puppets.

Philippe V., formerly Duc d'Anjou, second son of the Grand Dauphin, was born at Versailles 1683, and was thus seventeen years old at his accession to the throne of Spain.

Did no other record of his treacherous, joyless character exist, it could be accurately judged by the portrait of him now in the Louvre, painted by Rigaud the Court painter to commemorate his accession.[1] A slight sickly boy with pasty face and flaxen hair, an expression vacillating and weak, but not without the dignity born of self-esteem. He is dressed in the funereal black velvet of the Spanish Court, well suited to his melancholy temperament. The face gives the impression of indolence, but not of the monstrous sensuality which rendered him so easy a prey to his two wives, for with this sensuality was coupled a morbid piety which forbade him to take a mistress, with the result that they had over him an absolute power, and had only to refuse him their bed to gain whatever they asked.

Here is Saint-Simon's description of him at his departure from France: " The King was well made, in the flower of his first youth, fair like the late King and the Queen his grandmother, grave, silent, measured and reserved, as though born to live among the Spaniards." [2]

Here is a later description of one who knew him well—" Madame," his great-aunt the Princess Palatine, mother of Philippe d'Orléans, afterwards Regent of France:

Very hump-backed and ill-made . . . with pretty features and beautiful hair, and, what is strange, hair of a beautiful

[1] Dangeau quotes the following from the gazette *Le Mercure* of Dec. 1700: " The first of the month the Sieur Rigaud, famous painter, who has been appointed by the King to paint His Catholic Majesty, worked for the first time at the portrait of this monarch. All the Court was charmed at his first sketch " (Dangeau, vi. 442).
[2] Saint-Simon, viii. 103.

yellow, his eyes being quite black. His complexion is white and red, he has the Austrian lip, a loud voice and speaks with incredible slowness. He is good and peaceable, but rather obstinate when he gets an idea in his head. He loves his wife above everything, leaves her all the work and meddles with scarcely anything. He is religious and would think himself damned if he slept with any other woman than her. Without religion he would be a libertine, for he cannot do without women. This is why he loves her. The good King asks nothing more than to have a woman in his bed. He lets himself be led without difficulty, this is why the Queen will not let him out of her sight. . . . He has great need of being surrounded by clever people, for his own intelligence would not carry him far, but he has a good heart. He is rather melancholy, and nothing in Spain can amuse him.[1]

Melancholy certainly, but as for the good heart—we shall see!

Louis himself said of him that he was too cold and silent, and on Madame de Maintenon's nerves he had evidently got, for she wrote to the Duc d'Harcourt: "His voice and the slowness with which he speaks are very disagreeable. Perhaps they will be less shocked by it in Madrid than here at Versailles."[2]

That he was deformed, had one shoulder higher than the other, and was unsteady on his legs, we know from the Princess des Ursins, who wrote of him six years later: "He holds his head higher than he did and begins to be firmer on his legs. His figure is very much better and I hope in a short time that his shoulders will be entirely symmetrical."[3]

The terrible deformity of his later years, his body swollen to a balloon on frightful bandy legs, Saint-Simon himself describes when as Ambassador in 1721 he was in Madrid.

Such was physically this degenerate grandson of the handsome Louis XIV. His character was even more deformed than his person.

He was indolent, indifferent, tactless and stupid to an incredible degree. Selfish and self-centred, he would keep the Council waiting for hours without reason, and when there sit yawning and inattentive, indifferent to all that was going on. He would keep the Queen waiting two or

[1] *Mémoires de Madame la Duchesse d'Orléans, Princesse Palatine*, ed. Busoni, p. 244.
[2] Lavallée, *Correspondance de Madame de Maintenon*, iv. 350; letter of 3 Dec. 1700.
[3] Geffroy, 286; letter to Madame de Maintenon of 23 Dec. 1706.

three hours for meals, pass whole days without opening his lips, and often throw himself into a chair and shed torrents of tears for no reason. He would keep letters, even those he knew to be important, for weeks unopened in his pocket, and would not give himself the trouble to compose his own, even to his grandfather. " He had some curiosity in reigning," wrote Louville to the Duc de Beauvillier, " but do you know how he showed it ? By listening at the doors of the council-chamber behind the tapestry placed there for that purpose." [1] And again : " He has taken a fancy for Quintana " (one of his French suite) " and he kisses him all day long before all the others and that with a familiarity and foolishness which makes me sick." [2]

> The Prince [Saint-Simon thus excuses him], younger brother of an elder, quick, violent, impetuous, very intelligent but of terrible temper and outrageous obstinacy [the Duke of Burgundy], had been educated in a dependence and submission necessary to avoid troubles and assure the tranquillity of the Royal family. . . . His mind and all dependent on it was therefore nipped and suppressed by this indispensable kind of education, which, falling on a character gentle and quiet, habituated him neither to think nor act, but to let himself be easily led. . . . The great piety in which he had been carefully educated, not being allied to habits of judgment and discernment, nipped and suppressed him still more, so much that in spite of good sense, intelligence and speech, slow but just and well expressed, he seemed made expressly to be shut up and governed. To all these dispositions he united another, very extraordinary, born of the union of piety with an ardent temperament, with which last he was so liberally endowed that he was incommoded by it even to the peril of his life during his journey to Italy . . . and had no relief until he rejoined the Queen. Hence it may be judged how much he loved her and attached himself to her, and how well she knew how to profit by it.[3]

Thus Saint-Simon, prince of sycophants, excuses him because he was a king. Had he been a mere *bourgeois* he would have found him fit only for a lunatic asylum. On his so-called " ardent temperament " it is best not to dwell, but it is a fact that his first wife's death was due to his abuse of her complacence, as well as his own subsequent insanity. Half-monk, half-satyr, he would leave her bed to avow his

---

[1] Louville, *Mémoires*, i. 133.   [2] Ibid., i. 136.
[3] Saint-Simon, xi. 231.

weakness to his confessor and after absolution return again to her arms.

Feeble and irresolute, he resembles—hardly a puppet, for puppets respond briskly enough when their wires are pulled—but one of those bran-stuffed dolls which collapse unless propped up. In the case of Philippe V., machinist and prop were the Princess des Ursins. It was she who regulated his life, dictated his letters, sent him to the wars and forced him to remain on the throne in spite of himself and of all Europe, including Louis XIV. Thanks to her clear brain, energy, and ability, Spain was twice saved—first from becoming a mere province under the domination of France, and later from being partitioned out by Louis to half the European Powers to save his own skin, and it is due to her not only that the Bourbons still remain on the throne in independence, but that there is any Spain left for them to rule over.

How the miserable puppet she had helped to place on the throne rewarded her, will be the scandal of sovereigns as long as sovereigns exist. Jealous of his wife's affection for her, as long as she was alive to protect her he feigned friendship, esteem and even gratitude, accepted her devotion, whimpered over her absence, implored her counsel, and dissimulated his hate with such cunning as to deceive even her, and no sooner was the Queen dead than he schemed her ruin, setting the virago he married six months after to drive her with brutal insult from the country she had won for him, and close all the frontiers of Europe against her. History can furnish few examples of a monarch so treacherous and ignoble as Philippe V. of Spain.

Unfortunately he had for guide, philosopher and friend a man almost as ignoble as himself and less serious. The Marquis de Louville, thanks to the protection of his patron the Duc de Beauvillier, governor of the princes, had been his tutor in infancy and first gentleman of the bedchamber later. He had accompanied him to Spain as chief of his French household and had profited by his loneliness and home-sickness to worm his way into his confidence. Louville was arrogance and insolence personified, and despised everything that was not French. Under his influence the boy did not attempt to hide his own contempt for Spanish customs, so different to those of Versailles, and the enthusiasm which greeted his arrival soon turned to detestation. In order to retain his own influence Louville inspired him with the fear that they wanted to poison him, so that he refused to eat anything that was not cooked by his French *chefs*, or allow any Spaniard to approach his person. To the Spanish nobles he never condescended to address a word, and had it not been for the counter-policy of the Princess, who on her arrival saw how things stood, combated Louville's fatal influence and taught the young Queen to win back the hearts of his subjects, they would have flocked in a body to the standard of the Archduke Charles, and sent back their sulky sovereign whence he had come.

We will turn to the more agreeable picture of the Princess he is about to marry.

Marie-Louise-Gabrielle of Savoy, younger sister of the Duchess of Burgundy, and by her mother great-niece of Louis XIV., was a mere child of thirteen at the time of her marriage, but precocious to a degree which seems almost fabulous. Both sisters had been the constant companions of their father, and apt pupils in his ambitious politics, and she arrived in Spain thoroughly trained by him to serve his ends, which were to extract from Philippe the gift of the Milanese provinces and assume the title of King of Lombardy.

Everything that went on at Versailles was known to him, thanks to the Duchess of Burgundy, and his son-in-law's "ardent temperament" was no secret. Hence this child of thirteen, not yet a woman, had been educated by him to play on his sensuality with the cunning of an experienced courtesan, and it will be seen presently how thoroughly she had learnt her lesson. During their long journey side by side the Princess by skilful words had discovered these ambitions for the aggrandisement of her own house, and with characteristic promptness set to work at once to replace them with others more compatible with her own. She taught her that her personal welfare was bound up with that of Philippe, and so successfully did she use her eloquent tongue that not long after her arrival the child had no other thought than the glory of her husband and Spain.

The astonishing influence the Princess obtained over her seems to have been at first due, not so much to affection in the ordinary sense of the word, as to the Queen's appreciation of the benefits to be derived from her. Their relations were rather those of a mutual-aid society than of

F

gouvernante and pupil. Each desired to rule, each alone was incapable of doing so, the Queen from her youth and inexperience, the Princess from her subordinate position. Each achieved power by means of the other, and the sentiment arising from their appreciation of this mutual need served better to keep them united than affection, since it was self-interest and thus free from caprice.

The lessons of the Princess differed from those of the Duke only in the ends to be obtained. The means were similar—to play on the senses of her husband and get all she wanted by refusing him her bed. Thus the Queen ruled Philippe, and the Princess ruled the Queen, and domestic harmony was assured. The situation suited them both, and the antipathy they felt for each other at their first meeting soon gave place to the friendship which has grown proverbial and ended only with the Queen's death.

It is doubtful whether the Princess ever really loved the Queen—or whether indeed she was accessible to so futile an emotion—but that the Queen grew later to adore her Camarera Mayor is not open to doubt in spite of Louville's malignant verdict to the contrary.[1] Her nature was noble and generous, her heart warm and enthusiastic. The Princess was her only friend in a land of strangers, the only reliable person she knew, and the Princess, as we know, had " a charm impossible to resist when she wished to be seductive." The Queen, everyone who saw her agreed, was astonishing in the precocity of her intelligence and her unique personality. She was astonishing in this also, that where most people begin by being warm-hearted and generous and end by growing cold, she did exactly the reverse.

She had the same taste for popularity as her sister the Duchess of Burgundy, and the same charm and tact in winning it. On her arrival in Spain, where the marriage was unpopular, she had only to show herself to be adored. Without opening her lips, merely by her vivacious grace and charm, she won the hearts of the most hostile of the grandees, and as for the people, she was their idol, their

[1] " She cared little for the Princess although she made of her her favourite. If she allowed her to govern it was to assure her own empire. She regarded her as an instrument necessary to her will, and rightly, for without this woman, so learned in the art of seduction and gaining her ends, how could a Queen of fourteen make herself obeyed?" (Louville, i. 251.)

Madonna, for whom they would have given their lives. Finally she was courageous to a degree amounting to heroism, and, always frail and delicate, supported with cheerfulness perils and hardships which would have taxed the endurance of the most robust men.

But the reverse of the medal, the verdict of her enemies, chief among whom was Louville, must not be omitted.

According to him her temper was uncontrollable, and when it got the better of her she lost all dignity and even decency. He relates how on one occasion while at her toilette, overhearing him and the Princess in the antechamber discussing the character of Cardinal d'Estrées, whom she detested, she flew into the room naked to the waist, began to scream and gesticulate like a little fury, and would neither be stopped nor retire in spite of the remonstrances of the Princess and his own embarrassment. "She has an impetuous temper which the least contradiction increases to violence," he wrote, " and then nothing can stop her, not even Madame des Ursins." [1]

" Choleric little demon. Intrepid doll," is Michelet's summing-up, and impetuous and passionate she certainly was, if these are faults. But if at times her temper got the better of her and she forgot her dignity in the violence of her emotions, it gave her also the courage to defend her friends with an ardour which held in respect even Louis and Madame de Maintenon, and if Spain escaped being swallowed up entire or parcelled out piecemeal by the former, it was due almost as much to her violent temper as to the courage and ability of the Princess.

The feverish excess of vitality she had in common with her sister the Duchess of Burgundy seems to have been with both the result of ill-health. The Duchess could never be still, must all the time be hunting, dancing, or in violent movement of some sort or excited by high play. Constantly ailing, upset by the least excess in a life made up of excess, she was carried off by a trifling illness at twenty-seven. The Queen of Spain, suffering all her life from a malady of the glands, died of consumption at twenty-five.

The descriptions of her appearance vary. Louville, who grew to detest her almost immediately as the friend of his *bête noire* the Princess, wrote on her arrival that she looked a true sovereign—grace, intelligence, discernment, nothing

[1] Louville, *Mémoires*, ii. 51 and 95.

was lacking, that her figure was noble and perfectly made although small, that her complexion was dazzlingly white and her expression of the greatest sweetness.[1]

The Princess, however, was disappointed in her appearance on first seeing her, and wrote of her slightingly as too small, ill-dressed, with badly-arranged hair and an ugly mouth. But she, like the rest, was struck by her extraordinary intelligence and vivacity.[2]

[1] Louville, i. 99. [2] Saint-Simon, ix. 104.

CHAPTER X

THE MARRIAGE (1701)

THE marriage of these two royal puppets took place by proxy in the palace of the Dukes of Savoy at Turin on 11 September, 1701. The Queen was thirteen, the King eighteen — two children. The regulations for the ceremony and journey to Madrid were arranged to the minutest detail by the high priest of etiquette at Versailles, over whose newly acquired province they were nominally to rule, and everyone received orders for the rôles they had to play, like actors on the stage. At first it was arranged that the Princess should receive her charge from the hands of the Duke her father in Turin, but these orders were changed and she was told to go straight to Villefranche and await her there.[1]

" The day before yesterday," Dangeau notes in his *Diary* under the date 16 September, " a courier arrived from Turin, from whom we learnt that the Prince de Carignan, charged with the procuration of the King of Spain, has espoused the Princess of Savoy. She left Turin last Tuesday to go and meet the King her husband at Barcelona, where he is awaiting her. The Queen will be eight days on the road from Turin to Nice, where she will embark on the galley of the Comte de Lemos, which is entirely gilded and very magnificent." [2]

The Princess began her long journey from Rome some time before the Queen, going straight to Genoa where she remained for a week, and then proceeded by sea to Villefranche, which she reached on 14 September. Here she stayed for a fortnight on board her galley and only set foot on land to receive the Queen from the hands of her Piedmontese lady-in-waiting, the Princess de Massaran. Such

---

[1] "Madame la Princesse des Ursins before leaving Rome has sent a courier here to receive the King's orders. She will not go to Turin. She will go straight to Genoa and continue her journey to Villefranche and the Princess de Massaran will conduct the Queen to Villefranche" (Dangeau, viii. 172).

[2] Dangeau, viii. 195.

were the Royal orders from Versailles which she fulfilled to the letter.

The journey began most unfavourably. Neither was pleased with the other. The Princess found her charge badly dressed and provincial, the Queen thought her duenna haughty and severe. The weather was stormy and the Queen very sea-sick, and the ship, notwithstanding its gilding and magnificence and its attendants clad in silk and silver cloth, was infested with bugs! To complete the catastrophe, a frightful tempest put an end to the journey and almost to their lives, for the vessel was nearly overturned. They succeeded, however, in reaching Antibes, where the Queen's temper got the better of her and she absolutely refused to set foot again on board.[1]

Dangeau continues: "7 October, 1701. The Queen of Spain has experienced a bad storm and been obliged to put in at Antibes, and as she was very much incommoded by bugs on the galley and besides suffered greatly on the sea, she landed and has been lodged in the castle. The wind continues contrary, so she will not arrive at Barcelona as soon as was thought."[2]

From Antibes the Princess wrote to her friend the Prince of Monaco in Rome: "We do not yet know when we can get out of this port, the wind being contrary. It is very sad to be stopped so soon and not at least to have been able to reach a more agreeable place than this. I have every reason to be pleased with the Queen, for she shows me much kindness and perfect confidence."[3] This last phrase was a sop to her own pride, for the little Queen had as yet shown neither kindness nor confidence and was sulkily brooding over her woes and her departed Massaran.

It was easy to stamp her foot and refuse again to embark on the bug-infested vessel, but not so easy to change the programme of the despot of Versailles. A courier was dispatched at once with prayers that the journey might be continued by land, but to go and come was a matter of at least a fortnight, and meanwhile both ladies were heartily

---

[1] "Madame" Princess Palatine wrote on 12 Oct. to her sister: "Apropos of bugs, they have almost entirely eaten up the young Queen of Spain during her journey on the Spanish galleys" (Brunet, *Nouvelles Lettres de la Duchesse d'Orléans* (Paris, 1853), p. 28; letter of 12 Oct. 1701).

[2] Dangeau, v iii. 204.

[3] Trémoïlle, i. 91; letter of 30 Sept. 1701.

sick of Antibes. It was boredom rather than obedience probably which made them try once more to carry out the Royal orders and re-embark, but another violent tempest overtook them and they were again forced to land, having advanced no farther than Toulon.

On 12 October Louis wrote pompously to his grandson in Madrid: "The navigation of the galleys has seemed so fatiguing to the Queen of Spain and is even so dangerous at this season that she wishes to finish her journey by land from Marseilles to Barcelona. I have consented."[1]

His consent, however, took several weeks to reach the travellers, and they were already at Marseilles when it arrived. From there to the Spanish frontier the journey seems to have gone smoothly enough, agreeably, too, one may suppose to the child-Queen with a cicerone so charming and well-informed. As for the Princess, she profited by the enforced intimacy to study her pupil, and having arrived at her conclusions prepared her system of education.

Louville had been sent to greet the Queen at Montpellier, and, having as yet no reason to detest and fear the Princess, seems to have been favourably struck by her. "At the Queen's side triumphed Marie-Anne de la Trémoïlle in all the haughtiness of her rank, intelligence and pride," he wrote. "She had not yet renounced her right to homage and she had been so beautiful in her youth that her pretensions did not seem absurd even to those who most condemned them."[2]

But Louville was also the bearer of the unwelcome news that at the Spanish frontier all the Queen's Piedmontese suite must return whence they had come, not even excepting her *femmes-de-chambre*, a wise precaution against the probable intrigues of the Duke her father. At Perpignan she was informed of this order and her despair may be imagined. She stormed and raged like a little demon, lost all self-control, and, considering the Princess responsible, abused her with so much vehemence that in defiance of etiquette she lost patience and scolded her roundly.

"We have had a very disagreeable scene at Perpignan," she wrote to Torcy. "On Tuesday evening we had to tell the Queen that the King had ordered us, the Marquis de Castel-Rodriguez and myself, to dismiss all the Piedmontese household. The news rendered her completely desperate.

[1] Trémoïlle, i. 93.   [2] Louville, *Mémoires*, i. 205.

She would not sup and passed nearly all the night weeping."

She goes on to relate how the Savoy Ambassador who accompanied them had also complained, and with so much insolence that she had been forced to leave the room, how she had tried her best to make the Queen see the political necessity of the step, but had been answered so haughtily that she had been obliged to administer a sharp reproof, or, as she worded it, "profited by the occasion tactfully to make her understand the difference which exists between a King of Spain, grandson of our King, and a Princess of Savoy."[1]

But a pleasanter incident soon dried the child's tears and brought sunshine back to her face, momentarily at least. Near Figueras, where the nuptial benediction was to take place and where Philippe had already arrived, a horseman appeared in the distance galloping at full speed towards them. The Princess and her charge, each brooding over the disagreeable scene at the frontier, sat silent and paid no attention, till the cavalier, a boy with pale face and black eyes, threw himself from his horse in front of the coach and kneeling with doffed hat in the dust cried out that he was a messenger from the King of Spain, sent by him to salute the Queen in his name. The Queen, still sulking, seemed hardly to hear, but the Princess, to whom his face was familiar, stared, pressed her arm and whispered that it was Philippe V. himself. Tears and frowns vanished as if by magic, and before the Princess could stop her she had sprung from the coach, seized the King's hand and pressed it to her lips. Philippe's joy at finding his bride so charming can be imagined. Enchanted with her beauty and delighted with the spontaneity of her act, he murmured a few words of welcome, sprang on his horse and was out of sight before the Queen had recovered from her joyful surprise.[2]

But this ray of sunshine was momentary only, and at the thought of her departed suite her tears again began to flow, and notwithstanding that the glimpse she had had of her boy-husband had charmed her, she reached Figueras in the lowest spirits, which another disagreeable incident on her

[1] Saint-Simon, ix. 388.
[2] Combes, *La Princesse des Ursins* (Paris, 1858), p. 83. The incident is related by the Spanish Secretary of State, Ubilla, Marquis de Rivas.

arrival increased, bringing matters to a crisis so unpleasant as to necessitate the interference of Louis XIV. himself.

Philippe, detesting the highly spiced food of the country and trained by Louville to suspect poison in everything, would eat nothing which was not cooked by his French *chefs*, and these had therefore been transported to Figueras to prepare the bridal supper, which was composed entirely of French dishes with only two or three that were Spanish. This the grandees and ladies of the palace resented as an affront to their country, and had arranged a plot to show their displeasure.

Only the Camarera Mayor had the right to serve the King and Queen, who ate side by side in solitary state, the ladies of the palace receiving the dishes from the hands of the pages and handing them to her as she stood behind their chairs. On this occasion, in crossing the room, one after the other, they either tripped over their long skirts or let the dishes fall, so that of all the meats and *entremets* only those which were Spanish reached the Princess's hands. Saint-Simon describes the scene with his usual vividness:

On arriving at Figueras they were married by the bishop of the diocese with very little ceremony and soon after sat down to table for supper,[1] which was served by the Princess des Ursins and the ladies of the palace, half the dishes being Spanish, half French. This mixture displeased these ladies and many of the Spanish lords, with whom they plotted to make a scandal. And a scandal in fact it was. Under one pretext or another, the weight or heat of the dishes or the awkwardness with which they were presented to the ladies, not a single French dish arrived at the table and all were upset, while the Spanish dishes on the contrary were served without mishap. The vexed and afflicted manner (to say no more) of the ladies was too evident not to be remarked, but the King and Queen were wise enough to seem not to see and Madame des Ursins, very astonished, said not a word.

After a long and gloomy repast the King and Queen retired. Then what had been suppressed during the supper burst forth. The Queen began to weep for her Piedmontese. Like the child she was, she thought herself lost to be in the hands of ladies so insolent, and when it was a question of going to bed said flatly she would do nothing of the sort, and wanted to go back to her own country.[2]

[1] The Queen arrived at Figueras at five o'clock in the afternoon and the marriage took place almost immediately after. The usual hour for supper at the Court was half-past six.
[2] Saint-Simon, ix. 106.

From certain facts which transpired later, it would seem that her fury was not spontaneous nor entirely due to the burlesque affair of the supper, but to more serious matters. So serious indeed did the Princess think them that she dispatched Louville the next day to Versailles to report them to Louis and ask his counsel.

For it appears that on being left alone with her husband, ardent and impatient, instead of returning or even permitting his caresses, she had absolutely refused to admit him to her bed unless he would first promise to grant her request, which request was nothing less than that he should resign to her father, the Duke of Savoy, the command of the Spanish troops in Italy.

It had been arranged for some time that Philippe should go in the early spring to join the Duc de Vendôme in Lombardy to take command of his army and win his spurs according to custom. But the Duke of Savoy coveted the post of generalissimo above all things and, aware of the King's temperament, had made his daughter promise to allow him no conjugal familiarity till it was granted. It seems incredible that a child of thirteen, not yet arrived at womanhood, should have had it in her power to impose such conditions, yet no one, not even the Princess, seems to have considered it strange. However, with all his impatience to consummate the marriage, Philippe, revolted at her exactions, refused without hesitation. The result was that the Queen locked her door in his face and that he had to pass his bridal-night in tears alone in his own apartment.

Next morning, seeing him appear with swelled eyes and dejected mien, Louville questioned him as to the cause, but, shamefaced and timid, he would answer nothing but that " the Queen had insisted on talking politics."

He would gladly have kept the scandal to himself, but the Princess, hearing from the Queen what had passed, insisted that Louis should be told, as she considered it a form of blackmailing to which a stop must immediately be put. Therefore, Louville was taken perforce into Philippe's confidence and sent with the following letters to Versailles:

I send Louville to Your Majesty to bear the news of my marriage [Philippe himself wrote to his grandfather], and as he will relate everything in detail I will add nothing more. All I can tell you is that the Queen arrived in good health, that she

appears to be very intelligent and that her face is pleasing.
I have sent back all her household to Turin and have allowed
no one, either man or woman, belonging to that Court to enter
Spain. I have no time to say more, except that I am so disturbed by what happened to me to-day that I must refer you
to Louville for the rest.[1]

"My feeling is," the Princess, on her side, wrote to
Torcy, "that the Queen must from the first be made to
understand that she will gain nothing by this kind of
artifice."[2]

But how to punish a child so high-spirited and precocious? A grand conclave was held in the Princess's apartment at which the French Ambassador and all the Spanish
ministers were present. The conclusion arrived at was
that the child must be punished by the *lex talionis*, that
Philippe in his turn should shut his doors and that she
should be left alone in disgrace till her spirit was broken.
"They were of opinion," writes Saint-Simon, "that the
King in his turn should refuse to sleep with her the following
night in order to mortify and reduce her. This was done.
They did not see each other alone all that day and at night
the Queen was miserable. Her pride and vanity were
wounded." And he adds: "Perhaps also she had found the
King to her taste."[3]

Meantime, laden with dispatches on the momentous
subject, Louville was hurrying across the Pyrenees, and
with such speed that he reached Versailles the following
week.

Monsieur de Louville arrived yesterday [Torcy wrote to the
Princess on 13 November], the King received him immediately.
... His description has not destroyed what has been heard
on all sides of the personal qualities of the Queen, but you will
easily understand that the scene of the wedding-day was not
at all agreeable. ... His Majesty sees all the importance of
preventing from the first the ascendant which it seems the
Queen desires to take over the King of Spain's mind by artifices
so much beyond the simplicity habitual at her age.[4]

For two days Philippe succeeded in dominating his
"ardent temperament," refusing even to see his bride, with
the result that the poor child, alone among strangers, in
disgrace with everyone, including the Princess, with no one

---

[1] Trémoïlle, i. 94; letter of 4 Nov. 1701.   [2] Saint-Simon, ix. 389.
[3] Ibid., ix. 109.   [4] Ibid., ix. 392.

she knew to advise and console her, submitted and sulked no more, at least as far as the King was concerned. But considering the Princess to be responsible for her punishment and the dismissal of her suite, she would have nothing to do with her and tried to prevent the King from seeing her alone. "I await with impatience," the Princess wrote a week later to Torcy, "the confidence of her I serve. It comes very slowly, though I do all I can to attract it."[1]

Philippe was enchanted at the change in his favour. "It is with great pleasure that I make known to Your Majesty," he wrote to his grandfather the same day, "that the Queen's little grief lasted only half a day. Since then she has been always very reasonable and we live in perfect harmony."[2]

Whether because she felt lonely, or that she began to realise the use she might make of the Princess, the child's attitude towards her soon changed, and jealousy and anger gave way to confidence, if not as yet to affection.

The Queen shows me more confidence [the Princess wrote with satisfaction to Torcy the following week]. I saw at once that she had been prejudiced against me. . . . She makes me little presents sometimes. She is incredibly intelligent and sharp-witted. . . . The scene of which the Marquis de Louville saw the beginning has not been repeated. She has very well understood that this kind of way would not succeed and since then has thought only of pleasing the King. It was certainly the result of the bad counsels of Turin. One must not expect simplicity from her, she is cleverer than you can imagine.[3]

And ten days later:

The Queen loves the King very much and since our stay in Barcelona it is certain that I have gained much influence over her. She listens willingly to the advice I take the liberty to give her, and I see that she even follows it. As she is by nature suspicious and secretive, time alone will give her entire confidence in me, but I think I am on the high-road to it.[4]

Thus have the three, who began with so much quarrelling, realised the necessity of union and their mutual errors as to each other's character, shaken into their places and accepted the situation. From many remarks in her letters it

---

[1] Saint-Simon, ix. 391; letter of 12 Nov. 1701.
[2] Ibid., ix. 391.
[3] Ibid., ix. 394; letter of 19 Nov. 1701.
[4] Ibid., ix. 407; letter of 28 Nov. 1701.

THE MARRIAGE

is evident that in desiring the post of Camarera Mayor the Princess's design was to subjugate, not the Queen of whom she knew nothing, and regarded with negligence as a mere child, but Philippe himself, with whose special characteristics she was well acquainted. It is even probable that she, who had retained so much of her physical charm in spite of her fifty-nine years, had hoped to win the boy by his senses, and through him to govern Spain, and that, with characteristic energy and rapidity of action, seeing the passion he had immediately conceived for his young wife, she had promptly changed her tactics and directed all her forces to dominate her instead.

In any case the result was that harmony had replaced discord at the Court of Spain, and everyone, including Louis, was satisfied. Philippe, who asked nothing but to lie idle at the feet of his beloved, was in Paradise. The Queen was happy because each day she was gaining fresh influence over him, and the Princess because on her side she was gaining fresh influence over the Queen.

The ancient castle of the counts of Barcelona and kings of Aragon was to be their home for the present, since it was decided that they should take ship from there in a few weeks *en route* for Naples, the first part of the programme of Philippe's military début, and it was from Barcelona that the Queen wrote her first letters to the Dowager Duchess of Savoy, her "très chère grandmaman." The Princess's influence is already visible in the interest she shows (at thirteen!) in politics.

" You were surprised to hear of the King's seriousness," she wrote. " It begins to diminish a little, but what I want above all to make him do is to talk more when he is with the Spanish, for it would be a great pleasure to them." [1]

For the Princess, on her arrival, had been horrified at the contemptuous attitude of Philippe towards his subjects, due to Louville's training, and had not lost a moment in counteracting it and instilling into the receptive mind of her pupil the necessity, if she wished to remain Queen, of winning the good graces of the people she was to rule over, and realising the effect her charm would have on the straitlaced but chivalrous nobles, had already made several happy innovations.

" The Princess des Ursins," wrote the Ambassador

[1] Trémoïlle, i. 96 ; letter of 18 Nov. 1701.

Marsin to Louis, "allows some of the principal Spanish lords to enter the Queen's room from time to time after her toilette, which has not been done hitherto, and which gives them great pleasure and has a good effect."[1]

The result of this policy was that in a very short time the child had won the heart of everyone in Barcelona. The grandees in the palace, the citizens in the streets and the peasants in the surrounding country all adored her, and even Philippe, though still disliked, profited by her popularity.

Marsin told Louis of the happy effects of the Princess's education, and Torcy wrote her letters of warmest approval, at which she was radiant. "In truth,"—she herself confirmed the Ambassador's eulogies—"I have done marvels. I have already won the hearts of all the Catalonians. Men, women, and children perpetually fill my antechambers, and scarcely leave me time to take a bad meal during the few moments of leisure the King and Queen allow me."[2]

And later, to the Maréchale de Noailles: "I receive nothing but praise and very great kindness from everyone . . . and if I can put faith in what I hear, I am considered a kind of marvel."[3]

So well indeed had she played the first act of her rôle of guardian angel to the Royal babes he had confided to her, that Louis wrote to his Ambassador that she was to have absolute authority over the Queen, and he was to do nothing without consulting her.

They remained in Barcelona for nine months, the chief amusements of the Queen and Princess being to visit the convents and gardens in the neighbourhood while the King hunted. But quiet though the life was, it was excessively fatiguing to the Princess, with the multifarious duties of her office, as the following letter to the Maréchale de Noailles (written, however, in the highest spirits) during their stay at Barcelona bears witness:

> In what an office, bon Dieu, have you placed me! I have not the least repose and cannot find time even to speak to my secretary. There is no question of being able to rest after dinner nor of eating when I am hungry. I am only too happy to be able to snatch a bad meal hurriedly, and even so, it is

---
[1] Trémoïlle, i. 96; letter of 19 Nov. 1701.
[2] Saint-Simon, ix. 393; letter to Torcy of 19 Nov. 1701.
[3] Geffroy, 121; letter of 16 Dec. 1701.

very seldom that I am not called away the moment I sit down to table. Certainly Madame de Maintenon would laugh heartily if she knew all the details of my charge. Pray tell her that it is I who have the honour to take the King of Spain's dressing-gown when he gets into bed and give it him with his slippers when he rises. So far it is well, but that every evening when he goes to the Queen's bedroom the Comte de Benavente [1] should load me with His Majesty's sword, a *pot-de-chambre*, and a lamp which I generally upset over my clothes, that is too grotesque. Never would the King rise if I did not go to draw the curtains and it would be a sacrilege if anyone but me entered the Queen's room when they are in bed. Recently the lamp went out because I had upset half the oil. I knew not where were the windows and thought I should break my nose against the wall, and the King of Spain and I were nearly a quarter of an hour knocking against each other trying to find them.

I am on the best of terms with the King [she continues]. I tease him about his timidity . . . and His Majesty has grown so used to me that he sometimes does me the honour to call me two hours before I want to rise in order to see me. The Queen takes part in these jokes but I have not yet gained the same confidence she had in the Piedmontese ladies who served her before me. This surprises me, for I wait on her better than they and I am sure they did not wash her feet nor take off her shoes so quickly as I.[2]

Besides these duties she was bound, by the terms of her office, to be in constant attendance on the Queen, and at Louis' special order never to leave her alone for a moment, either with the Duke of Savoy's ambassador or the Spanish ministers, for since the affair of the wedding night intrigues were suspected. She had, besides, to arrange and keep in order the thirty ladies of the palace with their numerous underlings, in all three hundred females, all her mortal enemies and full of spite and intrigue. It is a marvel that she found either time or energy to cultivate her ambitions and prepare her batteries for the conquest of Spain.

[1] The grand chamberlain or mayordomo mayor.
[2] Geffroy, 113; letter of 12 Dec. 1701.

CHAPTER XI

FIRST INCIDENTS OF THE WAR

IT is no part of my design to trace in any sort of detail the fluctuations of the long and wearisome War of Spanish Succession which followed on Louis' acceptance of the crown of Spain for his grandson Philippe d'Anjou, yet since it forms the background to the figure of the Princess, a brief summary of its principal battles and incidents cannot be omitted in their place.

Louis' annexation (for he intended it to be nothing less) of a crown to which he had no right is one of the chief stains on his glory, and like most similar crimes brought its own punishment, for to maintain his claim France was drained of her blood and gold and with no compensating profit, since Spain, when at length, thanks to the courage and tenacity of the Princess, she did raise her head, refused to be annexed and insisted on her independence, and all that Louis gained, he who in his youth had been acclaimed as a demi-god, was in his old age to be hated and condemned by his subjects, and leave his country a prey to the indignation and rebellion which ended a century later in the Revolution. Madame de Maintenon, with her clear head, her prudence and innate political acumen, did well to hesitate when asked her opinion on the advisability of accepting the testament. She would have done better openly and fearlessly to express what was in her mind.

The arrogance he had shown since his conquest in Flanders grew more exaggerated at this fresh success, and his imprudences more flagrant. The testament wrung from the demented King expressly stipulated that on mounting the throne of Spain the Duc d'Anjou should renounce his rights to that of France in order to prevent any possible union of the two countries. In his exuberance Louis set this deliberately at defiance so far as publicly to confirm these rights, thus increasing the suspicions and hostility already excited against him, and as though to offer a direct challenge to England and Holland he refused to recognise

William and Mary, and ostentatiously offered his protection to the deposed sovereign. He trampled thus on all forms of international union and forced the European Powers to unite against his arrogant pretensions. On 7 September, 1701, Great Britain, Holland and Austria signed a treaty of alliance which was followed later by Denmark, Prussia, Savoy and the whole of the German Empire, with the exception of Bavaria and Cologne. All Europe was thus in arms against him, sustained by the inexhaustible wealth of England and Holland and the inexhaustible troops of the Empire, and with the great soldiers Eugène of Savoy-Carignan and the Duke of Marlborough pitted against his own inferior generals.

War broke out soon after Philippe's accession with the invasion of the Milanese territory by Prince Eugène, who, though half French by birth, since his father was Comte de Soissons,[1] had thrown himself on the side of Austria from anger that Louis in his youth had refused him employment. The Duc de Vendôme, most competent of the French generals, had been sent to oppose him and the occasion was considered good for the young King of Spain to receive his baptism of fire and learn the art of war under his guidance.

It was Louis' system of military education in his family to send the boys at an early age to the war, nominally in command, actually to learn their trade as princes of the blood. The Bourbons, with all their faults, were brave, even Philippe V., and the proudest and happiest moment of their lives was when they rode forth, untried generals, to win their spurs in Flanders or Italy. Philippe had begged for and obtained permission to take command of the Spanish troops in Italy at the New Year, and but for a slight attack of the smallpox, from which he suffered in February, would already have joined his cousin Vendôme. As it was, the expedition had been postponed and it was not till a month later that the preparations for departure were begun.

There was no question of separating from his young wife. He and the Queen were to travel together in state and pay official visits to their Italian possessions, beginning with Naples, after which the King would proceed to Lombardy to take his place at the head of his army. The Princess des Ursins naturally was to accompany them, and all three were

[1] His mother was Olympe Mancini, niece of Cardinal Mazarin.

looking forward with the greatest delight to the expedition, the Queen because she was home-sick and counted on a long visit to Turin, and the Princess because she intended to display her new grandeur among her old friends in Rome. The journey from Barcelona to Naples was to be made by sea, and the only flaw in the happiness of the Queen and Princess was the dread of a repetition of the bugs and tempests of their last voyage.

However, when the grandees heard that not only Philippe but the Queen were preparing to leave the country they raised a hue and cry. It was bad enough that Philippe himself should go, for the Kings of Spain were like a fetish or idol, to be kept permanently in its shrine, but that the Queen also should leave them was inadmissible. So violent were their outcries that Marsin, Louis' ambassador, was forced to transmit their objections to the supreme arbiter, with the result that to Philippe's despair she was ordered to remain behind.

The Queen, Louis ordered his grandson, must stay and represent him during his absence, and not in Barcelona but Madrid, where she would be better employed governing his subjects than following him to Italy. The Spaniards were right in being afraid that if both King and Queen were absent the Emperor would swoop down on the country. Also it was a question of economy, for a Queen could not travel without the pomp and ceremony due to her rank, and the treasuries of both France and Spain were empty. Besides, she could not accompany Philippe to Lombardy and live among the soldiers in camp, and what would become of her in Naples alone among strangers? Finally he hinted in his despotic way that if all these arguments did not convince his grandson and he still insisted on taking her, he would have to renounce the campaign altogether.[1]

The Princess had already felt the justice of the grandees' objection and, even before Louis' letter reached Philippe, had accepted the position, and with the promptness of action which characterised her had determined to profit by the occasion to consolidate her own position. Already, for several months, she had been performing the duties of Camarera Mayor without either the official position or appointments, and she began to think it was high time to enjoy both. Marsin the Ambassador, at first prejudiced

[1] Trémoïlle, ii. 15; letter of 3 March, 1702.

INCIDENTS OF THE WAR

against her by Louville, had quickly succumbed to her fascinations and was now her humble slave. Him, therefore, she now prompted to act as her intermediary with Louis.[1]

What you say about the Princess des Ursins that no one in the world is so capable as she to fill the post she occupies [he wrote to Torcy], is so true that it is absolutely necessary that she take the title of Camarera Mayor, to which she has always objected and will refuse unless the King shows her firmly and kindly that he desires it. . . . A letter written by himself would do marvels for she would be flattered by it . . . and the life she is obliged to lead here, which is that of a dog or at least a street porter, merits well some distinction and gratification. . . . It would be well also that the King, in his letters to the King and Queen of Spain, should advise them to urge her strongly to accept this post. It is impossible to express how extremely necessary she is to them, above all at these commencements.

And he ends by repeating, "The charge is excessively fatiguing. . . . The King and Queen cannot do without her. They would be very embarrassed, and we also."[2]

The letter, obviously written at her own dictation, had not for the moment the effect desired, for thanks to Louville's influence Philippe had made himself and the French in general too unpopular for the appointment of a Frenchwoman to be politic. The post was too important and too much coveted by certain Spanish ladies of the highest rank and influence, chief among whom were the old Marquise de Castel-Rodriguez, the Duchess of Medina-Sidonia and the Comtesse de Palma, the latter a niece of Porto-Carrero and leader of all the Court intrigues against the Princess.

It has been already stated and we shall have occasion to remark it again and again, that the Princess, far from being discouraged by failure, was stimulated by it. Since the title of Camarera Mayor was refused her she would claim that of Regent for her puppet the Queen. To consolidate her position and dictate with authority during the King's absence had been her aim, and this means was as good or even better than her own appointment. Therefore she wrote to Torcy to propose it, not as her own wish but that of the grandees.

---

[1] The Comte de Marsin was a soldier rather than a diplomatist and had been appointed *pro interim* when the illness of the Duc d'Harcourt necessitated his retiring.

[2] Trémoïlle, ii. 5; letter of 24 Jan. 1702.

A child—yes, she forestalled objections, but the Spaniards were bent upon it, and Ubilla the minister who, according to her, was the mouthpiece of Porto-Carrero himself, had declared that it was the custom of the country and that were she but one year old he would still demand it.[1]

Naturally Louis objected. It would be surprising if he had not. But the Princess had the wisdom not to insist for the moment, and to distract his mind and gain his favour, expatiated on the Queen's obedience and the resignation of both his grandchildren to his will.

"The Queen becomes every day more reasonable," she wrote to Torcy announcing her renunciation of the journey to Italy. "Her confidence in me could not be greater and I think that I shall always be sufficiently the master to make her do all I want by taking certain measures."[2]

What these measures were can be easily guessed. As the Queen obtained from Philippe all she wanted by playing on his senses so the Princess dominated the Queen by flattering her ambition. It was the moment for decisive action and she seized it. She instilled into her pupil's ambitious soul the most dazzling prospects—Regent, practically ruler of Spain at thirteen, and with the Princess des Ursins, that is to say, Intelligence personified, for Prime Minister. What between them could they not achieve! A kingdom to subjugate, a people to win, during the absence of him who had done his best to lose both. So she dazzled her with visions of glory and power unlimited, and at the age when most children are reading of fairy godmothers, magic wands and the like improbabilities, this child found herself actually the heroine of such tales with the fairy godmother at her side to fulfil her desires. Her adoration for her Camarera Mayor dates from this moment.

Louis on his side was delighted at their submission, for nothing irritated him so much as opposition to his will. The episode of the bridal-night had alarmed him, for it was not at all to his taste that his newly-acquired province should be surreptitiously interfered with by the Duke of Savoy. So pleased was he that he wrote to his grandson: "Regard your marriage henceforth as the greatest happiness of your life. The submission of the Queen, her gentleness and reasonableness, are no less rare than extraordinary in a

[1] Trémoïlle, ii. 18; letters of 5 and 9 March, 1702.
[2] Ibid., ii. 19; letter of 5 March, 1702.

person of her age."[1] And the Princess, to whose wise guidance this submission was due, received a lion's share of praise and thanks.

Her letters to Versailles concerning the Queen's regency are masterpieces of diplomacy. Louis continued to object, found it fantastic, and she agreed with him that it was. She even took the initiative and declared that in her opinion a Queen should never meddle with State affairs. Not only was it unwise but also she dreaded the effect of so much responsibility on the child's health, and was doing her best to combat the appointment. But how was she, alone and a foreigner *without any official position*, to fight against the loudly-expressed will of an entire nation? Government and people insisted so violently that it might be dangerous to thwart them, and after all it would be an honorary title merely, since the true Regent would naturally be her " official adviser " the Cardinal Porto-Carrero.

Thus she reasoned, with arguments worthy of Louis himself, and to forestall further opposition persuaded Philippe on the eve of his departure, hardly knowing in his grief at the separation what he was doing, to sign the official document appointing his wife Regent of Spain during his absence.

On 8 April he tore himself from the arms of his Dalila with grievous lamentations and many tears and embarked on board a French galley, accompanied by his evil genius Louville and Marsin the Ambassador, both of whom were to accompany him, thus leaving the Queen nominally, the Princess actually, in possession of the field.

[1] Trémoïlle, ii. 25 ; letter of 22 March, 1702.

CHAPTER XII

THE ART OF REIGNING (1702)

THE Court had remained at Barcelona only while awaiting Philippe's embarkation for Italy, and now that this had taken place Madrid began to murmur and exact the presence of the Regent in the capital. But first Aragon, one of the twenty-three kingdoms, each with its separate rights and privileges, of which the Spanish monarchy was at that date composed, claimed her presence to preside at the opening of their Cortes, and shortly after Philippe's departure the Princess with her Royal charge left Barcelona for Saragossa, its capital.

They arrived on 25 April "amid all possible demonstrations of joy," the Archbishop and all the notables in robes of ceremony driving far out on the road to meet them. Next day the Queen gave audience to the chief personages of the kingdom and drove in state to the cathedral, the famous Notre Dame del Pilar, to take the solemn oath to maintain the privileges of the State. On the next she presided at the opening of the Cortes, where her speech—little Regent of thirteen—was read by the Protonotary. Thus she entered into her kingdom.

Meantime the Princess, thanks to Marsin's appeals and her own hints, had received the official title of Camarera Mayor. Their seven weeks' stay in Saragossa was her début in the art of governing and she made the most of it. She lost no time in asserting her authority and continuing the reformation she had already begun at Barcelona. Her objects were twofold, first to gain the goodwill of the people so alienated by Louville's policy, and at the same time to wage war against the antiquated customs and unhygienic habits of the Court. Already at Barcelona she had begun her campaign by replacing the French, who filled all the principal posts, with Spaniards, a policy which won most of the grandees to her side, but at the same time her war against the etiquette and customs of the country offended many.

The Spanish Court was solemn and sombre, and rigid Oriental customs regarding women prevailed. Their windows were concealed by wooden screens as in the Orient, and their coach windows were heavily curtained. At the theatres the sexes were separated by a curtain down the centre. No amusements. For public recreation bull-fights and *autos-da-fé*, at which all the Court ladies assisted with pleasure; for home diversion, the munching of chocolate and other sweetmeats during interminable visits of their female friends. The palaces swarming with arrogant dwarfs with huge heads and misshapen bodies and minds still more deformed, source of all the dissensions and scandals of the Court.[1]

In the palace no chairs except for the King and Queen. The ladies sat on cushions on the floor and the men stood. Even in their own houses and at meals they sat on the ground—only the master of the house had his arm-chair. No hygienic accommodation of any sort, not even a *chaise-percée* except for the King and Queen. Everything was thrown from the windows, so that at night in the unlighted streets the pedestrian had to pick his way carefully.

The *tontillo*, against which the Princess waged special war, was a long heavy train, short at the back but long in front and at the sides, invented to hide the feet of the ladies as they sat on the ground. Mahomet guarded hair and breast from the eyes of the profane, Spanish husbands fiercely protected the feet. It is true that, according to Madame d'Aulnoy, these were the most attractive part of their bodies. "They are very small," she writes, "and when the ladies walk they seem to be flying. They press their elbows into their sides and slide along the floors without raising their feet." Graceful enough, but in so sliding the *tontillo* raised clouds of dust which disgusted the Princess and made the little Queen, already delicate in her lungs, cough violently.

To be fat was considered the worst of crimes. "They cultivate leanness," writes Madame d'Aulnoy, "and swathe their bodies with bandages like babes to prevent their breasts developing, and not content with daubing their faces

[1] "The females are frightfully ugly, their heads larger than their bodies, with hair reaching to the ground. They wear magnificent clothes and are the confidantes of their mistress from whom they obtain all they ask. Indispensable in a great house" (Comtesse d'Aulnoy, *La Cour et la Ville de Madrid vers la fin du XVIIIe siècle*. Paris, 1874).

with heavy fards they rouge their shoulders also, and even the cheeks and shoulders of the statues in the palace were rouged."

Every noble had his mistress, generally an actress or singer, and openly boasted of the maladies contracted from them, with which they infected their wives, so that nearly all the children were born scrofulous.

Here is a picture of the Court, written by the Princess herself several years later:

> The Queen is alone almost literally from morning till night, for her ladies never come to the palace before five, and when it is hot even later, because most of them only rise at eleven or twelve, dine at two or three, and then sleep. When they are in her room, after kneeling to kiss her hand, they seat themselves on the floor mostly in silence. We ask them if they dance, sing, play an instrument, if they like walking or playing cards? They answer, "No!" What, however, they do admirably is to ask continually favours for themselves, their lovers and servants. When these are granted they say that it is just and could not be refused, and often in thanking for one favour they ask another. When they do not obtain it they complain loudly. They have besides the good quality of never doing anything at all. There are some who wear chaplets round their necks, the Agnus on their shoulders, little crosses, several relics, and hold a rosary in their hand.[1]

Such was the semi-Oriental Court which the Princess had the mission to modernise.

"I think I shall have no fewer adventures than Don Quixote in the enterprise you give me to destroy the etiquette here!" she wrote to Torcy not long after her arrival.[2]

Her own and the Queen's French costumes and her condemnation of the *tontillo* had passed more or less unnoticed in Barcelona, where the Court was on a very small scale and the etiquette less rigid, but she soon discovered that in Madrid she would have to battle against a formidable clique of enemies, at the head of which was the Comtesse de Palma already mentioned. She began to regret Philippe's absence and to feel her position precarious, she, a foreigner against a nation of enemies. Courageous as she was she hesitated to enter the lists against so many, and on one pretext and

---

[1] Bossange, *Lettres de Madame de Maintenon et la Princesse des Ursins*, iii. 441; letter to Madame de Maintenon of 21 March, 1707.
[2] Saint-Simon, ix. 386; letter of 6 Sept. 1701.

another put off leaving Saragossa in spite of the urgent appeals of Porto-Carrero and Louis' insistence.

"I expect to find purgatory, if not worse, in Madrid," she wrote to Torcy. "The Comte de Marsin predicted that I should have a thousand difficulties based on the affair of Don Miguel, which he attributed to the cabal against me."[1]

Of this affair we have the following account:

While in Barcelona she had as secretary (and also lover) a certain Don Miguel Salvador, young and handsome but with a bad reputation, "full of bad qualities and very dangerous," according to Porto-Carrero. Anonymous letters had reached Versailles blaming her for admitting to a post in which State matters were no secret, a man who had been in the service of the Emperor and was suspected of being a spy of the Queen-Dowager, and she had been forced to dismiss him. To indemnify him she had persuaded Porto-Carrero to appoint him governor of Potosi, the most important city of Peru, on hearing which Louis had sent her, through Torcy, a severe reprimand with the order to have the appointment cancelled and to expel Don Miguel from the country.

But the Princess, now practically Regent and conscious of her power, was no longer a submissive slave and began to resent the authority assumed by the King of France. So instead of obeying, as was her wont hitherto, she flew like a lion to the defence of her lover, refused to expel him and wrote back to Torcy with more clearness than suavity that if Louis wished it he might do it himself.

Don Miguel she defended with ardour. Son of an apothecary he might be, but of one ennobled for his services to the Crown. Dismissed from his post of Secretary of Finance —possibly, but because Philippe was too poor to pay his appointments. Friend of Austria he had certainly been, but had returned to his allegiance on Philippe's accession. Finally, she says that she knows perfectly well from whom these attacks proceed, that they are directed more against herself than Don Miguel, that it is not the first time the Comtesse de Palma had attacked her and would not be the last.[2]

Louis' orders were formal, that they should leave immediately for Madrid. The capital too insisted, and no further

[1] Trémoïlle, ii. 51 ; letter of 29 May, 1702.
[2] Ibid., ii. 41 ; letter of 14 May, 1702.

postponement was possible. The date for the journey was fixed, therefore, and she prepared to arm herself for a furious tussle, not only with the Comtesse de Palma and her clique but with Porto-Carrero and the French Embassy itself.

For on Porto-Carrero, her quandam lover and benefactor, she had turned the cold shoulder. The Cardinal himself had been looking forward to renewing their friendship and had busied himself in having her apartment in the palace magnificently redecorated and furnished, but she was untouched by his devotion. As "Official Adviser to the Regent" his position in the kingdom during Philippe's absence was supreme, and since she intended to occupy that place herself, his suppression was absolutely necessary. Therefore she had systematically snubbed and ignored his authority and neglected all his demands for their return to Madrid. As for Blécourt, acting as ambassador during Marsin's absence with the King in Italy, he had the insolence to reprove her for her attempted suppression of the *tontillo*, a matter which now assumed the proportions of a political feud.

"The mere threat dismays all the ladies of the highest rank here," he wrote, "and to put it in execution would alienate the affection of everyone from Her Majesty." He insisted that, instead of trying to alter Spanish customs, the Queen and herself should adapt themselves to them, and even went so far as to propose that they should make their entry into the capital in Spanish dress and order all the ladies to do the same, to cancel the bad impression she had caused.[1]

To this the Princess replied with a curt and haughty refusal. The Queen, she answered, refused absolutely to wear the *tontillo* or to have her hair dressed *à l'espagnole*, and would enter Madrid in French costume with her hair in curls *à la française*. The Spanish ladies might wear what they liked in the procession, but the Queen forbade the *tontillo* while in attendance on herself, "for it embarrasses their service and raises clouds of dust which is bad for her lungs. The Queen is astonished," she ends disdainfully, "that these fashions appear to the Madrid ladies such a privilege that it is impossible to reform what is so inconvenient and ridiculous."[2]

Blécourt, humiliated and furious, wrote to Versailles to

---

[1] Trémoïlle, ii. 56; letter of 14 June, 1702.
[2] Ibid., ii. 57; letter of 17 June, 1702.

complain, "So, in order to be in the fashion, the ladies must abandon the *tontillo* which prevents their legs and feet from being seen when they are seated on the ground," he deplored. "But it is a crime here to show the feet and there are husbands extravagant enough to say that they would rather see their wives dead than that their legs should be seen."[1]

Louis, appealed to on this weighty question, though to destroy the etiquette was one of the special missions of the Princess, decided in favour of Blécourt. The *tontillo*, he ruled, must on no account be abolished. On the contrary he desired that the Queen herself should wear it occasionally in order to content the nobles.

The cabal was already at work and Blécourt was not the only one to complain to Louis of her attack on Spanish customs. "They are more upset at this proposed change than they would be at a descent of the English on all the Spanish coasts and the loss of the chief forts in the kingdom!" Torcy wrote to her disdainfully, but at the same time insisting on her capitulation.[2]

However, she refused to yield, and she and the Queen entered Madrid in French costume with their hair curled, belaced and beribboned, to the horror of the grandees and the spiteful fury of their wives.

"There were nor husbands nor wives who did not shudder at the sight of the ribbons (*fontanges*) and laces they wore in their hair," the Minister of Finance, Orry, wrote to Torcy. "They considered it a tacit order to themselves, assuredly very capable of changing friendly sentiments." And, though a friend of the Princess, he expressed his earnest hopes that the Queen would in future dress her hair *à l'espagnole*, that is to say without any ornament.[3]

This sensational entry took place on 30 June, and after the first shock was over, curls, *fontanges* and Paris clothes were forgiven and everyone succumbed to the charm of the sinners, except naturally the Comtesse de Palma and her clique. The Princess even succeeded in subjugating Blécourt, who, more soldier than diplomatist, was an easy dupe. His dispatches henceforth are full of her praise. "It does not appear that Madame des Ursins wishes to meddle

[1] Trémoïlle, ii. 64; letter of 24 June, 1702.
[2] Ibid., ii. 64; letter of 3 July, 1702.
[3] Ibid., ii. 65; letter of 4 July, 1702.

with business—quite the contrary," he wrote to Torcy a fortnight after their arrival. "There is not the least complaint and everyone considers it an effect of Providence to see the Queen in the hands of a person so wise, so disinterested, and so capable of inspiring in her all that is necessary for the good of the monarchy."[1]

In spite of these conquests, however, her group of enemies caused her some anxiety, and she wrote to Torcy to put him on his guard against probable intrigue and calumnies, naming those most likely to attack her: first and foremost the Comtesse de Palma, very influential on account of her relationship with Porto-Carrero, the Duchesse d'Ossone, young and pretty, attractive to men and very friendly with Blécourt, and a certain Madame d'Aguirre, a spy in the pay of her enemies in France. These three had sworn a solemn oath to get her expelled from Spain by inventing "all that the blackest malice could conceive. Through them," she wrote, "you will know all that I shall never do and probably never think!"[2]

The friction between her and Porto-Carrero had developed to open warfare. According to her he had turned completely against France and systematically opposed all her suggestions of reform. She had been in Madrid three weeks before he condescended to pay her his official visit.

Even without enemies it was no easy matter to govern a country so divided and full of discord as was Spain at this time. Since the outbreak of the war the French had become very unpopular, the grandees and ministers maintaining that Europe was hostile to Spain only out of spite to France, and they regarded the authority of a Frenchwoman, known to be the official agent of Versailles, with intense disapproval. The country was divided into three parties: the partisans of Austria headed by the Queen-Dowager, who held a kind of rival Court at Toledo where she had been exiled on Philippe's accession; the Nationalists, in revolt against French authority, which included all the grandees and most of the nobles; and the partisans of France, every day growing less. With the arrival of the Queen and Princess a fourth party speedily took shape — the partisans neither of Austria nor Spain nor France, but of the Princess des Ursins.

[1] Trémoïlle, ii. 66; letter of 13 July, 1702.
[2] Ibid., ii. 67; letter of 15 July, 1702.

THE ART OF REIGNING 95

The Queen, playing with great earnestness at the game of ruling a kingdom, served admirably to strengthen her authority by her childish charm which fascinated her austere but chivalrous opponents. Twice a day she presided at the Giunto or Council, sometimes for six hours at a time. So far, etiquette forbade the Princess's attendance in the room, but it is more than probable that she was present, concealed behind some convenient piece of tapestry. In any case she was kept well informed of everything which went on there and the government was practically in her hands. Her policy for the moment was simply to gain the hearts of the people, and she had at her command the most irresistible of baits, the attraction of a child who made herself loved because she desired it.

What Spaniard could resist it? With her marvellous precocity the Queen had at once grasped the situation and played her part to perfection. She had not been long in Madrid before everybody, friend and foe, was at her feet. "She was born intelligent," writes Saint-Simon, "and in this early youth, with a mind wise, firm and consistent, capable of counsel and restraint, she possessed everything to make herself adored and thus became the divinity of the Spaniards." [1]

Even those most prejudiced against her as the great-niece of Louis XIV. and more than half French by blood, even the grandees of the old school, found her irresistible and wagged their heads with pleasure when she presided at the Giunto. This child, not yet fourteen, took her place gravely at the head of the table among the wise old counsellors (extremely foolish, according to the Princess) and listened patiently but not without criticism to their divagations, irrelevancies and general imbecilities. And often, weary with their long futile discussions and unable to disapprove openly, she would bring her embroidery, and when the speeches were too wearisome would thread her needle and begin to sew.

The first time [wrote the Princess to Torcy], they were very astonished, but she told them with her usual grace that as they spoke often of things which had nothing to do with the business in hand and did not interest her, she would employ her time in needlework. All immediately understood her meaning. They looked at each other in amazement and

[1] Saint-Simon, xi. 244.

laughed. Since then they keep more to the point, and when, from bad habit, they forget, the Queen either says with a smile that she will take her needlework or else she takes it without saying anything, and everyone laughs.[1]

"Marie-Louise de Savoie was grace personified when she presided at the Giunto, needlework in her hand, with an attention nothing could distract," writes the author of Louville's *Mémoires*, "keeping a modest silence during the deliberation which she broke now and again by remarks full of sense and justice. All the Council was on her side."[2]

A strange life for a child at the age when others were playing with their dolls. Twice a day for three hours presiding at the Council and after giving audience private and public to the ladies of Madrid.

Often [she herself wrote to Louis] I have no time to take air, and only a moment in the evening after my supper to amuse myself a little with my ladies. This I employ in playing *Colin-Maillard* (blind-man's buff) and *Compagnie-vous-plaît-elle?* To speak frankly, I am very impatient that the King, when he has beaten the Germans, should return and retake the care of the State so that I might have nothing to do but enjoy seeing him and think of amusing myself.[3]

Judging from what is known of her character, however, it is not likely that she was so well amused playing *Compagnie-vous-plaît-elle?* whatever that may be, as presiding at the Council, but it was the Princess's policy to hide her pupil's passion for governing. Louis did not approve, as Madame de Maintenon declares over and over again, of women meddling with business, except under his own direction. As for Philippe's return, that wish was genuine on the part of both Queen and Princess, for the latter had realised that with an idle, uxorious monarch behind her, who had no wish but to be spared the trouble of reigning, but whose authority none dared dispute, she would be better able to hold her own against her enemies and had no fear that he would interfere with her schemes of government.

It was a perfect partnership, this woman of sixty with her ability and experience and the docile intelligent child who obeyed her implicitly. The Princess kept well in the background behind her tapestry and allowed her pupil

---

[1] Trémoïlle, ii. 80; letter to Torcy of 19 Aug. 1702.
[2] Louville, i. 360.
[3] Trémoïlle, ii. 76; letter of 27 July, 1702.

THE ART OF REIGNING

to receive all the praise for their happy success. Versailles only was aware of the truth.

I think you will easily judge the pleasure it gives me to learn that the Queen of Spain merits in reality the praises bestowed on her [Louis wrote]. If it is due to you, I know that you hide it with the greatest care, but in any case you respond so perfectly to my confidence that you must be assured that I am as grateful to you as you could wish for your wise conduct, and that it increases the esteem and affection I have always had for you.[1]

Had he guessed that she was working with quite other aims than his glory and aggrandisement he would have been more sparing of his praise.

Thus, in less than two months and in spite of the *tontillo*, she had succeeded in winning all Madrid, and the little Queen was their idol. Blécourt was her slave, Louis was pleased, Madame de Maintenon approved, Torcy was never tired of singing her praises. Everyone spoke well of her, which, her enemies said, is precisely what always happens at the beginning to those of whom everyone ends by speaking ill.

The immensely long ciphered letters she wrote once a week to Torcy are veritable official dispatches, touching on everything military, political and financial. They are written with the lucidity and conciseness of a practised statesman, while the reforms she proposes are extraordinarily able and courageous. No doubt Orry, whose admiration for her outlasted her disgrace, counted for much in them, and her political education in general; Orry the competent, man of many resources, who shared in her triumph and ruin. As for Porto-Carrero he was completely ignored, and his name figures as little in her dispatches as though he and his office did not exist. Yet all the while he was there ostensibly presiding at the Council, but so ignored by the Queen that he hardly dared to open his mouth. He was rarely admitted to her presence and had not the least authority over her, the Princess, or the State. His rôle was reduced to querulous complaints to all who would listen, that his office had been wrested from him by the Princess, that she kept him in complete ignorance of what went on, made not even a show of consulting him, and ignored his remonstrances.

[1] Trémoïlle, ii. 77; letter of 30 July, 1702.

He was seventy-three and had never had much intelligence. Now he had become too feeble to be capable of holding his own against a rival of the force and ability of the Princess, and if he continued to support his humiliation and did not retire at once to his archbishopric of Toledo, it was because he hoped that at Philippe's return she would be relegated to her proper sphere.

It will be seen presently whether that miracle was accomplished. Meantime we must leave him and the Princess to their struggle for the mastery and follow the King in his campaign in Italy.

CHAPTER XIII

PHILIPPE V. IN ITALY (1702)

WAR had been openly declared by England, Holland and Austria on France and Spain, and Prince Eugène, full of spleen against Louis for having disregarded his military genius, had been appointed commander-in-chief of the allied armies in Italy. He had already defeated the combined French and Spanish troops at Carpi and Chiari, and taken nearly the whole of Mantua, and the Duc de Vendôme, Louis' only reliable general, had been sent to oppose him. It was to learn the art of war under this successful general that Philippe V. left his kingdom fifteen months after his accession and his young wife five months after his marriage.

Accompanied by the Ambassador Marsin and his evil genius Louville he arrived in Naples on 17 April, having been little over a week on the voyage. The Neapolitans had been looking forward impatiently to his presence, for they had long been groaning under the yoke of viceroys harsh and avaricious and had many grievances. Some, however, were in favour of the Archduke, and these had prepared a plot for his assassination. But when he arrived and the conspirators saw, instead of the brutal Bourbon they expected, a frail gentle boy with yellow curls and black miserable eyes, they were touched and had not the heart to kill him. One of them even betrayed the plot, with the result that a special guard was appointed to protect him, but the officers of this guard, bought by the imperialists, in their turn plotted to give him up to the Austrians, which was luckily discovered in time.

Whether from vexation at these intrigues or grief at his separation from the Queen, or from physical causes already alluded to, before he had been a month in Naples he fell into a fit of melancholy so profound as to assume the proportions of insanity. He refused to see anybody, shut himself up in his apartment with his doctors and confessor, would attend none of the fêtes organised in his honour, and showed himself so morose and disagreeable that his Italian subjects were thankful when, after six weeks, he took his departure. Louis' order was that he should proceed to Acqui, near Milan, to join the Duke of Savoy, and afterwards take his place at the head of his troops under the command of his cousin the Duc de Vendôme.

Leaving Naples he proceeded by slow degrees by sea to Livorno where he landed and continued his journey in a post-chaise as far as Alessandria. Here his father-in-law awaited him and they went together to Acqui, where the rest of the ducal family was assembled.

Amédée II. was enchanted with this opportunity of attacking his son-in-law on the subject he had so much at heart, the command of his Spanish troops, and seeing him so young and inexperienced and so unlike a soldier, thought it would be easy to persuade him to renounce it in his favour. And in Philippe's present mood he might perhaps have succeeded had it not been for Louville, who disliked and mistrusted him, and was so opposed to his having any authority whatever in the Spanish army that Philippe gave in. And since Louville was for the moment the master, he worked with such success that not only he nipped in the bud all the Duke's hopes of command, but caused a rupture between him and Philippe which proved fatal to the interests of both France and Spain.

Charles-Auguste d'Allonville, Marquis de Louville, was at this date (1702) thirty-four years old. He had been in Philippe's service since the Prince was a child, as tutor and gentleman of the bedchamber, and had accompanied him to Spain as chief of his French household. On his arrival the boy, as has been said, was lonely and miserable and threw himself for consolation on the one person to whom he was accustomed, so that he attained an authority which neither his position nor character warranted.

Louville more than any other was the depositary of his soul [writes Saint-Simon]. He had been recommended to the King (Louis) by the Duc de Beauvillier as a man wise, well educated, full of good sense, intelligence and resource and worthy of all confidence. Louville had in fact all these qualities and was besides gay and full of amusing jests, highly flavoured but with judgment, which roused the King from his natural cold solemnity and were a great resource to him on his arrival in this foreign land. He became director of the monarchy. He knew the King of Spain thoroughly, was sole confidant of his heart and distributor of his favours. He governed Spain and the King and passed for being Sovereign Arbiter of everything in the country. It was he who wrote all his private letters to the Court of France and everything passed directly through his hands.[1]

The portrait is too favourable. Here is the man as he has revealed himself by his words and acts.

Quick-tempered to the point of violence, self-assertive and arrogant, loyal to his master as long as it served his interests, but always ready to abuse and depreciate him, hasty and superficial in his judgments, narrow and presumptuous, obstinate as a mule and vain as a peacock. He despised everything and everybody not French, and was never so happy as when fomenting discord. Intelligence he had and wit and vivacity, and his letters show him gay and amusing. But he was the last person to have been placed near Philippe at so critical a moment as his accession, and his unpopularity during the first year of his reign, before the advent of the Queen and Princess, was due to his pernicious influence.

The Duke of Savoy, who was even more intelligent than Louville, soon discovered that it was more important to gain his favour than that of his master, especially in Philippe's present state of health, and tried his utmost to win him by all kinds of flattery. "He was cringing in his politeness," writes Saint-Simon. But Louville was not easily moved from his point, and he had conceived, not it must be owned without reason, a violent mistrust of the Duke.

" It was worth seeing," writes the author of his *Mémoires*, "with what marvellous art the Duke of Savoy mingled respect with familiarity, reserve with frankness, and with what tact he made himself agreeable to the meanest of the King's suite, how he conversed to cover the King's embarrassment, how he jested and recounted the gossip of Versailles as though he lived there." [2]

For the Duke was not only intelligent but knew how to make himself charming, and Versailles with all its inhabitants was exceedingly well known to him, thanks to the indiscretions of the Duchess of Burgundy.

But even the gossip of his old home did not succeed in rousing Philippe from his lethargy. His malady, which he called the " vapours," was gaining ground every day. He

[1] Saint-Simon, ii. 241. [2] Louville, i. 283.

shut himself up here as in Naples with his confessor and doctors, and refused to speak or move. He thought probably of nothing else than his beloved Queen, but her name had never passed his lips since his departure from Barcelona. He complained that his head felt hollow and as if it were going to drop off, and although his appetite was good and he slept well, he was under the impression that he was dying. All these symptoms so alarmed Louville that he wrote to Versailles that if he were not allowed to return to his wife he would certainly go mad, and implored Louis to send him one of his doctors.

But, as is well known, the maladies of others were the last of Louis' cares, and he refused either to allow his grandson's return to Spain or to send a doctor. "The vapours of which you complain," he wrote indifferently to Philippe, "are disagreeable but not dangerous."[1] And he insisted on his joining the army immediately.

Philippe's meeting with his father-in-law was cordial, flattering on the part of the Duke and solemnly polite on that of Philippe, but thanks to the malevolence of Louville their friendly relations did not last long, and a disagreeable incident brought about a complete breach and was the direct cause of the Duke's rupture of his alliance.

Presuming on their relationship he wanted to violate the strict etiquette of the Spanish Court which exacted that kings might eat only with kings, and at the supper he had prepared for his son-in-law had ordered a *fauteuil* for himself to be placed at the Royal table, whereas he had no right to be seated at all while the King ate and never except on a *tabouret* in his presence.

Louville, going to supervise the banquet in his official capacity, discovered this arrangement and, exasperated at what he considered the Duke's insolence, went at once to inform Philippe. But the boy, either from timidity or indifference, refused to make any objection, and Marsin the ambassador took his side. Louville, however, obstinate as a mule, and accustomed to have his own way in everything, persisted with so much energy that finally the King gave way and allowed him to order the second *fauteuil* to be removed.

Presently Philippe entered the banqueting-hall. He

[1] Baudrillart, *Philippe V. et la Cour de France*, i. 108; letter of 7 June, 1702.

PHILIPPE V. IN ITALY   103

saluted his father-in-law in passing and then seated himself at the table without taking any further notice of him, so that the Duke was forced to stand with the other courtiers behind his chair. He succeeded in controlling himself during the meal, but the result of Louville's meddling was that next morning he sent word that he was retiring to Turin with all his troops, and would take no further part in the war. So offended was he that he left without bidding farewell, wrote to both his daughters of the humiliation he had suffered, and immediately after broke his alliance with France and entered into negotiations with the Emperor. It will be seen that, in consequence of this affair, he became one of the most vexatious and even formidable enemies of France and Spain during the long war which followed.

Louville, however, was charmed at his departure and boasted to everyone how he had snubbed his arrogance; but he lived to repent his folly, for he made two enemies even more formidable, as far as he was concerned, than the Duke himself — the Duchess of Burgundy and the Queen of Spain, neither of whom ever forgave the humiliation to which he had subjected their father. The Duchess left Louis no peace till he sent an order for his recall and the Queen became his mortal enemy in Spain. Thanks to the intercession of the Duc de Beauvillier and Torcy his recall was countermanded, but only on condition that he changed his tactics completely and behaved with less insolence, and he received a severe reprimand, not only for this affair but for his Spanish policy in general and the bad influence he had acquired over the King. As for Philippe, at the time he was indifferent to everything and seemed hardly to notice the Duke's departure or that of his troops, but on his return to Spain the Queen forced him to withdraw his protection and favour from Louville.

But this is to forestall. For the moment, instead of congratulating himself on having escaped dismissal, he was furious at the reprimand he had received, especially as to the damage he had done in Spain, and attributing it to the Princess's complaints, became thenceforth her mortal enemy.

At the first talk of her appointment as Camarera Mayor he had dreaded in her an antagonist and rival, and through the Duc de Beauvillier had endeavoured that the Duchesse de Ventadour should receive the appointment. He had witnessed her influence with the King and Queen with the fiercest jealousy, and had left Spain in terror at the importance she would assume when alone in authority. From all he heard, things had proved even worse than he anticipated, and this last straw so upset his equilibrium that he answered Torcy with violence that he would resign his post rather than submit to the authority of the Princess, to whose jealousy he owed his disgrace. "She foresaw," he wrote, " that I should never allow the King of Spain to be attached to her gilded skirts (*sa jupe dorée*) and easily persuaded the Queen that I should be a dangerous rival to her credit with the King." [1]

Meantime the order arrived from Versailles that Philippe, in spite of his vapours, must proceed at once to Cremona and take his place at the head of his troops, an order which he promptly obeyed. Arrived at the camp, his malady vanished as if by magic with the excitement and activity and the open-air life, and he recovered his health and spirits and behaved with courage and energy at the Battle of Luzzara which took place on 15 August.

The Duc de Vendôme, generalissimo of the French armies, had naturally received orders that so precious a life should be exposed to danger as little as possible and a place had been reserved for him at the rear, but during a hot skirmish he managed to escape from his staff and galloped off alone to the front, where he remained under a heavy fire during one of the fiercest encounters of the battle. This was his ordeal of fire, and he bore it bravely and well and merited the name of *El Rey Vencedor* which his Spanish troops gave him, though no one ever rightly knew which side had conquered. "Never," writes Saint-Simon, "was combat so keen, so hot, disputed with such violence, never was such valour on either side, never resistance so obstinate, never fire or struggle so continuous, never success so uncertain. The King of Spain remained a long while under the heaviest fire with perfect tranquillity, watching the reciprocal attacks of the armies and laughing at the fear he perceived among his suite." [2]

Letters of congratulation poured in from all sides, but probably the one which gave him most pleasure was from the Queen, notwithstanding that in it she announced that his own coasts had been attacked by the enemy.

[1] Louville, i. 341.   [2] Saint-Simon, x. 222.

PHILIPPE V. IN ITALY

Yesterday [*yer*, she wrote, with her amusing spelling], after holding the Council in the morning as usual, I assisted at another which lasted from eight in the evening till nearly midnight. . . . Now I am going out walking, for it is an infinitely long time since I have been out. Good-bye, therefore, my dear King, I doubt not that when the campaign is over you will no longer be amused, but you will come back to find your little wife who loves you better than herself.[1]

Louis was delighted. His grandson had obeyed his orders, had won his spurs, and proved himself worthy of his Bourbon blood and might now return to his wife, all the more that the state of his country demanded his presence. For besides the attack on the coast to which the Queen alluded so lightly, other and graver troubles had occurred. A revolt had broken out in Catalonia and showed every sign of spreading, and one of the most important and trusted personages in the kingdom—the Amirante of Castile—had played the traitor and fled to Portugal to join the enemy. It was time that a country given up to revolt and confusion should no longer be left in the hands of a child of fourteen.

Since the resignation of the Duc d'Harcourt the post of ambassador had been filled only temporarily, for Marsin had neither the rank nor the qualifications for so important a place. The Princess had already been asked to recommend a successor, but she had been too long out of France, she said, to know who was most suitable and could only suggest the Duc de Gramont. Louis, however, had cast his eye on a man of much greater importance and experience, no other than her old lover the Cardinal d'Estrées.

The Cardinal, now an old man of seventy-four, in bad health, with nothing to gain since he was immensely rich and laden with all the honours it was in the power of Louis and the Pope to bestow, was not tempted to accept a post so onerous and it was only under great pressure that he consented, and on condition that he should be aided by his nephew the Abbé d'Estrées, a young fellow of whom more than enough will be heard. Always haughty and arrogant, old age and ill-health (he suffered from the stone) had exaggerated these defects so that his temper had become insufferable and he would support no contradiction. Even Louville, his ally and flatterer, said of him that " always sad, morose and discontented, when he was not apathetic

[1] Trémoïlle, ii. 95; letter of 1 Sept. 1702.

he was foaming with fury and uttering nothing but complaints and curses."[1]

"The Abbé, his nephew, was a young man," writes Saint-Simon, " well made, *galant*, with a very commonplace mind, intoxicated to fatuity with himself, his talents and the high position and brilliance of his family, honourable and well-intentioned, but often mistaken and making himself ridiculous. His morals had excluded him from a bishopric. . . . He was not rich and was anxious to succeed." And again: " L'Abbé d'Estrées was singularly complex, a handsome face, some sort of wit, avaricious and at the same time magnificent. A great opinion of himself, occasionally absurd. For the rest, good-natured and a man of honour, with a superficies of fatuity which was a pity. He had very much the manners and jargon of the great world, which he knew well through his uncle the Cardinal, who was very fond of him, but could not sometimes resist mocking him. His morals, which were not clerical, had excluded him from a bishopric and sent him to the embassies."[2]

In spite of their old friendship the Princess had regarded the Cardinal's appointment with dismay and done her best to prevent it, for besides that she dreaded the authority of a statesman so important, his policy was that of Louville, namely, that Spain should be entirely under the domination of France.

These fears she made known, on first hearing of his nomination, to Louis and his ministers, tactfully and through the medium of the Maréchale de Noailles: " I am afraid that this nation, naturally haughty, will consider it a mark of contempt on the part of France that one of the greatest minds living should be sent them, not to counsel but to rule, and that it will increase the dislike they already have for the French."[3]

However, since to rule in Spain was precisely Louis' intention in choosing d'Estrées, her objections had little weight, and all the concession she obtained was that he should not be officially nominated until after his arrival with Philippe, but should slip quietly into his post as she herself had done into hers.

As she anticipated, the appointment was very unpopular with the grandees for the reasons she gave. Porto-Carrero,

[1] Louville, ii. 51.   [2] Saint-Simon, xi. 407.
[3] Geffroy, 127 ; letter of 14 Oct. 1702.

too, was strongly opposed to it, but chiefly from jealousy. He was, besides, bitterly disappointed, for he had counted on Philippe's arrival to put the Princess in her place, and the presence of her former lover would, he feared, only strengthen her position. Old and infirm as he was, he finally decided that rather than enter on fresh struggles with d'Estrées he would retire from political life and take refuge in his archbishopric of Toledo.

The Cardinal d'Estrées, arrogant and fully decided to make the most of the authority given him by Louis, joined Philippe in Milan on his way back to Spain. Louville naturally lost no time in flattering and paying him an obsequious court, and as he was an amusing companion his advances were accepted. His theme was always the Princess des Ursins and her crimes, the petticoat government to which Spain had been subjected since Philippe's departure, her hatred of the French and manœuvres for popularity, the authoritative airs she gave herself and the fatal influence she had over the Queen, to all which d'Estrées listened with interest and increasing disapproval.

At Genoa Marsin took his leave and returned to France, and at Perpignan they were joined by the Abbé d'Estrées arrived from Versailles.

He had been Louville's fellow-student, and as they had much in common in character it was not long before they swore eternal friendship. The Abbé was at once initiated into all the crimes and follies of the Princess, and the two, encouraged by the Cardinal, undertook a veritable campaign for her ruin. They persuaded Philippe to announce officially before his arrival in Madrid that the Cardinal's authority must be absolute, that he was to be first at the Despacho or Privy Council, and that no business of any kind should be transacted without his knowledge and approval, that in fact he should unite the prerogatives of First Minister with those of Ambassador of France, a combination exactly opposed to the will of the Spaniards and the policy of the Princess.

When this proclamation reached her ears she understood at once that it was a plot directed against herself, and with her usual promptness lost no time in checking it. Her counterplot was that the Queen by her charms and caresses should keep Philippe so secluded in her apartment, to which no one could pass but through her own, that access to him would be impossible, and that thus all affairs between him and the Ambassador should of necessity pass through her own hands.

The result of these rival intrigues was the most formidable quarrel of her life, a battle in which for the time she triumphed, but which had the gravest consequences later, for in her impatience of any authority she lost sight of the importance of the man she attacked, and forgot that, though a Louville might be disgraced and a Porto-Carrero humiliated, the Cardinal César d'Estrées, great prince of the Church and chosen friend of Louis XIV., was not so easily disposed of.

While Philippe was proceeding by what seems incredibly slow stages for an eager husband returning to his wife and a monarch to his kingdom on the verge of a revolution, an event occurred which swamped for a time all minor considerations. This was the destruction in the port of Vigo by the English and Dutch of the Franco-Spanish fleet laden with treasure from the Indies, a loss incalculable at such a moment when every penny was needed to prepare arms and ammunition for the struggle with Austria. Yet notwithstanding this fresh anxiety and the growing difficulties political and financial she had to face, it was with dread rather than relief that the Princess received the news of the King's approach and prepared for the tussle which she knew to be imminent.

CHAPTER XIV

STRUGGLES FOR THE MASTERY (1703)

IT was an ill day for the Princess when the trio of conspirators set foot in Spain. The Queen, eager to greet her husband, had decided to go with all the Court to Guadalaxara, sixty miles from Madrid, to meet him, but so unpopular had he become that, in spite of the Princess's entreaties, the grandees and ministers refused to go farther than Alcala, and would have preferred not to disturb themselves at all, but await him in the palace at Madrid.

At Alcala the quarrel broke out. After the speeches of welcome and hand-kissing the King retired with the Queen to her apartment, the Princess remaining according to custom on guard in the antechamber, where all the grandees were assembled. Hardly had they entered than the Cardinal, without taking the least notice of her or the rest, stalked arrogantly in behind them. This was bad enough, for the Queen's apartment was sacred even to the ambassadors who had their right of entry to the King's, but when, with a simper and dandified air, the Abbé followed, she lost all patience and rose to prevent him. It was an open declaration of war, and she responded to it as such. She attacked the Cardinal on his return and angrily asserted that "though his office and years gave him liberty to act as he thought fit, his nephew was not yet of an age to have such free access to the apartment of a young Princess." To which the Cardinal replied haughtily that his nephew was ambassador as well as himself and had the same rights. That day the Abbé, ostentatiously and without any pretext, with an insolent smile entered the Queen's apartment three or four times, which so enraged the Princess that she wrote a formal protest to Louis.

A few days later, after their arrival in Madrid, the Cardinal, passing her in the antechamber on his way to the Royal apartment, asked her mockingly whether she would permit him to wish the Queen good-evening. Feigning to take him seriously she rose and said she would inquire. Whereupon, before she could reach the door, he pushed past her roughly and entering exclaimed, "This is an example of your etiquette which I have orders to abolish. Another time I will bring my baptismal register that it may be known who I am!"[1]

Meanwhile Louville's share in the concerted programme was to write violent letters to the Duc de Beauvillier, who would naturally show them to Louis, filled with abuse of both the Queen and Princess, of which the following extracts are a specimen:

> If the King does not take prompt measures to drag the Catholic King out of his slavery he is lost. First of all Madame des Ursins must be dismissed—of that there is no question. The King and Queen must be told to dismiss her for having given them bad counsels out of personal ambition. The Queen hates all the French, and she and the Princess have so well understood that she will not be able to govern absolutely as long as there are any French here, that they have resolved not to suffer any to remain. The Queen feels that her husband is an imbecile who thinks and desires nothing of his own will, and that she has only to keep him shut up to make him say, write and think all she wishes. He must therefore be guarded absolutely and it must not be allowed that the Queen guards him, since if she does it will be the Duke of Savoy who will govern Spain as now he governs her, and I know the King well enough to affirm that within a year, when there will no longer be any French here, if she or his father-in-law wish to make him sign a treaty with England, Holland and the Emperor against France, with the cession of the Netherlands and everything they would like for their commerce, he would do it without hesitation. And to this extremity we are reduced by a wretched Frenchwoman (*malheureuse française*) who, for her personal ambition and in lightness of heart, wishes to separate two nations and inspire a French Prince with an extreme aversion for France. If I could talk with the King for half an hour a day in private and were supported by France I could frustrate all her schemes, but I have no great wish to play that part, for if you would give me two millions in gold and make me eighteen times grandee to remain here in my present situation, I would not stay, for I think the pains I suffer are next only to those of Hell. What I most fear is that if the Princess is recalled she will not obey, and that no one will know how to force her, since she has the King and Queen in her pocket.[2]

[1] Trémoïlle, iii. 11; letter from the Princess to Louis XIV. of 20 Jan. 1703.
[2] Saint-Simon, xi. 506; letter of 27 Jan. 1703.

The following week he continues in the same strain :

Since my last letter things have gone from bad to worse with such fury and explosion that there is no one who does not say openly that the King and Queen are resolved not to suffer any French at the Court of Spain. The Queen monopolises the King to such a point that she scarcely lets him hunt, for the sole reason that the Abbé d'Estrées and I sometimes go and she fears we might talk to him. It seems that the King, infatuated though he is, has remarked this obsession, for he said to me the other day that when he wanted to hunt she said to him in a sour voice which he imitated, "Is it possible that after so long an absence you still want to be gadding about" (*courir la pretentaine*). Now this "gadding about" consists only in hunting every other day and all the rest of the time he is shut up night and day in her room, where no one ever approaches him except the Queen, Madame des Ursins, and Monsieur d'Aubigny.

It is certain that if Madame des Ursins is allowed to remain here to govern the King and Queen, all is lost beyond recall. But how force her to leave if the Queen, haughty as she is and governing the King absolutely, take her part ? The hatred of Madame des Ursins for the French and all that regards France is so notorious and of such long date that no one is surprised. When I was in Rome nothing else was talked of. She was brought up by a rebel father who apparently educated her badly as regards her duties. She married a husband who, after fighting a duel, took refuge in Spain. While she was in Rome she always flattered the Spanish even when we were at war with them, and during that time was arranging honours for herself at the Court of Vienna,[1] and the Cardinal d'Estrées knows it as well as I. Since then she was in France, where she declares she was not well treated, and when she was chosen to be near the Queen she meant never to return. I pray God never to show me any mercy if I do not think as I say and if she does not give me reason to think so, and if I were dying I would affirm the same.[2]

Not content with abuse founded perhaps on facts, he employs calumny, and accuses the Queen of having "strange morals, very singular and impossible to write," and insists that the Princess should be replaced by "another French-woman who should watch her and keep her in order." [3]

Porto-Carrero, terribly jealous of the Cardinal and despairing, between him and the Princess, of regaining his authority, lost not a moment after Philippe's arrival in sending

[1] See p. 14.
[2] Saint-Simon, xi. 511 ; letter of 13 Feb. 1703.
[3] Ibid., xi. 513 ; letter of 22 Feb. 1703.

in his resignation as President of the Despacho, giving as his reason that he " could not get on with the persons he would meet there," and not all the King's persuasions could induce him to remain.

This was a trump-card for the Princess and she made the most of it, for these "persons" clearly meant the new Ambassador and his nephew, and she insisted that if the d'Estrées were allowed to assist at the Council alone, the Spaniards would inevitably conclude the Government to be entirely in the hands of the French, and persuaded Philippe to exclude them also, and hold it alone with the Spanish secretary, the Marquis de Rivas.

The Cardinal's fury when he received the official announcement of this decision knew no bounds, and he and the Abbé insulted the Princess so grossly that she lost all patience and sent in her resignation as Camarera Mayor. " The Cardinal and Abbé breathe fire and flame against me," she wrote. " They accuse me of wishing to govern the King through the Queen, of seeking too much to please the Spanish, of not sufficiently opposing the etiquette, and of being the cause of the King's decision to hold his Despacho alone till he hears what Your Majesty advises, and they seem disposed to make everything go wrong in order to throw the blame on me." And she ends by declaring that it was impossible for her to remain any longer with an Ambassador openly her enemy, and begs Louis to accept her resignation.[1]

A week later she wrote to Torcy that the attacks of the two d'Estrées had become a veritable persecution, that their chief occupation was to set everyone against her, that they accused her of sequestrating the King and keeping him perpetually shut up with the Queen, so that no one might have access to him but herself, that they treated all her friends "like dogs" and excited the Spanish against her by accusing her of wishing to govern the kingdom. "The Abbé," she continues, " is a giddy fellow preoccupied with himself and the most conceited person in the world. The Cardinal is no longer what he was. His mind is very much deteriorated, his vivacity has degenerated into fury and often his conversation is very far removed from good sense. You can have no idea to what an extent the Spaniards are discontented with them both. These gentlemen preach

[1] Trémoïlle, iii. 9 ; letter to Louis XIV. of 21 Jan. 1703.

STRUGGLES FOR THE MASTERY 113

nothing but the destruction of etiquette. I also wish it destroyed, but to me it does not seem that everything which is not French should be called etiquette." Finally she reiterates her decision that either they or she must leave Madrid.[1]

The following week she has even worse to relate. The d'Estrées menace the French who are friendly towards her so that they dare no longer visit her. They insult her openly and exact that when they are with the Queen she shall retire. The Queen herself they treat with the greatest discourtesy and leave her eighteen days without paying their respects. As for her, hardly a day passes that the Cardinal does not find means to insult her, affecting to ignore her presence and passing her without salute, and she implores Torcy to persuade Louis to allow her to retire, that she " may be delivered from so outrageous a persecution." [2]

The Queen, with her usual impetuosity, threw herself into the fray and wrote to Louis urging the d'Estrées' recall. Philippe too was dragged in, though it is doubtful if he did more than sign the letters they gave him. One of Louville's accusations, which Louis had most resented, was that all his letters were composed by the Princess, and these now arrived frequently, filled also with complaints of the Cardinal's insolence and imploring his recall. "Never a day passes," he wrote, "that I have not to support his haughty ill-humour."

Louville declares that the Princess's resignation of her post was nothing but a feint to force Louis to recall the d'Estrées, and that Philippe had confided to him that she never had the slightest intention of leaving Spain. This seems improbable. She was not the woman to play her cards so badly, and there is a ring of sincerity in her letters which points to genuine discouragement. In any case Louis, who liked and esteemed d'Estrées and counted on him to assert his own authority, not only accepted her resignation but did so with such severity as almost to merit the name of a disgrace.

I chose you to be near the Queen of Spain [he wrote], persuaded that nothing could be better for her and the interests of my grandson than your perfect accord with my Ambassador in Madrid. I valued no less the spirit of harmony of which I

[1] Trémoïlle, iii. 16 ; letter of 1 Feb. 1703.
[2] Ibid., iii. 21 ; letter of 8 Feb. 1703.

thought myself assured, than the other qualities I found in you. But your letters of the 21st and 26th of January destroy the opinion I had. If harmony cannot be established between the Cardinal and you, I cannot force you to support all the annoyance you foresee from a quarrel very damaging to public affairs, and rather than expose you to the fresh embarrassment you fear, I hereby accord you permission to come hither to give me an account of the matter before going to Rome, since you wish to retire there to rest.[1]

Philippe also received a severe scolding :

I chose the Cardinal as the most consummate and enlightened statesman that I could place near you, whose wisdom and experience would serve you best. He sacrificed for me his repose, his health, perhaps his life, with no other design than to prove his gratitude and zeal. And when you have most need of his talents, when it is most indispensable that he should take prompt measures for your safety and that of your kingdom, you show an unfortunate facility all at once for thinking you can govern alone a monarchy which the wisest of your predecessors would have difficulty in directing in its present state. I name facility in you what I should regard as presumption in another. . . . Choose then which you prefer, the continuation of my aid or the self-interested counsels of those who desire your ruin. If the first, order the Cardinal Porto-Carrero to re-enter the Despacho, if only for six months, and continue to allow the entrance of Cardinal d'Estrées. Do not shut yourself up in the shameful voluptuousness (*mollesse honteuse*) of your palace. Show yourself to your subjects and listen to their requests. . . . If you choose the second I shall be terribly afflicted at your ruin which I shall look upon as imminent.[2]

To the Cardinal he wrote a friendly apologetic letter excusing his grandson, bidding him at all costs persuade Porto-Carrero to re-enter the Despacho and assist at it himself, and promising that if the Princess did not alter her conduct he would recall her, and on the same day he wrote to Porto-Carrero himself begging him to assist at the Despacho and not deprive his grandson of his valuable services.

Torcy expressed the King's sentiments on the matter still more clearly to the Princess :

I cannot sufficiently express to you how much the King has been personally annoyed that the Cardinal d'Estrées, whom he esteems and likes, who undertook so disagreeable a journey solely

[1] Millot, *Mémoires de Noailles*, ii. 173 ; letter of 9 Feb. 1703.
[2] Ibid., ii. 159 ; letter of 4 Feb. 1703.

out of zeal, should receive on his arrival an affront in the face of all Europe, and that it appears to be you, Madame, who have counselled the King of Spain to treat him as he has done.[1]

And this was not all. Smarting under these unjust reproofs, the Princess could at least console herself with the thought that, summoned to Versailles, she would be able to defend herself *a vivâ voce*, but a little later—probably at the instance of Madame de Maintenon, who did not want her at Versailles—this invitation was revoked and she received orders to proceed direct to Rome. To which she haughtily replied that the season would make this impossible since the great heats would have already begun, and proposed remaining till the autumn at Orleans, where her relative the Cardinal de Coislin would give her shelter.[2]

But with the wires of her puppets in her hands she was more than a match for her adversaries, and her next move was to set them in motion. Philippe she directed to write to Louis with an arrogance which must have considerably surprised his grandfather. The Cardinal, he complained, had cruelly slandered him and had no other object than to ruin the Princess, " who is so necessary to the Queen's happiness. However, since the King desires her departure that is sufficient, and we will make that cruel sacrifice to the Cardinal and Abbé d'Estrées, but it will cost the Queen dear and she very much hopes that in recompense she will be delivered from these two cruel enemies."[3]

And a fortnight later:

Whatever repugnance I may have to speak to you further on the subject of the Princess des Ursins after the sharp reproaches this disagreeable affair has drawn on me, I think nevertheless that it is my duty to inform you that the rumour of her departure causes numerous and general complaints. All the Queen's household is in an indescribable state of despair. Nobles and people all speak of it with resentment.[4]

At this point the Queen, "choleric little demon," flies to the defence of her husband and replies to Louis' accusations with incredible audacity.

"*Mollesse honteuse!*" she blazes out. "The King kept

[1] Baudrillart, i. 138 ; letter of 4 Feb. 1703.
[2] Trémoïlle, iii. 24 ; letter of March (date not specified), 1703.
[3] Baudrillart, i. 14 ; letter of 18 Feb. 1703.
[4] Trémoïlle, iii. 26 ; letter of 2 March, 1703.

shut up in the shameful voluptuousness of his palace! What an outrage! How dare the Cardinal write such lies! How unfortunate to be in the clutches of so vile a man!"

The attack on the Princess she takes, or pretends to take, to herself.

Self-interested counsels of those who intend his ruin! What and whom does the Cardinal mean by that? If it is me, judge, I pray you, of his audacity. To say that *I* desire the King's ruin—that *I* keep him in *mollesse honteuse*—is that to be borne? I, whose sole happiness consists in his glory—I, who hid my tears not to prevent his going to Italy!

Passionately she defends the Princess:

By what right does the Cardinal attack her—she who has always counselled me well, she who is esteemed by everyone in Spain? To my mind this man is a monster. He excites nothing but discord and gains the hate of everyone by his haughty manners. He boasts everywhere that he has brought mortification upon us from the King our grandfather, and this by the blackest impostures that have ever been invented.[1]

And three weeks after:

I suffer tortures so cruel that if Your Majesty has not the goodness to protect me I shall certainly be the most unhappy Princess in the world. The Princess des Ursins, in whom I had placed all my trust, is forced to abandon me, and the same persons who persecute her so unjustly, after having behaved disrespectfully to the King and me, have again been able by their impostures to make you think ungrateful, presumptuous and voluptuous a Prince whom I love as he merits and who is your grandson. . . . I do not know if you have been informed of the bad effect the departure of the Princess has produced.[2]

And so miserable was she at the threatened loss and Louis' attack that she fell ill with fever and grew so thin with fretting that all the Court remarked it, as the Princess wrote to Torcy. To defend him from the charge of *mollesse honteuse* which had specially upset her, she had herself prepared a paper which she enclosed, showing how he had passed each day since his arrival from Italy, a childish document apparently of her own composition. It is headed:

[1] Millot, ii. 169; letter of 18 Feb. 1703.
[2] Trémoïlle, iii. 30; letter of 8 March, 1703.

RELATION OF WHAT THE KING HAS DONE THE FIRST
DAYS AFTER HIS ARRIVAL AND HOW HE IS AT PRESENT
OCCUPIED

The King arrived the 17th in the evening, which he spent in giving his hand to be kissed by everyone and trying to persuade the Cardinal Porto-Carrero to change his mind.[1]

The 18th, after being dressed and hearing mass, he passed the rest of the morning with all his Court. In the afternoon he went to Notre Dame d'Atocha, from whence he returned late and finished the evening with the Cardinals on the same subject.

The 19th the King passed the morning as before and saw besides the Cardinals on the same matter. In the afternoon he hunted from one to six, after which the Cardinal d'Estrées came to speak with him as to the way he should hold the Despacho.

The 20th the King passed the morning as before, again strongly urging the Cardinal Porto-Carrero, and in the afternoon was again at the hunt as before. In the evening he spoke with the Cardinal d'Estrées on the bad effect which he feared his entry alone in the Despacho would have. After which he held his Despacho.

The 21st he held Despacho morning and evening, was at the chapel in the morning and walked in the afternoon.

What the King does at present is to hold his Despacho morning and evening, show himself three times a week in public in the chapel, dine twice a week in public, give public audience twice a week, go every morning through all his apartment to see all his Court, hunt nearly every day even in bad weather, give private audiences to all who desire them, and go out in his coach or on foot every Sunday and holiday, which are the days he does not hunt.[2]

An exemplary life certainly, and far from voluptuous. Louis himself had spent his own youth much less virtuously.

But Philippe had to support a still worse humiliation. Louville, whom he had dismissed at the Queen's prayer, headstrong as usual, dared to attack him with incredible brutality, told him that he was ruining himself in his grandfather's eyes by taking part in the cabals against his Ambassador, blamed him for " passing all the day shut up in his palace among two hundred women as in a seraglio," playing at childish games, for which everyone mocked him, declared that it was deplorable that his fine qualities should be tarnished by an indolence and weakness so extreme that people began to say he was more debased than his predecessor

---

[1] On the subject of the Despacho.   [1] Trémoïlle, iii. 35.

Charles II., with other home-truths applied with so much violence that Philippe burst into tears.[1]

Meanwhile the vehement championship of the Queen and Louville's accusations as to her treasonable plots with her father had had a curious effect at Versailles. Louis began to realise that his grandson was a nonentity but that she was not, and that if he wished to retain a hold on Spain she would have to be reckoned with. He and Torcy, sitting in council in the apartment of Madame de Maintenon, decided that it was better not to exasperate her further by depriving her of her Camarera Mayor and thus perhaps push her into the arms of the Duke of Savoy. And the result of the confabulation was that Louis deliberately ate his own words (a feat which habit had taught him to do with a certain dignity) and wrote to the Cardinal that notwithstanding her bad conduct the Princess must retain her post and that he must reconcile himself with her.

> You must remember [he wrote] that if the Queen receives this mortification of having her torn from her she will never pardon my want of consideration, and also that it would be impossible without the Princess to be kept informed of her acts, that she would be capable of advising the King her husband badly before one could be warned in time to prevent it. . . . For these reasons you must at once give her a pretext to remain, letting her, however, understand that she may not do so unless she be reconciled to you.[2]

A week later he wrote to his grandson, giving him official permission to retain the Princess, but insisting that he use all his authority to put a stop to " these quarrels disagreeable and injurious to your service." [3]

This letter was accompanied by a " project of reconciliation " between the adversaries which is worth quoting :

PROJECT OF RECONCILIATION BETWEEN MADAME DES URSINS AND THE CARDINAL D'ESTRÉES. VERSAILLES, 18 MARCH, 1703

1. That the King of Spain declare to His Eminence that he never had the intention of deciding anything without him.
2. That His Eminence express himself enchanted to see that

---

[1] Baudrillart, i. 142 ; and Louville, ii. 16 ; letter from Louville to the Duc de Beauvillier of 28 Feb. 1703.
[2] Trémoïlle, iii. 37 ; letter of 9 March, 1703.
[3] Ibid., iii. 39 ; letter of 18 March, 1703.

his exclusion from the Despacho did not arise from want of confidence.

3. That Madame des Ursins declare that in giving her advice she did not act from mistrust of the Cardinal.

4. That on these declarations the Cardinal and Princess be reconciled.

5. That the Princess abandon her severity in the observation of etiquette.

6. That she recognise the good intentions of His Eminence in demanding free access to the Queen.

7. That the Queen grant this demand.

8. That the King accord all liberty for an arrangement of the matter.

9. That His Eminence express his gratitude to Their Majesties.

10. That the Cardinal be allowed to examine all affairs.

11. That the King do his utmost to persuade the Cardinal Porto-Carrero to return.

12. That Madame des Ursins on behalf of the Queen take the first step to persuade him.[1]

This amusing document was obeyed in the letter rather than the spirit. An official reconciliation did actually take place. The Cardinal, accompanied by his nephew the Abbé, paid the Princess a visit of ceremony and was kept waiting for an hour in her antechamber. When at length admitted he saluted her, according to the Princess, "with the air of one who pardons rather than repents an outrage," and she, according to Louville, received him coldly and haughtily, spoke of indifferent things and avoided all allusion to the quarrel.[2] And the result was that in less than a fortnight it broke out again with greater violence than ever.

So much for reconciliations according to Royal orders.

[1] Trémoïlle, iii. 39.
[2] Ibid., iii. 41 ; letter of 23 March, 1703 ; and Louville, i. 378.

CHAPTER XV

THE QUARRELS CONTINUE (1703)

STRONG in the Queen's protection the Princess still haughtily refused to remain and ostentatiously continued her preparations for departure, declaring that nothing short of an express order from Louis himself could change her decision. She continued to abuse and complain of the Cardinal and even dared to write to Louis himself, insisting that she came to Spain only out of deference to his order, and that in so doing she had sacrificed her own interests. She was hurt also that he desired her to remain only because the King and Queen wished it, and not because he valued her services. Finally she exacted that, if she consented to stay, he should "explain himself more favourably towards her." [1]

Which order Louis obeyed by return of post!

> If I doubted your zeal and fidelity [he wrote], I should not have counselled the King and Queen of Spain to keep you in Madrid. As I am assured of them, I have reason to believe that your remaining there will be useful for the good of my service and that of the King my grandson. [2]

A triumph which we may be sure she did not hide from her enemies.

In proof of the change in her favour at Versailles we have the following letter to Louville from the Duchesse de Beauvillier, warning him to moderate his abuse of her:

> She has powerful friends here [she wrote], Monsieur d'Harcourt, Madame de Maintenon and Chamillart, and I see that she will remain whatever happens. The King wishes to support the Cardinal d'Estrées and writes clearly to the King of Spain that he will not recall him, but between ourselves, Madame des Ursins is considered necessary and useful. Monsieur de Marsin, who has been consulted, thinks so, and it is the opinion which reigns here. [3]

Sincere or not the Princess continued to insist on resign-

---
[1] Trémoïlle, iii. 42; letter of 30 March, 1703.
[2] Ibid., iii. 48; letter of 22 April, 1703.
[3] Saint-Simon, xi. 516; letter of 9 March, 1703.

THE QUARRELS CONTINUE

ing her post. She is desperate, she says, at being forced to remain. " Nothing could be more disagreeable than to be exposed to fresh calumnies from those who have made me understand only too well their power and ill-will." [1]

Never was situation more disagreeable than mine since the return of the King to Madrid [she wrote to d'Harcourt]. Outraged in every way by those who ought on the contrary to praise my zeal and bear witness to the painful life I lead, I have received nothing but letters full of reproaches and threats, as if I were the most criminal of women. I have seen my adversaries, occupied only with the task of ruining me, triumph in their unjust designs by the approval given them.[2]

The so-called reconciliation was a mere façade behind which the hatreds, envies, and intrigues continued with greater virulence than before. Obedient to Louis' order both d'Estrées and Porto-Carrero attended the Despacho, but the Despacho existed no longer except in name. For form's sake Philippe presided at a table at which they and the Secretary Rivas were seated, but nothing of any importance was discussed and the real Privy Council was held by the Princess in her own apartment with Orry and her secretary d'Aubigny—"three heads under one bonnet," as Louville called them. But soon even this phantom Despacho grew intolerable to her and the Queen, probably because it necessitated Philippe's presence, and a fresh plot was formed for its suppression. Knowing that both cardinals, old and infirm as they were, went to bed early, she ordered that it should be held, not as before in the morning, but at ten o'clock at night.

Porto-Carrero [writes Saint-Simon] received every day all possible slights about all business matters, and the Cardinal d'Estrées also. Accustomed to be master, the Cardinal Porto-Carrero could no longer support all he had to suffer. His mildness, patience and mediocre mind were at the end of their tether. In order to be rid of them, Madame des Ursins conceived the idea of holding the Council from ten to eleven at night to fatigue these old men by the late hours.[3]

Things are going from bad to worse since the pretended reconciliation [Louville wrote to Beauvillier]. The Queen and Madame des Ursins restrain themselves no longer and the poor

[1] Trémoïlle, iii. 44; letter of 10 April, 1703.
[2] Hippeau, *Avènement des Bourbons au Trône d'Espagne* (Paris, 1875), p. 99.
[3] Saint-Simon, xi. 400.

cardinals are without any consideration or authority. Also the King is shut up even more than before and no one enters the palace. And what makes my heart bleed, the King is so despised that his name is not even mentioned in the orders they give. Something happened on Holy Thursday which should have made him die of shame if he had as much heart as his good servitors. As he was making the stations[1] on foot in the streets with the Queen, all the people cried *"Viva la Reyna!"* and nobody *"Viva el Rey!"* . . .

Now I am going to tell you something which will make you understand in what shameful dependence the King lives as regards the Queen. Yesterday as he left his bed to dress, Hersent, his valet, asked him what costume he would wear. The King replied with an embarrassed air that he did not know. Hersent said sharply: "But, Sire, whom then am I to ask?" He hesitated for some time in silence and then said, "Wait!" He went into the Queen's apartment, took her order and came back saying "*En golille.*" Three hours after the Duc de Medina-Sidonia came to ask if he would hunt. He had the same embarrassed air as with Hersent. Three times the Duke asked him without receiving an answer. Finally he went again to the Queen's apartment and then came back saying he would go. . . .

I heard this morning that he had had a fresh dispute with the Queen, and I think they even beat each other. He came to the Despacho with his eyes swelled as big as my fist. . . . I knew already that they had cruel quarrels. You may judge by this how unhappy he is and how discontented with his chains, unable, however, to break them.[2]

Notwithstanding her return to favour Torcy continued towards the Princess as severe as before; begged her to avoid in future "quarrels as disagreeable to the King as they are contrary to his interests," and adds that so far he "sees in her letters little disposition to do so and awaits a change with impatience." [3]

He might wait a long while for any change in her attitude towards the Cardinal, and her letters both to Torcy and Louis continue as before, haughty, reproachful and filled with complaints. She had been too brutally insulted to pardon him and her one idea, since she could not get him recalled, was to force him to resign. Towards the Abbé, however, she was visibly softening. He was paying her an assiduous court with a traitorous design which will be seen presently, and visited her every day, flattered her vanity and pretended to have been won over entirely to her side.

[1] The Stations of the Cross.
[2] Saint-Simon, xi. 516; letter of 7 April, 1703.
[3] Trémoïlle, iii. 47; letter of 22 April, 1703.

It is curious that a woman of her intelligence and experience should have fallen into the fresh trap set for her, and says much for the Abbé's powers of dissimulation. Not only did he gain her confidence so far as to be admitted to private audience for two or three hours each day, but he even persuaded her to pardon Louville whom Philippe had dismissed. This dismissal she now made him revoke at the Abbé's request and he retained his post of chief of the French household and was even employed on a secret mission to Versailles, where we may be sure he spared neither abuse nor calumny.

She had confided to him that the true reason of his dismissal was the Queen's jealousy, who had been told that, in order to counteract her influence, he had sent for two actresses, Mademoiselle Marchand, a French singer, and Madame Lévèque, a Milanese dancer, whom he entertained in his country-house with the view to seduce Philippe, by their charms, away from her. This Louville denied vehemently in a letter to Beauvillier, accused the Princess in retaliation of having expelled them from Spain because d'Aubigny was their lover, declared that the latter slept in her apartment at Buen Retiro, the summer palace, and that he and the Duc de Medina-Sidonia had seen him washing his teeth at her window, hinted that she had tried to make love to himself and ended these calumnies by saying that when one has light morals (*mœurs à l'escarpolette*) one should not attack one's neighbours.[1]

But though the Abbé had wormed his way into her confidence, the Cardinal became every day more aggressive, and two weeks after the pseudo-reconciliation the quarrel broke out with greater violence than before.

"Whatever I do, whatever indifference I show to his insults," she wrote to Torcy, "every day the Cardinal's rage against me increases, every moment I find myself burdened with some fresh calumny. No one goes to see him but either he turns me into ridicule with bitterness or says outrageous things about me, as though his fury had turned his brain." She relates that he had succeeded in setting all the people of importance against her by repeating or inventing things she had said against them. Thus he had told the Duc d'Albe, just appointed ambassador to Versailles and whose opinion, therefore, was of value to her, that she

[1] Saint-Simon, xi. 518; letter of 11 May, 1703.

wrote every day long letters to Torcy against him. The Marquis de Rivas he persuaded that she wanted to turn him out of his post as Secretary to the Despacho, with the result that he was scheming to get rid of her first, and that he had ordered the Comte de Palma to make out a list of her crimes to be submitted to Louis.[1]

She accuses him of having fomented dissension and rebellion everywhere and of having estranged the whole country from France by his arrogance and contempt. "He would set hell in motion to overturn the kingdom and ruin everybody in it without distinction," she wrote to the Maréchale de Noailles.[2]

"It seems as though he had no other object in this country than to persecute me, since he neglects all other matters to give himself up entirely to his extravagant fury," she complained to the Duc de Gramont.[3]

And at the same time the Cardinal was writing to Louis :

> I could never have magined that the greatest, most dangerous and irremediable of all my anxieties would be stirred up by a person whom my brother and I loaded with obligations, who came to Rome, widow of her first husband, whom her mother and family could not attract to France, because she would only appear there with distinguished rank, which she sought in the Courts of Spain and Vienna under the protection of the Cardinals Nidhardt, Porto-Carrero and the Empress-Dowager, whom we served, so to speak, like a kind of orphan separated from all her kin, and contributed so much, under Your Majesty's protection, to establish in the highest position in Rome. . . . Her worst crime is that to acquire the favour of the Spanish nation at the expense of ours, she has not only abandoned the French but conspired with the Spanish to expel them all. . . . It was she who dictated or caused to be dictated all those furious letters (of Philippe and the Queen) five or six weeks ago. She has proclaimed her absolute authority and that of the Queen, and in doing so has made the King fall into so great discredit that the evil is irreparable.[4]

Torcy, whose partiality for Louville is not to his credit, wrote to ask his opinion as to which of the belligerents was in fault, thus giving him the opportunity to recapitulate

---

[1] Trémoïlle, iii. 61 ; letters to Torcy of 27 June and 17 and 30 Aug. 1703.
[2] Geffroy, 157 ; letter of 28 July, 1703.
[3] Trémoïlle, iii. 61 ; letter of 28 July, 1703.
[4] Saint-Simon, xi. 502 ; letter of 10 Aug. 1703.

THE QUARRELS CONTINUE 125

all his calumnies and invent others, which he did *con amore* with his usual vehemence.

The Queen is no less dangerous than Madame des Ursins [he wrote in answer]. She is the most dangerous Princess in the world, the worst enemy of France and the French, attached only to her own House, little person of fourteen of immeasurable presumption and ambition, false, avaricious, malevolent and deceitful to excess, directed by Madame des Ursins, governed by Monsieur de Savoie, and all-powerful over the mind of a husband feeble, timid, irresolute, without will, with little sentiment, who has to be decided at every moment on every individual matter, not from lack of intelligence and knowledge but because the mainspring which decides men is not in him, and because God has given him a mind subordinate and, if I may say so, slavish, which will make him always dependent upon somebody. . . .

Consider, I pray you, a young Prince of nineteen, amorous of his wife, enchanted to see her again, who arrives with her in Madrid, where he is imprisoned from the day of his arrival in the grasp of a woman, clever, false, cunning and experienced, who entangles him on all sides and in every way. This Prince is no sooner arrived than all artifices are employed, including those of the Queen, to persuade him that the Cardinal d'Estrées is a man ambitious, haughty, intractable, who wishes to dominate him with harshness and severity, that he is in his second childhood, full of ill-humour, that he is hated by all the Spanish and especially the grandees. The Prince in this state never goes out and sees no one. The only servitor who spoke freely with him (Louville himself) has no more access to him, being himself in disgrace. The Cardinal and Abbé have no access to him, his doors being forbidden. He is always with the Queen, shut up with their enemies. . . .

In God's name, do all that depends on you, if you care for the two monarchies, to give the Prince the succour of which his feebleness has need. Before everything the Princess des Ursins must be dismissed. The King our Master receives no letters from the King his grandson, but instead those of the Princess and Orry, which the King copies without changing a single word.[1]

He goes on to accuse the Princess of the most ignoble acts, of selling appointments and titles, of appropriating the money allowed her for the Queen's wardrobe, of causing stones to be thrown at the windows of the Cardinal's palace, of having scandalous morals and being the mistress of d'Aubigny. "Choose one of three things, for a fourth is not possible," he ends: "Either have her carried off by

[1] Saint-Simon, xi. 526; letter of 16 Aug. 1703.

force or chase her away or make her leave of her own accord."¹

The Princess on her side regarded Louville with the utmost disdain and wasted little powder on him. "It should not be permitted to so insignificant a person to outrage a woman of my rank. The Duc de Beauvillier is deceived if he thinks him worthy of esteem. Only the debauched could give importance to such a man," is all the notice she deigns to take of him.

The Cardinal renewed his attacks with ever-increasing violence. He loathes her, loathes her *protégé* Orry, loathes Spain itself—"this country fertile in calumny and falsehood!" It would almost seem, as the Princess said, that in his fury at his defeat he had lost his mental balance.

For defeat it was, and there was no longer any doubt as to who was conqueror in this Homeric battle. The Princess, strong in the Queen's protection and the respect she inspired at Versailles, took no more pains to humour him and her royal puppets did not hide their aversion. The Queen, to quote Louville, "treated him in public like an old dog," and she and Philippe wrote letter after letter to Louis to "put an end to their torture" and recall him. "Our hatred is so extreme," she wrote, "that if we were asked whether we would remain on the throne of Spain with the Cardinal for ambassador, I assure you that I know not what we should decide."²

Such a state of ebullition at a time so critical for the country could not be allowed to continue and Louis had perforce to give way and decide his recall. But old and infirm though he was, and feeling himself unequal to the combat, it needed more than one letter to persuade him to abandon the field and then only on condition of leaving his nephew behind him to carry on the feud, and it was not till 10 October that he finally consented to leave Spain, so furious with the Queen that he omitted the courtesy of paying her an official farewell.

The Princess was charmed to be able to write that he had been mobbed and insulted by the people on his departure, that his palace had been bombarded with stones, all the windows broken, his servants wounded and his grooms

---

¹ Louville, ii. 100 ; letter to Torcy of 15 Aug. 1703.
² Baudrillart, i. 159 ; letter of 28 July, 1703.

massacred. It is true that Louville accused her of having herself organised the attack.

So ends the first part of this amazing quarrel for the government of Spain. The Cardinal, sorely wounded, retired from the field, but only to continue his attacks from a safer distance. The second part is the continuation by his nephew the Abbé, more robust and unscrupulous than himself, whom the Princess was imprudent enough to accept as ambassador in his place.

CHAPTER XVI

THE ANNOTATED LETTER (1703)

IN accepting the post of Camarera Mayor the Princess had, tacitly if not openly, pledged herself to work as Louis' agent in the administration of the affairs of a country which he considered as much his own as though he had conquered it by force of arms. At what precise epoch and for what reason did she resolve to break this contract?

On her arrival in Spain she had immediately seen how strong was the popular feeling against France and taken all possible measures to regain the favour of the Spanish, but it would seem that only on the arrival of the Cardinal, with his insistence on Louis' complete authority, had she realised the full danger of such despotism and decided the exclusion of the French from any share in the government.

It would be absurd to attribute this attitude to motives of personal vengeance. The Princess had higher aims in view. She wished to govern Spain and knew that, had Louis insisted on keeping d'Estrées or any other viceroy as his representative, not the grandees only but the whole country would have flocked to the standard of the Archduke Charles.

She had her own ideas of the qualifications she desired in the Ambassador of France—nothing overwhelming in the way of rank or prestige, honesty (towards herself at least), a good head and perfect obsequiousness to her authority. All these were ready to hand in the person of the financier Orry, but she dared not propose him, for his origin was obscure and his antecedents more than doubtful. His virtues and fitness for the post, however, she constantly vaunted to Torcy, and with a persistence which left no doubt as to her wish. "You have sent me a man whose intelligence, profound, solid and resolute, is what is required in this country—Monsieur Orry!" she wrote as early as the autumn of the preceding year, and nearly all her letters contain similar praise. But Versailles had remained deaf, for how could the Roi Soleil be represented by a man of the people who was not even born?

Since the embassy was out of the question, that of First Minister was actually proposed by her and taken so seriously into consideration that Torcy wrote to ask Louville his opinion, and as Orry was one of the few people for whom he had esteem he replied favourably enough.

The idea of Orry as First Minister of Spain is not what is most burlesque in the steps taken [he replied]. True, it is ridiculous, but after all it is the least bad, and he would be much better than Monsieur d'Aubigny, for he has more intelligence, capacity and a sort of probity than he. He is besides French both by birth and inclination . . . and would do nothing against the interests of France. He wants to protect the French and the others want to ruin them. He has besides ideas and talents and is an indefatigable worker.[1]

But not even Louville's rare praise could prevail over the caste sentiment of the epoch, and Orry remained, for the present at least, with no higher post than that of superintendent of the armies. The Princess, however, was not one to renounce her projects for the sake of a mere title, and he attained under her auspices a position of even greater authority than had he been nominated ambassador or first minister. For he formed, together with her and d'Aubigny, one of the famous Triumvirate—"three heads under one bonnet"—which settled all the affairs of the country and prepared the official documents which it was Philippe's rôle to sign at the Queen's bidding.

Jean Orry, Seigneur de Vignori, was at this time sixty-one years old. He was named counsellor-secretary to Louis XIV. in 1701 and had been sent soon after to Spain to examine into the financial state of the country and see if his genius could save it from total bankruptcy. This mission, with no special denomination, he had fulfilled so successfully that he had remained there as superintendent of the army and later Minister of Finance.

He was of the dregs of the people [writes Saint-Simon contemptuously], very intelligent, who had tried all sorts of trades, first in order to live and afterwards to put by money. First *rat-de-cave*,[2] then agent of the Duchess of Portsmouth,[3] who found him out cheating and dismissed him. Returning to his first trade he made himself known to important financiers

[1] Saint-Simon, xi. 534 ; letter of 28 Aug. 1703.
[2] Vintners' clerks were called so by the people.
[3] Louise de la Querouaille, mistress of Charles II. of England, who returned to France in 1685.

who gave him various commissions which he executed to their liking and recommended him to Chamillart.¹

He paid his court to Madame des Ursins. His intelligence pleased her. She found him obsequious and of a humour to work under her authority . . . and they worked together as mistress and servant.²

Her secretary d'Aubigny, third (or, according to Louville, first) of the Triumvirate, had increased in importance since we made his acquaintance in Rome. Almost immediately after her arrival in Spain she had had him appointed equerry to the Queen. Philippe took lessons in fortifications under his direction, and by these means he had access to both. He was no longer le Sieur d'Aubigny but El Señor Don Luis, a person of so much consideration that Louville asserted that he governed the country and everyone in it, including the Princess. The Abbé d'Estrées relates a scene which took place at one of their councils during a discussion about a bodyguard of musketeers to which the Spanish were opposed. Orry was for it, d'Aubigny against. The Princess had the casting vote and she sided with Orry. Whereupon d'Aubigny jumped up from the table and left the room, exclaiming violently: "Ah, Madame! when one acts so one should not meddle with business!" ³

It is not the last time we shall have to relate similar insolences. His antagonism to Orry, due to jealousy, was the cause of his ultimate betrayal and abandonment of the Princess in her ruin.

It is time to say a few words about this d'Aubigny who played so large a part in her life, who had at this date been in her service for at least eighteen years, and was trusted by her implicitly.

"He was a tall, handsome fellow," writes Saint-Simon ("Handsome as paint," he says elsewhere), "very well-made and supple in mind and body. By degrees he became the Princess's equerry, private secretary, intendant and general confidant. He disposed of everything in her house including herself, and had over her the influence of those who supply the deficiency of a husband." ⁴

He was of humble birth, son of a notary, but here in Spain

¹ Minister of War, by whose recommendation he was sent to Spain.
² Saint-Simon, x. 389.
³ Trémoïlle, iii. 85 ; letter to Torcy of 3 Oct. 1703.
⁴ Saint-Simon, xi. 243.

she had made a noble of him. He had his apartment in the Royal palace next her own, the apartment formerly occupied by the wife of Louis XIV. herself, but neither large nor grand enough for this *parvenu*, who had it enlarged. He was popular with the Spaniards and a favourite with the King and Queen. "Great and small, all bow the knee to him," and even Madame de Maintenon spoke well of him, from all which it may be gathered that he was intelligent enough to make himself agreeable.

All-powerful as was this Triumvirate, Spain could not do without a representative of France. The Duc d'Harcourt was willing to return, but in spite of their friendship and his recent championship he found no favour in the eyes of the Princess. "She fears him as much as the Cardinal," Louville wrote, "knowing that he wants to govern as despotically as herself. She knows also that he would not fail to bring his wife here, who, being sweet-tempered and insinuating, might after a time suit the haughty humour of the Queen as well as herself." [1]

Another of her friends, the Maréchal de Tessé, had also been proposed, but him also she considered too authoritative and important. The fact is, she would willingly have had the post remain vacant and the French expelled in a body, Ambassador and all, so much did she dread a repetition of the Cardinal's despotism. For this reason she preferred to bear those evils she had in the shape of the Abbé, whom she hoped without his uncle would acknowledge her authority. He was far from ideal certainly. "He comes out of a school where he has not learnt to speak the truth where I am concerned, nor allow others to live in peace," she wrote to Torcy.[2] But she did finally accept his nomination, thus falling into the trap set for her by himself, Louville and the Cardinal, not unknown, one is inclined to think, to Torcy himself, for there is little doubt that the Abbé's change of attitude towards her was due to an intrigue that he should replace his uncle in the embassy to play the spy on his behalf.

Nevertheless she had enough suspicion to make him sign a paper promising to cease persecuting her, to maintain harmony, and not erect himself as censor against her—in

[1] Saint-Simon, xi. 518 ; letter to the Duc de Beauvillier of 11 May, 1703.
[2] Trémoïlle, iii. 84 ; letter of 25 Sept. 1703.

his own words, to act more as a courtier than an ambassador. But in the same letter in which he announces this covenant he broke it by fresh calumnies. "The King," he wrote, "shuts himself up with his Secretary of the Despacho, hears what he has to say, takes his papers, and without saying a single word, carries them into a little cabinet where, shutting himself up with Madame des Ursins and the Sieur Orry, he decides all matters public and private."[1]

The harmony, if it ever existed, did not last long, for less than a week after quarrels again broke out between her and the Abbé. "Nothing can equal the way the Abbé is treated since he is ambassador," Louville wrote on 8 October. "A scullion would not wish to be ambassador at such a price. Everything great and small is hidden from him. . . . The Queen and Princess call him only 'Monsieur l'Ambassadeur de France,' with inexpressible ridicule and contempt, and I think they want to dishonour him in order that Orry may remain sole envoy of France without an ambassador."

He asserts that the Princess forces him and the Abbé to speak well of her in their letters to Versailles, that she stands over them while they write, that she and the Queen detest all the French with the exception of Orry and d'Aubigny, and that the Princess's confessor confided to one of his servants when he was drunk that she was married to d'Aubigny and that the two were putting by every penny in order to go and live brilliantly in Rome.

As for the Queen [he adds], she is more false if possible than the Princess, and has taught the King to be so also. He who never lied in his life, lies at present from morning till night out of fear of their threats. . . .

D'Aubigny pushes his insolence to the extreme limit, ruins the Princess by his evil counsels and insolence, decides everything with absolute authority and the Princess dares not even breathe. All the streets are filled with pasquinades and rhymes against him and her.

But the worst calumny he had yet invented was to insinuate that d'Aubigny was the lover of the Queen herself. "He is shut up night and day with her, even while the King is at the hunt, and lodges in the apartment of the Infantas, which they have caused to communicate with hers." After which incredible attack he accuses them both—d'Aubigny and the Queen—of being in league with the Duke of Savoy

[1] Trémoïlle, iii. 85 ; letter of 3 Oct. 1703.

in his recent alliance with Austria. " The Queen," he wrote, " loves her father madly and esteems him still more. She says that what they call his treason is only that he wants to procure in Italy a little advantage to his House, which she loves more than her life, and that if he has turned against France it is because he wants to save Spain from being engulfed." And this collection of infamies he winds up by calling d'Aubigny "a brute-beast, with no knowledge of any sort, though it is he who directs everything." [1]

The Abbé on his side had begun his intrigues by feigning humility, asked the Princess her advice upon everything, begged her to supervise all he wrote to Versailles, and when he had flattered her to the top of her bent, insidiously persuaded her to affix her signature, together with that of Orry, to his official dispatches. It is incredible that the Princess should have fallen into a trap so obvious, but either from vanity or inadvertence she did as he desired.

It was the moment when things were at their worst. The Duke of Savoy had thrown himself openly on the side of Austria, the Archduke with all his armies was marching on Spain. There was hardly a soldier in the country and Louis had been implored to send troops to the rescue.

It was this important dispatch that the Abbé with Machiavellian cunning had persuaded the Princess and Orry to countersign, and Louis' anger at an innovation so arrogant may be imagined. By this one false step she had justified the Cardinal's accusations, and it was accepted as an open declaration of her dictatorship.

However, being under the protection of the King and Queen, she was not directly attacked, but the Abbé received an angry reproof from Torcy intended for herself. " Though I exhorted you to harmony with Madame des Ursins," he wrote, " I do not advise you to continue to allow your letters to be signed by any other than yourself. I am writing this also to Orry, and Chamillart is scolding him severely for having dared to sign your dispatch." [2]

Even before this letter reached Madrid the Princess had realised her folly and begun to suspect a trap. The Abbé was all honey, but she divined venom in his heart and determined at all costs to know the truth. The costs were

[1] Saint-Simon, xi. 537 ; letters of 8 and 10 Oct. 1703.
[2] Trémoïlle, iii. 97 ; letter of 19 Nov. 1703.

heavier than she anticipated, and this fresh imprudence was the cause of her first disgrace.

In concert with Philippe and the Queen, the messenger bearing his dispatches to Versailles was waylaid by order of the King and his bags seized and taken to the Princess. She broke the seals without any effort at concealment and discovered that, far from being the grateful *protégé* he feigned, he was continuing his attacks and accusations with more virulence than before.

This violation of the diplomatic seals was bad enough, but she did worse: she had the imprudence to make a copy of one of these letters and with her own annotations and denials send it to her brother the Marquis de Noirmoutier, begging him to show it to Torcy as a proof of the Abbé's perfidy.

The opening of the diplomatic bag she laid to Philippe's charge, whom she directed to write to his grandfather that, having heard that the Abbé was in the habit of abusing the Princess while professing to be her friend, he was determined to find out the truth and ordered his dispatches to be brought to himself, that he had opened them and found them to be full of calumnies against her, and that he had even written that his only sentiments towards her were implacable hatred and contempt.[1]

Her brother in all loyalty did as he was bid and sent the annotated copy to Torcy, but the latter, always her enemy and probably in league with the d'Estrées, took the violated bag to Louis with a formal complaint that in opening the ambassadorial dispatches she was guilty of *lèse majesté*, and excited him to such a pitch of anger that her disgrace was then and there decided.

Such is the truth as revealed by the documents concerning the famous *lettre apostillée*, or annotated letter, exaggerated by Saint-Simon into a very improbable tale which has been copied by all the biographers and has become the best-known incident in the life of the Princess.

Here is her own relation of the affair to the Maréchale de Noailles, who, as a relative by marriage of the d'Estrées, had taken their side during the quarrels:

It is certain that the Abbé during several months has written, and caused to be written against me, infamies which I ought never to have pardoned, and no less true that from the

[1] Millot, ii. 273; letter of 3 Dec. 1703.

moment he seemed to wish to be my friend, in spite of all prudence and solely to please you, I begged Their Catholic Majesties to demand him for ambassador, and that the same day on which I rendered him this service he wrote to the Duc de Beauvillier and Torcy that I had sent two couriers to France behind the back of the ministers to prevent his embassy; that I was a traitor and worked with a cabal of evil-intentioned people to exclude the Cardinal from the Despacho; that it was absolutely necessary that someone should control me, and that to put a stop to " the frivolity which I have in common with all women," he considered that the King should write to Their Catholic Majesties to take violent measures against me at the next quarrel he should hear of. . . . I begged my brother to make known to Torcy the wrong he did me and, that he might understand the matter, sent him a copy of the intercepted letter, with notes in the margin, merely to destroy the lies advanced against me.[1]

To the Duc d'Harcourt she wrote:

All that I receive from the Marquis de Torcy shows so great a partiality for my enemies that I fear to lose the King's esteem through his bad offices. There are no calumnies which the Cardinal d'Estrées has not openly recounted or caused to be written against me, nor any means he has omitted to make me enemies in this country. Having persuaded Their Catholic Majesties to ask the King that the Abbé might remain here as ambassador, I did not expect that as long as his uncle was here his conduct towards me would change, but I hoped that after he had left his good faith would return and he would abandon his plan of ruining me, won by the service I had rendered him.

I was deceived. The more easy I have been in forgetting his outrages the less he has responded to my hopes, continuing always to set people against me and trying by his lies to make a quarrel between me and the Marquis de Torcy. Most certainly there does not exist in the world a life more painful or disagreeable than mine! I kill myself physically and mentally to make the King and Queen loved by their subjects. They are both young and I have to be always on the watch as to what they do and ought to say. As long as I could flatter myself that Torcy was impartial I have kept some tranquillity in the midst of my sufferings. Now that it is impossible to doubt that he gives entire credence to the Abbé, I die of fear that the loss of the King's esteem will be my reward for my incredible application to his service, the many fatigues I suffer, the debts I make every day, and the disorder in which I left my affairs in Rome. I am weary to the last degree of being everybody's servant and still more disgusted by all I receive from France. . . . I have nothing but vexations, which kill me and make me regret a thousand times a day not to have left when the King gave me

[1] Geffroy, 164; letter of 25 Dec. 1703.

permission. . . . From Monsieur de Torcy I get nothing but harshness which shows me only too well that the impudence of certain rascals weighs more than my loyalty, and the least insinuation from the Abbé, who at bottom is nothing but a feather-brain, full of arrogance, and a bad man, draws upon me threats from the King which make me die of grief. . . .

It appears that my crime is that the King of Spain opened a private letter of the Abbé and that I had some share in the matter. This I deny, and as a proof that I speak the truth, I confess that I am very capable of taking such a liberty without compromising the King of Spain. . . .

For a year by nearly every post I receive from everybody in France defamatory libels invented against me by Messieurs d'Estrées and Monsieur de Louville. The rank of ambassador does not give the Abbé the right to dishonour with impunity a woman like me. . . . Monsieur de Louville is assuredly the greatest rascal living. I know for a fact that it is he who by his lies has caused all these quarrels which still continue here. . . . It is astonishing that two virtuous men like the Duc de Beauvillier and the Marquis de Torcy should be taken in by so ignoble a *débauché*. They have always imagined that his zeal for the service of the King of Spain drew on him the hatred of the Spanish. Nothing is farther from the truth. Self-interest only, and the desire to dominate His Majesty in order to make his own fortune, were his only aims, and he would have ruined the monarchy had he not been recalled. His mouth is always filled with the worst of filth, a thousand infamies against me which he vomited continually to all the French here, and Madame de Maintenon fared no better because he imagined it was she who protected me. . . .

All honest people praise my moderation and patience in supporting what every day they invented to make me despised. If I had had to do with bears and tigers I should have tamed them by my patience. Unfortunately I know not how to exorcise demons, and one can call no otherwise those who sacrifice everything to their passions, to whom lies cost nothing, and who think it impossible to rise without crushing others. . . .[1]

I cannot close this chapter without inserting Saint-Simon's version of the *lettre apostillée* which he recounts no less than three times at the greatest length, of which three narratives the following is a *résumé* much condensed :

One day the Princess, wishing to speak in private with Louville and the Duc de Medina-Cœli and to see them without being interrupted, led them to a retired chamber of her apartment. D'Aubigny was there writing, with his back turned to the door, and at the sound of her voice and without looking up,

[1] Hippeau, *Lettres de la Princesse des Ursins* (Paris, 1862), pp. 13, etc.; letters of 17 Nov. 1703 and 1 Jan. 1704.

began to swear and apostrophise her with epithets of houses of ill-fame and a violence more than marital, asking why the devil she took it into her head to come and worry him and never leave him an hour's peace, calling her by the strangest, most familiar names, so rapidly and impetuously that all was over before she could show him she was not alone. All four remained stupefied. The Duke and Louville looked elsewhere to give the Princess time to recover and also to recover themselves. No excuse was possible and she attempted none. She grew red, began to laugh, and said very loudly: "Messieurs, you see at least that d'Aubigny does not like being interrupted." And immediately in an authoritative voice bade him leave the room. He fled, and she then continued the discussion for which they had come as though nothing had happened.

The story ran like wild-fire through the palace, thanks to Louville, who rushed off to tell the Abbé, and the latter, charmed with the scandal, wrote to Torcy at once stating that d'Aubigny, her servant of mean birth, took part in the secret councils from which he himself was excluded, that he pillaged with both hands, was the only male who slept in the palace, and that his authority was so great that everyone concluded the Princess had married him.

The Princess, he continues, had the habit of opening all the Abbé's letters, and this among others was brought to her. The graver accusations of treason and disloyalty to France she passed over, but that of marriage to her own servant touched her pride and so enraged her that she scrawled (in her big firm handwriting so characteristic of the woman): "Pour mariés—NON!" She then took the letter so annotated to the Queen and, "with strange clamours," showed it to her and the King and many of the courtiers, after which, without attempting to reseal it, she sent it to Louis enclosed in another from herself full of furious complaints against the Abbé.

Now when the letter thus violated was opened at the State Council before the King and his ministers the amazement was tremendous. Their first impulse was to laugh, because by denying only the marriage with d'Aubigny she had tacitly admitted the truth of the other accusations, but laughter soon gave way to anger at such incredible audacity. Louis was furious and even Madame de Maintenon was too scandalised to interfere in favour of her *protégée*, whose recall was immediately decided.[1]

[1] Saint-Simon, xiii. 66 and v. 502, etc.

Saint-Simon alone is responsible for this sensational version of the matter, and his variations are sufficiently disproved by the facts that the Princess employed d'Aubigny in missions to Versailles later, which she would hardly have done had he been the hero of a scandal which brought about her disgrace, that he was received with kindness by Madame de Maintenon, who presented him to Louis and mentioned him often in her letters to the Princess with praise of his intelligence and good manners.

CHAPTER XVII

FIRST DISGRACE OF THE PRINCESS (1704)

THERE were many other causes besides the violation of ambassadorial dispatches for the Princess's disgrace. She had been imprudent enough to humiliate a man of great importance and greater pride, liked and trusted by Louis. Such an enemy was more formidable absent than present, at Versailles than at Madrid. On his arrival on 4 December Louis had received him "with open arms and kisses on both cheeks," and with the gift of the rich Abbey of Saint-Germain-des-Prés in compensation for his recall.[1] He had his *entrées* to his private cabinet at all hours, and it may be imagined that on the subject of Spain and its misgovernment, of Philippe and his *mollesse honteuse*, of the Queen's fatal influence and the Princess's many crimes he had much to say and Louis to hear. His accusations *a vivâ voce* were enough without other reasons to have decided her disgrace.

Other reasons, however, there were which appeared unfortunately to justify the Cardinal's attacks. In sending troops to Spain at the demand of his grandson, Louis had commissioned one of his generals, the Comte de Puységur, to make inquiries into the state of the country, and his report was crushing for the Princess and her favourite Orry. According to him the money sent by Louis for the campaign had disappeared and both were suspected of appropriating it. No preparations had been made, no provisions or ammunition sent to the camp. As to the King and Queen: "Nothing is more pitiable," he wrote, "than the state of the Spanish Court. There is no dignity, no government." "The King drives out in a ridiculous old coach with liveries partly of Louis' own Court, partly Spanish of the date of the late King. The King and Queen are two prisoners of importance of whom Madame des Ursins is the gaoler."[2]

Such evidence could not be ignored and Louis' decision was taken. Prudence was necessary, however, for the Queen in her devotion was capable of going to any length to pro-

[1] Dangeau, ix. 368.
[2] Baudrillart, i. 172 ; letters of 22 Jan. and 10 Feb. 1704.

tect her Camarera Mayor, even of exciting Philippe to disobey his orders and throw himself on the side of his father-in-law the Duke of Savoy. It was expedient to separate the two before he hurled his thunderbolt. He wrote to Philippe, therefore, ordering him to proceed at once to the camp to take his place at the head of his troops. The campaign had not yet begun, but Philippe unsuspectingly obeyed, and no sooner was he well out of the way than the Princess received orders to leave Spain.

By the same messenger the Abbé also received a letter containing this welcome news, but his triumph was short-lived, for it announced also his own recall.

"The complaints against the Princess des Ursins," Louis wrote to him, "have reached such a point that at last it has become necessary to take final steps. I see the evil of her remaining in Spain and the time has come to dismiss her. I should not have deferred it so long had I only consulted the good of the State, but it was necessary to wait till the King of Spain had left Madrid. I had reason to foresee that he would be too sensible to the Queen's tears, and that they might have prevented him from obeying my counsels promptly enough, and it was, therefore, necessary to wait till he was separated from her so that reason only should influence his mind." The letter continues with the threat that if Philippe resists, he, Louis, "weary of maintaining a monarchy where he sees nothing but confusion and contradiction," might make peace with Austria to the detriment of Spain.

"They have not ceased to injure you with the King my grandson," he concluded, "and their bad offices have made so great an impression that he has already begged me several times to recall you. You will now be still more odious in his eyes, because he will think you the chief cause of the order I give to the Princess des Ursins and will have no more confidence in you. You can be assured that your fortune will not suffer, and that in sending another ambassador, as I am resolved to do soon, I shall remember the services you have rendered and all they merit." [1]

To Philippe at the camp he had already written the week before :

I have given you many marks of my friendship, but none stronger than to have mastered the pain it gives me to ask you

[1] Millot, ii. 284 ; letter of 19 March, 1704.

FIRST DISGRACE

to dismiss immediately the Princess des Ursins. Do not hesitate to make this decision. It means everything for you. Contribute at least to calm the interior of your kingdom while I am employing all my force and care to sustain in your interest so painful a war. . . . I am persuaded that you will believe me in a case where your own ruin would be the result of resistance to my counsel. I beg you to communicate my letter to the Queen. I send you what I have written to her. Your Majesty must immediately appoint another Camarera Mayor. . . . I am thinking of sending you another ambassador. . . .[1]

The Queen he treated with more deference. He would not have exacted the Princess's dismissal, he wrote, had it not been absolutely necessary. She might come to France or return to Italy as she thought proper. He hoped that his grand-daughter would obey him and give him fresh reason to esteem and love her even more tenderly than heretofore.[2]

The Duke of Berwick, now Marshal of France, had been sent to Spain as generalissimo of the combined French and Spanish forces, and had received orders to try to get to the bottom of the "animosities." Being an old friend and a man of honour, his verdict, as it appears in his *Mémoires*, is altogether in her favour. Here is his relation, slightly condensed :

The Abbé, having a strong desire to become ambassador, paid his court with all his might to Madame des Ursins, blaming his uncle's behaviour to her and working so well that by dint of promises that he would never do anything but what pleased her and would depend entirely on her will, she engaged His Catholic Majesty to write to France to demand that he might succeed the Cardinal. This was accorded and apparently the new Ambassador lived in perfect understanding with her. But the Princess, suspecting his good faith, engaged the King of Spain to have his letters to Torcy seized at the post. There she found the enlightenment she sought, for the Abbé abused her conduct and lamented the dissimulation to which he was forced. Madame des Ursins, after having taken a copy of this letter, sent it herself by one of the King's messengers complaining bitterly of the Abbé's perfidy and calumnies. But what she did was also very displeasing at the Court of France, which considered her action as an attack on the rights of men, the ambassadorial dispatches being always held sacred.

On my arrival each tried to have me on their side, the Queen did not disdain to solicit me. . . . I persuaded the King to leave Madrid the 4th of March for the frontier. It is true that

[1] Millot, ii. 288 ; letter of 10 March, 1704.
[2] Ibid., ii. 289 ; letter of 10 March, 1704.

nothing was yet ready for the opening of the campaign, but as the Abbé had received orders to hasten his departure I thought it my duty to second him. The King [Louis], who was very irritated against Madame des Ursins, desired to separate his grandson from the Queen in order to obtain more easily the Princess's dismissal, and to this end the Abbé received a letter for the King of Spain, but as the King had an amazing aversion for him it was feared that he would not be able alone to execute his commission. My orders were to support him if necessary and employ the strongest means to engage His Catholic Majesty to consent to the King's will. . . . In spite of his love for the Queen and friendship for the Princess he did not hesitate an instant to obey, and thus the Abbé had nothing to do but give his letter, nor I than to console the King who was penetrated with the grief it would cause the Queen. I wrote to Madame des Ursins to tell her of my sympathy in her misfortune and at the same time counsel her as a friend to obey with all the promptness and submission possible, for in spite of the King's consent we were not sure of what the Queen might do—Princess of immense vivacity, sensibility and pride.

Madame des Ursins did not hesitate, and to show her obedience left Madrid the day after she received the order. The Queen was furious with rage and grief, and breathed fire and flame against her enemies. . . . Their Catholic Majesties, irritated at what the Abbé had done, wrote so strongly to the King against him that they obtained the promise of his recall, and in fact the Duc de Gramont was nominated, but as he could not arrive before June, the Abbé remained with the army until then.[1]

Here is his letter of condolence to the Princess, written on 8 April:

It is with the greatest grief that I have learnt that the King orders you to quit Spain. This news will be very painful to you, all the more that you will be separated from the Queen, towards whom you have rightly so much attachment and all imaginable friendship, and though I know that your good sense and respect for the King's orders will not allow you to hesitate an instant in obeying them, I am too sincerely your friend not to implore you to conform to them immediately, since the least delay will ruin you entirely in the King's mind. . . .[2]

"This thunderbolt," writes Saint-Simon, "rendered the Queen desperate without overwhelming her on whom it fell. . . . The Princess understood that for the moment nothing was to be done, but she did not despair of the future. She paid her farewell visits in the town, regretting

---

[1] *Mémoires du Duc de Berwick*, i. 227, etc.   [2] Geffroy, 171.

FIRST DISGRACE

nothing, she said, but the Queen, keeping silence as to the treatment she had received and supporting it with a courage vigorous and circumspect, without haughtiness but without the least humility."[1]

She chose to fill her place, her friend the Duchesse de Béjar, a lady of mild and humble mind, devoted to herself and not likely to intrigue against her during her absence nor dispute the post at her return. On 11 April, having instructed the Queen in all she had to do, and put order in all the affairs of her post, she left Madrid without any complaint or manifestation of grief, as though she were leaving of her own accord for a well-earned rest. The Queen accompanied her two leagues on the road, so that her departure seemed rather a triumph than a disgrace.

Once out of the capital, however, and the letter of the King's order obeyed, she did not hurry herself further, and remained for some time at Alcala, only a short distance from Madrid—about as far as Fontainebleau from Paris, writes Saint-Simon. Here she was in constant communication with the Queen, and even, according to him, returned several times to see her in secret. At Alcala all her household, her coaches, gentlemen and pages—all the paraphernalia of her rank, assembled, and she dispatched d'Aubigny to the Maréchale de Noailles to beg Madame de Maintenon's intercession with Louis that she might be allowed to come to Versailles to justify herself.

"Finally, after five weeks of obstinate sojourn in Alcala," continues Saint-Simon, "when all her plans were well prepared and assured, with a presence of mind never enough to be admired at a moment so filled with sorrow, rage, and grief, and the prostration due to such a terrible fall, she advanced towards Bayonne, travelling as little each day and resting as often as she dared."[2]

On 19 April, Dangeau notes in his *Journal*: "The Princess des Ursins has left Madrid for Alcala where she will remain eight days to assemble her equipages. The King of Spain has sent her one thousand five hundred pistoles for the journey and allows her eight thousand crowns pension. . . . The Queen has given her her portrait enriched with magnificent diamonds."[3]

Before leaving Spain she wrote a letter to the Maréchale

---
[1] Saint-Simon, xii. 76.   [2] Ibid., xii. 97.
[3] Dangeau, ix. 49.

de Noailles, intended naturally to be shown at Versailles, full of resentment at the treatment she had received.

"At last lies have triumphed over truth, and though I can affirm that no one will ever serve the King with more zeal and probity than I, I see myself treated like a criminal who has betrayed the State, while my accusers triumph. It is easy for men, as cunning as the Cardinal d'Estrées and as vile as his nephew, to intrigue successfully against a woman who has no other support than a little intelligence and much loyalty of heart. But I am surprised that those I thought my best friends, whom I have always honoured and who would be sorry to pass for unjust, should work my ruin." And she ends: "Permit me these reproaches. I have still courtesy enough to be sorry to have made them, but seeing myself sacrificed to a band of rascals, I have not moderation enough to suppress them."[1]

At Bayonne, in answer to her request to be allowed to come to Versailles she received a peremptory refusal with the order to go straight to Italy, but a journey to a distance where communication with the Queen would be impossible was not at all in her programme, and she replied coldly that the great heat—it was already June—rendered it impossible.

Wherever she went spies from Versailles were on her track. At Pau, where she remained for some time, she fell into the hands—not unkind ones, it must be owned—of a certain lawyer and novelist, Jean de Préhac by name, in the secret service of the War Minister Chamillart, who had been deputed to extract from her as much as possible. As she had known him in her youth it was easy enough for him to worm his way into her confidence and hear her own version of the d'Estrées's quarrels, and it is evident that her irresistible charm and eloquence had won him to her side.

On 19 July he wrote to Chamillart:

> The continual care I have for all that regards the King's service obliges me to tell you what I have learnt from the Princess des Ursins, who has been staying here and left yesterday for Toulouse, where she has permission to wait till the great heat is over. I knew her very well in Rome and Paris, but best twenty-five years ago when I was secretary to the Queen of Spain [the Queen-Regent, wife of Charles II.] and taught her Spanish. She wanted to be her *dame d'honneur*. Fifteen years later she wanted to be that of Madame la

---

[1] Geffroy, 169; letter of 23 May, 1704.

FIRST DISGRACE

Duchesse de Chartres, but a delay of three weeks which she demanded to write about it to her husband spoiled everything. These different matters having given me close relations with this Princess who was very upset over Spanish affairs, she was very pleased to find me here and open her heart.

Here is his report of her confidences, much curtailed:

The Cardinal d'Estrées having been nominated ambassador in Spain, the Cardinal Porto-Carrero was in despair and asked leave to retire, and neither the prayers of the King nor the Queen could turn him from his resolution.

From the first the Cardinal, who intended to govern despotically, regarded the Princess as an obstacle, and in spite of their old friendship resolved to get rid of her. Monsieur de Louville, who on his side wanted to govern the King and who in Italy had insinuated himself into his confidence by all sorts of complacencies, did not find the same facilities in Spain and, attributing the change to her, united with the Cardinal to ruin her. The Abbé arrived whom the King received gladly, and allowed him, so said the Abbé, to enter the Queen's apartment whenever he chose. To this the Princess objected and the Abbé wrote against her furiously to Versailles. Shortly after he told her that the Amirante of Castile had plotted to have the King assassinated at the hunt and that she and the Queen must prevent him from going. The Queen therefore begged him with so much insistence to abstain for some time from hunting that finally he promised. A fortnight after he received a letter from his grandfather reproaching him for his idleness and voluptuous life and for remaining always shut up with women, and the Princess at the same time received an angry letter from Torcy. She complained to the Abbé and they quarrelled. The King on his side was in despair but she calmed him and even found means to reconcile him to the Abbé. But the King warned her that he had discovered from several things that the Abbé was a rascal and assured her that he was deceiving her. He ordered his letters to be brought to him and, having opened them, found one to Torcy full of cruelties against her. The Princess, who has always relied on Torcy, wrote to him about it, but he replied that the Abbé was her best friend and always praised her in his letters. Knowing the truth this was a thunderbolt to her, for she judged that Torcy, who had received the letter, had acted in concert with her enemies. Shortly after Philippe, of his own accord and without telling anyone, insisted on the recall of the Abbé, whom she described as the blackest rascal in existence.

She continued that Philippe had been forced by his grandfather to leave Madrid a month earlier than was necessary in order to get rid of her more easily, and that had she not been prudent enough to show her submission and leave quietly, the people would have risen and prevented her departure by force.

He goes on to say that she receives every day very tender letters from the Queen, that the King had sent her ten thousand pistoles for her journey, and having thus pleaded her cause in a dozen pages, he ends by saying that it is the Princess's own narration, for the truth of which he is not responsible.[1]

The Princess left Pau on 18 July, and thus retreating by slow degrees arrived at Toulouse, convenient resting-place between the two Courts, where she obtained permission to remain temporarily. It was destined to be the last stage of her retreat. When she again takes to the road it is towards Versailles and triumph.

From Toulouse she wrote several times to the Maréchale de Noailles, letters as usual intended for the eyes of Madame de Maintenon, full of melancholy, feigned or genuine. The Maréchale, in spite of her disapproval of her quarrels, had proved herself a good friend, had exerted herself that her pension should be paid, and sent her consolatory messages from Madame de Maintenon. Nevertheless there is a lingering reproach in the Princess's letters, in her allusions to Rome and the tranquillity she hopes to enjoy there. "I have found so much falseness everywhere that I confess I am very tired of the world and have a great longing to live in Rome, because there one sees only those one wishes and the climate is soft and agreeable to a lazy woman who likes to be well lodged, to hear the best music that exists, and seeks also to pass the rest of her life in some tranquillity."

Her health, she wrote, had been seriously affected by her disgrace. Her eyes were in a lamentable state, and she was devoured by fever, the result of worry, enervation and uncertainty as to her fate. For all these ills she was taking her favourite remedy of asses' milk which, according to her, " sweetened the blood so often embittered." [2] We must leave her there for the moment and return to the Court of Madrid and the forsaken Queen.

[1] Saint-Simon, xii. 544, etc.; letter of 19 July, 1704.
[2] Geffroy, 179; letter of 4 Nov. 1704.

CHAPTER XVIII

THE DUC DE GRAMONT (1704)

THE Queen of Spain's submission to the despotic recall of her favourite did not last long and soon gave place to an access of grief and rage which found vent in a hurricane of vehement letters to Louis, Madame de Maintenon, her sister the Duchess of Burgundy—everyone in fact whom she thought likely to help her to regain her.

The Abbé had been replaced in Madrid by the Duc de Gramont, who was an old acquaintance of the Princess, and whom she had even proposed for the embassy before the nomination of the d'Estrées.

But Gramont, composed of the same clay as Louville and the Abbé, was not one to remain friends with those in disgrace. He had received instructions from Louis to do all in his power to combat her influence with the Queen, and these orders he executed with more zeal than tact, abusing her continually and with so much venom that he made a mortal enemy of the Queen immediately after his arrival.

Here is his own description of one of the angry scenes between them:

> The Queen was in great grief, complaining that all her habits were changed by the absence of the Princess and her authority in the eyes of the people very much lowered
>
> "What has the poor woman done," she cried passionately, bursting into violent tears, "to be treated so disgracefully! All the accusations against her to the King my grandfather are false. And is it not sad that he, wisest and most prudent of men, should credit the venomous tales of people full of gangrene rather than his own grandson who knows the rectitude of Madame des Ursins' conduct?"[1]

Not only did he profit by his position to try to set the Queen against the Princess, but had the baseness to invent calumnies and write them to the Princess herself with the intention to cause a breach between the two.[2]

[1] Millot, ii. 301; letter to Torcy of 28 May, 1704.
[2] Trémoïlle, iii. 10; letters from the Princess to Gramont of 3 Aug., etc., 1704.

Antoine de Gramont was great-nephew to Philibert of the famous *Mémoires*, the favourite of Charles II., and grandson of Henri IV. and la belle Corisande. "He had in his favour," writes Saint-Simon, "nothing but his name, his dignities and an advantageous figure. He had the handsomest face and the most manly that it is possible to see."[1] But Spannheim, envoy of the Elector of Brandenbourg, less influenced by externals, sums him up thus: "Loves women. Loves wine. Brutal. Much wit. Vain. Ambitious. Loves pleasure. Hot-tempered."

"He treated the most important matters with an impertinent frivolity, was too French in the quickness of his judgments, jumping at conclusions before examination," is the verdict of the Abbé Millot[2]: and that of the Maréchal de Tessé: "He imagined that he had been sent to Spain to govern it according to his own will and that everything must give way before him."[3]

He had been a favourite at Versailles and Louis had even at one time given him permission to write his history, but as perseverance was not his strong point he had soon given it up. "His pen was not trimmed for so vast a subject," writes Saint-Simon. Shortly before his appointment he had had the folly to make a secret marriage with the woman who had been his mistress for years, a *femme-de-chambre*, and after his nomination to the embassy of Spain, anxious to take her with him, he had avowed it to Louis, who was naturally indignant and would not hear of her accompanying him to Madrid as Ambassadress. Such was his position on his arrival at the Spanish Court.

He had immediately excited the Queen's anger not only by abuse of her favourite, but also because, in obedience to Louis' orders it is true, he had secretly tried to persuade Philippe to forbid her to meddle in the government. This Philippe had naturally repeated to her and thenceforth it was war to the death between them.

On his arrival, however, he had been favourably impressed by her and had sent the following description of her to Madame de Maintenon:

The Queen of Spain is almost as tall as the Duchess of Burgundy and has the same delicate figure and graceful manners. Her air is altogether noble and majestic. Her eyes are neither

---

[1] Saint-Simon, xii. 83. [2] Millot, ii. 299.
[3] Tessé, *Mémoires*, ii. 136.

very large nor very bright, her complexion beautiful but pale, the mouth small, the teeth white but irregular. One could not call her a beauty but I assure you that her face must please everyone of good taste.

So much for her body. I will speak now of her mind. I have been astonished at her intelligence and the elegance and justice of her answers to all the articles of a long speech I had the honour to make her in the name of the King, and it surprised me that a person not yet sixteen was able to place words gracious and solid with ease and readiness. She is a very extraordinary person.[1]

A very extraordinary person indeed, as we learn on all sides, capable not only of governing her feeble husband, but of attacking and vanquishing Louis himself; loyal, too, and frank in an epoch when such virtues were rare.

"So ardently does she desire the Princess's return," wrote the Maréchal de Tessé, "that she is capable of upsetting the Kingdom and going all lengths if the King does not consent to allow it."[2]

Upset the kingdom she actually did during the eight months of her favourite's absence. "The Queen," writes Saint-Simon, "desired the recall of the Duc de Gramont, guilty of the crime, unpardonable in her eyes, of being opposed to the return of Madame des Ursins. She had persuaded the King her husband to oppose all his grandfather's orders, and to neglect ostentatiously his counsels. Her aim by this system was to weary him and make him understand that nothing but Madame des Ursins, well-treated and sent back all-powerful, could replace things as before and make him obeyed in Spain as formerly."[3]

She forced Philippe to abandon the campaign at the risk of Louis' withdrawing his troops. She did her best that everything in the State should go wrong to prove his mistake in dismissing the one person capable of making them go right. She systematically opposed all Gramont's suggestions and rendered his position so untenable that, seeing he must either give way or resign his embassy (which did not suit him as, on account of his marriage, he was in semi-disgrace at Versailles), he changed his tactics, wrote to Torcy that the Princess's absence had done more harm than good, that she was more dangerous absent than present and her influence over the Queen more fatal; finally, that it would

[1] Baudrillart, i. 178; letter of 14 June, 1704.
[2] Tessé, *Mémoires*, ii. 57.   [3] Saint-Simon, xii. 391.

be better to allow her to return. "Her counsels are indispensable," he wrote, " to bring the Queen to the state of mind desired by France. She will have her back at the cost of the overthrow of a hundred monarchies."

But the d'Estrées were at Louis' elbow to thwart such prudence or good intentions as he may have had, and his severity towards the Princess at this time was undoubtedly due to them. The Cardinal's hatred of her had become a veritable obsession, the mania of persecution, and as he had his entries at all hours it is not surprising to hear that Louis grew sick of her very name.

Everything that went wrong was laid at her door, even the capture of Gibraltar, which took place at this date (24 July, 1704), a fortress hitherto considered impregnable, but which was so carelessly guarded, Gramont wrote, that "it was taken for the mere trouble of climbing up." "Here you may see," he added, " the result of the fine administration of Canalez (War Minister in Spain) and the Sieur Orry, who both deserve to have their heads cut off."[1]

Louis' ill-humour was not diminished by the bad news which arrived shortly after of the defeat of his own troops at Blenheim in Bavaria, one of the most important battles of the war (13 August).[2]

Orry was immediately recalled without explanation in spite of the prayers of the King and Queen, who liked him and appreciated his services. But Spain since the Princess's departure was governed not by its own King but by the King of France, and he remained inflexible. He refused to see him on his arrival and even threatened to have him hanged. His anger towards the Princess redoubled, and this time not all the Queen's letters could soften him.

> Hitherto [so he vented his ill-humour on his grandson] you have given your confidence to people either incapable or self-interested. I ask you to dismiss Canalez, I recall Orry, and meet with nothing but resistance and opposition. You see the result of their work by the fate of your armies and fortresses. It seems, however, that your interest in these individuals occupies you entirely, and at the time when you should have none but great aims you debase them to the cabals of the Princess des Ursins, of whom they never cease to weary me. Show that there is a King and a Council in Spain, that you

[1] Millot, ii. 315 ; letter to Louis XIV. of 10 Aug. 1704.
[2] Called by the French the Battle of Hochstadt.

THE DUC DE GRAMONT

command it and that the individuals who have abused your confidence are not the masters of your monarchy.[1]

But though Philippe, separated from his wife, was too timid or too indolent to resent his grandfather's attacks, the Queen at Madrid was neither. She continued to urge and insist on the return of her favourite until by dint of persistence she finally got her own way.

Not for some time, however. "The Queen of Spain," Dangeau notes in his *Diary* on 3 September, "continues to insist strongly in favour of the Princess des Ursins. She asks that she be sent back at once to Spain or at least be allowed to come to Versailles in order to justify her conduct. But the King, who is displeased, refuses one and the other and desires that she return to Italy." [2]

She attacked Madame de Maintenon and implored her intercession, but received nothing but a sermon and a scolding. "Your friendship for the Princess should have limits and you should allow it neither to disturb your peace nor your good understanding with the King," was her answer.[3] And so incensed was Louis at her persistence that he relieved his mind by writing her a letter even more severe.

Whether he thought better of it or that Torcy warned him of its imprudence, this letter was never sent, but it is worth quoting as expressive of his irritation against her at this time:

The results which I foresee [he wrote] are too serious for me to forbear explaining myself to Your Majesty with my natural sincerity and with the freedom of a grandfather speaking to his grand-daughter. I gave you the Princess des Ursins because of the esteem I had for her, which made me think she would be capable of forming the mind of a young Princess and inspiring her with all those sentiments worthy of so great a personage as yourself. However, forgetting our common interests, she has given herself up entirely to an animosity of which I was ignorant, and has thought only of thwarting those who have been charged with my affairs. If she had had a faithful attachment to you she would have sacrificed her resentments, well or ill founded, against the Cardinal d'Estrées instead of drawing you into them. . . . I had then either to recall my Ambassador, abandon you to her and leave her to govern your kingdom alone, or recall her. It is this last which I have thought necessary in the hope that you would defer to my sentiments and

[1] Millot, ii. 317; letter of 20 Aug. 1704.   [2] Dangeau, x. 114.
[3] Geffroy, *Madame de Maintenon*, ii. 33; letter of 5 Oct. 1704.

that, the Princess away, you would lose in part the impressions she has given you. It is not true that she has ever been suspected of any intelligence with our common enemy. By these insinuations she wishes to make herself meritorious in your eyes. She is accused of having wished to govern Spain and of not having inspired in you those sentiments which it seems you should have for me, and to have had friendships and enmities where she should have had no other interests than yours. She is accused of continuing in her absence with even more bitterness and less discretion what she did while she was near you.

I judge the counsels she has given you by their results. You have often opposed my suggestions, you have no confidence in my ambassadors, you love and hate as the Princess inspires you, you wish at fifteen to govern a large and unsettled monarchy without advice. . . .[1]

The letter is docketed in Torcy's handwriting: "This letter was not sent."

That history repeats itself is a truism, but it is not often that within two years precisely the same things happen alike in all details. After the above explosion, as before, Louis thought fit to eat his words, and having hurled a thunderbolt at each of the three rebels in turn, deigned to give the Princess permission to come to his feet and plead her cause.

Again, what was the reason of this sudden change?

Madame de Maintenon claimed the merit, as we learn from her own words to the Queen, who had written to thank her for the great service she had rendered her [2]; but if finally she had acted as intermediary with the King, it would seem to have been that she was so harassed by the attacks of the Queen and Duchess of Burgundy that she was forced to yield. In any case the Princess's return was decided in Louis' mind as early as October.

In the archives of the Comtes de Gramont-d'Aster are letters and instructions addressed to Gramont during his embassy at this date. They are docketed in his own handwriting as being from Louis XIV. under different names, thus: "From the King under the name of Baron de la Roquerie." "From the King under the name of 'L'Épine blanche,'" etc. None, however, are in Louis' own hand and are probably from Torcy. In these documents the Princess is designated as *l'absente*, or *la confidente*, Philippe as *la*

[1] Baudrillart, i. 191; letter of 20 Sept. 1704.
[2] Trémoïlle, iii. 112.

THE DUC DE GRAMONT 153

bonté, the Queen as *l'esprit,* while poor Orry figures as *le sujet à caution.*

Here are a few extracts concerning the Princess.

The first is dated 14 July, thus when she was at Pau on her way to Toulouse, and throws considerable light on the Queen's attitude after her departure.

Paris, 14 July, 1704. Wise men see with grief the obstinacy of *l'esprit* [the Queen]. It is useless to think it will pass so quickly. It seems best to ignore it and to execute your orders exactly, more gently but without weakness. The feebleness of *la bonté* [Philippe] is the cause of much grief. *Le sujet à caution* [Orry] has orders to leave at once and I know from a good source that he will not return. . . . Le Baron de la Roquerie.

Paris, 15 August, 1704. The mind of *l'absente* [the Princess] still dominates and her inspirations will last a long time. You must weaken them gradually and without letting it appear that you think about it. You must apply yourself and use all your efforts. Le Baron.

Paris, 31 August, 1704. You must continue to humour *l'esprit.* Above all do not quarrel with her and by your tact avoid everything which might make quarrels. . . . He [Louis] is persuaded that you say what you think about *la bonté,* but he finds it difficult to believe. [Gramont had written that Philippe really detested the Princess and was opposed to her return, of which more presently.] I think that you might well act towards *la confidente* as you propose. One must take time and not throw oneself at her head at the wrong moment. L'Épine blanche.

Paris, 20 October, 1704. Things are going more smoothly with *la confidente,* and by what I gather I think that steps will soon be taken to do as you propose [steps for her return which Gramont had finally advocated].

Paris, 22 October, 1704. I am sorry that your good relations with *l'esprit* have lasted so short a time. You must try to repair what the letter of *la confidente* has spoiled. It is true that it was wished to hold her responsible for the conduct of *l'esprit* and that she was told that she embittered her, but she exaggerated when she wrote that it was wished to force *l'esprit* to abandon her. The permission given to the Maréchal de Tessé to see *la confidente* shows clearly that things are going better for her, of that you can assure *l'esprit.* Try to soften as much as possible the too great vivacity of this person. I hope we may win her by means of *la confidente* and our own care. L'Épine.

Paris, 16 November, 1704. I am told that a letter has been sent you for *l'esprit* which ought to give her great pleasure since it tells her of the journey of *la confidente* to Paris and that the order has been given and sent to Toulouse.¹

Thus for the second time the violence and persistence of the young Queen have triumphed and her favourite is to return, this time to no secondary post but to become veritable dictatress of Spain.

¹ Geffroy, 469, etc.

CHAPTER XIX

TRIUMPH OF THE PRINCESS (1704-5)

WE left the Princess on 4 November at Toulouse drinking asses' milk, in constant communication with the Queen, but apparently ignorant of the sudden turn things had taken in her favour—so little aware indeed that she was preparing to leave for Marseilles—or so she said—when she received a visit, as welcome as it was unexpected, which altered her plans.

Her old friend the Maréchal de Tessé had, at the persistent prayer of the Queen, been appointed by Louis to succeed the Duke of Berwick as generalissimo of the armies in Spain and had demanded and obtained permission to stop at Toulouse on his way to announce to the Princess that she might proceed to Versailles in order to justify herself to the King.

More than Madame de Maintenon, it would seem to have been the Duchess of Burgundy whose mediation had brought about the change in her favour. Seven years before the Maréchal had been sent to the Court of Turin to arrange her marriage and, appointed her chief equerry, had conducted her back to France. He grew to adore his little charge—she was only eleven, and since then had considered himself her knight, her special property, and would have killed himself to give her pleasure. The Queen of Spain had implored her sister to intercede in favour of the Princess, which she had done so successfully that she had won over Madame de Maintenon, "ma tante," she called her, who loved her for her cajoleries and could refuse her nothing, and, aided by Tessé, for whom Louis had a great esteem, had succeeded in persuading him to give her at least a hearing. Louis had allowed Tessé to make a détour on his way to Spain to bear the welcome news.

He related his interview to Louis with more sympathy for the Princess than truth.

" She was not at all heated," he wrote, "nor did she give

vent to reproaches against those she considers responsible for her disgrace. She did not even mention them, and either from affectation, vanity, innocence, contempt, dissimulation or virtue, contented herself with saying, 'If I am guilty let me be punished; if innocent, I should be worth very little if my *amour propre* did not exact full justification.' "[1]

To Torcy also he wrote in the same strain : "I was never once able to get her to speak a word about Messieurs d'Estrées. She neglected mentioning them, and considering herself gravely offended will neither complain of nor accuse them. . . . Is it dissimulation, virtue, vanity, magnanimity, weakness ? Decide for yourself, for I neither can nor will. I consider that she deserves your consolation."[2]

But by the same post he wrote to Chamillart, his intimate friend not likely to betray him: "If some day you should be curious to know thoroughly the history of the intercepted letter, what was added to it and all that the demon of intrigue and ambition could invent, I could write a volume as big as the *Mille et une Nuits*."[3]

His arrival in Madrid was the greatest consolation to the abandoned Queen smarting under Gramont's abuse of her favourite, and his relation of their interview is told with sympathy and pathos.

"I cannot nor ought to hide from you," he wrote to Louis, "that the Queen spoke to me almost with tears in her eyes of the Princess des Ursins and that she said word for word: 'You see, Monsieur, she was my *dame d'honneur*, my *gouvernante* and my friend. I feel my head bewildered since she is no longer with me.' "[4]

As for Gramont he was furious when he learnt that Tessé had been sent to Toulouse, and thought it high time to make his peace with one about to be restored to favour. He wrote at once to congratulate the Princess and insisted that he and he alone was responsible for it. "Monsieur de Tessé wished to be the announcer of the happy disposition in your favour in which I have put the King, but if he has claimed the merit he robs me of what is due to my work alone."[5]

To which the Princess, aware of his treachery, replied

[1] Saint-Simon, xii. 561, appendix xi. ; letter of 20 Oct. 1704.
[2] Ibid., xii. 561, appendix xi. ; letter of 11 Dec. 1704.
[3] Ibid., xii. 561, appendix xi. ; letter of 20 Oct. 1704.
[4] Ibid., xii. 561, appendix xi. ; letter of 12 Nov. 1704.
[5] Geffroy, 465 ; letter of 2 Nov. 1704.

curtly: "Once for all, be persuaded that I know what to think concerning you."¹

On 26 October Dangeau wrote in his *Journal*: "A rumour is abroad that we shall soon see Madame la Princesse des Ursins, and even that she will make a fairly long stay in Paris, but it is not thought that she will return to Spain though the Queen continues to insist strongly that she be allowed to do so."²

And on 17 November : " The King has sent a courier to the Princess des Ursins at Toulouse to tell her to come to Versailles, where she is expected to arrive before Christmas."³

This permission she received with the same dignity she had shown in her disgrace. She did not hurry herself and wrote with apparent indifference to the Maréchale de Noailles on 8 December that owing to the bad roads and short days she should be nearly a month on the journey.⁴

"I leave for Paris to-morrow," she wrote to Gramont, "where I hope to arrive the end of the month. I have chosen the Limoges road as the shortest and where there are fewest large rivers to cross. I have reason to believe that I shall be well received, since the Marquis de Torcy has so assured me."⁵

The Maréchale de Noailles drove out to meet her several miles outside Paris. She was the first, but by no means the only one, to welcome with enthusiasm her on whom all were prepared to turn the cold shoulder only a few weeks before. Everyone knew that Louis intended to reinstate her in her post, and everyone, especially those who had been most eager to condemn her, tried to retrieve their error by hurrying to welcome her. " They prepared themselves for a sort of sunrise which was about to change and renew everything in Nature," wrote Saint-Simon, himself among the first to pay his court to the rising sun.⁶

All Versailles, male and female, flocked to greet her, the courtiers with doffed hats sweeping the ground, the ladies with shrill screams of welcome. The Spanish Ambassador, the Duc d'Albe, and his wife, drove in official pomp to

---

¹ Trémoïlle, iii. 113 ; letter of 7 Dec. 1704.
² Dangeau, x. 165.   ³ Ibid., x. 180.
⁴ Geffroy, 181 ; letter of 8 Dec. 1704.
⁵ Trémoïlle, iii. 113 ; letter of 7 Dec. 1704.
⁶ Saint-Simon, xii. 399.

receive her on the road, lavished on her all the honours at their command, and insisted that she should remain at the embassy and partake of a sumptuous banquet prepared in her honour.

Out of deference to their post she accepted this hospitality, but for one night only. The following day she took refuge with her own people in the house of Mademoiselle de Cosnac, now Comtesse d'Egmont, whom it will be remembered she had chaperoned as a young girl. Here in her hotel of the Rue de l'Université, worn out with fatigue, and perhaps not a little disgusted at the shallowness of humanity, she shut her doors to everybody and for the first few days did not go out.

On the day of her return—4 January, 1705—Gramont's secret correspondent wrote to him in Madrid:

L'esprit [the Queen] goes too fast and presses the return of *la confidente* before she has been seen. *L'ami* [Louis] will think what is best to do. Meanwhile dissimulate and flatter *l'esprit* so that she may not be embittered. You must continue to be patient and arrange things in our favour with *la bonté* [Philippe]. He must not cause a quarrel between us and *l'esprit* by telling her of the good counsels you may give him.[1]

From which it would seem that the intrigues had not ceased and that Philippe was no stranger to them.

The King and Court were at Marly when she arrived, but all the courtiers flew from there to the Rue de l'Université to pay their respects, the Duke of Burgundy among the first. The crowd before the door was so great that half the coaches could not be admitted. It was the fashion to go and see the Princess des Ursins.

The excitement among the courtiers at the arrival of the Princess was inconceivable [writes Saint-Simon]. All eyes opened wide and everyone realised its importance. People who had never known her boasted of being her most intimate friends. Those who had been the strongest partisans of the two d'Estrées feigned to be transported with joy, and her real friends were enchanted at her return.[2]

The first official mark of the Royal favour was the order given to Torcy in his capacity of Foreign Minister to pay her a visit of ceremony. Torcy, her enemy, friend of Louville and the Abbé, who had so ardently counselled her disgrace, was furious, but had perforce to obey, and the

[1] Geffroy, 474. [2] Saint-Simon, xii. 399.

TRIUMPH OF THE PRINCESS 159

Princess's satisfaction may be imagined. She received him with haughty coldness, and so far from seeking to justify herself turned the tables and took the attitude of one who accuses and condemns.

It seems that she herself was surprised at the completeness of her triumph and confided to Saint-Simon her contempt of those who, without transition or shame, had passed from bitterest enmity to cringing flattery.

On 14 January Gramont's secret correspondent wrote to him:

> The letter I write to-day will be short but strange. I have heard of the sudden and surprising decision which has been taken to send back *la confidente* at the prayer of *la bonté* and *l'esprit*. This has not been decided without mature deliberation. . . . It is desired that you shall give the news to *l'esprit*, to put you in her favour until the arrival of *la confidente*, who seems in no hurry to depart.[1]

A week later the Princess herself wrote to tell him of her "gracious reception," hinting, she also, her hesitation to return. "Although everybody tells me that it is a triumph for me, I assure you that I should infinitely prefer to go and live quietly in Rome. . . . If I must return to Madrid I shall not leave before the spring. I am very fatigued with the journey I have just made. The season alarms me and I have some family affairs I wish to finish if possible. I have represented all these reasons to the King, who wishes that I shall leave in a fortnight."[2]

But the supreme triumph was still in reserve. Her reinstatement in her post had been decided out of deference to the Queen, but her reception by Louis was a homage to her own personality and astonished herself as much as the Court. It is indeed difficult to account for the exaggerated cordiality which he lavished upon her to whom he had behaved with so cruel an injustice only a few weeks before. Was it policy? Hardly, for the Queen was fully satisfied that he received her at all. Remembering the attraction she had had for him fifteen years before and in view of other events to be related presently, the most probable explanation seems to be that Louis XIV., aged sixty-seven, had again fallen a victim to the irresistible charms of the Princess des Ursins, four years his junior, an attraction which seems to have been either physical or a kind of

[1] Geffroy, 475.   [2] Trémoïlle, iii. 116; letter of 21 Jan. 1705.

personal magnetism, since when she was away it lost all efficacy.

Here is Saint-Simon's account of her reception at Versailles and her subsequent visit to Marly. Saint-Simon may be relied on in his narrative since he was an eye-witness, constantly in her society, and at this time among the most enthusiastic of her toadies.

The King returned to Versailles on Saturday [10 January] and learnt that the Princess des Ursins had arrived and had spent all the afternoon at Saint-Cyr alone with Madame de Maintenon. She was lodging in the town with d'Alègre.[1] The day following she dined alone in her own house and went to see the King, with whom she spent two hours and a half in his cabinet alone.

She entered the Royal presence with a very assured air and not at all like one about to try and justify herself. She came out radiant, and from that moment her triumph began.[2]

What took place during that interview of two hours and a half to make her, usually so self-contained, radiate her joy in public? Did she employ her irresistible eyes as well as her eloquent tongue? And did Louis, "remembering that he had been *galant*," again succumb to the charms of this enchantress, "impossible to resist when she wished to be seductive"? It would certainly seem so.

The Court [continues Saint-Simon] returned to Marly where many balls were given, and it goes without saying that Madame des Ursins was of the party. Her air of triumph was incomparable at the constant attention the King showed her, honouring her as though she were Queen of some foreign state. She never appeared but he seemed at once preoccupied in trying to entertain her, showing her things and seeking her approbation with a never-failing air of gallantry, even of flattery. The frequent private interviews she had with him in the apartment of Madame de Maintenon which lasted for hours, those which she had very often in the morning with Madame de Maintenon alone, made her the idol of the Court. The Princesses surrounded her whenever she appeared and went to see her in her room. Nothing was more astonishing than the servile attention shown her by the highest, most important and most honoured personages. Her glance was counted an honour and even the most distinguished ladies received a word from her with rapture.[3]

It would be interesting to know if the Cardinal and

[1] The old Marquis d'Alègre, whose daughter was one of her great friends.
[2] Saint-Simon, v. 504. [3] Ibid., xii. 434.

TRIUMPH OF THE PRINCESS

Abbé d'Estrées witnessed these genuflexions of the supple courtiers.

As an admirable example of her discretion, Saint-Simon relates that instead of receiving the mob of courtiers during her toilette and hairdressing according to the fashion of the day, she never allowed herself to be seen except fully dressed and with her hair arranged.

Saint-Simon, prince of snobs, was naturally one of the first among the servile courtiers.

I was flattered [he writes] at the kind behaviour of the Dictatress of the Court. It excited remark which attracted me immediate consideration. Besides that many of the most distinguished people found me alone with her in the mornings, she often called me to her in the *salon*, where at times I said a word in her ear with a free and easy air which all envied and few dared to imitate. She never saw Madame de Saint-Simon without going up to her, praising her and drawing her into the conversation of those surrounding her, often leading her to a mirror and rearranging her hair or part of her dress as though she were her daughter. Often, too, she drew her aside and talked to her in a low voice for a long time. . . . People asked with surprise and many with envy whence arose so great a friendship which nobody had suspected, and what most excited their curiosity was that Madame des Ursins, leaving the room of Madame de Maintenon with the King and her, seldom failed to go up to Madame de Saint-Simon if she found her in the ante-chamber, take her into a corner and talk to her in a low voice.

Among the many balls where Madame des Ursins was always treated with the same distinction, I wish to speak of one to which she had with some difficulty obtained an invitation for the Duc and Duchesse d'Albe. I say with difficulty because no ambassador nor stranger had ever been admitted to Marly, excepting once Vernon after the marriage of the Duchess of Burgundy, and to do honour to Monsieur de Savoie of whom he was the envoy.

The balls were held in a large square *salon*, at the upper end of which was the King's *fauteuil*. . . . The Duke and Duchess arrived at four o'clock and went to the apartment of the Princess des Ursins, who had received permission to take them to Madame de Maintenon before the King went there. This was a great favour to Madame des Ursins, for Madame de Maintenon never received any foreigners nor ambassadors, and the Duc and Duchesse d'Albe had not yet seen her face.

Nothing could equal the air of triumph worn by Madame des Ursins at the servile eagerness of all those of importance around her, at the care of the King to distinguish and do her honour, as to a miniature Queen of England, and the majestic way she received it all, with a mixture of grace and courtesy seldom seen now and which recalled the earliest days of the Queen-Mother. The King was admirable in giving full value to everything which in itself had none. She placed herself near the high chamberlain and looked at everyone through her eye-glasses. Every moment the King turned to speak to her. Madame de Maintenon, who in her honour came sometimes for a quarter of an hour to the balls before supper, took the high chamberlain's place that she might be next her and close to the King, and the conversation between the three never ceased. The Duchess of Burgundy joined in it often and she also talked to no one but Madame des Ursins and evidently sought to please her. . . . Her prodigious favour was the more accentuated by a little spaniel which she carried under her arm as if she were in her own house. . . . No one could recover from their amazement at a familiarity which even the Duchess of Burgundy would not have dared to risk, so much do trifles strike one when they are without precedent. And to see the King many times caress the little dog! In short, never has such a success been seen. One could not grow accustomed to it, and those who witnessed it and know the King and his Court are still, after all these years, amazed at it. Since then Madame des Ursins is hardly ever seen at Marly without this little spaniel under her arm, the highest symbol of her favour and distinction.[1]

And as the favour of Louis meant that of the entire Royal family, one and all paid an extravagant court to the new favourite. Madame de Maintenon ostentatiously took the lead, but privately was terrified at the new caprice of her King. However, she kept her fears to herself, and much of her time was spent with the Princess in the little dark room allotted to her (for Marly was small and over-crowded with guests), so often alluded to by both in their letters. Here was organised that partnership in which they signed a treaty, half serious, half jesting, the Princess pledging herself to keep Madame de Maintenon informed of all that went on at the Court of Madrid, and Madame de Maintenon on behalf of the King promising never again to listen to scandals against her. " I have still in my casket the treaty of articles you drew up in my room at Marly," she wrote two years later.[2]

It was at this date that Madame de Maintenon began to assume an interest so keen and an attitude so dictatorial in Spanish affairs that all Europe commented upon it. How-

[1] Saint-Simon, xii. 436, etc., and 512.
[2] Bossange, i. 180 ; letter of 20 Oct. 1707.

ever, as the enormous mass of her correspondence shows, her interests were in the Church rather than the State, and all her energies engaged in governing her three hundred and fifty embryo saints at Saint-Cyr. It is known that after the Princess's return to Spain all the Spanish dispatches were taken by Torcy to her apartment and opened and discussed there in her presence by himself and Louis, and her authority over Spain has been exaggerated on that account. Louis' objection to any interference with his government is well known, and it is most likely that, disgusted at the results of his grandson's accession, at his feebleness and the Queen's obstinacy, and weary of the quarrels and intrigues of the Spanish Court, he had placed her as a kind of buffer between himself and them to save his dignity, and that she did no more than transmit his orders. She herself denies having either any influence or even any knowledge of affairs of the State. How often in her correspondence with the Princess the following phrases occur: "I know nothing of affairs. It is not wished that I should interfere with them and I myself have no desire to do so." "This is what I have heard and which I repeat like a parrot without understanding." "It is not suffered here that women meddle with business," etc., all of which are generally cited as so many examples of her hypocrisy. That Louis told her everything is certain, and that he consulted her upon most things is probably true also, for he esteemed her reasonable mind and disinterestedness, but no one, not even Madame de Maintenon except in personal matters, had any influence over him, and that she was allowed to govern Spain at a moment so critical for France is contrary to all probability.

Dangeau catalogues thus the series of the Princess's triumphs at Marly and Versailles:

Versailles, 11 January, 1705. The King gave an audience of two hours and a half in his cabinet to the Princess des Ursins, and said in the evening to Madame de Maintenon that he still had many things to say. The Princess went from there to the Duchess of Burgundy, who took her into her small cabinet and they were shut up for a long time.

Versailles, 12 January. The Princess des Ursins was shut up a long time with Madame de Maintenon.

Versailles, 13 January. The Princess des Ursins was again shut up with the King and Madame de Maintenon. It seems that His Majesty is pleased with her and that she will probably be sent back to Spain.

Versailles, 15 January. The Duchess of Burgundy sent for the Princess des Ursins to Marly and shut herself up in a cabinet with her.

5 February. The Colonel Bozzo Boino, sent by the King and Queen of Spain, arrived to thank the King for the good reception he has given the Princess des Ursins and for his decision to send her back to Spain. The Duc d'Albe has orders to pay the Princess a visit in grand ambassadorial state to rejoice with her at the hope of seeing her soon again at Madrid. She will not, however, leave till April. She wishes to remain for some time in Paris to re-establish her health and put some order in her affairs.

Marly, 19 February. Ball at Marly. Madame de Maintenon came and caused to be placed near her the Princess des Ursins whom the King has brought on this visit.

Marly, 23 February. The Duc and Duchesse d'Albe arrived and descended at the apartment of the Princess des Ursins, who has received permission from Madame de Maintenon to take them to her room. The Princess and Duchess supped with the King at his table.

Marly, 18 April. After dinner the King was shut for a long time with Madame de Maintenon, the Princess des Ursins and Monsieur Amelot, whom the King sent for from Paris. He will leave in a week for his embassy in Spain.

Marly, 29 April. The Princess des Ursins has left Marly, but will stay a fortnight longer in Paris and will come to Versailles to take leave of the King before going to Spain.

Thus for over three months she was in constant and close contact with the King and Court and in the full blaze of his favour, which not long after took a more substantial form in benefits to herself and her family.

On 15 June Dangeau continues:

Versailles, 15 June. In the evening in Madame de Maintenon's apartment the King was shut up for a long time with the Princess des Ursins, who took leave of him on her return to Spain. The King gives her many considerable favours.

Versailles, 16 June. The King increases the pension of the Princess des Ursins by ten thousand francs. She already receives ten thousand. He gives her twelve thousand crowns for the journey. He creates her brother Monsieur de Noirmoutier duke.[1]

[1] Dangeau, x. 229, etc,

CHAPTER XX

VISIONS OF A CROWN (1705)

THUS did the Princess triumph in spite of the d'Estrées. Thus were her enemies crushed beneath the wheels of her chariot, and not only was she reinstated with all honour in her post, with money and titles showered on herself and her family, but she refused to return unless her own conditions were complied with, these conditions being the recall of the Duc de Gramont and the appointment of the Ambassador of her own choice, Amelot, and the reinstatement of Orry in his post. With all these exactions Louis complied, but still she hesitated, still she remained in Paris. "*La confidente* seems in no hurry to depart," Gramont's secret correspondent had written to him in January, and in June she was still there.

With the Queen clamouring for her return, Louis himself urging it, and Madame de Maintenon insisting, it might have been expected that she would have flown back on the wings of duty if not of love, but she showed no inclination to move. Amelot had already arrived in Madrid, Orry followed him in a week, but still she lingered.

Excuse followed excuse. First, "The season is ill-suited." And when the winter was over, "My health languishes." When summer arrived, "I must put order in my affairs"; and it was not till supreme pressure was put on her, Versailles pushing, Madrid pulling, and her brother and wise friends advising and arguing, not till the middle of June, five months after Louis had consented to her return, that she finally tore herself away.

I have already declared to the Princess [Louis wrote to his grandson in January] that it is necessary she return to Spain, that both you and the Queen desire it so earnestly that out of friendship for you I could not oppose what it seems would give you so much pleasure and which I thought would have such useful results. She appeared to me surprised and even vexed, said that her return to Spain would suit nobody, that her health was bad, that she lacked the strength and would die in Spain.

Nevertheless she promised me to go, but not immediately as the season was ill-suited.¹

On 28 May she herself wrote from Paris to her old friend the Maréchal de Villeroy: " I am hardly in a fit state to write and I know not when I can leave, for my fever has not left me. I had again yesterday an access of quartan fever preceded by several very violent attacks of colic in the stomach. . . ."

A fortnight later Madame de Maintenon wrote to the Comte d'Ayen, now Duc de Noailles, who had married her niece: " There is something about Madame des Ursins which I cannot understand. She cannot be persuaded to go back." ²

What was the reason of this caprice?

Saint-Simon, echoing the rumours of the Court, thus explains it: " Madame des Ursins found herself in her own country so far above all she could have anticipated, that she hesitated to return to Spain. The eagerness of the Queen touched her no more and the frivolous insinuations which began to be made she eluded. The age and ill-health of Madame de Maintenon tempted her. She would have preferred to dominate here than in Spain." ³ Which being interpreted means that Louis' favour and flattery had turned her head to the point of renewing her dream of thirteen years before of supplanting Madame de Maintenon in his affections.

Why not? she might reason. She was in no way her inferior; on the contrary, she was of higher rank, was seven years younger, gayer, more intelligent, and had marvellously preserved an agreeable physique and ardent temperament. It was the epoch of Ninon de Lenclos, seductive at eighty. Madame de Maintenon, with impaired digestion, rheumatic, toothless, deaf, " dried up with sadness," as she describes herself at this date, was not an amusing companion for the man of pleasure Louis still remained. Her talents had always been of the educational order. She was essentially (to her credit be it said in that age of egoism and frivolity) unworldly, conscientious and altruistic, and, as she herself realised, more in her element at Saint-Cyr than in his brilliant courts of Versailles and Marly. Louis was a

¹ Baudrillart, i. 204 ; letter of 16 Jan. 1705.
² Geffroy, 184 ; letter of 12 June, 1705.
³ Saint-Simon, xiii. 17.

curious mixture of piety and worldliness. By nature he was egoistic, sensual and cruel, but these innate characteristics were tempered, sometimes even, especially in his old age, overbalanced by superstition and his absolute faith in the theological doctrines of his confessors, their promises of heaven and menaces of hell. This fear of God (fear in the most literal meaning of the word) made him as he grew older look upon his cruelties to his cast-off mistresses as so many bribes to the Deity, and the chief influence Madame de Maintenon had over him was that, sincere believer and thoroughly good woman as she was, she represented to him the path to heaven, not unstrewn with flowers since she had besides a physical attraction for him. The Princess des Ursins was the exact opposite of Madame de Maintenon. Her practical good sense despised the sterile emotions of mysticism. Though a Catholic by birth and education, she was unconsciously a complete pagan in her indifference to everything apart from physical life on this planet, as is easy to gather from her letters. Above all, where Madame de Maintenon, probably owing to her early suffering, was devout to a point which, seeming incredible in that age, has gained her the stigma of hypocrite, the Princess was a worldling after Louis' own heart. He loved gaiety and wit, and it was these which had kept him so long at the side of Madame de Montespan in spite of her hysterics and jealousies. From all accounts the Princess was equally brilliant and amusing, and with her irresistible tongue and eyes may well have seduced him to dream of fresh infidelities.

" Madame de Maintenon," Saint-Simon continues, " was not without anxiety to see the King so pleased with Madame des Ursins, so delighted with their long and frequent *tête-à-têtes* and so careful to distinguish her in public with the air of one who remembers that he has been *galant*. These delays appeared to her superfluous and she saw no good reason for them." [1]

That the rumours of the Court had reached the ears of Madame de Maintenon herself, the following words written to the Princess a year later prove : " It is said that your design is to take my place near the King either in getting me into trouble at Court, or in poisoning me, or awaiting my death, which cannot be far off." [2] The jesting tone of

[1] Saint-Simon, xiii. 60.   [2] Bossange, i. 28 ; letter of Aug. 1706.

this allusion does not conceal its bitterness to those acquainted with the style of her letters.

And who knows but if such were her aspirations they might not have been realised had the age and infirmities of Madame de Maintenon fulfilled their promise? It was impossible to foresee that this invalid of seventy, who describes herself as " a phantom dragged about from bed to bed," had still fourteen years of life before her, that she would outlive her King and most of her contemporaries and remain queen of Saint-Cyr and her three hundred and fifty *demoiselles* well on into the Regency.

In any case it is certain that if Louis had not actually fallen a victim to the mature charms of the Princess, Madame de Maintenon suspected that he had, and did her best to get rid of so dangerous a rival, and fortunately the Princess had level-headed friends to warn her and prevent her from adding to her many imprudences the crowning folly of remaining longer in France. These wise counsellors were her relative Daniel de Cosnac, Archbishop of Aix, and her brother the Duc de Noirmoutier.

" She dared not avow her hopes," writes Saint-Simon, " but they guessed them and combated them by dwelling on the extreme fragility of her position at Versailles and the solidity and permanence of her state in Spain. They told her that, blinded by the prodigious brilliance of her surroundings, she forgot that she owed it to Madame de Maintenon's interest in governing Spain through her, which could only be satisfied by her return thither, that if she did not return Madame de Maintenon in her disappointment would soon cause all the seductive brilliance to vanish and make her feel the effects of her jealousy if the King continued his favours, and that then she would find herself as abandoned as now she was courted and adulated." Finally, that the sooner she departed the better if she wished to keep her place in Spain and her favour at Versailles.

"The solidity of these arguments persuaded the Princess. She thought no more of what had been in her mind but as a temptation and dangerous seduction and resolved to fix the day of her departure." [1] And he adds elsewhere : "So did this great soul, ambitious and energetic, miss her goal for the second time from having tried too suddenly to attain it."

[1] Saint-Simon, xiii. 20.

CHAPTER XXI

TREACHERY OF PHILIPPE V. (1705)

AND how did the King and Queen, forsaken puppets, receive the news of her return?

Gramont, as has been seen, had received orders to announce the good news. The messenger arrived on 21 January, at nine o'clock in the evening, and he lost not a moment in demanding an audience of the Queen. Here is his official description to Louis of the interview :

> It was quite a fortnight since she had looked at me and hardly saluted me. I entered her private apartment after having asked permission, and said that I came to know, since it was post day, whether they had any letters for Your Majesty. They answered yes and said they would go and fetch them. As the Queen a moment after gave me one for Your Majesty I said that I had already the answer to it in my pocket, that you had the gift of answering your letters beforehand and I, your unworthy ambassador, that of having sought in vain the means to please her. Then I gave her Your Majesty's letter, which she read very eagerly, and remained in what is called an ecstasy, almost fainting. A little more and she would have thrown herself on my neck in the presence of the King. Her tongue was then loosened and, shedding a torrent of tears, what did she not say of Your Majesty! . . .
>
> So much for the emotions of the Queen. Those of the King were different. He seemed as though thunderstruck, grew pale as a corpse, and could not conceal his surprise and grief. Thus he thinks very differently to the Queen about the return of Madame des Ursins. . . . You know, Sire, what I have already told you on this subject. I implore Your Majesty on my knees that only you and Madame de Maintenon shall know of this. The King your grandson confided it to me and he would die of grief if the Queen should ever hear the least hint of it. The return of Madame des Ursins is admirable for the Queen, the King dreads it and the healthiest part of Spain will see it with sorrow and lament loudly.[1]

To the secret correspondent in Paris he wrote as follows :

You would not believe the astonishing effect produced here by the recall of *la confidente*. No one great or small but cries

[1] Baudrillart, i. 202 ; letter of 22 Jan. 1705.

out that *l'ami* [Louis] cares for them no longer and wishes to sacrifice them since he abandons them thus. Not a single woman of quality has been to kiss the hand of *l'esprit* and congratulate her on the news, which has put her in a fury. At least do not think that what has been done is a matter of indifference to the country, for it may cause great embarrassments, and I can assure you, as one who knows what he is saying, that if *la confidente* does not entirely change her game and mix at least three parts water with her wine, she will pass a bad time, which will afterwards recoil on you. Beware above all, whatever may be said to you, not to send back *le sujet à caution* [Orry]. He is held here in horror by everyone and it would be the way to complete the ruin. You know what *la bonté* [Philippe] has told you of him. He is a lawless madman and of an ambition completely beyond his sphere, the sole cause that *la confidente* lost her head and came out of her place. I know her well. She has a good heart. Her intentions are naturally straightforward, but she is weak and frivolous.[1]

The Princess des Ursins weak and frivolous!
To his friend the Prince de Vaudémont he wrote:

I have been treated by the Queen, and between ourselves by Madame her Camarera Mayor, like a thorough rogue and have received continual thrashings. I have supported everything without a word, but I should lie if I told you I had not resented it. Madame des Ursins returns here. The Sieur d'Aubigny her favourite accompanies her. The Sieur Orry, the execration of Spain, will return with her I give you my word, for she will insist on it so that her triumph may be complete. . . . The Sieur Orry will return Patriarch of Spain and d'Aubigny the distributor of favours.[2]

And to Torcy:

I cannot resist repeating to you that I am too devoted and really attached to the King not to be sensibly touched by the too hasty decision which has been made on totally false premises, and to assure you that the ground here is completely unknown. I have searched it to its innermost recesses, but more credence has been given to words more self-interested than mine. They cannot support me and never will, because they recognise that I am sharp-eyed and faithful, and perhaps the only man in France capable of inspiring life in a man naturally lethargic, whom I should have certainly delivered from the fetters of slavery. . . . The cabal is prepared to govern more despotically than ever. The King of Spain will be imprisoned and bound more tightly than he has ever been.[3]

---

[1] Geffroy, 475; letter of 28 Jan. 1705.
[2] Ibid., 476; letter of 4 March, 1705.
[3] Trémoïlle, iii. 118; letter of 10 Feb. 1705.

And this at the same time that he was claiming gratitude for her return to favour.

The Princess, who was never deceived by the double game he played so unskilfully, had made his recall one of the conditions of her return, but it is probable that Louis, recognising his incapacity, would of his own accord have replaced him. He had been sent to undermine the Princess's authority, and by his tactless abuse had increased it. He had been ordered neither to quarrel with the Queen himself nor be the cause of her quarrelling with Louis, and by his intrigues had nearly caused a breach between the two Courts. He had been told to treat her with the greatest consideration as the most important of the two sovereigns, and to satisfy his personal spite had tried to excite Philippe against her. Worse than all, he was now to be found guilty of encouraging the latter in dissimulations towards his grandfather which Louis found unpardonable.

In a moment of more than usual weakness Philippe had confided to him under pledge of secrecy his dislike and jealousy of the Princess, and that so far from wanting her to come back he was really thankful for her absence and had feigned sorrow only to gain the Queen's favour. This the unscrupulous confidant revealed to Louis as if it were his own discovery, but was not believed. "He [Louis] is persuaded that you think what you say about *la bonté*, but has difficulty in believing it," the secret correspondent had replied. And again: "What you say of *la bonté* would give great joy to *l'ami* [Louis] if he could believe it."

Louis either could not or would not believe in such duplicity on the part of his grandson who had been clamouring so persistently for the Princess's return, and Gramont, to prove himself right, had persuaded Philippe to write himself to his grandfather imploring him not to send her back, which he did directly her return was announced. "I know," he wrote, "that the Spanish have regretted her but little and wish as little to see her again. Thus when I asked you for her return it was not for my own satisfaction, but only not to have dissensions with the Queen."[1]

A month later he wrote more openly, again at Gramont's instigation, declared that he had never desired her return, that he would not be at all pleased to see her again, and that the Spanish had never regretted her, and suggested

[1] Millot, ii. 345; letter of 3 Jan. 1705.

that she should remain at Versailles as *dame d'honneur* to the Duchess of Burgundy, " where she would be quite in her place." [1]

To these foolish letters Gramont had himself added the following :

SIRE,—The King your grandson writes you the absolute truth, all that he thinks and wishes on the subject of Madame des Ursins. I have written the same to Your Majesty more than once, and it must be understood that her return cannot and never will be regarded with indifference, but as causing the worst suffering to the greater part of the people and those who compose the Court. To tell you the contrary would be to deceive you.[2]

After Philippe's letter doubt was no longer possible, and Louis, thoroughly disgusted at such treachery, wrote him a severe reprimand :

Being the Master it ill becomes a person of your rank to seek bypaths to express your true sentiments. The fear of domestic difficulties is too feeble a reason to oblige you to disguise the truth. It is better to support some contradiction and speak with authority than force yourself to write in two ways entirely opposed.[3]

Philippe was terrified at this severity and felt that the moment had come to shift the blame on the right shoulders, so he wrote again trying to excuse himself for his treachery, a letter full of contradictions and absurdities, probably the only one in existence which he ever composed without help, and which reveals his character in all its foolish puerility.

He began by asking pardon for acting against a person whom he liked and esteemed as he did the Princess. Never had he thought her return opposed to his interests, on the contrary, he had always considered her very useful, and this, added to his friendship for her, made him ardently desire it. Why then had he written against her? Because he feared that once more in Madrid the Queen—" this Princess who makes all my happiness "—would be so pleased to have her back that she would send him away. The Duc de Gramont had perceived this sentiment and had persuaded him to write it privately to his grandfather.

"I was blind," he continues, "and fell with open arms

---

[1] Baudrillart, i. 206 ; letter of 1 Feb. 1705.
[2] Trémoïlle, iii. 117 ; letter of 5 Feb. 1705.
[3] Baudrillart, i. 206 ; letter of 1 Feb. 1705.

TREACHERY OF PHILIPPE V 173

into this trap, and it was owing to this blindness and the empire the Duc de Gramont has assumed over me in flattering my feebleness, that I wrote to you as I did, not only against the Princess's return but also that of Orry." Finally he writes that, having returned to his senses, he repents infinitely of having acted against a lady to whom he is under so many obligations, whom he would never forget and loved so much, and begged his grandfather to pardon him for the embarrassment his contradictory attitude had caused him. "Have pity on my feebleness," he whined in conclusion. "Do not betray me to the Duc de Gramont, and above all do not let the Princess des Ursins ever hear of it."[1]

For the first time he had revealed himself to Louis as he was—jealous, deceitful and abject. Jealous, not only of the Queen's affection, but probably also of the Princess's superiority, and her authority in the State where he himself had none.

However, instead of being disgusted at the foolish ignoble letter, Louis seems to have been touched by it, either from pity or pleasure that his grandson's rebellious spirit was broken. "The confession you have made me of what you call feebleness," he answered him, "is a sign of your confidence in me, and I am far from condemning your uneasiness based on the idea that the Queen's tenderness for you would be divided when the Princess des Ursins is back with you. . . ."[2] A touch of irony is, however, perceptible in his concluding words: "The health of Madame des Ursins will perhaps delay her departure, but I press it as much as possible. I hope she will increase your happiness."[3]

In face of such proofs of his treachery and unscrupulousness it is probable that without the Princess's exaction Gramont's recall was decided. In any case, on 21 March he received the following from the secret correspondent: "*L'ami* [Louis] always thought you were deceived about *la bonté* and that he would never have the strength to resist *l'esprit*. It is foreseen that this Government will have its inconveniences, but they would be still greater if *l'esprit* were not reckoned with. After all, she can have no other interests than those of *la bonté*." And the letter ends with

---

[1] Baudrillart, i. 207; letter of 10 March, 1705.
[2] Ibid., i. 208; letter of 23 March, 1705.
[3] Geffroy, 476; same letter, words not cited by Baudrillart.

the summary dismissal: "It is understood that you can no longer serve in the place where you are."[1]

Thus were the intrigues of this incompetent Ambassador frustrated. During the few months of his embassy he had committed nothing but follies, but he bore a great name and could not be humiliated as he merited. He left Madrid, therefore, laden with honours, Philippe bestowing on him the Order of the Golden Fleece ("*ce mouton là*," he called it disdainfully) and many magnificent gifts, including three portraits by Titian, and was shortly after appointed to the important governorship of Navarre and Béarn, in which capacity he was in constant relation with the Spanish Court, including the Princess, who was obliged by her office to keep up an official correspondence with him.

He was furious at his recall, however, and on his arrival wrote to her as follows:

I wish you success, although the manner in which I have been dismissed from the capital of Spain between you and me was a little severe and unmerited, for if I had served my God with the same zeal, ardour and disinterestedness that I have served the King and Queen of Spain, I should be the greatest saint in Paradise. And you know what their gratitude has been and if they could have dismissed any differently the wretched envoy of a miserable little Lucca. I should lie if I hid from you that I have keenly resented it.[2]

To leave his sting behind him, on the eve of his departure he wrote the following criticism of the King and Queen and principal personages of the Court for Torcy's delectation:

Here is the portrait true to life of the King of Spain, the Queen, and most of the grandees that I have known in Madrid.

The King of Spain has intelligence and good sense. He thinks and speaks always with justice. He is naturally kind and good, and incapable, if left to himself, of doing harm, but timid, feeble and idle to excess. His weakness and fear of the Queen are so great that, though born virtuous, he would sacrifice his word without hesitation if he thought it would be the means of pleasing her. I have proved it more than once. Thus you may believe me and rely upon it once for all, that as long as he is with her he will never be anything but a child of six and never a man.

The Queen has intelligence beyond her years. She is proud, arrogant, deceitful, impenetrable, haughty and implacable.

[1] Geffroy, 476; letter of 21 March, 1705.
[2] Ibid., 468; letter of 30 Aug. 1705.

At sixteen she loves neither music, nor the theatre, nor conversation, nor walking, nor hunting; in a word, none of the amusements suitable to her age. She desires nothing but to dominate as a sovereign, to keep her husband always in leading-strings, and depend as little as possible on the King her grandfather. This is her nature and character, and whoever thinks differently has never known her.

Then follow malignant criticisms of all the friends and partisans of the Queen and Princess. Veraguas is arrogance personified, full of artifice, "as must be one who has attained the grade of favourite to the Princess. He hates France openly and despises it as well as Spain."

Aguilar has about the same character and desires the extinction of all the French in Spain and the arrival of the Archduke in Madrid. "These personages are the right arm of Madame des Ursins and sole confidants of the Queen."

"Medina-Cœli has the pride of Lucifer and his head is full of wind and extravagant ideas. . . . Monterey, a weathercock turning with all winds. . . . Palma, an ox whose only merit in Spain is his hatred of France. Lemos, a brute-beast quite incapable of his post, which the favour of his wife with Madame des Ursins procured him." In a word, the only persons who find grace in his sight are those with whom the Camarera Mayor is on bad terms.

Thus the Duc de Medina-Sidonia is "of great probity, faithful and attached to Philippe as a shadow to its body," but cruelly persecuted because his wife is supposed to aspire to the post of Camarera Mayor.

Porto-Carrero is "of great probity, faithful and attached only to his master, staunch and firm for the good of the State, a slave to his word. It is he who placed the crown on the King's head and who in spite of all has kept it there, but having had the misfortune to displease Madame des Ursins he is treated with shame and ignominy, which makes the nobles and people groan."[1]

On hearing that his recall was due to the Princess, he stayed three days at Bayonne on his way back to France in order to pick a quarrel *a vivâ voce* with her, but as she did not arrive he was forced to content himself with another letter of reproach.

As to your accusation that I have tried to sow discord between the King and Queen of Spain, permit me to say that

[1] Baudrillart, i. 686, etc.

the character of traitor and slanderer never was nor will be that of the Duc de Gramont, and the King of Spain, who is truth personified, can tell you that never a word escaped me tending to destroy the entire confidence and tender friendship he has for the Queen. I have never desired anything but his welfare and glory. I was attached to him by inclination and cherished him like a mistress. I have omitted nothing that might please the Queen. I have not been able to succeed. It is not my fault. No one, I think, knows the reason better than you.

I have never harmed anyone. On the contrary, all my life I have thought of nothing but to please and give pleasure to everyone, but I could not be worse repaid than I have been for my good and upright intentions, for always people have sought to injure and crush me, and though I have been in no one's way, they would have succeeded had I not had to deal with the justest and most equitable of men—the King, who knows my heart and my upright conduct since fifty years.[1]

It cannot be said that the King of France was fortunate in his ambassadors.

[1] Trémoïlle, iii. 122 ; letter of 1 Sept. 1705.

CHAPTER XXII

RETURN OF THE PRINCESS (1705)

"THUS, covered with honour and glory, she completed her triumph in France to go and reign openly in Spain without contradiction or rivalry." [1]

Certainly no triumph could be more brilliant, more complete. No longer limited to her post of Camarera Mayor, she returned with a Viceroy's sceptre in her hand, plenipotentiary of the King of France and with his representative as humble slave and secretary, for Amelot, her *protégé*, was appointed ambassador on the express understanding that he should act in perfect agreement with her and the tacit menace that if he did not he would be recalled.

Michel-Jean Amelot, Marquis de Gournay, was a man after her own heart, honest and serviceable and an able statesman.[2] "He is good all round," she once wrote of him, "he has conscience, heart and intelligence."

A man of honour, hard-working, of great sense and intelligence [writes Saint-Simon, for once praising a man of no birth]. He was gentle, courteous, supple, firm, and very wise and modest. He was State councillor, had been ambassador in Portugal, Venice, and Switzerland, and had succeeded everywhere, made himself liked and acquired a great reputation. He belonged to a family of lawyers, and consequently was eligible neither for the Golden Fleece nor the Grandeeship. Madame des Ursins thought she could do no better than have under her an ambassador of no family and with no other protection in France than his own merit, who in virtue of his office could aid her in all business matters, and who as a matter of fact was nothing but a powerful secretary, sheltered by whose position she could act with all authority in Spain and all confidence in France. He was well with the King and Madame de Maintenon. . . . She decided therefore on him and obtained his appointment, with express orders that he was to act only in concert with herself and, to put it shortly—under her.[3]

[1] Saint-Simon, v. 506.
[2] Amelot began his career as councillor to the Parliament. He was appointed ambassador to the Venetian Republic in 1682, to the Swiss Republic in 1688, State councillor 1693, director of commerce 1699.
[3] Saint-Simon, xii. 442.

Here are his official instructions concerning her:

His Majesty has been so content with the solid intelligence of the Princess des Ursins and with her knowledge of Spanish affairs, that he has considered he could do no better than send her back immediately to Madrid. The Sieur Amelot is witness to the solemn promise she made to the King to act in all things in perfect agreement with his Ambassador, who will respond by an entire confidence in her.[1]

On 30 March Dangeau notes in his diary: "Monsieur Amelot, councillor of State, has been declared Ambassador to Spain. He refused for some time out of modesty to accept the post, but the King insisted and he obeyed."[2]

It would be interesting to know if this hesitation was really due to modesty, or, given the fate of his predecessors, to a fear of collaboration with so authoritative a chief.

She left Paris on 16 June and was nearly two months on the journey. Her health was still bad. She suffered much from her eyes and a cough which grew worse as she proceeded. It would have been surprising if all the emotions and agitations—the uncertainties, triumphs, aspirations and disappointments, of the last six months had not left their mark, and the journey was long and very fatiguing at this hottest season of the year.

Her letters written on the way are anything but cheerful, and show plainly that so far from being glad to return to Spain and her " marvellous Queen," as she calls her, she was vexed and irritated to have been forced to leave France and its still more marvellous King.

With every league covered by her procession of coaches she left farther behind the kingdom over which her inordinate ambition had given her the hope to rule, and notwithstanding that her return journey was triumphant as a Royal progress, her vexation increased as she advanced. The weekly correspondence with Madame de Maintenon arranged at Marly begins at this date, and her first letter was written from Bordeaux on 7 July, nearly a month after her departure from Paris. In this, as in the rest, one divines beneath the perpetual complaints a bitterness more profound than can be attributed to " the insupportable heat which kills even the beasts," " the abominable inns where repose is impossible," " the fatigue and a cold

[1] Baudrillart, i. 221 ; instructions to Amelot of 24 April, 1705.
[2] Dangeau, x. 290.

RETURN OF THE PRINCESS

in my head which grows every day worse," and " the dust capable of blinding the eyes and spoiling the lungs."

She travelled slowly, and only at night on account of the heat, starting at six in the evening and resting " in some bad inn " till sunset. She speaks of a terrible thunderstorm which overtook her at Villa-Fagnan, rain and hail such as she had never seen, lasting for three hours, during which the light chaises, following with the servants and baggage, were all overthrown and broken.[1]

Yet in spite of the adverse elements the journey was not without compensations had her disappointed soul allowed her to appreciate them, for her advance was a series of triumphs. Everywhere she passed rejoicings in her honour. Flowers were strewn before her coach. Clergy, civic magnates and nobles all left the towns and came to meet her on the road in robes of state, and harangued her in speeches full of eulogy and welcome. At Bordeaux, which she reached 5 July, all the officials and notables did her homage. At Bayonne, where she did not even deign to alight, a salute of cannon was fired as to a royal personage. At Saint-Jean-de-Luz, where her equipages as Camarera Mayor awaited her, a guard of honour was placed before the door of the palace prepared for her and nobles and populace vied with each other to show her the most honour. Here was formed the superb state procession with which she was to enter Spain, a procession as pompous and long as though she were the Queen herself.

The fashionable gazette of the day—*le Mecure galant*—thus describes the pageant:

At Saint-Jean-de-Luz the Queen's coaches had been awaiting her for several days, and many Spanish gentlemen and officers were assembled. All the cities and villages through which she passed were under arms, and the people crowded to meet her and mounted guard at the house where she was lodged. She left Saint-Jean-de-Luz the 13th, with a suite of eighty persons. Orders were given and very well executed to furnish her and her household with all the commodities capable of diminishing the fatigue suffered at this season in crossing the mountains and burning plains leading to Madrid. Many distinguished persons, even some grandees among them, met her on the road to escort her. Dances, games, bull-fights, salutes of artillery, celebrated her return wherever she passed. I exaggerate nothing in saying that her path was strewn with flowers thrown with full hands from overflowing baskets.[2]

[1] Bossange, iii. 186 ; letter of 7 July, 1705.   [2] Geffroy, 192.

But all these glories left her more than indifferent—irritable. Her letters are filled with lamentations and complaints—of a violent fever which had attacked her the day she left Paris and increased with every stage of the tiresome journey, a journey "long, dangerous, painful, and very bad for my health at a season when even the most robust can scarcely support the intolerable heat." Even the pomp of her numerous equipages annoys her—"it is an entire household I have to drag about after me."

At Vittoria, six days' journey over the mountains from Saint-Jean-de-Luz, the Queen-Dowager sent one of her equerries to congratulate her on her return, and this is the first thing on the journey which seems to have given her any pleasure. The Queen-Dowager was her bitter enemy always, but strangely enough she appears up to now not to have suspected it, and received her cajoleries with pleasure. "The Queen-Dowager has always honoured me with much kindness," she wrote to Madame de Maintenon. Not many months after she grew more suspicious and placed spies to watch over her, and less than two years later these suspicions became a certainty and she understood the reason of this flattery. "She pushes her expressions of tenderness for me so far that I am ashamed for her and myself. All I can say does not change her, and she continues to treat me as though we were comrades and good friends, which flatters in no way my vanity, for I like everyone to keep in their place."[1]

Yet, even in writing this, she was still far from suspecting to what a point the Queen-Dowager carried her hatred.

To return to her journey.

On crossing the frontier she deigned to show some pride at her reception by the Spanish, less from the pleasure it afforded her than to discredit those who declared she was detested in Spain. "It would be impossible to express the joy everyone shows when I pass," she wrote to Madame de Maintenon, "not a single village on the way where they did not present arms. Everywhere they danced under my windows and let off fireworks as though I were the Queen."[2]

But this pride was of short duration. At Burgos, which she reached a day or two later, her complaints recommence. The sandy roads raise clouds of dust which ruin her eyes

[1] Bossange, iii. 426; letter of 7 March, 1707.
[2] Ibid., iii. 195; letter of 21 July, 1705.

and lungs. She is discouraged at all she hears of the state of the country. "In truth it needed all my submission to the King's will, and my attachment to Their Majesties Très-Chrétienne et Catholique, to return to the Court of Spain at a moment so difficult."[1] Even the Queen's impatience to see her irritated her: "She wants me to do in one day a journey that should take three."[2]

Hardly a word of the supreme honour prepared for her—the arrival of the King and Queen themselves to meet her on the road, an honour without precedent in the history of Spain. She alludes to it only in passing as though it were the most natural thing in the world, and the contrast is great between her own indifference and the emotion it excited in others.

They drove to meet her to Canillas, two leagues from Madrid, and had sent before them the Royal cooks and officers of the kitchen to prepare a sumptuous feast. Amelot, the ambassadors, and all the ministers were assembled to honour her return, and at the close of the banquet a letter was brought her from the Queen announcing the arrival of herself and the King the same evening at six o'clock. It was not without remonstrances and black looks from the Spanish ministers that the sovereigns took a step so contrary to the customs of the country, but the Queen was ready to sacrifice even her popularity to do honour to her favourite and could not be dissuaded.

At the appointed hour, therefore, the Royal coach, escorted by the entire Court, arrived. The King got out. The Princess knelt at his feet. As for the Queen, beside herself with joy, she threw herself into her arms and kissed her over and over again on both cheeks like the impetuous child she was.

After an hour's rest they continued their journey to Madrid, the Queen imploring the Princess to ride with her and the King in the Royal coach, which would have been the climax in the numerous breaches of etiquette. But this she prudently declined and followed in her own official coach directly after. The procession extended all the way from Canillas to Madrid and proceeded slowly between the double rank of coaches which lined the road on either side

[1] Geffroy, 189; letter to the Maréchale de Noailles of July 1705.
[2] Bossange, iii. 200; letter to Madame de Maintenon of 25 July, 1705.

—the most numerous and splendid cortège that had ever been seen.

But all these things we learn from others. In her own letters hardly a word of this magnificent reception. "The King is in good health." "The Queen has grown taller and thinner." "Her gland malady is much worse and she has developed an air of melancholy new to her." "My cold is much worse and I have lost my voice to such a point that I had hardly enough left to acknowledge the welcome of Their Majesties." "In order that I might rest, the Queen took me to a convent of two hundred nuns, and only my joy at seeing her again enabled me to support this fresh fatigue."[1]

"I preserve in my great prosperity the same moderation as when I appeared so criminal," she excused herself for her lack of enthusiasm, but as moderation in expressing her emotions was not one of her special qualities, we may be allowed to suspect that it was due rather to the failure of her projects and the contrast between the brilliant Court she had left behind with the dreary discomfort of that of Madrid.

[1] Bossange, iii. 201, etc.; letters of 5 and 28 Aug. 1705.

END OF PART I

PART II

PART II

CHAPTER I

IN DEFENCE OF A MONARCHY (1705)

WHETHER the Princess accepted her mission to work for the supremacy of France in good faith, or with the definite intention of breaking with Louis, or only as a means of realising her personal ambitions, are questions difficult to resolve. My own conviction is that the former must certainly be dismissed, for she was too experienced in Spanish affairs not to be aware of the danger of French domination, and she had been treated too harshly and unjustly to feel much compunction in breaking her word. It is possible that in accepting it she was moved by a real desire to do well for the country of her adoption and aid its independence, but more probable, from all we know of her character, that her main motive was personal ambition.

If she returned with the design of saving Spain, not only from the clutch of Austria, but from that of Louis also, her hesitation is explicable, for the task was formidable. Spain was menaced by all the European Powers, and having neither army nor money was entirely at the mercy of France. Louis consented to give his gold and troops only on condition of servitude so complete that, as has been seen, not the smallest detail public or domestic could be decided without his intervention, a position intolerable to a proud people like the Spanish. From her first entry into public life the Princess's aim had been to diminish this authority, and this policy she now at her return continued with more energy than ever, ousting the French from all posts in the Government, at the same time that she made use of French gold and blood to free the country from its other enemies, an audacious combination against which Louis opposed all his efforts, but in which, by dint of courage and perseverance, she succeeded. Madame de Maintenon might groan over the transfusion of French blood into Spanish veins, bewail her France writhing in the throes of starvation and poverty to maintain the armies of Spain, weep over her King forced to retrench on his banquets, melt his gold plate and abandon his mania for building. A will stronger than hers or his insisted, persisted, and menaced to such good effect that troops and gold continued to cross the Pyrenees, that Austria was eventually forced to abandon her claim, and Louis his despot's grip, and that, in spite of his thunderbolts, Madame de Maintenon's wails, and the ignoble indifference of Philippe himself, she fought on, fought till she got the troops and gold she needed, and saved Spain from the clutch of Austria and the fetters of France, a country shorn of its foreign possessions it is true, but intact within its frontiers and henceforth free and independent.

For the Spain to which she returned was in the throes of revolution and surrounded on all sides by enemies. During the two preceding years the war had been like a game of see-saw, alternate defeat and victory on either side. In September 1703 the French troops under Villars and the Elector of Bavaria had defeated the Imperialists at Hochstadt, but the arrival of the two great Generals Marlborough and Prince Eugène had speedily put a stop to their success, and at the Battle of Blenheim the following year Hochstadt had been retaken, and the French with heavy losses forced to recross the frontier. In May 1705 the Emperor Leopold had died and been succeeded by his son Joseph, and the Archduke Charles his brother received all his aid in his efforts to conquer Spain. The country, completely alienated by Philippe's attitude and Louis' despotic interference, was ready now to accept him as their sovereign and nothing but their chivalrous affection for their young Queen, and respect for the Princess's authority, had kept them hitherto loyal. With her departure they had grown more sullen and menacing and with good reason; for the country was in no case to combat such a coalition as Austria, England, Holland, Prussia and Portugal. The treasury was empty and such army as existed unpaid and half-starved. Their only salvation, if they retained their Bourbon King, was in Louis' consent to aid them with men and money, and they were well aware what price he would exact in payment. They had no choice but to submit to Austrian rule or that of France, and the former found more favour in their sight.

LOUIS XIV.
From a portrait by Rigaud in the Musée du Louvre.

IN DEFENCE OF A MONARCHY 187

The problem the Princess had to face on her arrival was to extract from Louis troops and gold enough to free the country from the menace of Austria, and at the same time preserve it from his own domination. A hopeless case it would have seemed to another. To her its difficulties only served to stimulate her energies and genius.

She reached Madrid on 4 August and found everything prepared for her reign. The Duchesse de Béjar, Camarera Mayor *pro interim*, had abdicated with due humility. Amelot was installed at the French Embassy, Orry at the Ministry of Finance and Commerce, Tessé at the head of the armies. All three were her friends and entirely devoted to her. All her adversaries, Spanish as well as French, had been dismissed, and nothing remained but for her to arrange her pieces for a supreme checkmate to the enemy.

Without losing a moment she took her place at the board. She would have no domination from either side. Above all no disastrous peace with slices of Spain thrown to fill the jaws of the Allies, which had been already proposed and which Louis had begun to consider. She would have either victory, with her puppets firmly established on their throne in independence, or an honourable defeat with the ground disputed inch by inch.

Temperamentally optimistic, at first she seems hardly to have realised the desperate state of the country and declared that she had come in time " to arrest the torrent which was hurling it over the precipice." But the torrent was not so easy to arrest for the entire kingdom was ripe for revolution, and her optimism soon vanished before the disasters which followed in quick succession after her arrival. The people, disappointed in their hope of peace, revolted in masses and opened their gates to the armies of the Archduke. In October Aragon and Valencia yielded, and Catalonia recognised him a sits sovereign. At the same time the Portuguese attacked Badajoz, on which the fate of Madrid itself depended, and on every side fresh perils surged up.

To her prayers for help the replies of Madame de Maintenon grew ever more cold and constrained. To her representations of the terrible state of Spain she opposed the terrible state of France. To her clamours for troops and gold she replied with groans over the poverty of France. It is true that her statements were not exaggerated. France was also in a desperate state and had need of all her gold and men to guard her own frontiers. Presently it was whispered that Louis was in treaty with the enemy for peace — and what a peace! Nothing less than the partition of Spain among the enemy with a poor little sovereignty such as Sicily and Sardinia allowed to his grandson out of his immense empire. To save his own skin Louis was willing to sacrifice Spain.

She could hardly believe her ears when this rumour reached Madrid. It seemed too monstrous a treachery, and she dispatched Amelot in hot haste to Versailles to know if it were true. Louis received him coldly, denied the report but said that "it was not surprising that people should suppose him to be weary of exhausting his own kingdom to support another which seemed bent on running to its ruin." [1]

Such a reply was equivalent to an avowal and so the Princess considered it. Disgusted at such treachery she took the bit in her teeth, openly threw off all allegiance and faced Louis *de couronne à couronne*, as an equal power. Through his ministers and Madame de Maintenon she spared him neither reproaches nor even threats. Her demands for men and money took the form of exactions and without deigning any more to ask for counsel or permission she gave her orders, and directed the ministers and generals in Spain as though her dictatorship was publicly acknowledged.

Philippe she dispatched to Aragon, nominally to take command of his army, but probably because she thought him better out of the way. The Queen she made him appoint Regent during his absence, nominally also since it was she who governed, and supported on either side by her two creatures, Amelot and Orry, she took her place openly at the head of the Government. It was she who planned the campaign and defences, with no more regard for the Generalissimo Tessé, Chamillart complained, than if he had been a mere captain of infantry. It was she who provisioned the army, prepared the attacks and chose the officers, and she did it, even her adversaries own, with the skill of an experienced general. Louis having failed her, she concentrated all the forces at her command, and with marvellous ability resisted the enemy during eight long years, pushing her way slowly but surely towards victory

[1] Baudrillart, i. 239.

in the teeth of opposition, not only of the enemy, but of Louis himself, and of the feeble boy whose throne she was so ably defending. For in spite of a show of resistance which deceived no one and consisted mainly in copying letters dictated by the Princess, Philippe would gladly have put off from his head a crown so thorny, and instead of mounting his charger at the head of unreliable troops, have retired to Naples or Sicily, there to bask peacefully in the arms of his beloved Queen.

Poor Madame de Maintenon, if, as the popular voice asserts, she had really sent the Princess to Spain as her lieutenant or viceroy, had created a Frankenstein like to cost her dear. She was caught between two fires, between Louis, sick of a country which bid fair to be the ruin of his own and appalled at the menacing attitude his subjects had begun to assume, and this dictatress who dared dispute his will and refuse to allow Philippe to abdicate, which was the only possible way to save France. It was a difficult position for a woman worn out with the exigencies of her despotic husband and longing for peace and tranquillity, and it is no wonder that her letters grew cold and her jealous fears of the Princess as a rival increased to absolute aversion.

And the position of Louis himself it must be owned was terrible and almost excuses his treachery. In placing his grandson on the throne of Spain he had thought to annex the immense empire as a province for his own aggrandisement, and had chosen Philippe precisely that his feeble character might ensure obedience in case of failure, for, far-seeing politician as he was, it is impossible that he had not reckoned on the opposition of Europe and the possibility of having to capitulate. It was a game of hazard which from the first he had been forced to realise was going against him, and had it not been for the Princess's tenacity would certainly have ordered his grandson to abdicate, accept the crown of Sicily (so much to the good in any case) and allow the Archduke to reign in Spain, with probably a slice of the coveted Netherlands as compensation for himself.

His treasury was so empty that he was forced to melt his plate for the daily expenses, forced to abandon his hobby of building fabulous palaces and to make all sorts of sordid economies. His people, sick of his ambitions which cost them so dear, were on the eve of a revolution

and his troops, for which the Princess was eternally
clamouring, were needed to repress the riots consequent
on the lack of bread. Matters had reached the point when
he must choose between surrender or ruin. He had no
choice but to withdraw his army from Spain, abandon his
grandson, and accept such conditions as the allies thought
fit to impose. To this humiliation he had resigned himself—he, who had posed as the conqueror of Europe—but
even the right to surrender was denied him, for here, behind
his grandson, the weakling who asked nothing better than
to obey, had surged up a champion more obstinate than
himself, fully determined that Philippe should not abdicate
but remain on the throne if humanly possible, that Spain
should not be partitioned out among the Allies at Louis'
good pleasure but handed on intact to Bourbon heirs. Here
was his own paid agent, the woman to whose fascinations
he in his senility had succumbed only a few months before,
turning on him like a tigress, defying his omnipotence,
and forcing his grandson to defy him also. Here was a
will for the first time opposing his, obliging him to continue
to his own ruin this disastrous war, ready to continue it
without him if need be.

CHAPTER II

THE FLIGHT TO BURGOS (1706)

THE disasters of 1705 were nothing to those of the following year both for France and Spain. Pressed and importuned by the Queen and Princess, Louis had grudgingly sent his grandson fresh troops, under the command of the Duke of Berwick and the Comte d'Ayen, now Duc de Noailles, to protect the Portuguese frontier and defend Catalonia: troops he could ill afford, for his own armies were being decimated in Flanders by Marlborough and in Italy by Prince Eugène. On 23 May at Ramillies the Maréchal de Villeroy was defeated by Marlborough, with the loss of twenty thousand men and the chief cities of Brabant and Flanders, and on 7 September the Duke of Savoy, now in open alliance with Austria, at the head of the Emperor's troops inflicted a bloody defeat on his armies in Italy. The Duc de Vendôme had been recalled to Belgium to face Marlborough and, profiting by this, Prince Eugène had immediately emerged from the mountains and hurried to Turin, where he joined forces with the Duke of Savoy, and the two defeated Marsin and La Feuillade in one of the bloodiest battles of the war, in which the Duc d'Orléans, who had nominally the command, nearly lost his life. This defeat practically put an end to the war in Italy for the French were forced to evacuate the country, an event which turned eventually to the benefit of Spain, as will be seen presently.

At present, however, the kingdom seemed on the verge of complete devastation. The Austrians occupied Naples, the English Sardinia, and the Pope recognised the Archduke as King of Spain. Alcantara had been captured and ten battalions made prisoner. Salamanca and Carthagena had yielded without even a show of resistance. Many of the grandees declared themselves openly in favour of Austria and revolt was general in the country. Every day hundreds of soldiers deserted and the greater part of the country fell into the hands of the Archduke who entered

Barcelona and was proclaimed King, as Charles III., on 2 July.

As this series of misfortunes reached one after the other the ears of the Princess, for the first time she lost courage. "A kingdom attacked in so many places, a spirit of revolt everywhere, unreliable subjects who blame everything one does—all this is capable of turning a better head than mine," she wrote to Madame de Maintenon, and each letter of this date ends with the same desperate prayer: "More troops or we perish!"[1]

On the official recognition of the Archduke as King of Spain in Barcelona, the Spanish historian San Phélipe wrote with curious superstition:

> The heavens announced by prodigies how fatal was this epoch to Catalonia. On a clear day in September suddenly there appeared over Barcelona a globe of fire the centre of which was blood-red, surrounded by a light cloud, and this surrounded by another so dark as to inspire horror. This fatal meteor appeared during one hour in opposition to the sun. The dark cloud then insensibly spread over all the country which it veiled in obscurity. The centre, from which the flame issued, devoured with incredible rapidity the matter surrounding it, then a crash was heard and frightful noises, which did not resemble thunder but cannon-shot and musketry fired alternately. For if the noise ceased one instant it redoubled immediately after, and the clouds crashing one against the other, a noise as of drums and the clashing of arms was heard. The heavens were agitated thus during an entire hour. There was no lightning but sparks of fire and a noise as of the crackling of bay-leaves thrown on the fire, until, the matter being entirely consumed and the flames spent, the lighter of the clouds covered all Catalonia. This obscurity remained on the horizon for more than two hours. Finally it disappeared, the vapours being raised to the highest region of the atmosphere. But the day remained charged with clouds and the horror inspired by this phenomenon was dissipated only by the shades of night.[2]

To return to more serious matters.

Porto-Carrero, who had retired in anger from the capital, found the occasion good, under the influence of the Queen-Dowager, to take a sweeping revenge for the humiliations he had suffered and went over to the Archduke. He declared publicly that the French had proved themselves tyrants, and that he had made a mistake in supporting Philippe's claims to the throne. He was at his bishopric of Toledo,

---

[1] Geffroy, 252; letter of Feb. 1706.   [2] San Phélipe, i. 243.

THE FLIGHT TO BURGOS

in constant relation with the Queen-Dowager, who had her residence there when the Portuguese entered in triumph, and he welcomed the general with open arms, had his palace illuminated, caused a *Te Deum* to be sung in the cathedral, and celebrated the event with so much enthusiasm as to rouse the suspicions of the Portuguese themselves, who found it difficult to account for so sudden a change in the man who more than any other had been instrumental in placing Philippe on the throne. The Queen-Dowager, with more reason, was radiant at her nephew's triumph. She threw off her widow's weeds for the first time since the death of Charles II., dressed herself in gala costume, opened her palace to the general and vied with Porto-Carrero in showering gifts and favours on the conquerors.

And as a crowning misfortune, the Archduke himself, with an army of twenty thousand men, marched on Madrid with the intention of being proclaimed king in the capital with all pomp and ceremony.

Philippe, flying with the remnants of his vanquished army, was forced to re-enter Madrid by way of France, all the roads in his own country being in the hands of the enemy. He re-entered it in May, but only to fly again almost immediately at the approach of the Archduke.

The grandees, more ready to forsake their French King than they had been to accept him, tried to persuade him to remain quietly in Madrid, to surrender the throne and submit to such conditions as the Archduke thought fit to impose, which he would probably have done had it not been for the Queen and Princess. They themselves wished to defend the city and refused to leave, but Amelot insisted on their flight and they were finally persuaded. But fearful that the grandees would force them to remain as prisoners, they kept their departure secret till the last moment so that no preparations for the journey were possible, and this added greatly to the physical hardships they suffered.

Travelling in Spain in those days was like moving house, for there were no inns nor any sort of accommodation on the roads and everything, even to the beds, had to be carried with the traveller. It is hardly surprising to hear that on their sudden departure, unfurnished with the most elementary necessaries of life, the ladies of the palace preferred to remain comfortably in Madrid and pay their court to the new sovereign. A few only followed them into exile, and these complained so loudly and constantly over the bad food and lodging that both Queen and Princess heartily wished they had not.

As for them, the courage and cheerfulness with which they supported these hardships were admirable, all the more when it is considered that one of them was a girl of seventeen, the other a woman of sixty-four, and neither in good health.

Here is one of the letters written by the Princess to Madame de Maintenon on the journey:

BERLANGA, 24 *June*, 1706.

We have been forced at last to quit Madrid, and as we wished to keep a good face up to the last and not let people know our intention, we left without taking even the most necessary things. The Queen was without a bed the first days. . . . She had only two eggs for supper, and the next day was no better. . . . She has with her no one but myself, one woman and a *femme-de-chambre*, the lack of money having reduced her to these, and most that we have is borrowed. The King has just sent to tell her to send his jewels to France either to sell or engage. Among these are the famous pearl called *La Pelégrina* and the diamond which the Spaniards call *l'Estanque* [the Pond]. The Queen has added all her own jewels.[1]

Here is the Queen's letter to Madame de Maintenon on arriving at the Royal palace in Burgos, capital of Castile:

BURGOS, 6 *July*, 1706.

I arrived here yesterday evening very tired from having always got up before sunrise, from the heat and horrible dust and the lodging which could not be worse—so bad that a wall fell down in the house where I was, in a place where everyone had to pass. You may judge by this of the rest. We hoped on arriving here to find a little more comfort and cleanliness, but we have found neither. In spite of this, if the King could conquer his enemies, we should be gay, but the worst is that every day brings us some bad news. Saragossa has revolted without having seen the enemy. Carthagena is lost and the Portuguese are establishing themselves in Madrid.[2]

[1] Bossange, iii. 304; letter of 24 June, 1706. " We have seen the jewels with tears in our eyes," Madame de Maintenon wrote in answer. " Everyone is touched in their different way. The pearl and diamond are so extremely beautiful that they will be difficult to dispose of here, and I think will be kept and restored to you " (Bossange, i. 15).

[2] Millot, ii. 418.

THE FLIGHT TO BURGOS 195

She could even jest over her misfortunes:

Not a day passes [she wrote to Amelot, who had insisted on their flight] that the Princess des Ursins and I do not abuse you, when we think that it is you who made us come to Burgos, not a day that we do not love the Duc de Gramont a hundred thousand times more than you, and shall love the Abbé d'Estrées also if you do worse things to us. Neither of them would have had the severity to send us to a place where we cannot go out in the streets for fear the houses should fall on our heads, where the mosquitoes sting us the whole day long, rats eat in the rooms where we are, and bugs and fleas suck our blood all night.¹

The Princess wrote in the same high spirits a few days later to Madame de Maintenon:

To amuse you a little I must give you a description of my apartment. It consists of a single room twelve or thirteen feet square. A large window which will not shut, exposed to the midday sun, nearly fills one wall. A low door leads into the Queen's room and another narrower still into a winding passage where I dare not go, though there are always two or three lamps burning, because it is so badly paved that I should break my neck. I cannot call the walls white for they are filthy. My travelling-bed is the only furniture I have, with a folding chair and deal table which serves me alternately for my toilet, my writing-table and for eating the Queen's dessert, having no kitchen and perhaps not enough money to keep one up. Her Majesty only laughs, and I laugh also. I have been much worse off in my travels.²

As a contrast to this cheerfulness and courage Madame de Maintenon at Versailles was groaning over the horrors of war, the sufferings of the people and the visible anger of God, whom in the anguish of her soul she even dares to reproach. Her letters of this date are filled with such phrases as the following: "Our two Kings defend religion and they are unfortunate. Our enemies attack each other and they triumph." "The designs of God are incomprehensible. Three great and very Christian kings [the third was the Pretender] are abandoned by Him. Heresy and injustice triumph." "Your Spanish are traitors, our Flemish abandon us and God seems offended with us." ³

And not only did the Princess support misfortune with cheerfulness, but combated it with admirable energy. For

¹ Trémoïlle, iii. 145 ; letter of 11 July, 1706.
² Bossange, iii. 317 ; letter of 15 July, 1706.
³ Ibid., i. 3, 5 and 9 ; letters of 5 and 20 June and 4 July, 1706.

O

example, money was absolutely indispensable not only to maintain the starving troops, but for their own daily expenses, and no one had any. Louis was silent when appealed to. Madame de Maintenon responded with groans over their own sad fate. The Princess herself had nothing, for neither Versailles nor Madrid had paid her pension for over a year. Yet money had somehow to be found.

With a courage truly admirable in that priest-ridden country, she issued a decree calling on the bishops of each diocese to raise what she euphemistically called a "voluntary loan," and as bishops in those days were courtiers as well as priests, she reckoned rightly they would be either ashamed or afraid to disobey. The Pope was furious and sent orders to the clergy to refuse, and even Louis protested. But the Pope might hurl anathemas and the Jesuits menace her with flames here and hereafter, she remained firm and fearless, laughed at their threats and succeeded by this means in raising no less than four million francs, enough to pay and feed the army and keep some part of it at least from deserting to the enemy. It needed but a little, as she herself said, that she did not order the church plate to be melted down for the benefit of the troops.

And as money attracts money, other semi-loyal provinces now came to the rescue. Seville, Cordova and Granada of their own accord raised an army of four thousand horse and fourteen thousand infantry, and the wealthier cities of Andalusia collected large sums. The tide of luck had turned, momentarily at least, for the French troops, forced to evacuate Italy after the defeat of Turin, now arrived and drove the Austrians from Madrid, so that Court and Government were able to return there in October.

The Princess, who often, in describing soul-stirring events, finds place for charming interludes, relates how Philippe, who had returned to Madrid before them, drove out to Segovia to meet the Queen. "Their joy at meeting was inexpressible," she wrote. "The Queen ran down into the street to embrace her King, his coach being unable to enter the narrow courtyard of the house. It rained in torrents and she was wet through, but she had the joy of embracing him a moment earlier than if she had awaited him at the door, and she wished to profit by it." [1]

[1] Bossange, iii. 388; letter of 26 Oct. 1706.

THE FLIGHT TO BURGOS 197

Arrived in Madrid they were welcomed with the utmost enthusiasm by the fickle people who had acclaimed the Archduke only a few months before. "Their cries of joy, which rent the clouds, will deafen me for more than six months," the Princess wrote to Torcy.[1] The crowd in the streets was so dense that it took three hours for the Royal coaches to traverse the city. The mob pillaged the palaces of the Archduke's most prominent partisans, cast all the furniture into the streets and set fire to it, saying that they did it, not to enrich themselves, but to punish the traitors.[2]

One of the Princess's first acts was to dismiss all the ladies of the palace who had refused to accompany them into exile. They tried to excuse themselves by saying that they had intended to follow but found the roads no longer free, but she showed no mercy. She had always found them intractable and insolent and it was besides a notable economy, for the palace ladies, including their own attendants, formed an army of more than three hundred souls to feed and pay.

The Queen-Dowager with her Court of traitors was exiled beyond the frontier to Bayonne, a punishment which she attributed to the Princess, unjustly, since, in fact, she did her best to plead for her. Porto-Carrero, her companion in guilt, escaped with no punishment at all, in consideration of his former services. On their arrival in Madrid he awaited them in fear and trembling at the entrance to the palace, but was kindly greeted by both King and Queen and even by the Princess herself. As he will appear no more in our history, we may add here the few facts of the three years he had still to live. He tried to regain favour by spending vast sums on repairing the damage caused by the Portuguese in Toledo, resumed gradually his old life in Madrid, and had even the honour of baptising the first-born son of the sovereigns he had betrayed—the little Prince of the Asturias, whose birth we have now to record. He died three years later, and the Princess mentions his death to Madame de Maintenon as follows: "Poor Cardinal Porto-Carrero ended his rôle yesterday. He had conversed with his nephew, the Comte

[1] Trémoïlle, iii. 166; letter of 27 Oct. 1706.
[2] Bossange, iii. 326; letter to Madame de Maintenon of 12 Aug. 1706.

de Paluce, till midnight. Two hours later he called one of his people and went to sleep. At six o'clock his *valet-de-chambre* opened his curtains and found him dead. Although he was over eighty-one he appeared so robust that one would have given him still many years of life." [1]

He had at least a just appreciation of his own shortcomings, for he ordered to be carved on his tomb the following epitaph: HIC JACET CINIS PULVIS ET NIHIL.

[1] Bossange, iii. 332 ; letter of 15 Sept. 1709.

CHAPTER III

BIRTH OF THE PRINCE OF THE ASTURIAS (1707)

IN the midst of the war which was shaking Europe to its foundations the Princess remained courageous and optimistic. Her letters strike always the same note: "All is not lost if one has courage." "Our misfortunes are great but not without remedy." "Fortune will change in our favour."

The year 1706 had been dark for both countries. France had suffered the heavy defeat of Ramillies and been forced to evacuate Italy. Spain had lost many of her provinces, and more than half her people had gone over to the enemy. But with this new year a ray of sunshine broke momentarily through the clouds, when on 12 February the Queen's pregnancy was officially announced, a fact joyful enough in itself but particularly so at this crisis, since the prospect of an heir born in their own country, and therefore Spanish, warmed the hearts of the people and brought back their loyalty and affection.[1] Spanish custom exacted that besides the official announcement the Queen herself should offer a public thanksgiving to the Virgin of Atocha, a ceremony which is thus described by the Princess:

> The Queen was in one litter, I in another. The *dames d'honneur* were in coaches followed by the officers of the household. Down the centre of the streets, which were strewn with sand to prevent accidents, painted barriers were erected from the palace to the church and lined by officers and armed soldiers, with now and again trumpets and hautboys. All the streets were hung with beautiful tapestries, the balconies

[1] The Queen did not arrive at womanhood till 28 August, 1703; thus more than two years after her marriage. The ceremony announcing this event, which was the custom at the Spanish Court, took place on this day, and is thus described by Louville in a letter to Torcy of 28 August, 1703: " The Queen has at last had the *agréments* of her fourteen completed years. The fête on such an occasion is great in this country and it was celebrated with great brilliance. There was general hand-kissing, and Vazet (Philippe's valet) entered solemnly in the midst of all the assembled Court and cried with a loud voice: '*Messieurs! La Reyna tiene sus reglas!*' A wonderful thing is Spanish etiquette!" (Louville, ii. 107.)

covered with rich carpets of different colours as well as the windows from top to bottom. In certain places silver plates, mirrors and paintings were hung on crimson taffeta which had a most beautiful effect. Many fountains were ornamented with statues in the midst of foliage interlaced with flowers. An immense crowd sang the praises of the King and Queen. Some wept with joy and prayed that Their Majesties might have fifty children who should outlive the world. Others laughed and made very grotesque grimaces. Some, on seeing the Queen, were so transported with joy that they carried their folly so far as to cry that they loved her more than God. All the grandees surrounded Her Majesty on foot. There were some who could scarcely drag themselves along, and she in her goodness ordered them to go back, but they could not be persuaded and accompanied her even to the Chapel of the Virgin where the *Te Deum* was chanted. The King awaited her and gallantly opened the door of her litter, having preceded her in his coach with the chief officers of his household and his guards. Their Majesties returned in the same manner, and although the function lasted over four hours the Queen was not at all fatigued.[1]

The event added not a little to the Princess's work and responsibilities. It was she who had to choose doctors, wet-nurses and the *gouvernante*, to prepare the room in which the great event was to take place, and supervise the choice of the cradle and layette. In the midst of all her political duties, with the entire weight of the Government on her shoulders, and at a moment of such storm and stress, it is amazing that she found time to attend to all these details. But she accepted her new charge with the greatest cheerfulness and the care and forethought she shows in her letters of this date prove the order and method of her mind.

For example—Spanish etiquette exacted that a female, not a doctor, should assist at the lying-in, but this she would not hear of, nor indeed that any Spaniard, male or female, should be employed, being all, she declared, very incompetent. It was poor Clément of Paris, *accoucheur* to the Duchess of Burgundy, who was to be dragged across the Pyrenees at the arrival of the Prince of the Asturias— for Prince it would certainly be, she affirmed in her optimism. The room in which he was to be born must be gay and freshly decorated with hangings and furniture of pale blue silk embroidered with gold and silver. " The

[1] Bossange, iii. 399; letter to Madame de Maintenon of 14 Feb. 1707.

Queen has only two beds," she wrote to Madame de Maintenon, "one old one for the winter, white and gold and very shabby, one for the summer of plain taffeta, which I do not think a woman of the provinces with an income of ten thousand francs would keep in her room."[1] In such a bed evidently the heir to the twenty-three crowns of the Spanish Monarchy could not be born.

But the cost of a blue silk cradle and furniture embroidered with gold and silver was no less than twenty thousand crowns, and Madame de Maintenon would not hear of such extravagance. The layette, which she had commissioned the Duchesse de Beauvillier to choose, would cost more than fifty thousand—"nothing certainly for the Prince of the Asturias, but too much for the present state of affairs!" The Princess had to content herself with hanging the room "with pictures by good painters, which will decorate the walls and give an air of freshness in the summer," and a layette "of ordinary linen, but a quantity of it." As for the responsible post of *gouvernante*, since it was a position of authority offering great facilities of intercourse with the King and Queen, she jealously guarded that for herself.

But the task the most onerous was the choice of the wet-nurses and this preoccupied her entirely, for it seems it was impossible to find, except in the mountains, women free from the malady then called the pox, now by the more euphonious name of syphilis. Nearly everybody, populace as well as nobles, suffered from it, husbands infecting their wives and mothers their children, so that nearly all were born with some hereditary taint. Thus the Princess insisted that the twelve from whom her choice was to be made should be sent from the Navarre frontier, and subjected to a rigorous examination, not only of their bodies, but their private life, antecedents and surroundings, before they were sent.

On 23 May she wrote to Madame de Maintenon: "The wet-nurses will soon be arriving. It will be a goodly company and a pretty occupation to torment me, when they are brought to bed, to satisfy them and prevent their tearing each other's eyes out, and see that they eat reasonably. . . ."[2]

---

[1] Bossange, iii. 396; letter of 7 Feb. 1707.
[2] Ibid., iv. 6; letter of 23 May, 1707.

A week later she wrote again:

Eleven wet-nurses with their suite arrived yesterday at Retiro,[1] and the twelfth comes the day after to-morrow. Seven have brought their babies with them but the other five have not had theirs. I thought that too much honour could not be paid them, that the people must get accustomed to respect the creatures to be employed in nourishing a prince or princess of the best blood in the world. Besides two or three of the Queen's coaches which were sent to meet them, I sent a gentleman to compliment them officially. They made their entry through Madrid, where the people heaped blessings on them and came down to this palace through a garden where only Their Majesties pass. I went to receive them at the end of a gallery in the apartment of the Queen who was in the balcony. I embraced them all heartily and then led them to Her Majesty who deigned to come forward to meet them. It was then that all the babies they held in their arms began to make marvellous music and announce by the strength of their voices the goodness of their mothers' milk. They threw themselves on their knees to kiss the Queen's hand, some wept for joy, others were in an ecstasy, and the rest showed their delight by a thousand flattering and spontaneous words, which would certainly have touched you as much as they did me. . . . Afterwards I led them to their apartments which are surrounded by gardens. In one room they found a grand collation of which they had need. When they had finished I settled them into their rooms, which are magnificently hung and where I had caused all necessaries to be prepared, very clean and convenient. Some time after, the King and Queen wished to go there also. The nurses had fresh transports at seeing themselves at the feet of their King. Afterwards they had to sup. To accustom them to my presence I took my place at the head of the table on a very pretty straw chair, and they on the carpet after the fashion of the country. I wished to taste myself that their food was neither too highly spiced nor too greasy. I found it to my taste and profited by it to sup with them. We drank to the health of all the Royal House and the Prince about to be born. Never have I enjoyed so agreeable a meal. . . . I shall assist at their lying-in and apply myself energetically to learn everything relating to these matters so that I may be more experienced and better able to serve the Queen when her turn comes. . . .[2]

The little Prince arrived safe and sound on 25 August, " strong as a Turk with the most lovable face in the world, the most charming Prince of the Asturias that has ever been seen," the Princess wrote to the Duc de Gramont.[3]

[1] Buen Retiro, the summer palace near the city.
[2] Bossange, iv. 11 ; letter of 30 May, 1707.
[3] Trémoïlle, iv. 20 ; letter of 25 Aug. 1707.

THE PRINCE OF THE ASTURIAS

It was forty-six years since an heir had been born to the Spanish throne. The Princess showed him to the people for a moment every evening at sunset on the balcony and they were mad with joy, ran hither and thither about the town singing and shouting, and the proprietors of the booths which served for shops overturned their goods into the streets for them to scramble for. Never was birth so welcome.

The baptism took place on 8 December, the ceremony being performed in the palace chapel by the Cardinal Porto-Carrero, the Princess standing sponsor for the Duchess of Burgundy and the Duc d'Orléans for Louis XIV. The Princess describes it with great charm:

> I had the honour to hold the Prince in a litter all mirrors and gold brocade. We passed through the corridors of the palace, hung with the most beautiful tapestries the King possesses, and entered the chapel, which was entirely covered with rich carpets. Two bishops assisted the Cardinal in the function. All the grandees were there and in the procession they walked in front. As I had the honour of holding the Prince I ordered them in his name, since his *gouvernante* served as his interpreter, to put on their hats. In descending from the litter I quitted this honourable title for another still more so, for I had the honour to represent one of the greatest Princesses in the world [the Duchess of Burgundy]. I should very much have wished to compensate by the nobility of my person for the lack of beauty and youth, so as to be less unworthy to represent so beautiful a personage, and I have never before felt the grief of being old and without charm as in filling the place of so amiable a Princess. Monseigneur le Duc d'Orléans, who had luckily received the night before a very beautiful costume from Paris, was covered with admirable diamonds and lacked nothing to please all who saw him. I should have been pleased with everything if our little Prince had not had his face covered with a rash. But I was a little consoled that he cried with so loud a voice that no one could doubt as to his health.[1]

[1] Bossange, iv. 125; letter of 12 Dec. 1707.

CHAPTER IV

THE DUC D'ORLÉANS (1707)

WE must leave the little Prince in his room hung with Titians, with his twelve wet-nurses in attendance, and return to the wearisome war in the midst of which he made his entry, and it must not be imagined that during the seven months since the official announcement preparations for his advent alone had occupied the Princess. The situation was indeed so critical that it is a marvel how either she or the Queen could abstract their minds from its perils to think of cradles and diet. The Duke of Savoy, intoxicated with his triumph at Turin, had besieged Toulon to the great grief of his daughters. Spain was attacked on all her coasts and frontiers. Catalonia had severed itself completely from the rest of Spain and Naples had yielded. Revolt and civil war were rending the remainder of the monarchy. Nearly all the Spanish possessions in the Netherlands were in the hands of the enemy and Gibraltar was occupied by the English. On all sides the outlook was of the blackest, and the burden and responsibility of all was on the shoulders of the Princess.

One of her most appreciative critics, the Marquis de Courcy, writes of her work at this date:

> The domination exercised by Madame des Ursins was at the same time legitimate and beneficial. Legitimate because it was due to the incontestable superiority of her intelligence, the remarkable force of her will, the unshakable firmness of her resolution and the quite exceptional and virile cast of her character. Beneficial because in every circumstance she protected the feebleness and hesitation of the young King and masked with discretion his lamentable failures. It manifested itself in general by acts noble and bold, very rarely unpolitic, nearly always useful and fruitful; in the greater part of the important steps taken by Philippe's ministers, reforming the finances, repressing the criminal attempts of the grandees, winning for the new King his people's affection, putting a stop to ecclesiastical abuse, establishing an administration central and strong, reconstructing the military defences—in a word, laying the foundations in Spain of the Bourbon Dynasty.[1]

[1] Courcy, *L'Espagne après la Paix d'Utrecht*, p. 31.

THE DUC D'ORLÉANS

And this epoch of the birth of the little Prince, these months during which she could give her mind to the trimmings of his cradle and diet of his nurses, was the beginning of the crisis which must result in the existence or annihilation of Spain as an independent monarchy.

Louis himself, attacked on all sides, at the end of his capacity for furnishing fresh troops to protect Spanish territory all over Europe, had turned restive and desired now nothing more ardently than peace, even at the cost of losing Spain, and one of the hardest of the Princess's tasks at this time was to prevent his parcelling it out to fill the jaws of his own enemies. Even before the defeat of Ramillies he had tried to obtain terms of peace at the cost of Philippe's territory and win back the Duke of Savoy by offers of his Milanese states. He had even gone so far as to suggest to his grandson that it would be best to sacrifice all his outlying possessions and content himself with Spain and the Indies. To all which Philippe, *alias* the Princess, had replied that he would abdicate nothing, and that it would be terrible that his states should be dismembered before he had even tasted the pleasure of enjoying them.[1]

One of the most formidable of the Princess's enemies, not only because of his high rank but his lack of scruple, was Philippe d'Orléans, nephew of Louis XIV., and afterwards Regent of France. Son of Philippe, Louis' effeminate brother, and his second wife, Charlotte-Elisabeth of Bavaria, better known as "Madame" or the Princess Palatine, he combined the *ruse* and irresponsibility of the one with the brutal coarseness of the other.

He had the same or even a better claim to the throne of Spain than his cousin Philippe, and on the death of Charles II. his election had been seriously considered. As grandson of Anne of Austria, wife of Louis XIII., who was daughter of Philippe III. and sister of Philippe IV. of Spain, he was also in the direct line of succession and was besides brother-in-law to the late king, whose first wife, Marie-Louise d'Orléans, was his half-sister. Thus his claims were stronger than any other of the Bourbons, and he and his father had been bitterly disappointed that Louis had preferred Philippe d'Anjou. Two years after Philippe's accession he had moved heaven and earth

[1] Baudrillart, i. 273.

that at least his right to succeed him in default of heirs should be established, a claim which Philippe recognised and to which Louis consented.[1]

While this question of his eventual succession was pending he had asked Louis for the command of the French army in Spain, probably even then with the intention of conspiring against his cousin, but at that time Louis had prudently refused.

According to the Princess he was born under an unlucky star. His military career began with defeat at the Battle of Turin, in which he was seriously wounded and nearly lost his arm, but this disaster did not prevent him from again at this date demanding the command in Spain, and to everyone's surprise Louis now consented.

The Princess could hardly believe her ears when she heard this, not so much on account of his incompetence as his pretensions to the throne, which were notorious. She wrote at once to remonstrate, declared that it was the height of imprudence to send to a country rent by civil war a possible, if not probable, pretender to the throne—one besides, she might have added, who by his brilliant personality offered so marked a contrast to the weakling already installed there.

She mistrusted the Duke profoundly. Philippe also detested him, not so much on account of his pretensions to the throne as from motives more petty and personal. He was jealous of his handsome person, his gaiety and intelligence, and dreaded the impression he might make on the Queen. But the nomination once made, neither he nor the Princess dared oppose it further, the latter, however, reserving to herself the right to organise a system of supervision by which his least act should be reported to her, and during his visits to Madrid, on pretext of installing him royally, she ceded him part of her own apartment so that all his movements and the visits he received could be watched.

His first move justified her suspicions, for instead of coming straight to Madrid and from thence to the army,

[1] Under the date 9 November, 1703, Dangeau notes in his *Journal*: " The King of Spain has made a declaration by which the Duc d'Orléans is called to the succession to the crown of Spain in default of descendants of the Queen Thérèse, and that as a grandson of the Queen Anne, who have rights to this crown preferably to all other princes not of the House of France " (Dangeau, ix. 344).

known to be awaiting his presence for the important attack on Almanza, he lingered at Bayonne to pay his court to the Queen-Dowager which, considering the part she had recently played at Toledo, was, to say the least, indiscreet. Moreover he was received by her with such exaggerated honour, and remained so long at her Court, that people began to hint that he intended to divorce his wife, marry her and share with her the throne of Spain— a simple way certainly of putting an end to the war.

But the Princess, already on the defensive, seized the opportunity to put a first spoke in his wheel. The Duke of Berwick, acting as generalissimo till his arrival, was impatient to begin the attack, and without warning the Duc d'Orléans, she now sent him the peremptory order in the King's name to wait no longer. Berwick, irritated at the Duke's appointment, needed no encouragement and, put on his mettle, immediately obeyed, attacked the Portuguese and put them ignominiously to flight, thus obtaining one of the most brilliant successes of the war— the famous Battle of Almanza in which nine thousand prisoners were taken and few of the enemy left to carry back the news of their defeat. The booty was immense —all the cannon and provisions, over a hundred flags and a huge quantity of ammunition. So complete was the victory that Torcy claimed it to have been the turning-point in the war, and to have established Philippe on the throne of Spain.

The Duke meantime had arrived in Madrid where he remained for two days without the least suspicion that Berwick would dare begin the attack without him. The Princess said nothing, and it was only when the battle was over and the victory complete that he first heard of it. Naturally he was furious, and rightly attributing it to the Princess became from that moment her bitter enemy and, as will be seen, one of the chief instruments of her ruin.

From beginning to end of his two campaigns in Spain, the Duke would seem to have taken command of the armies with the deliberate intention to avoid fighting, probably at Louis' order with the design to force Philippe to abdicate. Now, after Berwick's victory, instead of following it up, punishing the rebels and retaking Lerida and Tortosa, which was its natural sequence, he remained absolutely inactive at the camp, and far from punishing the Spanish traitors made his first move for popularity by proclaiming a free pardon to all. Beside this, he assumed all the airs of a sovereign, levying taxes and bestowing posts and appointments without any reference to Philippe or his ministers.

Owing to his high rank the Princess could do nothing except complain to Chamillart the War Minister, but this she did with so much acrimony and insistence and also with so much justice, that he received something in the nature of a reproof, on which, furious at her interference, he on his side attacked her, accusing her and Orry of gross mismanagement in the preparations for the campaign, in the provisioning of the army and the supply of arms and ammunition. So bitter on either side did the letters become that the quarrel bid fair to be a repetition of that with the d'Estrées.

No open rupture, however, took place between them. The hostilities were carried on by letter through the Minister and their personal relations during the Duke's visits to Madrid were stiff but formally polite. They could even stand as co-sponsors before the font at the baptism of the little Prince of the Asturias without apparent hostility. His visits were however rare, for most of his time was spent at the camp trying to win the suffrages of the army. As for fighting, nothing seemed farther from his thoughts, and the attack on Lerida was postponed from week to week on various pretexts, to the ever-increasing fury of the Princess, and when at her appeal Chamillart remonstrated, he turned the tables, laid the blame of the delay on her, and declared that it was a plot to ruin him. He thus managed to let things drag on till the middle of October, when finally public opinion insisting, he attacked the town, which, as the Princess had predicted, fell with hardly any resistance.

During the eight months of the campaign this was his only action. Naturally the Princess's suspicions that he was following out a programme increased, but the Duc d'Orléans, nephew of the King, was too highly placed to be openly accused, and all she could do was to increase her army of spies in the hope that in one of his drunken orgies he might betray himself.

Another mystery! To her amazement, soon after the

capture of Lerida he announced his immediate return to France which, as Berwick had already been recalled, left the army without a chief at the moment when, with a little energy, Barcelona might have been retaken and the Archduke forced to quit the country. No remonstrances had any effect and he left Madrid in December, leaving behind him, in the minds of Philippe and the Princess at least, the conviction that he had come to Spain with quite other aims than to defeat his cousin's enemies or establish him on the throne.

CHAPTER V

SECOND CAMPAIGN OF THE DUC D'ORLÉANS (1708)

THE comparative respite of 1707 had enabled Louis to collect his forces for a fresh struggle in Flanders, while the evacuation of Italy had allowed him to send the defeated troops to the aid of his grandson with the happy result of the victory of Almanza, so that on the whole the year had not been an unlucky one for France and Spain. In the following spring Vendôme at the head of an army hardly inferior to that of the enemy retook Ghent and Bruges, so that of all the Spanish possessions in the Netherlands lost since 1706 only Oudenarde remained to be retaken. And this too might have succeeded had he not ceded to the prayers of the Duke of Burgundy and permitted him to join his cousin and assume the nominal command of the army. The Duke of Burgundy, as Saint-Simon tells us, was "impetuous, of terrible temper and outrageous obstinacy"; the Duc de Vendôme also. The result of the double command was disastrous. The Duke of Burgundy opposed his ignorance and inexperience to the military genius of his cousin, and insisted on one thing when Vendôme ordered another. Their quarrels and the consequent hesitations and indecisions caused them to miss every opportunity offered by their opponents, with the result that Oudenarde was lost after a terrible tussle on 11 July, Marlborough and Prince Eugène forcing them to retreat in disorder with the loss of over fifteen thousand men.

Meanwhile in Spain matters had dragged on without the possibility of action since the armies were without a chief. The Archduke every day received fresh reinforcements and each day's delay was a gain to him and a loss to Philippe. Worst of all as far as the Queen was concerned, her father the Duke of Savoy was attacking Toulon at the head of his own and the Emperor's troops, an event which caused her and the Duchess of Burgundy the utmost consternation and embarrassment.

In February, Madame de Maintenon in response to one

CAMPAIGN OF THE DUC D'ORLÉANS

of the Princess's letters, sparing neither reproaches nor exactions, wrote sharply: "We have to support the attacks of the Duke of Savoy who insists on invading France, of Marlborough who declares he is coming to Paris, of Prince Eugène who is on his way to Germany with immense forces. If you take all our troops, what will become of the other menaced places?"—a sharpness not at all in keeping with the usual suavity of her style.[1]

The poor young Queen in despair at her father's cruelty tried her best to awake in him some vestige of paternal sentiment, and wrote him the following letter which would have certainly moved his heart had he had a heart to move:

Why do you think, *mon cher papa*, that I am no more your friend and even that I have forgotten you? I am very offended, being as I am so far from such a thing, for I can assure you that I have always tenderly loved you. It seems to me that it is much more for me to reproach you since you are always doing your best to rob me of my crown and thus show me few signs of the tenderness you ought to have for me. How long, *mon cher papa*, do you intend to persecute your daughters and make them suffer all imaginable things? Could anything be more cruel than that one's father whom one loves should make war on one? Put an end to my unhappiness, love your child who deserves it. It rests only with you to make me the happiest Princess in the world; will you refuse me? Is your heart hard enough for that? No, my dear papa, I cannot believe it, and I hope you will let yourself be touched by a daughter who is penetrated with grief at all which is happening, who loves you truly and desires only your prosperity, which you will find if you will be our friend.

The child's artless remonstrance ends here and it is the Princess evidently who dictates the rewards he may expect in payment for a cessation of hostilities, namely the whole of the Spanish territory in Lombardy together with the title of king, which, as both she and his daughter knew, had been his ambition from his youth.

Let your answer console me [the child continues] and be a proof of your tenderness which I deserve so much, my dear father, by what I have for you. I think you will be surprised, remembering your little Louison, the name I have borne so long, to read a letter like this, but in spite of myself you make me serious. I am very serious indeed, because it seems to me I am no more permitted to call you my dear papa. Be my

[1] Bossange, i. 224; letter of 12 Feb. 1708.

dear papa, however, and let me be your Louison and let us love each other like good friends.¹

Amédée of Savoy must certainly have been what the Maréchal de Tessé called him, " a real bundle of thorns," to remain untouched by so pathetic an appeal, for not only did he leave the letter unanswered but responded by fresh attacks on the two countries.

One thing was every day growing more certain, that Louis was fully decided to abandon Spain. Reduced to the last extremity he had no other resource than to sue for peace. The dread of losing his own country made him indifferent to the fate of his grandson, and he persisted in his attempts to make him abdicate as the only means to save his own skin.

Had Philippe been alone he would certainly not have resisted, for he was as weary of the war as Louis himself, but behind his throne stood one fully determined that he never should yield, formidable by her influence over the Queen, who herself had no idea of resigning her crown and who by forbidding him her bed had it in her power to make his life intolerable.

To all Louis' persuasions, therefore, the Princess dictated refusals which Philippe obediently copied and signed, probably with a quaking heart. "I shall quit Spain only with my life. I am incapable of descending from the throne where God has deigned to place me! As long as one drop of blood remains in my veins I shall die defending my states rather than abandon them like a coward! " ²

And again, after three months of pressure and argument:

It is an outrage even to imagine that I can be forced to leave Spain as long as I have a drop of blood in my veins. Certainly that will never happen! The blood which flows in them is incapable of supporting so great a shame. I shall make every effort to maintain myself on a throne where God and you have placed me, and nothing but death shall tear me from it or make me resign it! I shall remain on the throne or quit it only with my life! ³

Noble words truly, of which no one at Versailles doubted the authorship. " His Majesty knows that the firmness

---

¹ Baudrillart, i. 308 ; letter of 31 Jan. 1708.
² Ibid., i. 321 ; letter to Louis XIV. of 6 Aug. 1708.
³ Ibid., i. 323 ; letter to Louis XIV. of 12 Nov. 1708.

CAMPAIGN OF THE DUC D'ORLÉANS 213

shown by the King in his letters is the work of the Princess," wrote Torcy later.

Amelot at her dictation dared even to remonstrate with Louis and she herself wrote to Madame de Maintenon representing the danger for France itself if the Allies were enriched by the cession of Spain; wise reasonings to which Louis was, however, too discouraged to listen. He had decided to abandon the country which had brought him nothing but disaster, and since Philippe refused to abdicate by fair means he must employ foul.

The armies were still without a chief and notwithstanding the prayers of the Princess he deferred the departure of the Duc d'Orléans from week to week, unwilling to irritate the enemy by fresh preparations for war, and it was not till the end of February that he grudgingly allowed him to return.

Who knows with what instructions he undertook the new campaign, and what secret intrigues to force Philippe to abdicate were in his orders? One thing is certain, that fighting was absent from the programme. Arrived in Madrid, he lingered there for another month, seeming to have forgotten that the army existed, eating, drinking and making merry with his friends to the despair and fury of the Princess, who retaliated by a rival intrigue and caused to be spread at Versailles the report that he remained to pay his court to the Queen his own niece, with whom he had fallen in love—a masterly stroke, since it had the effect of increasing Philippe's jealousy and enraging Louis, the Dauphin and the Duchess of Burgundy. "The scandal," writes Saint-Simon, bewailing it, "reached the provinces and all foreign countries excepting Spain, where it was not spoken of because there was no evidence of its truth." [1]

It reached the ears of Philippe, however, and was nearly the cause of an open rupture between the cousins. It is amusing to read that the Princess, without doubt the author of the scandal, in a letter to Madame de Maintenon denied its truth. "I know not for what reason such reports are invented," she wrote, "they are so vulgar and so far from the truth that they bring shame only to those who spread them. His Royal Highness has always shown the Queen the respect due to her, and which she attracts

[1] Saint-Simon, xv. 160.

by her air, as modest as it is majestic. The King is generally in her room and I also when he comes, and he speaks to Their Majesties sometimes of business, sometimes of agreeable trifles, and always with a reserve and politeness very worthy of his rank." [1]

The campaign of 1708 under the Duke's command was a repetition of that of the preceding year—the same delay in attacking, the same complaints of the lack of preparation. From the time of his arrival at the camp no action of any sort was attempted till July when Tortosa was taken, another easy victory, the benefit of which was destroyed by his again granting a free pardon to all the rebels.

But if he was idle regarding the interests of Spain he was by no means so regarding his own. At the camp before Tortosa, with no other general than his own creature the Comte de Bezons, he had every opportunity of carrying on his conspiracy. The Princess's spies reported that he was making all efforts to gain the suffrages not only of the rebels but of the enemy; that he encouraged complaints and mockery of Philippe; that he was on the friendliest terms with the English and Dutch officers and that he and Stanhope, the English general, supped and got drunk together every night in his tent. They had been friends before the war, and Stanhope one of his boon companions at his orgies in the Palais Royal, and these orgies they now revived to the immense scandal of the Spanish.

More important still, his secretary Regnault and one of his aides-de-camp Flotte,[2] whom she had suspected on account of their frequent journeys to and from the camp, had been tracked to Holland where they delivered and received dispatches.

The Duke soon became aware that he was being watched, and the feud between him and the Princess finally broke out, according to Saint-Simon reaching a climax in the famous toast when, more than half drunk, he dared publicly to offer the grossest insult to her and Madame de Maintenon.

One evening [he relates the incident], after having worked all day as usual since his arrival seeking expedients to repair the

[1] Bossange, iv. 168; letters of 19 Nov. and 17 Dec. 1708.
[2] Regnault or Renaud des Landes had acted as the Duke's secretary during the campaign of 1708. Joseph de la Flotte-la-Crau, a Provençal of good family, had been his aide-de-camp in Italy.

CAMPAIGN OF THE DUC D'ORLÉANS 215

complete neglect of even the most indispensable preparations for the campaign and make some progress, he sat down to table with many Spanish lords and the French of his suite, preoccupied with anger against Madame des Ursins, who governed everything and had thought of nothing concerning the campaign. The supper grew gay, a little too gay, and the Duke, rather the worse for wine and always absorbed in his indignation, took a glass and looking the company full in the face, exclaimed—I apologise for being so literal—" Messieurs, je bois à la santé du c—— capitaine et du c—— lieutenant! "[1]

The words struck the imagination of the guests. No one, however, not even the Prince himself, dared comment on them, but laughter seized everyone and was stronger than prudence. They drank the toast without repeating the words, and the scandal was tremendous. Half an hour after at most Madame des Ursins was told of it, and understood that she was the lieutenant and Madame de Maintenon the captain. . . .

Behold her now transported with rage and writing the incident with the exact words to Madame de Maintenon, who on her side was furious. *Inde iræ!* Never have they pardoned the Duke, and we shall see how nearly they succeeded in ruining him. All the rest of the King's life, and up to his death, he did not cease to feel what a cruel and implacable enemy he had in Madame de Maintenon, by all kinds of persecutions she excited against him.[2]

Elsewhere he adds:

The shouts of laughter were general at a joke so amusing and at the same time highly flavoured. The words ran through Madrid, and it may be judged whether the jealous Princess had not more than one spy at these suppers, and if the words so cruelly directed were not at once reported to her and the use she knew how to make of them. She sent them at once to Madame de Maintenon, and the fatal joke ruined the Prince in Spain and in France. The Princess restrained herself no longer and, the campaign ended, the Duke took leave of Spain for ever and left Madame des Ursins triumphant and more absolute than ever.[3]

It is difficult to believe that the Duc d'Orléans even drunk could publicly have offered so gross an insult to the wife of Louis XIV. and the favourite of the Queen of Spain. Saint-Simon alone is responsible for the story, yet considering his intimacy with the Duke it is probably

---
[1] The omitted word is too gross to print and impossible to translate. The words " I apologise for being so literal " are Saint-Simon's own.
[2] Saint-Simon, xvi. 161.   [3] Ibid., v. 508.

true, and it is certain that Louis' coldness towards him dates from this time.

Thus the year dragged wearily to its close. The Duke left towards the end of November, leaving Bezons in charge of the army, and returned to France where things were going worse than ever. The quarrels and indecisions of the generals in Flanders had enraged the people to the verge of a revolution. The Duke of Savoy, now general in the Austrian army, was marching at the head of forty thousand infantry and ten thousand cavalry on Dauphiné and menacing Lyons. In Spain also the outlook was of the gloomiest, and even the Princess lost her optimism. As for Madame de Maintenon, in her fear and morbid piety she even dared for the first time to blame her King. " Our King was too proud, God desires to humiliate him. France had grown too large—perhaps unjustly. He will confine it within narrower limits. Our nation was insolent and lawless. He will punish and abase it." [1]

[1] Bossange, i. 367 ; letter of 23 Dec. 1708.

CHAPTER VI

CONSPIRACY OF PHILIPPE D'ORLÉANS (1709)

THE veritable year of calamity was still to come, the fatal year when Madame de Maintenon's pessimism seemed justified, for with the New Year the fabulously cold winter of 1709 crept up and completed the ruin of France. All the rivers, even in the south, were frozen and even the sea round the coasts. The people died off like flies from cold and hunger. Sentinels were frozen to death at their posts. All public offices, theatres, factories and schools were closed. All vegetation was killed, even the olives and vines of Provence, and the terrible frost gave no respite, but lasted well on into the spring, and when finally it ceded to the summer sun, hail and floods ruined such vegetation as was spared.

Rebellion and revolt were in the air and Louis, more and more discouraged, had already in March made overtures for peace at The Hague, and renewed his efforts to persuade his grandson to abdicate, this time even employing threats. But the Princess was on the watch, and his answer was a repetition of that of the preceding year: " God has placed the crown of Spain on my head and I shall maintain it there as long as I have a drop of blood in my veins. Whatever happens, never will I sign a treaty unworthy of me. Never will I quit Spain living, and I prefer without comparison to perish disputing the ground inch by inch at the head of my troops than to take a part unworthy of me, and which would for ever tarnish the glory of our House."[1]

The Duc d'Orléans was in disgrace. Full of his conspiracy he had begged to be allowed to return to Spain, but was refused. However, his creature the Comte de Bezons was there together with Regnault and Flotte, so that the plot was continued in his absence, and the Princess, determined to bring matters to a crisis, increased her army of spies

[1] Baudrillart, i. 341 ; letter to Louis XIV. of 17 April, 1709.

and had all three carefully watched. It was soon reported to her that every night Regnault and Flotte went to the enemy's camp and were admitted to the headquarters of General Stanhope. Moreover, they were overheard making overtures among the Spanish troops in favour of the accession to the throne of the Duc d'Orléans, whom they declared had a better right than Philippe, and promising them liberal rewards if they supported his claim.

This was enough to justify their arrest, but the two rogues got wind of their danger and decided on flight. Regnault disappeared at once, and Flotte seized the opportunity of the departure of the victualling commissioner to take the spare place in his coach, Bezons, who was in the plot, giving them an escort of twenty dragoons.

But they had not gone far before two squadrons of cavalry sent by the Princess stopped the coach, sent back the escort and conducted Flotte to Madrid, where he was searched and thrown into prison. Regnault was also arrested as he attempted to cross the frontier.

Bezons made furious complaints to Philippe, declaring it was an insult to the King of France thus to arrest his servants, but without effect. The Princess held her prey and had no fear of the consequences, for the papers seized on them justified her act. Several letters to Stanhope in the Duke's own handwriting were found as well as Stanhope's replies, revealing the plot to be even worse than she had suspected. His inaction during the two campaigns was explained, for it appeared that he had offered to surrender Tortosa and Pampeluna to the English, cede to the Archduke his rights to the throne of Spain, and allow the Austrians to occupy the rest of the country on condition that he should be recognised King of Carthagena, Valentia, Navarre and Murcia.[1]

Threatened with torture, the two conspirators confessed that when arrested they were on their way to negotiate matters with General Stanhope, and, to the amazement and horror of the Princess, declared that the Duke had told them he was acting at the order of Louis XIV. himself.

Louis' first movement on learning of their arrest seemed to confirm this incredible accusation, for he wrote immediately in great anger to Amelot demanding an explanation of what he was pleased to call "the lack of consideration

[1] San Phélipe, *Mémoires*, ii. 298.

and respect due to himself" in arresting his subjects.[1] In reply to which Philippe, at the Princess's direction, wrote back revealing the whole affair and formally accusing the Duc d'Orléans, first of conspiring with his subjects to dethrone him and seize his crown, next of negotiating with the enemy to surrender to them parts of his kingdom, and third of having made use of Louis' name to give weight to the conspiracy.[2]

It is difficult to believe the Grand Monarque guilty of treachery so base towards his own grandson, but no less difficult to account for his attitude if innocent. On receipt of this letter his principal idea seems to have been to hush up the affair and the next to spare the two rogues Regnault and Flotte. Here is an extract of his answer to his grandson:

> I have received in your letters of the sixth and fourteenth of this month the explanations you sent me about the intrigues of Regnault and Flotte, for I cannot yet resolve to attribute them to my nephew. . . . Would to God it were possible to deprive our enemies of the pleasure of hearing of this unfortunate affair, but since my nephew has been capable of giving them notice of his intention, it is to be feared his confidence has gone farther. It is, however, prudent and to our common interest to act as though they were entirely ignorant of a secret which I should like to hide for ever. . . .
> My intention is to speak to my nephew. I wish to engage him to make me a sincere confession as to his projects and secret intercourse. . . . I cannot sufficiently praise your wise conduct on an occasion when scandal would be so pernicious, but so natural in your just resentment. I restrain my own anger and force myself to be silent though my name has been employed to authorise a cabal against you and your states.[3]

Later on he wrote again that he had spoken to the Duke, and was more than ever convinced of his innocence, and insisted that Philippe should hush up "a scandal which has already done only too much harm, not search more deeply into it, and prevent its being talked of any more in Spain."[4]

But the Princess was not at all disposed to hush up an affair so much to the confusion of her enemies, among

---
[1] Baudrillart, ii. 79; letter of 13 July, 1709.
[2] Ibid., ii. 79.
[3] Ibid., ii. 81; letter of 26 July, 1709.
[4] Ibid., ii. 95; letter of 5 Aug. 1709.

whom she was now inclined to include Louis himself, and she made Philippe write back with a spirit and indignation which left no doubt from whom the letter emanated.

I confess that I was very surprised [he wrote] at your letter about the conversation you have had with the Duc d'Orléans and cannot persuade myself that you found him innocent or that his words can have effaced in your mind the proofs I sent you and which seem to me more credible than all he can say, since they are founded on fact. How can he say he had no intention to harm me when, not content with collecting partisans to try to establish himself on the throne of Spain, he began by trying to make me contemptible to my subjects, and has often spoken of me before my officers in a way that scandalised them to such a point that they desired no longer to serve under him ?

As for keeping the matter secret, it is of too much importance to me to know which of my subjects are concerned in the plot for me not to try to discover the whole truth. . . . Therefore I beg you not to be surprised if I take measures to extract by force from Regnault and Flotte what cannot be extracted by gentler means.[1]

It was not often that Louis had received so sharp a refusal to obey his orders, and he must have realised disagreeably that nothing but the certainty of his own complicity could account for such audacity.

It would seem also that the menace of torture terrified him, for he wrote immediately both to Philippe and Amelot insisting that they should be interrogated by no one but himself, and ordering peremptorily that they should at once be sent to France. This order the Princess disdained to notice, and the two conspirators remained in prison for more than six years.

It will probably always remain a mystery whether in his desire for peace Louis did actually consent to the Duc d'Orléans' conspiracy against his grandson, by which his own country would have been delivered from the horrors of war. In his favour it must be stated that he was furious with the Duke and treated him with such coldness and severity that his position at Court became impossible. He forced him to resign his rights to the eventual succession to the throne of Spain which he had obtained only a few years before, and even, at the Dauphin's insistence, consented that he should be judged before the Public

[1] Baudrillart, ii. 97 ; letter of 16 Aug. 1709.

Tribunal. "Never," writes Saint-Simon, "never was clamour so universal! Never was such a din! Never such isolation as that in which the Duke found himself!"[1]

According to him it was his own wit which saved the Duke from the public ignominy of the tribunal. He relates how he found the Chancellor walking up and down the room agitated to the last degree at having to judge so great a personage. "Think of it, a Prince so near the throne! What can be done to avoid so terrible a scandal?" "Why," replied Saint-Simon, "that is easy enough. The Duke is accused of *lèse majesté*, but since the *lèse majesté* is to a foreign sovereign it can be judged only by that sovereign, and since the accused is of the King's blood it is beneath the King's dignity to surrender him." This Portia-like verdict so enchanted the Chancellor that he gathered up his robes and hurried off to tell Louis, who was probably as enchanted as himself that a way had been found to avoid publicity.[2]

The trial was countermanded, but the Duke was not at the end of his troubles. Louis remained icy, and he was completely ostracised by the whole Court. When he joined a group at one end of the room it melted away to the other, and he remained always alone. Finally, it ended in his abandoning Versailles altogether and giving himself up to his orgies in the Palais Royal with his *roués* and *filles-de-l'opéra*. His mother, the Princess Palatine, attributed his disgrace entirely to the Princess, "this incarnate devil" as she calls her, and accused her of hating him only because he "found her too old to wish to be her lover."[3]

Thus did she mow down another enemy. It was her hour of vengeance. Alas! the Duke's was not far distant.

[1] Saint-Simon, xviii. 71. [2] Ibid., xviii. 78.
[3] Brunet, *Nouvelles Lettres de la Duchesse d'Orléans* (Paris, 1853), 184.

CHAPTER VII

DICTATRESS OF SPAIN (1709)

NOTWITHSTANDING the wretched state of affairs, the year 1709, so fatal to France and Spain, must be reckoned as the culminating point in the life of the Princess, for not only did she at this supreme crisis push her puppets into the background and openly assume the reins of government, but held in respect as one of themselves all the crowned heads of Europe. Her opponents were no longer cardinals and ambassadors, but their masters. The Duc d'Orléans was ostracised at her bidding, Louis dared not resent her insolence, and Madame de Maintenon quailed before her letters à feu et à sang.

In April of this year so full of incident, she asserted her authority by an act so flagrant in its open defiance as to put the final touch to the separation of the two countries.

All Spain knew that Louis had decided to abandon his grandson, withdraw his troops and sign an ignoble peace to the ruin of the country, consenting to its dismemberment and partition to the enemy to save his own. Naturally their hatred of the French increased to ferocity. All the blood of the hidalgos boiled in their veins. Never, they swore, should their country be thus disposed of by a foreigner, be divided piecemeal and thrown to stop the jaws of England and Holland from devouring France. The grandees raged and fumed when they passed a Frenchman in the palace, and in the streets the people could with difficulty be restrained from assassinating them and sacking their houses.

What such hatred meant in a people so vindictive and hot-blooded was not hard to foresee. There was but one way to save the situation, and that way the Princess took with her usual promptitude. Before the people had time to mass together for the revolution she judged inevitable, she forced Philippe to sign a proclamation dismissing every Frenchman who held office from his post and putting Council and Government entirely in the hands of the Spanish. No Frenchman except Amelot was to be admitted to the Despacho or allowed any authority in the State. Spain was at last to be ruled by the Spanish—she omitted to add, under the Princess des Ursins.

The Spanish were enchanted, but Louis was furious, and wrote to Amelot to know what was her share in the act. To which that wily Ambassador, more devoted to her interests than his, replied that she had had nothing whatever to do with it, the proof being that it rendered her own position as a Frenchwoman holding office so disagreeable that she felt bound to offer her resignation.[1]

As though to point the insult to France she now called to the Ministry of Foreign Affairs—the most important at this epoch in the Government—one of the bitterest opponents of the Bourbon succession, the Duc de Medina-Cœli, former Prime Minister under Charles II., and disgraced at Philippe's accession, a Nationalist and a great favourite with the Spanish.

The effect of this master-stroke was phenomenal. The War of Succession was in great part a civil war, rendered possible only by the ill-will of the Nationalists. Thus the Archduke had had little difficulty in entering and appropriating the principal cities, which preferred his rule to that of France, and the policy of the d'Estrées, Louville and Gramont in giving all the important posts in Government and Court to the French had driven even Philippe's adherents to his side. But already they were learning that his rule brought neither peace nor prosperity. The Archduke himself was unpopular and his army detested, composed as it was chiefly of Puritans, English and Dutch, who outraged their religious sentiments by committing all sorts of sacrilege. Many of the rebels had seized the occasion of the birth of an heir to return to their allegiance, and many more only awaited an opportunity. This by her *coup d'état* the Princess had furnished, and the expulsion of the French from authority in the State brought back nearly all the nobles to their King and most of the rebels needed but little persuasion to lay down their arms and swear fidelity. It is claimed that the victories of Almanza and Villaviciosa (to be spoken of later) were the turning-points in the establishment of Philippe on the throne. My own studies have led me to the conclusion that it was due to this master-stroke of the Princess.

[1] Trémoïlle, v. 12; letter to Louis XIV. of 30 April, 1709.

And, to set a seal on their allegiance, before the general enthusiasm had time to cool, she now arranged that the important ceremony of swearing fealty to the heir to the throne should take place, in spite of his sixteen months. The function, which she describes with great charm, took place in the chapel of the Retiro.

Joy shone in the faces of those who came to accept him as successor to the King his father [she wrote to Madame de Maintenon]. Cardinal Porto-Carrero officiated at High Mass. The Patriarch [of the Indies] confirmed the Prince, and the Cardinal had the honour to act as his godfather, at which he was transported with joy. . . . Never ceremony took place with more majesty, better order or more magnificence. Our pretty Prince gave his hand to be kissed of his own accord to all who knelt before him, and as it lasted nearly three hours and the wish to sleep and feed came over him he began to cry, unable any longer to support so great a fatigue. His nurse was sent for, and although very occupied with her breast, he did not cease to put out his hand to be kissed, so that everyone was charmed with him.[1]

But though by her *coup d'état* the Princess had saved Spain to the Bourbons, she had ruined herself and Philippe in the eyes of their chief. Since his grandson permitted so flagrant an insult to France he must be treated, if not as an enemy at least as a stranger, and at all costs forced to abdicate.

Philippe, absorbed in his dream of love—or sensuality, probably thought little and cared less whether his ministers were French or Spanish. His name in general, and especially during this year of action, stands for that of the Princess, whose authority was now absolute, his only act of sovereignty being to affix his signature to her decrees.

The rupture between the two monarchs was complete. Louis was ready to sign away the whole of his grandson's possessions to obtain peace for France, and the Princess, aware that no more help was to be had from him, began also on her side to work for a separate peace for Spain.

Philippe had as Superintendent of Finance in the Netherlands a certain Don Juan de Boeckhove, Comte de Bergeyck, whom Louis had also employed in his negotiations for peace. Him now at her dictation Philippe ordered to make overtures to England and Holland for a separate peace with Spain. He was also to try to persuade his

[1] Bossange, iv. 250; letter of 8 April, 1709.

Flemish subjects, on the ground that the rupture with France was complete, to return to their allegiance, and finally to propose to the Archduke that, if he consented to renounce his claim on Spain and the Indies, Philippe would cede to him all his Italian states including Naples and Sicily. And he received the strictest orders to let neither Louis nor his ministers know anything whatever of the matter.[1]

And by a curious coincidence, precisely at the same time Louis himself dispatched Torcy to The Hague with offers of all Philippe's possessions, including Spain and the Indies, if the Allies would agree to peace and allow him to retain the kingdom of Naples and Sicily, and offering on his own part all his Flemish states and the cession of Strasbourg.

Both negotiations failed. To these magnificent offers the Allies now turned a deaf ear, for Marlborough and Prince Eugène were profiting too much by the war to put an end to it, and they continued to exact that Philippe should hand over Spain with all its dependencies to the Archduke, and Louis Strasbourg and his Flemish states, merely as a preliminary to negotiations and to obtain an armistice of two months, at the end of which, if these conditions were not fulfilled, they would recommence the war, and they added insultingly that if Louis desired a guarantee of peace, he had only to send his troops and himself force his grandson to abdicate.[2] This last clause was too much for Louis' pride, and he haughtily refused further negotiations.

However, it did not alter his decision to withdraw his troops from Spain, for he had no longer any interest in supporting a grandson so rebellious. Moreover his people began to show their teeth. The terrible winter had left its mark. Famine was decimating the army. The plague, which was ravaging Italy, was now threatening France. The losses in Flanders had discouraged the most optimistic, and in their misery they grew menacing. Louis, once their idol, was now the cause of their woes with his mania for conquest, his gardens and palaces which engulfed their money, his banquets and costly hunts and his incessant

[1] Baudrillart, i. 350; letter of Philippe V. to Bergeyck of 15 Sept. 1709.
[2] Ibid., i. 363; letter of Louis XIV. to Amelot of 3 June, 1709.

journeys between Versailles, Marly and Fontainebleau, dragging after him an entire household at their expense. The street-singers abused and insulted him even at the gates of Versailles. Madame de Maintenon, never popular, was accused of buying up the corn and selling it at treble the cost for her own profit. She was ridiculed and menaced to such a point that she was afraid to leave the palace for fear of being stoned. "They complain of everything the King does!" she wrote to the Duc de Noailles. "His journeys to Marly are the cause of the ruin of the State. They want him to renounce his horses, his dogs, his valets. They attack his furniture. In a word, they want to begin by despoiling him the first. And yet he has retrenched on his food at Marly. He has sent his gold plate to the Mint and pawned his jewels. I was among the first to send my plate to be melted down, and if it were only a matter of eating off porcelain, we should be quit for very little." [1]

The famous "Pater" of this year is sufficiently eloquent of the popular attitude—

> Notre Père qui êtes à Versailles
> Votre nom n'est plus glorifié,
> Votre royaume n'est plus si grand.
Votre volonté n'est plus faite ni sur terre ni sur l'onde.
Donnez-nous notre pain qui nous manque de tous côtés,
Pardonnez à nos ennemies qui nous ont battus et non à nos
> généraux qui les ont laissés faire,
Ne succombez pas à toutes les tentations de la Maintenon mais
> délivrez-nous de Chamillart. Amen.

And Philippe too, sick of the war, was more than ready to yield and required incessant propping up and setting on his legs. He was sick of struggle and action, sick of being a soldier when he cared only to be a lover, sick of a throne so hard and a crown so heavy. But the Queen and Princess were sick of neither, and seeing him ready to give in to his grandfather's importunities took matters into their own hands with a vigour which left him no choice. "What, Sire!" the Princess is reported to have cried, forgetting etiquette in her wrath. "Are you a prince! Are you a man! You who give so little importance to sovereignty, and whose sentiments are weaker than a woman's." [2] And

---

[1] Collin, *Lettres de Madame de Maintenon,* iv. 165 ; letter of 9 June, 1709.

[2] Combes, 299; cited from *L'Histoire secrète de la Cour de Madrid.*

the Queen had it always in her power to enforce obedience and obtain his signature by refusing him her bed.

The weekly correspondence between the Princess and Madame de Maintenon, now open antagonists, had grown more strained since the former became aware of Louis' decision to abandon Spain, and after the discovery of his treachery in the Regnault affair, of which she at least had no doubt, open war between them was declared. Madame de Maintenon, acting always as buffer between her and Louis and certainly at his orders, warded off her adversary's attacks by feigning complete ignorance. To the Princess's reproaches for Louis' abandonment she opposed God's abandonment of France; to her demands for troops and money, the misery and poverty of France, the terrible winter, famine and pestilence, the people dying of hunger, the army fed on rye and the officers on black bread, her King pawning the crown jewels and retrenching on his food; and the Princess, goaded to fury by the opposition underlying all these lamentations, responded by irony, mockery, incredible insolence and audacity.

She refused to believe in the rye and black bread, refused to believe that France was sunk so deep in misery. Madame de Maintenon had cried wolf too often, and she had not forgotten similar wails of poverty while Louis was furnishing six thousand men and the necessary funds for the Pretender's raid on Dunkirk.

In May the Spanish had an important victory over the Portuguese, four thousand killed and many prisoners, which she joyfully announced. But her triumph met with no response; on the contrary, for every victory increased Louis' difficulty in dragging his grandson off his throne.

This reticence enraged the Princess, divining the cause. "You will perhaps be sorry for our victory," she wrote ironically, "fearing that it may confirm the King in his desire to defend himself at any price and thus embarrass the peace you desire so much."[1]

"I confess," Madame de Maintenon had once the imprudence to declare—"I confess that my fears had never before reached the point of foreseeing that we should be reduced to wishing that the King and Queen of Spain were dethroned."[2]

[1] Bossange, iv. 272; letter of 3 June, 1709.
[2] Ibid., i. 430; letter of 24 June, 1709.

Memorable words, never to be forgotten nor forgiven, thrown in her teeth perpetually and as often denied. " Is it possible that I wrote that I wished the crown of their Catholic Majesties to be torn from their heads—I, who would give anything to have it assured!" And again: "Why do you accuse me of wishing that Their Majesties were dethroned? I am very far from such sentiments."[1]

And yet the letter exists.

In June she announced the failure of the peace negotiations and menaced Louis' withdrawal of his troops from Spain, a threat which was fulfilled the same month by the recall of Bezons the traitor, now promoted Marshal of France.

Had the troops departed at this critical moment it is probable that the enemy, taking advantage of the exposed frontiers, would have concentrated all their forces and overwhelmed the country, which Louis had perhaps intended in order to free his own invaded states. Luckily an army is not so quickly transported and meanwhile the Princess still held a trump-card, which she now produced.

The Queen was again *enceinte* and expecting her child in August. Clément and Madame de la Salle the *accoucheuse* had again crossed the Pyrenees to assist at her confinement, and this circumstance she now made use of to move the hearts, if not of Louis and Madame de Maintenon, at least those of the Dauphin and Duchess of Burgundy. Before Bezons and his army had time to finish the preparations for their departure, the Queen, in a pathetic letter, implored her grandfather not to remove his troops at a moment so critical, thus leaving her and her unborn child at the mercy of the enemy or to die of the hardships of another flight, since, his help withdrawn, the Archduke would certainly march on Madrid. "What would become of me and my children?" she cried piteously. "Would it not be the cause of our death? And could you make me run so great a risk when it depends only on you to prevent it?"[2]

That Louis himself, indifferent as he was to the sufferings of others, was touched by this letter is doubtful, and the concession which followed was probably due to the intervention of the Dauphin and cajoleries of the Duchess of Burgundy. In any case, it had the desired effect and he

[1] Bossange, i. 441 and 448; letters of 21 July and 10 Aug. 1709.
[2] Baudrillart, i. 359; letter of 17 June, 1709.

DICTATRESS OF SPAIN

immediately countermanded his order to Bezons and told him to remain till further orders.

But though he had yielded on this point, it gave him the right to continue his insistence on Philippe's abdication. He wrote to Amelot that he must make him understand that the concession was temporary only, that the troops would remain only for a month or six weeks at the utmost, "to give him time to provide for his safety." In plain language, it was an ultimatum that if in six weeks' time he had not resigned his crown he would be left to the mercy of the enemy.

But in less than six weeks the child was born, for the Queen's anxieties had precipitated events, and she was prematurely delivered on 2 July. It was another son, but deformed, and fortunately died a week later. "This little angel departed to heaven a little before midday!" the Princess announced to Madame de Maintenon on 9 July in a brief cessation of hostilities.[1]

The lull was of very short duration and immediately after the duel recommenced with more acrimony than ever. "I cannot pardon you your wish that Their Catholic Majesties should be dethroned!" the Princess reiterated. "You have a hundred needs without that and you might instead, it seems to me, pray God that they might keep their crown, in spite of the complete abandonment in which the King considers himself obliged to leave his grandson." And giving her to understand that if she was expected to counsel him to abdicate they were very much mistaken in her intentions, for that she would rather die than do so, she ends by announcing her decision to resign her post and retire from Spain.[2]

[1] According to Dangeau the child's face and body were deformed and he had no nails (Dangeau, xii. 470).
[2] Bossange, iv. 301 ; letter of 18 July, 1709.

CHAPTER VIII

INTRIGUES TO FORCE THE PRINCESS TO RETIRE (1709)

THERE are many riddles in the life of the Princess, and one of the most difficult is whether in her threats of resigning her post which recur after every friction with Versailles, she was sincere or merely playing a part in order to strengthen her position. Her enemies and most of her biographers accept the latter. My own opinion is that they were genuine, the result of depression and discouragement very comprehensible when all the circumstances are considered, Her life in Spain was a perpetual struggle and sacrifice, ill repaid by everyone except the Queen, terribly fatiguing and with no compensating advantages except the satisfaction of her mania for domination. One is too apt, in dealing with an epoch of intrigue and the woman whom Saint-Simon has dubbed its high priestess, to suspect her good faith in every matter great and small, but on the whole she has shown herself on the contrary too frank and courageous in speaking her mind, being perhaps too disdainful of humanity to lie.

In any case, at the present moment her threat was displeasing to no one at Versailles, for Louis' one hope of peace lay precisely in her voluntary resignation. His chief desire now was that Philippe should descend quietly from his throne and retire as kinglet of Sicily or Sardinia, far enough from Versailles to be spared his reproaches. Nothing prevented this but the presence of the Princess. Therefore at her menace to resign her post he replied with cold indifference that she must do as she thought best for the good of the country.

Dismiss her he dared not after his last experience and the stormy attacks of the Queen, and his own domestic peace also was at stake. The Dauphin, who had bitterly resented the Duc d'Orléans' plot for his son's dethronement, and the Duchess of Burgundy whom he adored, were both enthusiastic in her praise, and indeed his honour would have suffered everywhere at such an act of injustice to the woman who was so ably defending his grandson's throne.

INTRIGUES AGAINST THE PRINCESS 231

Amelot, who had been expelled from office as the result of the Princess's *coup d'état*, had been allowed to remain in Madrid at the earnest entreaties of Philippe and the Queen, but now in his anger Louis recalled him and refused any longer to have an embassy at a Court whence his subjects had been so ignominiously expelled. Some form of representation was necessary, however, and Blécourt, who had experience of the country, was sent without any official title. The following instructions he received on his departure show that as early as the middle of July the Princess's departure was taken for granted.

The King desires that you live in the strictest union with the Princess des Ursins during the time she may still remain in Spain. There is reason to think that before long she will judge it suitable to depart, and let it be seen by this retreat that the King and Queen of Spain will really receive no other counsel than that of the Spaniards.[1]

But if the Princess was willing to resign her post voluntarily, the idea that pressure was put upon her would have irritated her pride and made her wish to remain. Louis, aware of this and preferring intrigue to force, employed, as it would seem, the Comte de Bergeyck, already mentioned as representing Philippe in the peace negotiations, to bring about the desired departure.

Bergeyck was devoted to his King, and though Flemish by birth (his mother was the widow of Rubens the painter), sincerely anxious for the welfare of the country, and as he considered the Princess's influence fatal to both, had willingly undertaken the commission.[2] In any case, whether he acted as Louis' instrument or from genuine disapproval of her influence in Spain, he did his best, first to persuade and, since that failed, to force her to leave.

He began his attacks by informing her in his capacity

---

[1] Trémoïlle, v. 28.

[2] Judgments as to Bergeyck's character differ. Saint Simon loads him with praise as the *protégé* of the Duc d'Orléans : " A man infinitely modest, equitable and disinterested, the truest of men, boldest in speaking the truth, loving and seeking good for its own sake, and most attached to his master's interests" (Saint-Simon, xxiv. 247). Fenélon, on the other hand, who, as Archbishop of Cambrai, had many opportunities of observing him during the negotiations, accuses him of treachery, intelligence with the enemy, of encouraging the war and obstructing peace (Saint Simon, xx. 302, note 7).

of plenipotentiary at The Hague that the allies refused absolutely to enter into any negotiations or even to believe that the separation between the two countries was genuine as long as she, the agent of France, remained in Spain, and suggested that she immediately leave the country since her presence was fatal to the interests of the King. He added that Louis and his ministers were of the same opinion and if she did not resign her post at once and quit Spain, even against the will of the King and Queen, she would incur universal reprobation.

Not content with this attack, he wrote at the same time to Philippe urging that it was decisive to his interests and that of his country that she should leave, since the enemy would always think Spain was governed by France as long as she remained. "This is the opinion of His Majesty, of all the ministers and persons of distinction at this Court," he repeated as emphatically as he had done to the Princess.[1]

This employment of Louis' name, which he would certainly not have dared without authorisation, appeared to the Princess like an official order, and she immediately wrote to Madame de Maintenon that she had in consequence resigned her posts, that of Camarera Mayor and *gouvernante* to the little Prince, and at the same time directed Amelot to announce her departure to the King.[2]

However, though she herself seems to have been ready enough to leave, the Queen was so desperate at the idea, and she and Philippe put such pressure upon her to remain, that she hesitated, and instead of quitting the country decided to retire to the Royal palace of Aranjuez, fifty kilometres from Madrid, and await the course of events.

But Bergeyck—or Versailles—was not satisfied with this pseudo-retreat, and he renewed his attacks with greater insistence. "His Majesty, his ministers and all those devoted to him think as I do," he reiterated; "thus you will be blamed by everyone if you defer your departure. You know well enough that everything is attributed to you."[3]

Matters had reached this point when an incident occurred which brought the rupture so long brewing between her and

[1] Bossange, iv. 339; letter of 12 Aug. 1709.
[2] Trémoïlle, v. 36; letter of 26 Aug. 1709.
[3] Bossange, iv. 338; letter of 31 Aug. 1709.

Versailles to a climax, and suspended for a time all talk of her departure.

The small army which Louis had consented to leave in Spain at the Queen's prayer was still under Bezon's command, the Spanish troops under that of the Comte d'Aguilar, a Spaniard with the interests of Spain if not of Philippe at heart. The two generals as well as their armies were at daggers drawn. "Never," writes San Phélipe, "was an army so disunited, everyone, from the two chiefs down to the last soldier, wanting the other to lose."

Generals and armies remained as usual inactive except for their quarrels. They were lodged in a fortress on one side of the River Ségré, the enemy on the other, an easy prey which they had only to cross the river to capture, since they were more numerous and better equipped. D'Aguilar, impatient at Bezon's inaction, put all possible pressure upon him to attack, and finally, enraged beyond endurance, wrote to Philippe to send a formal order. In spite of this Bezons continued to refuse. A second time a more peremptory order was sent, but Louis not Philippe was Bezons' master, and it would seem that his was on no account to attack. Presently the enemy, either in collusion with Bezons or concluding them to be weaker than they were, took the initiative, crossed the river suddenly and attacked them, whereupon Bezons, without even a pretence at defence, abandoned his fortress, took to his heels and fled with all his troops behind him. This was the famous —or infamous—battle of Fort Balaguer, in which three battalions of French were taken prisoners by an army of less than half their number.

It was the second act in the intrigue to force Philippe to abandon his throne and prove at the same time to the enemy the separation of the two countries. That in acting as he did Bezons had obeyed orders is proved by the fact that, far from being disgraced or even rebuked, on his return to France he was treated with the utmost benevolence, and that, notwithstanding Philippe's complaints to his grandfather, Louis maintained an absolute silence on the matter.

The Princess, certain now of his complicity in the Duc d'Orléans' plot, poured out her wrath in a letter to Madame de Maintenon, so insolent in its open attack on Louis himself as to be nothing less than a declaration of war. Here are some of its most scathing, if somewhat involved, phrases:

> If the Maréchal de Bezons has merely obeyed the King in acting as he has done, it is impossible nevertheless to attribute it to His Majesty without lacking in the respect due to him, to believe that a soul so generous has been capable of tarnishing his glory by an action which will be detested by all honest men. Therefore Their Catholic Majesties throw it entirely on his general, being unable to imagine that the King his Master ordered him to commit an act so cowardly. If the King desires to ruin his grandson entirely, at no matter what cost to himself and the French who have just dishonoured themselves, there is nothing to be said, but if on the contrary he does not wish to contribute to his ruin, as long as he leaves his troops in Spain at His Catholic Majesty's expense, they ought, without seeking to fight, at least to prevent the enemy from advancing and crossing rivers, when we are so much stronger in every way. It is a hundred to one that we should have gained a complete victory, that the Archduke would have been ruined and forced to quit Catalonia, that Portugal would have sued for peace, that everything would have changed, and that before the winter was over the war would have entirely ended, advantageously for France and leaving the King of Spain on his throne. . . . Everyone is astonished that Monsieur de Bezons has been afraid of offending the enemy by fighting when they sought it. . . . It is difficult to understand why the enemy should always be spared.

And she ends by announcing that Philippe is departing next day for the scene of disaster, leaving the Queen Regent, and that both have commanded her absolutely not to depart, so that in spite of her resolution she is forced to obey.[1]

To which Madame de Maintenon replied as follows:

" I have received your letter *à feu et à sang* and flew at once to Monsieur Voisin " (Minister of War who had replaced Chamillart) " to know what orders had been given to Bezons. He said that they were what was always given to the generals, that he was to do his best and not commit himself inopportunely." And she ends, not without menace: " We have reason to think that we bring you bad luck. Perhaps you will do better when you are without us." [2]

By the same post which brought to Madame de

---

[1] Geffroy, 370 ; letter of 1 Sept. 1709.
[2] Bossange, i. 461 ; letter of 14 Sept. 1709.

Maintenon the Princess's letter à feu et à sang, Louis received the following news from Blécourt:

"The Queen will remain governor during the King's absence and Madame des Ursins, under these circumstances, has not been able to refuse their Majesties to remain for some time longer with the Queen."[1]

But at such a time the Allies were not to be trifled with, and though she consented to remain she thought it prudent to adopt the somewhat ostrich-like method of retiring from public view. The Queen was for the third time appointed Regent and the Princess appeared no more before the scenes. On 9 September she wrote to the Duc de Noailles:

I have taken a part which I know you will approve. It is to shut my doors to everybody in general, without excepting anyone, even my friends, of whatever nation they may be, so that I may not be suspected of interfering in anything. It is only on this condition, if it is permitted to make conditions with a great King and Queen, that I have agreed to remain at their Court. I shall enjoy some rest, and in truth I am very tired of tormenting myself and being tormented by others.[2]

And on the same day she wrote to the Maréchale his mother:

Their Majesties having absolutely insisted that I remain here, I have decided to do so, provided that I hear no more of affairs, and may shut my doors to the world in general. . . . I have already begun to isolate myself in this solitude, which is the only way I can live in peace. I see Monsieur de Blécourt no more than my other friends, Italian, Flemish or Spanish, in order to treat everyone alike. Some are very angry, but they have to be patient, for I shall hold to my resolution or leave Spain.[3]

But this pretended retirement from public affairs was scarcely a blind to those acquainted with the Court of Madrid. According to the Princess all the burden of the State rested on the shoulders of the Queen, and she took the pains, even to Madame de Maintenon, who knew well enough who pulled the wires, to describe her days as spent in drudgery for the public welfare:

She rises at six. After having prayed and written to the King she goes to see the Prince and returns to breakfast at eight. At

[1] Trémoïlle, v. 36; letter of 1 Sept. 1709.
[2] Ibid., v. 38; letter of 9 Sept. 1709.
[3] Geffroy, 377; letter of 9 Sept. 1709.

this hour the couriers arrive and the two secretaries of the Despacho bring the letters. Her Majesty confers with them and orders that they be sent to the different ministers. Afterwards she dresses quickly, and while her hair is being done reads the dispatches. She hears mass, often High Mass, and goes to hold the Despacho which lasts generally till midday. When dinner is announced, if there are people who demand an audience, which she never refuses, before seating herself she hears them patiently and replies very graciously according to their merit and birth. Dinner does not last half an hour. I have the honour to serve her. Afterwards she returns to her apartment, where Don Joseph Grimaldo and Don Manuel Badillo, secretaries of the Despacho, bring her an infinity of affairs to examine. She decides a part of these and reserves the rest for consultation with the ministers. The Quarante-Heures are said in the chapel close to her room and she never misses assisting at them nor at Vespers. At five o'clock she makes a very slight repast, and twice a week, when it is over, the ladies come to pay their court, on Tuesday all those who have the *entrée* to the palace, and on Friday Her Majesty receives only those who distinguished themselves by their zeal in coming to Burgos. They remain about an hour and a half. If it is fine the Queen descends with the Prince to the terrace. He retires to supper at a quarter- or half-past seven when the Queen goes to take hers, and again gives audience to whoever desires. . . . After ten o'clock she retires to her cabinet to read her books of devotion, then says her prayers and goes to bed. . . . Such, Madame [she concludes], are the occupations of a Princess not yet twenty-one, born for the pleasures of life.[1]

If she imagined that her pseudo-retreat would put a stop to the intrigues of Versailles she soon discovered her mistake, for not only Bergeyck but Madame de Maintenon herself continued the attacks to force her to resign, the former with greater insistence, the latter by a series of hints and innuendoes very galling to a proud nature. Thus, she takes it for granted that she remains only during Philippe's absence, and that at his return she will leave the country, and betrays a keen anxiety to know the place of her retreat. She refuses to let her know anything of what goes on at Versailles, declaring that since the Princess has retired from affairs she herself takes no more interest in those of Spain, and attacks her with want of patriotism and forgetting in her zeal for the King and Queen that she is born French.

More and more irritated, the Princess threw aside every semblance of respect and replied with brutal insolence.

[1] Bossange, iv. 322, etc. ; letter of 8 Sept. 1709.

INTRIGUES AGAINST THE PRINCESS 237

In her anger at Louis' treachery she seems to have lost sight of the tragedies going on in his own country. Towards the end of June Tournai had been besieged by the Allies and had held out gallantly for over two months. Now on 3 September it had been forced to capitulate, the prelude to a much worse misfortune, for a week later (11 September) Marlborough and Prince Eugène attacked Malplaquet and defeated Villars in the most desperately contested battle of the war with a loss of twelve thousand men. It is true that the Allies lost themselves twenty thousand, so that Villars in announcing the defeat to Louis wrote: " If God gives us another defeat like this, all our enemies will be destroyed," but it was, nevertheless, a cruel blow to his prestige and pride.

But the Princess, brooding over her own wrongs, had little sympathy for his misfortunes, and responded to Madame de Maintenon's lamentation over the fall of Tournai by harsh recriminations.

" Since you always demand peace on your knees and accept any conditions," she wrote, "why expose the lives of good subjects by sending them to be killed uselessly? Monsieur de Bezons did better to fly before the enemy, that is to say, if he prefers life without honour. It seems to me to matter little if Tournai holds out more or less since peace will be made in any case." [1]

And again:

The King has returned without having been able to drive the enemy out of Balaguer, where Bezons had the kindness to admit them, though much superior to them and without having, so you say, other orders than those usually given to the generals—not to risk his troops uselessly. . . . You do not openly side with our enemies and make war on us because it would be too monstrous and would for ever tarnish the King's glory, but another way no less damaging is to keep at the King of Spain's expense thirty-seven battalions which complete his ruin, ravage his provinces, and of which he reaps no other benefit than to fly before the enemy. . . . You will be well caught if, in spite of all your efforts to ruin Spain, it will be preserved to Philippe V.[2]

It would be interesting to know the comments of Louis and Madame de Maintenon on receipt of these audacious

---
[1] Bossange, iv. 329 ; letter of 15 Sept. 1709.
[2] Ibid., iv. 344 ; letter of 6 Oct. 1709.

letters, the immediate result of which was a fresh insistence on her departure. Philippe was on the point of returning to Madrid, and the Queen had recovered from her confinement. There was, therefore, no further reason that she should remain, and Bergeyck, this time certainly at Louis' order, recommenced his attacks.

Weary of struggling against injustice and intrigue she would seem at this date to have sincerely decided to quit the game and abandon her post, but the Queen, in despair at the idea of losing her, once more took up the cudgels in her defence and wrote one of her vehement letters to Madame de Maintenon imploring her intercession with Louis to forbid her departure. What Madame de Maintenon replied is not forthcoming but, pursuing her tactics of ignorance, she wrote to the Princess as though it was the first time she had heard of her intention. "I have been horrified to see in a letter with which the Queen of Spain has honoured me that there is talk of your departure. I do not know why she tells me to beg you urgently to remain with her since it seems to me you are entirely your own mistress, and would not be so cruel as to leave her if you did not judge it to be necessary for her own interest."[1]

To which the Princess replied angrily that if, as Bergeyck insisted, Louis desired her to leave Spain, it would be better that he should send her the order himself so that she might be able to show it when she should be reproached for having abandoned the Queen in her misfortune.

But any kind of official dismissal being precisely what Louis wished to avoid, Madame de Maintenon as his intermediary continued to reply vaguely, and taking her departure as a matter of course, again demanded what she intended to do after quitting Spain.

You wish to know my plans [the Princess retorted]. Here they are! The situation in which I leave Their Catholic Majesties allows me little hope that they can hold out against so many enemies which include the King himself. Therefore I wish to remain as near the Queen as possible, and having crossed the Pyrenees shall remain in some town near, probably Pau, where I can have news of her. This is the project which has excited your curiosity. I am making others for the remainder of my life which I keep to myself, and which consequently you will not know.[2]

---

[1] Bossange, i. 456; letters of 8 and 9 Sept. 1709.
[2] Ibid., iv. 349; letter of 14 Oct. 1709.

INTRIGUES AGAINST THE PRINCESS

This mysterious allusion excited the curiosity of Versailles to the keenest point and Madame de Maintenon, doubtless interested on her own account from personal rather than political reasons, immediately wrote to Villeroy, as an old friend and confidant of the Princess, to ask his help in explaining the enigma. "I know not why she has not told us this project for the remainder of her life," she wrote, tortured probably with the fear that she intended to make Paris her home.

Subsequent documents have revealed the mystery. Disgusted at the treatment she had received, tired of Louis' injustice and foreseeing (what actually happened) that one day she would be forced to abandon her post, she was secretly preparing herself a retreat which should be at least compatible with her dignity, neither exile to Rome nor obscurity in Paris, but an independent Principality with all the rights and treatment of a reigning sovereign.

This sovereignty at the Queen's demand Philippe had promised her out of the wreckage of his Flemish possessions, and the deed of gift was already prepared and awaited only the close of the negotiations for peace to be signed and guaranteed. Such independent sovereignties were not uncommon in France at that date. For instance, the Duchesse de Montpensier, better known as "la Grande Mademoiselle," was sovereign of the Principality of Dombes which she left in legacy to Louis' bastard the Duc du Maine, and outside Royalty the Duc de Gramont was independent Sovereign of Bidache near Bayonne. To her it seemed a reward not at all disproportionate to the services she had rendered and, considering her rank, no undue assumption, but she considered it more prudent for the moment to keep it secret till it was more assured.

Madame de Maintenon has been severely criticised by the Princess's admirers for her hostility towards her from the date of her return to Spain and especially at the time of her disgrace. Yet logically her attitude cannot be disapproved. She was from convictions, practical as well as religious, a pacifist. She detested and disapproved of war as a crime against humanity and above all against the Deity who was her unique adoration, in comparison with whom even her King was insignificant. Thus when the Princess des Ursins proclaimed herself, on her assumption of the dictatorship of Spain, as a kind of Bellona, thinking or caring nothing of the misery entailed by the wars she fomented, she would have been untrue to her convictions had she not expelled her former *protégée* from her intimacy and protection. It is no wonder that she grew ever more cold and hostile as the belligerent attitude of the Princess increased. "Your friend in Madrid writes me sad letters," she wrote now to Villeroy. "Her mind is embittered against us and our relations become very painful."[1]

The Princess on her side, pagan and materialist as she was, filled with the autocratic prejudices of her ancestors, considered Madame de Maintenon as a hypocrite since she was unable to conceive that the wife of the greatest war-lover in Europe could hold views so, from her point of view, ignoble and bourgeois, and attributed her perpetual outcries for peace to animosity against Spain.

The Princess in her next letter accuses Louis of lack of frankness, of "seeking byepaths to make known his will," which Madame de Maintenon indignantly denies. Whereupon she appeals to Bergeyck himself to say frankly by whose authority he had so vehemently pressed her departure.

Bergeyck responded frankly enough that what he had written had been at Louis' advice, but that if she expected an official order from him she would be disappointed for he did not choose to give it, but that if she wished to please him she would leave immediately and go far enough away to allay any suspicions the Allies might have that she intended to return.

This letter, proof positive of Louis' complicity, she forwarded to Madame de Maintenon, remarking dryly that it was a pity he had not been more explicit, and demanding, since she was forced to leave, that she should be paid her due. For three years, she wrote, she had received nothing from him, only five thousand out of the fifty thousand francs of her pension and nothing at all from Philippe. She has not a sou and has heavy debts. "My destiny," she concludes, "is very strange. Five years ago I was recalled for being a bad patriot, now I am driven out by the Allies for being too devoted to France."[2]

Louis' complicity could have been no secret to Madame de

---

[1] Trémoïlle, v. 43 ; letter of 28 Oct. 1709.
[2] Bossange, iv. 372 and 382 ; letters of 16 Dec. and one undated, 1709.

INTRIGUES AGAINST THE PRINCESS

Maintenon since he had none from her, but it suited his plans that she should feign ignorance.

The Princess des Ursins [she wrote to Villeroy] has sent me copies of several letters from Monsieur de Bergeyck which seemed to me so sharp and strong that with all my simplicity I cannot help suspecting him to be prompted by her enemies. Not only does he desire her to leave Spain but insists that she shall go far enough that her intention to return cannot be suspected. She seems embarrassed as to what she shall do when she leaves. The power of the Germans in Rome disgusts her with that city. She has not a sou and has many debts. She wants me to ask Monsieur Desmarets [Minister of Finance] for some part of the twenty thousand francs due to her. Judge whether I can do it! I should not dare to write to her to come here. She would make too bad a figure and I think she has too much good sense to expose herself to it, but I know not what to tell her.[1]

[1] Collin, *Lettres à Villeroy*, vi. 44; letter of 17 Feb. 1710.

CHAPTER IX

THE PRINCESS REMAINS (1710)

IT is disappointing in the full swing of this battle between "the two *dominatrices* on this and that side of the Pyrenees," as Saint-Simon calls them, that the Princess's letters should suddenly come to an end. This is due, as we learn from Madame de Maintenon, to her own wish. Now that their mutual hostility is more or less openly declared she fears that they may be used against her and begs that those already in her possession may be given to her old friend the Maréchal de Villeroy, who has orders to destroy them, and that she should burn in future all that she receives. For the next ten months, therefore, we are forced to reconstruct them from the answers of Madame de Maintenon herself.

Madame de Maintenon's anxiety to know the Princess's plans and especially to what country she meant to retire, increases in proportion to the latter's reticence. At the first talk of her departure she herself had taken it for granted that she should return to Rome where she still had her palace and financial interests. But the promise of her sovereignty in the Netherlands had changed her plans, for Rome was too distant from her new centre of interest and it was in Paris that she decided to make her temporary home.

Madame de Maintenon was in despair. She had neither pretext nor right to forbid it since the Princess's departure was not in the nature of a disgrace, but she did her best to prevent it by intrigue and repeated over and over again to Villeroy, whom she knew would communicate her letters, that she would be ill received at the Court. "Our friend in Madrid is too proud and too sensible to come and make a sorry figure at Versailles."

Villeroy was the Princess's friend but he was also the *protégé* of Madame de Maintenon and as a courtier not free from egoism. The friendship of the King's wife was to him of more value than that of the Queen of Spain's favourite, so not only did he repeat these discouraging words but added others as though from himself, proposing places of retreat the most distant from Paris. Why instead of Paris, where she would make but a sorry figure, not make Languedoc or Provence her home?

But whether the Princess saw through these manœuvres and enjoyed terrifying her opponent, or that she actually did intend to make her temporary home in Paris until she could retire in pomp to her sovereignty, she continued to declare more decidedly than ever that Paris and Paris only should be her home when she left Spain.

Immediately Madame de Maintenon, who had been so cold to the Queen's prayers, so insistent on her leaving Spain, changed her tactics and interceded with Louis to allow her to remain with so much insistence that he consented. Perhaps Louis was himself terrified at the idea of her return or perhaps the reason given by Madame de Maintenon was the true one, namely that peace being impossible owing to the exigencies of the Allies, such a sacrifice on the part of the King and Queen of Spain would be superfluous.

I send you the letters I received yesterday from the Princess des Ursins [she wrote to Villeroy on 15 March]. You will see in them a bitterness which you know I do not deserve. The letters received yesterday from Holland and which allow us no more hope of peace, make us think that she is in too much haste to abandon Their Catholic Majesties. But in case she leaves them, what can I counsel her as to her future? Her plan of remaining in Pau seems to me the best. She is too proud and too sensible to come and make a bad figure at Versailles. That of living as a private person with her brother in Paris might be agreeable but would not be without its inconveniences.[1]

This letter like the rest was communicated to the Princess who saw at once which way the wind was veering, but for reasons on which it would be idle to speculate further maintained her resolution, and on 2 March wrote officially to Torcy announcing her resignation and her decision to leave the following month.

You are too well informed of the reasons which force me to this step for it to be necessary that I should enter into any details [she wrote haughtily]. I will only say that it costs me very dear on account of the great grief it causes the King and

[1] Collin, *Lettres à Madame de Maintenon*, vi. 47 ; letter of 15 March, 1710.

Queen and the damage to my reputation, since everyone will think that I abandon them because they are on the edge of a precipice. I am preparing to begin my journey, and if my health could resist the passage of the Pyrenees at this season, when they are covered with snow, I should not wait till the beginning of April to leave.[1]

And on the same day she wrote to Villeroy for the benefit of Madame de Maintenon:

I have finally decided to tear myself from Their Catholic Majesties. I have already announced my departure at the Court and am giving the necessary orders for the long and fatiguing journey which I shall commence the beginning of April. I know not what will become of me when I shall set foot in France. . . . Nothing is more dishonourable for me than to abandon Their Catholic Majesties at this moment. However, I am absolutely determined to do so. I could pass from the dictatorship to the plough without regret and, satisfied with myself, live more peaceably than most in a modest house in Paris, if the expense of a fresh establishment impossible to my purse did not prevent me.[2]

For Madame de Maintenon there was not a moment to lose. In less than a month the dreaded rival would be on her way to Paris. The time had arrived for decided action and before the month was over three letters, all bearing the same date—17 March, reached Madrid, putting a summary stop to decisions, indecisions and projects by the royal order, explicit enough this time, that the Princess des Ursins, subject of Louis XIV., must remain at her post at the Court of Madrid.

The first was from Madame de Maintenon to the Princess. " I received your two letters confirming your resolution to leave Spain," she wrote. "You will see that the King does not approve of it, and that I knew better than Monsieur de Bergeyck when I assured you he did not wish it. . . . I do not understand your reasons for letting yourself be guided by Monsieur de Bergeyck who wishes to separate you so far from Their Catholic Majesties that you could never rejoin them." [3]

Louis' letter to his grandson was as follows:

" I counsel you to make the Princess des Ursins remain with the Queen. It would be useless that you should allow

---

[1] Trémoïlle, v. 49 and 51 ; letters of 2 and 4 March, 1710.
[2] Villeroy, 95 ; letter of 10 March, 1710.
[3] Bossange, ii. 47 ; letter of 17 March, 1710.

her to retire, and if they tell you that her departure would facilitate peace they deceive you, for our enemies are obstinate."¹

And here is his order to the Princess:

"You will give me fresh proofs of the interest you take in what concerns me by remaining with the Queen of Spain, and I think I can give her no greater pleasure than to ask it of you. I should even command it if I did not know your anxiety to do all I wish."²

Thus after six months' persistent efforts to dislodge her, at the point of succeeding he veers round, eats his own words and gives the lie to the scapegoat Bergeyck, who we may be sure had not used his name without authorisation.

Saint-Simon declares the whole affair of her departure to be nothing but a stratagem to gull the Allies and that neither she nor Louis had any intention of her leaving. But Saint-Simon had not read the correspondence, which seems sincere on both sides and to prove that Louis was most eager for her departure, and yielded to the prayers of the Queen and the tardy intercession of Madame de Maintenon only when he found it to be useless. As for the Princess, the sincerity of her letters appears evident.

Louis' flattering order found her in bed with the measles, and it was d'Aubigny who announced to Torcy its reception but with no great demonstration of joy.

"I preserve in my prosperity the same moderation as when I appeared so criminal!" she had written after her first disgrace had turned to a triumph, and now that history had repeated itself in its smallest details, now that she had for the second time been attacked and had again conquered, she showed the same reserve. In her answers to Versailles there is no hint of any pleasure — rather the contrary. "It required no less than an order from the King to engage me to remain here!" was all her acknowledgment.³

What she wrote to Madame de Maintenon is among the destroyed letters, but, from the answer, would seem to have been anything less than grateful. "You become very unjust to me," that lady replied, "but all must be forgiven in a state so surprising as yours. You intimidate me, and

---

¹ Trémoïlle, v. 52 ; letter of 17 March, 1710.
² Ibid., v. 53 ; letter of 17 March, 1710.
³ Ibid., v. 55 ; letter of 7 April, 1710.

I dare no more speak of my sentiments for you, still less of what I feel for the King and Queen. I fear that our letters will become drier and shorter because we do not think alike and that I respect you too much to dispute with you." [1]

To Villeroy the Princess wrote: "The order I have received from the King not to quit the Queen of Spain, and the obedience I owe His Majesty, have made me alter my decision to leave. If it had arrived a few days later it would no longer have found me in Madrid, for I was on the point of beginning my journey." And she concludes ironically: "You give me great joy in telling me the way our generous friend [Madame de Maintenon] feels towards me, and though I have never doubted her straightforwardness and goodness of heart, one cannot hear pleasant things too often. I shall work with all my force to acquire fresh merit which may give me the hope of surmounting the ill-will of my enemies. It is the best way to revenge oneself." [2]

The best way possibly, but not the way of the Princess. Louis, Madame de Maintenon and Philippe d'Orléans, whom as Bergeyck's protector she suspected, rightly or wrongly, of having incited him to attack her, were too highly placed to be within range of her shot, but within her reach was one whom she supposed to have been their instrument, and on him with characteristic promptness she wreaked her vengeance.

On 14 April the Duke of Medina-Cœli, Prime Minister of her own making, was sent for at seven o'clock in the evening and received in private audience by Philippe. On leaving the palace he was arrested, and without any explanation thrown into a coach surrounded by guards, and driven at full gallop to the fortress of Segovia, where he was condemned to perpetual imprisonment.

The arrest of a man of such rank and so respected by the people excited intense curiosity, not only in Madrid but throughout Europe and especially at Versailles. He was known to be a friend of the Duc d'Orléans and a staunch ally of Bergeyck, and the rumour at once spread that his arrest was due to the vengeance of the Princess des Ursins. Spain was up in arms with anger and emotion. His numer-

---
[1] Bossange, ii. 53; letter of 31 March, 1710.
[2] Villeroy, 106; letter of 6 April, 1710.

ous relatives moved heaven and earth for his release, or at least to know his crime. Louis wrote to demand an explanation of his grandson. Madame de Maintenon attacked the Princess with acrimony. Villeroy and her friends warned her that it was attributed to her. In vain! All that Philippe was permitted to reply was that the Duke had abused his confidence and acted against his service. " I have reasons and proofs sufficiently strong," he wrote, " to push things even farther, if I chose to treat him with rigour." [1] " The King has discovered things of such importance as to oblige him to imprison him," the Princess contented herself with replying, and referred Madame de Maintenon for an explanation to Louis, who said he knew no more than she,[2] and the Spanish Government revealed nothing but vague accusations of treason.

[1] *Œuvres de Louis XIV.*, vi. 207.
[2] Bossange, ii. 77 ; letter of 15 June, 1710.

CHAPTER X

THE DUC DE VENDÔME IN SPAIN (1710)

NOTWITHSTANDING the negotiations for peace, the spring of 1710 found all the armies of Europe preparing for a fresh campaign, for the Allies were more than ever bent on dethroning Philippe and bringing Louis to his knees. Neither Marlborough nor Prince Eugène would hear of peace, each for his own private ends, the Prince out of hatred to Louis, Marlborough because he was amassing money. To every fresh overture or concession made by Louis, they replied by fresh exactions. The separation of the two countries was no longer sufficient. Now they exacted that he should use force to drag his grandson off his throne, and even if Philippe consented to abdicate would allow him only to retain the sovereignty of Sicily and Sardinia. Finally, if Spain and the Indies were not handed over to the Archduke within two months from the date of proposal, war against both countries would recommence.[1]

These conditions were too hard even for Louis to accept and he closed the negotiations, and to the immense satisfaction of the Princess withdrew his plenipotentiaries and prepared to continue the war. Since he was forced to fight, he sent word to the Allies he preferred fighting against his enemies than his own flesh and blood, and he, who would have sacrificed Spain and his grandson to prove the separation of the two countries, now wrote to Madrid of the necessity of closest union.

Nothing better marks the triumph of the Princess at this date than Torcy's servility. Torcy, who had always disliked and worked against her, now fawns upon her. He asks humbly whether it would be desired that Louis should renew his embassy, not in any way to meddle with state affairs but merely to represent his master and work for the desired union. If so, would the Abbé de Polignac be acceptable to her; if not, would she herself name those who would. To which she replied in Philippe's name, though Philippe was in Aragon and probably knew nothing at all about it,

[1] Trémoïlle, v. 77; letter of Torcy to the Princess of 21 July, 1710.

LOUIS DE BOURBON, DUC DE VENDÔME
From a contemporary engraving.

that, accustomed to Amelot, he had declared that Amelot and Amelot only would be acceptable.¹

But other and more important events than the choice of an ambassador claimed her attention. The darkest moment of the struggle had arrived, the moment when most people lose courage but when, according to her optimistic theory, light is certain to break through and disperse the clouds.

In the middle of April, Philippe, ill and depressed, had rejoined the army in Aragon, but his presence inspired no enthusiasm and the troops, looking on him since Louis' abandonment rather as an enemy, made no effort to oppose the advance of the Allies. On the contrary they began again to desert, and in less than a month over two thousand had gone over to the Archduke.

For several months the Princess, seeing their one hope of salvation in the return of the French troops under a competent general, had directed Philippe and the Queen to ask Louis to send them the Duc de Vendôme, who since the defeat of Oudenarde had been in disgrace and without employment. He himself had begged to be allowed to go, but as long as he had any hope of peace Louis had refused. Now that the negotiations had failed, the Queen, as Regent, wrote again with fresh insistence. Her letter, evidently dictated by the Princess, is worth quoting as showing the change of attitude in the once obsequious Spanish Court.

After a few preliminaries announcing "the sincere desire we have to help France sustain a war which the temerity of our enemies renders every day more necessary and just," she continues: "We have seen with infinite sorrow the part you have taken to abandon us, thinking by so doing to inspire more moderate sentiments in an enemy blinded by good fortune. Now that we may attribute to intrigue all the insinuations made to cause a breach between us, let us endeavour by quite different methods to regain what has been lost, and having no longer but one common interest, try by plans better organised than before, to obtain the advantages which may be hoped from the union of the two crowns." After which pompous preface she demands as "absolutely necessary" the immediate dispatch of the Duc de Vendôme to command the armies in Catalonia.²

¹ Trémoïlle, v. 86; letter of 18 Aug. 1710.
² Baudrillart, i, 4064; letter of 1 Aug. 1710.

Her prayer was granted even before this letter reached Versailles, for it crossed on the road one from Torcy to the Princess announcing the Duke's appointment.

Unfortunately, when the order reached Vendôme he was in bed suffering from a severe attack of gout and it was not till the end of the month that he was able to leave.

His advent in Spain had a double importance, for, as will be seen, not only did it put the final touch to the establishment of Philippe on the throne, but incidentally brought to the Princess misfortune and ultimate ruin. For in his suite came an Italian, by name Alberoni, officially his almoner and secretary, in reality pander, buffoon and even worse—an individual by birth and morals lowest among the low, but whom Nature had endowed with intelligence so prodigious and a power of intrigue so formidable that what he set himself to do he achieved, and the task he set himself to accomplish at the Court of Spain was to oust the Princess from her place and assume himself the dictatorship.

Was it presentiment which made her notice the existence of a man as insignificant as was Alberoni at this date? In any case she wrote to the Duc de Noailles when Vendôme was already on his way: "I beg you to tell me frankly what you know of the Abbé Alberoni. They speak well of him in Paris and assert that he has all the confidence of Monsieur de Vendôme."[1]

And since the Duke unconsciously, and the Abbé consciously, played so large a part in her final ruin, a slight description of them is necessary.

Louis de Bourbon, Duc de Vendôme, was grandson of Henri IV. by Gabrielle d'Estrées; thus, by a bastard branch, cousin-german of Louis XIV., with whom before his disgrace he had been a favourite. His lack of cleanliness and decency were proverbial in an age which could not boast much of either. His health—and nose—had suffered from his debaucheries, which were monstrous. He was brutal, arrogant, quick-tempered, and of a voracity which sounds fabulous. Such virtues as he possessed were purely military. He was courageous to recklessness, very popular with his troops, and was indeed the only general Louis had capable of holding his own against Marlborough and Prince Eugène.

[1] Trémoïlle, v. 97; letter of 5 Sept. 1710.

Here are a few extracts from Saint-Simon's descriptions:

Insolent to excess where he thought he could be so with impunity and familiar with the people. At bottom pride personified, this demi-god could be approached only by means of flattery, admiration and adoration. [Here follows a long relation of his tastes against nature which he satisfied with his valets and inferior officers.] His sloth was inconceivable, his filth extreme. His bed was covered with dogs and bitches which had their puppies while he lay in it. He ate enormously with an extraordinary voracity, liking best fish, and stinking fish better than fresh. His soldiers and officers adored him for his familiarity and the licence he tolerated to gain their favour, for which he compensated himself by immeasurable haughtiness towards his equals.[1]

This arrogance he showed even to the princes of the blood and had been deprived of his command and exiled from the Court for his insolence to the young Duke of Burgundy at the Battle of Oudenarde rather than for the defeat. Since then he had remained for two years in idleness at his Château of Anet, dainty home of Diane de Poitiers sullied by his debaucheries, in dire disgrace with the Duchess and consequently with Louis.

So much for the general who was to save the situation in Spain. His relations with the Abbé Alberoni must be passed over as lightly as possible. It is enough to say that, while the Duke was commanding the French army in Italy in 1706, the Duke of Parma wishing to treat with him, sent the Bishop of Parma, whom Vendôme received on his *chaise-percée* engaged in an act which most people accomplish in solitude. The Bishop, indignant, left the room immediately and refused to return. Alberoni, son of a gardener, who had himself been employed as bellringer in the Cathedral of Piacenza, half valet, half buffoon of the Duke of Parma, was charged with the mission in his place and was received by Vendôme engaged as before—a delicate way of showing his contempt for the little State of Parma. But Alberoni, who had no decency to shock, fulfilled his mission as though he perceived nothing, and desirous of making his way in France, so flattered and amused the General that he consented to all the Duke's demands, and soon after took him into his own service as secretary, from which post he rose, by complacence to his vices and cooking him succulent Italian dishes, to the rank of almoner and

[1] Saint-Simon, xiii. 280.

most trusted confidant. It will be seen later how, after
Vendôme's death, he remained at the Court of Madrid,
how he negotiated and brought about the second marriage
of Philippe with Elisabeth Farnese his master's daughter,
how he intrigued with her and the Queen-Dowager to hunt
the Princess from Spain and how he was rewarded with the
post of First Minister. Clever politician, supple adventurer and unscrupulous rogue, such was the man whom
she admitted to her confidence and loaded with gifts and
favours, thus paving the way to his ultimate success
and her own ruin.

The Duc de Vendôme, accompanied by this ecclesiastic
and a numerous suite, arrived in Spain the beginning of
September. None too soon, for matters had gone from
bad to worse with the armies, and had reached a depth from
which it seemed impossible the country could be extricated,
so hopeless that Louis was almost justified in renewing his
efforts to persuade his grandson to abdicate and sacrifice
his crown in the interest of peace.

It was the Duc de Noailles, nephew by marriage of
Madame de Maintenon, commanding the army on the
French frontier, who was charged with the mission.

> You are to persuade him [his instructions ran] that being
> unable to preserve Spain and the Indies, he has no other
> resource than to accept what his enemies are disposed to offer
> him—Sicily. There is certainly no proportion between the
> possession of Spain and the Indies and that of Sicily and
> Sardinia, but there is still less between the rank of a king
> possessing these two isles and the private life of a prince
> despoiled of his states. You will add that France is exhausted
> by the cruel war she has supported for ten years against all
> Europe, that His Majesty would never have been reduced to
> the humiliating steps he has taken to obtain peace if he had
> not seen for a long while that his people can no longer support
> the heavy burden he is forced to impose on them.

After attacking Philippe and the Queen with these arguments, he was to try to gain the Princess to his cause either
by promises of reward or threats.

> You have full liberty to promise her what you think she
> would most appreciate, provided it be conformable to order
> and reason. If, however, the assurance of the King's favour,
> protection and recompense does not move her, you must make
> her understand that he will henceforth regard her as the cause
> of the total ruin of his grandson, that he is aware of the abso-

THE DUC DE VENDÔME 253

lute power she has over the mind of the Catholic King and that the firmness he has shown in his letters and words is her work, that if up to now she has been worthy of praise she will be so no longer, but blameworthy for the evil counsels which will lead his grandson to the edge of the precipice.¹

Noailles had joined Vendôme at Bayonne to discuss with him the situation, when the news reached them that a terrific battle had been fought at Saragossa, the citadel captured with heavy losses, artillery, baggage, ammunition lost, that the Archduke Charles was marching on Madrid and that Queen and Princess, Court and Government had been forced to fly to Valladolid, whither Philippe with the remnant of his defeated army had already retreated.

Vendôme, suffering from fever and the gout, was too ill to stir, but Noailles, armed with his instructions, which this fresh catastrophe made more than ever urgent, hurried off at once to Valladolid to join the fugitives.

This flight, which took place at nightfall on 9 September, was less tragic than that to Burgos four years before. Then nobles and people were all antagonistic to the French King and his *Savoyarde*, as they contemptuously called the Queen, and eager to welcome one more of their own blood. Now all the nobles and citizens flocked after them, abandoning shops and houses. Those who had coaches, wagons or horses rode. Those who had none went on their feet, and the road between Madrid and Valladolid was thronged in its entire extent, according to San Phélipe. Before their departure the Queen, with the little Prince of the Asturias in her arms, came out on the balcony and spoke to the crowd with so much grace that her success was incredible.² What had happened in so short a time to work so important a change?

This. The greater part of the enemy troops engaged in this campaign were English and Dutch, fresh from the ferment of religious fanaticism, of No-Popery and Puritanism. These troops, in their detestation of the Popish practices they witnessed in this ultra-Catholic country with its legions of monks and priests, had vented their fury by inconceivable outrages. They had bivouacked in the churches, eaten and drunk out of the sacred vessels, rubbed down their horses with the consecrated oil, and committed other enormities so outrageous that the people,

¹ Millot, iii. 431.   ² Saint-Simon, xx. 118.

horror-struck, had thought Hell was let loose among them, and bitterly regretted their readiness to admit them. Too late they closed the gates of the towns and barricaded themselves in their houses and castles. But they were powerless to resist the influx of the fanatics or put a stop to their sacrilege. Horrified and terrorised they thought with regret of their Catholic King, and would have given their lives to be able to eject the Puritans and purge their polluted churches. The result was that when the Archduke, who had made his headquarters at the Pardo, arrived in state to take possession of the capital, he found the streets absolutely empty. The procession had started from Notre Dame d'Atocha with the greatest pomp, the Archduke on horseback in Royal robes surrounded by his generals, preceded by two thousand cavalry, and followed by his guards and household, glittering with gold and jewels. But there was no one to witness his glory. Even curiosity and the national love of pageant ceded to the popular detestation. All the houses and public buildings were shuttered and barred, streets and squares deserted except for a few decrepit old men who spat on them as they passed, and stray children attracted by the coppers thrown them, but who cried " Long live Philippe! " oftener than " Long live Charles! " The Archduke was so furious that he stopped the procession before reaching the palace, and refusing to continue his humiliating " triumph," shook the dust of the city off his horses' hoofs and returned raging to his quarters at the Pardo.

San Phélipe relates that all the infected prostitutes followed, went from one soldier to another plying their trade, and succeeded so well in their hideous vengeance that the hospitals were filled to overflowing with their victims, and that the surgeons and nurses, instead of healing, poisoned their wounds, so that no less than six thousand died within a week; and that in all dark places in streets and forests, outraged Catholics lurked and assassinated the sacrilegious troops as they passed, so that they lost more men in the two weeks of their so-called triumph than in any one of their battles.

As for King Charles III., nothing remained but to retreat as quickly as possible towards more friendly Barcelona with such of his army as survived the raid of the prostitutes, and hardly were they out of sight than as if by magic all the houses were flung open, the church bells set ringing, and such a shout of joy went up to heaven that the departing sovereign heard it and cursed.

Meantime the Duc de Noailles had arrived in Valladolid to fulfil his mission and was received by Philippe and the Queen alone—at least the Princess was invisible. But her puppets, carefully instructed, performed their parts to perfection. Noailles did his best to carry out his instructions, but at the first hint of abdication Philippe, assuming one of the noble attitudes of which the Princess alone had the secret, declared that nothing in the world should make him resign his throne, that it would be dishonourable towards the Spaniards who had so nobly supported him, that with Vendôme in command the army would recover, that in any case and whatever happened he would continue the war. The Queen, impetuous as usual, confirmed his words with more energy, and it may be guessed that the Princess behind the tapestry was not ill-pleased with her pupils. Nothing was left for the Duke but to send his messengers to Versailles announcing the failure of his mission.

At no time during the fluctuations of this long war did the Princess show so much judgment and foresight as now, not only in her insistence on Vendôme's command, but in the resistance she inspired in the King at a moment so discouraging. The turn of the tide in favour of Spain was due, not to chance, nor even so much to the good generalship of the Duke, as to her optimism and energy.

For the moment, bad as it seemed, was propitious. The Spaniards, appalled at the sacrilege of the Puritans, were ready to throw themselves into the arms of anyone likely to drive them from the country, and forgot political feuds in religious sympathy. Queen Anne was suspected of being on the eve of withdrawing from the alliance and even Holland seemed less bent on continuing the war. Vendôme, recovered from his fever, had arrived full of energy and determined to retrieve his prestige. There was no time to lose, however, for the Austrian armies were on the point of junction with the Portuguese, so without wasting a moment he sent the Queen and Princess with the little Prince of the Asturias to Vittoria for greater safety and marched Philippe off to Toledo.

The journey to Vittoria was long and painful. It was bitterly cold, and the piercing mountain winds froze them to the bone in their draughty palace with its ill-fitting doors and windows.¹

Louis' efforts to persuade his grandson to abdicate did not cease with Noailles' failure, and the Princess's reproaches on the subject to Madame de Maintenon must have been severe to extract from her the biting words with which she answers them. "I shall respect your grief in spite of the offensive irony with which your letters are filled, but might I dare conjure you to prevent as much as possible a veritable bitterness between our two kings!" ²

For things had reached the point when the obedient Philippe had shown himself openly rebellious towards his grandfather, and the scene with the Duc de Noailles had not added to the good humour of Versailles. France was in the lowest depths of misery and the blame of everything was laid at her door.

But if the sun was setting in France, in Spain, thanks to the Princess's energy, it was rising fast. Things were going admirably under the new general. The Archduke, discouraged at his reception in Madrid, was marching sullenly back to Barcelona. Vendôme, dragging Philippe in his wake, had cleared Toledo of the enemy and escorted him back to the capital where he made a triumphal entry on 3 December.

His reception was as enthusiastic as that of the Archduke had been antagonistic. All the streets were decorated, all the houses illuminated, and after sunset the city was ablaze with fireworks. The people were so joyful to be rid of the Puritans that they knelt down in the streets and with clasped hands prayed God to bless him. He was presented by the city with corn sufficient to feed the army for ten days and twenty thousand pistoles which had been concealed from the Archduke. The two days he remained were days of veritable triumph.³

On 6 December, Vendôme, still accompanied by the King, marched in pursuit of the Archduke, who, after setting fire to the greater part of Toledo, had retreated to Aragon. The English general, Stanhope, with sixty thousand men encamped in the little town of Brihuega, in Castile, was at once put to flight. Stahrembourg, the

¹ Trémoïlle, v. 105 ; letter to Torcy of 4 Oct. 1710.
² Bossange, ii. 109 ; letter of 10 Nov. 1710.
³ Geffroy, 398 ; letter from the Princess to Orry of 10 Dec. 1710.

Austrian general, flying to the rescue, Vendôme marched on his army, gave battle without a moment's delay and put them also to flight.

This was the famous Battle of Villaviciosa, a brilliant victory, all the more to Vendôme's credit that his army was very inferior in number to that of the enemy and due entirely to prompt decision and action. Stanhope and two other English generals were taken prisoner, the booty was enormous, the slaughter terrific. Four thousand were left dead on the field, nine thousand made prisoner, and out of an army of thirty thousand only six thousand remained to the Allies, for the deserters returned in a body to their allegiance. The revolt of the Spaniards, which alone had made the war possible, was over and the end of the war itself could not be far off.

The news reached the draughty palace in Vittoria in the middle of the night, and the Queen herself ran joyfully to wake the Princess and announce the marvellous victory so little expected—a real *coup de ciel* as she called it.

Vendôme's triumph was tremendous. At Versailles all his sins were forgiven and he became the hero of the hour. Everyone said he had achieved the impossible. In Spain he was hailed as the "Restorer of the Kingdom" and he became the idol of the populace. Philippe bestowed on him the title of Altesse, which in Spain carries with it the important prerogatives of a prince of the blood and which the Duke of Savoy had solicited in vain.

A charming anecdote is told of this man of whom so many filthy ones are known. On the night of the victory, while all the camp was celebrating it with feast and song, the officers appointed to serve the King were in consternation. The baggage-wagon containing the Royal bed had not arrived and the night was already half spent. Philippe, one may imagine, was not best pleased to pass the night wrapped in his cloak and probably began to sulk. "Sire!" cried Vendôme, coming to the rescue, "to-night you shall sleep on the grandest bed on which a sovereign ever laid his head!" And he gave orders that all the captured flags should be piled in a heap in the Royal tent.[1]

The Princess, as was her due, came in for a lion's share in the honours and public gratitude. At the same time as Vendôme she received the title of Altesse, with all the

[1] Villeroy, preface, xlii.

treatment of a Spanish Infanta, which included a guard of honour of twelve officers. All the Court was at her feet, and such enemies as she had—not a few according to San Phélipe—retired temporarily into the background. She had reached the summit of her glory. Alas! the decline was not far distant.

CHAPTER XI

SIGNS OF PEACE (1711)

THE victory of Villaviciosa was the turning-point in the fortunes of Spain, and the prospect of peace seemed already within view. Each day brought its bit of good news. On 3 January Stahrembourg abandoned Saragossa, on the 23rd the Duc de Noailles took Girone. In February Balaguer returned to its allegiance. There was no more talk of forcing Louis to dethrone his grandson, and a growing discord among the Allies became apparent. England had for some time shown signs of being anxious to retire from the Coalition, and Holland now seemed growing weary of the war. In the words of the Princess: "Everyone began to see that the arrogant Coalition would at last be humiliated and the *vilains Hollandais* reduced to repent their insolence."[1]

In February the Queen and Princess with the little Prince had gone to Saragossa to join Philippe, where for a change they gave themselves up to amusement and gave a Court ball at which the King and Queen "danced with all their heart, being so little accustomed to amuse themselves that they are easily contented," the Princess wrote to Torcy.[2]

At the beginning of the year also, Madame de Maintenon, losing her severity at the prospect of peace, wrote words of rare praise to the Princess: "It is astonishing that you do not succumb under all the different rôles you fill. You have all the affairs of Europe on your shoulders, you take the keenest interest in two kings and are not indifferent to the reinstatement of a third.[3] You are the entire help, counsel and pleasure of a great Queen and in all the details of her service and that of a precious babe. Your heart is in all you do and—you travel in winter where there are no roads!"[4]

[1] Trémoïlle, v. 154; letter to Torcy of 3 March, 1711.
[2] Ibid., v. 150; letter of 17 Feb. 1711.
[3] The Pretender.
[4] Bossange, ii. 135; letter of 12 Jan. 1711.

In April an important event occurred which made the prospect of peace almost a certainty. An epidemic of small-pox had been for some time ravaging Europe, making hundreds of thousands of victims. On 15 April, the Dauphin, Philippe's father, succumbed to it, and two days after died the Emperor Joseph, brother of the Archduke.

This death, entirely unexpected, since the Emperor was only thirty-three, brought the preparations for war to a standstill, for having no sons the Archduke succeeded him, and since in the natural course of things he would be candidate for the Holy Roman Empire, the addition of Spain with its immense dependencies was a worse menace to the equilibrium of Europe than if it remained in Bourbon hands.

It was a death-blow to the Coalition. One after the other the Powers withdrew, England the first. If Queen Anne had continued the war from anger that Louis refused to recognise her sovereignty, her wrath had been effectually quenched in the torrents of blood shed on Austria's behalf, and but for Marlborough's rapacity she would long ago have withdrawn. But now Marlborough was in disgrace, the Tories in power, and the last obstacle was removed.

In October the Archduke was elected emperor, and all Europe expected that he would abandon his little Court of Barcelona, withdraw his troops from Spain, and settle down to the enjoyment of his new honours. But the speciality of this Prince being obstinacy—his admirers call it tenacity of purpose—he would do neither. On the contrary, he claimed his rights with more insistence than ever, and when Philippe, at Louis' advice, wrote to him on his accession with propositions of peace, his letter was returned with the seals unbroken. He retained the title of King of Spain and forced Venice, Tuscany and Parma to recognise his sovereignty, although he now possessed nothing in the country except a small part of Catalonia. There, at Barcelona, he still held his Court and seat of government, and even after his accession to the imperial crown his wife remained there as regent, and nothing, not even the siege, menaced by Vendôme, could dislodge her.

For this siege, as early as the beginning of February, the Duke had begun his preparations, but as money was scarce they dragged on without much effect till the autumn, and since the conquest of Saragossa nothing of any importance had been done. Philippe remained with Vendôme at the camp and the Queen and Princess in Saragossa, unwilling to return to Madrid till things were more settled. The hardships and emotions of the past years had told severely on the Queen's health, and the swelling of the glands in her neck had increased so much that already the preceding year the doctors insisted on a cure, and it had been arranged that she and the Princess should take the little Prince to Bagnères in the Hautes-Pyrenées. It was easy to make plans, but not so easy under the eye of Versailles to keep them. Louis forbade their advent on his territory on the pretext that the absence of the future King would be construed into a flight by the Spaniards, but in reality because he wished to avoid fresh difficulties for himself with Austria. Bagnères had therefore to be abandoned, and the victory of Saragossa and the Queen's desire to join Philippe there had caused her cure to be indefinitely postponed. In April, however, she fell so dangerously ill with high fever, that there was serious fear for her life. It was the first manifestation of the tuberculosis which carried her off three years later, but as she recovered it gave no serious alarm. In June she left her bed and went for a change of air to Corella, a little town in Old Castile famous for its bracing climate. Here, while Philippe hunted, she and the Princess took long walks and drives, and little by little it seemed as though all danger was over.

In spite of the brighter outlook in Spain, Louis was as bent as ever on forcing his grandson, if not to abdicate entirely, at least to cede enough of his possessions to obtain an immediate peace with Austria. In June Torcy wrote to the Princess with a touch of his old severity: "Understand if you please that peace is absolutely necessary, that the need of it increases every day, and that it is essential for the Catholic King that we do not again fall into the state in which we were two years ago. I think that all sacrifices will be good if they still assure the quiet possession of Spain and the Indies."[1]

To enforce his will, instead of Amelot, whom the Princess had demanded, Louis sent as ambassador the Marquis de Bonnac, with the special mission to persuade Philippe at any cost of the necessity of peace. His instructions con-

[1] Trémoïlle, v. 198; letter of 22 June, 1711.

cerning the Princess are worth quoting in proof of her absolute authority at this date.

FONTAINEBLEAU, 5 *August*, 1711.

The Princess des Ursins appears up to now to possess completely the confidence of the King and Queen of Spain. Since it is impossible that a favour so distinguished should not excite a large number of jealousies, she has for some years affected to retire from affairs. But this retreat has not diminished her credit nor slackened the eagerness of the Spanish to address themselves to her to obtain favours from the King their master. They know that this Prince deliberates and decides his principal affairs between the Queen and her, that this private council rules the destiny of the State, that the others are merely a matter of form and that those only can be regarded as having a share in the government whom the Princess des Ursins is pleased to summon to her consultations.[1]

On 4 September Bonnac arrived in Corella to deliver his credentials. His first audience was with the Princess and she listened with great attention, he wrote in his dispatch, while he proved to her that France was a greater loser than Spain by the exactions of the Allies and the necessity for both countries of immediate peace.

Having learnt wisdom by experience she had adopted the methods of Versailles, and shielding herself behind the Queen pretended to be fully convinced by his arguments and ready to use her influence as Louis desired. Bonnac was quite taken in.

The danger is not with her [he wrote], nor with the King, who cannot or will not decide anything of himself. The danger lies with the Queen, who is of a character entirely opposite. She thinks with arrogance, takes her part immediately, and is incapable of changing when necessity requires. The misfortunes she has suffered and the way she has emerged from them have given her an opinion of the good fortune of the King and herself which makes her regard with indifference and contempt all the representations one can make her on the evils to which they may be exposed in future. Madame des Ursins, who alone is capable of moderating this sentiment, thinks with more sobriety, and as long as her delicacy is not offended and she is allowed to think that nothing can be done except through her, I hope that with patience Your Majesty's wishes will be accomplished.[2]

[1] Trémoïlle, v. 207.
[2] Ibid., v. 213; letter to Louis XIV. of 20 Sept. 1711.

In the midst of more serious matters he gives a charming picture of the home life at Corella.

I had only seen the Prince of the Asturias in passing and I asked Madame des Ursins to be kind enough to let me see him more at leisure. She led me herself to his apartment. Although children are generally embarrassed by strangers, he asked to be given a little gun made on purpose for him, and began to do the musket exercise with the grace and precision of a musketeer, after which with the same grace he did the pike exercise. They then gave him a little drum on which he beat the march with great accuracy. Afterwards they brought the kettle-drums, with which he accompanied nearly all the airs they sang to him, for he has a marvellous ear and appears to have a taste for music. After that I retired, but the Queen, his mother, coming in a moment later to assist at his dinner, sent for me that I might see him dance. He makes the steps of the minuet as well as his age permits and shows in dancing a grace and accuracy of ear far beyond his age.[1]

[1] Trémoïlle, v. 218; letter to Torcy of 13 Oct. 1711.

CHAPTER XII

THE SOVEREIGNTY (1711)

IT will be remembered that in answer to Madame de Maintenon's question as to her plans after leaving Spain the Princess had written: "I am making other projects for the remainder of my life which I keep to myself, and which consequently you will not know." An answer which had excited the keenest curiosity and not a little suspicion.

Sovereignty with all its accessories and independence had always, as we know, been her obsession from her first effort to obtain from the Emperor the rank of Princess of the Empire up to her attempt to replace Madame de Maintenon at Versailles. To reign concealed behind the throne as she actually did in Spain was not enough. The high rank of Altesse, with its brilliant accessories of Royal guards and sentinels, was not enough. To be dictatress in the antechamber of Royal puppets was not enough. She must wear the crown and wield the sceptre in complete independence, and this ambition the Queen had satisfied, on a small scale, it is true, by extracting from Philippe the promise of a principality with sovereign rights in his states in the Netherlands.

In her present desire for independence other reasons than ambition had, however, a share. Her life since she left Rome had been one long struggle in the service of kings, who had rewarded her by injustice and ingratitude; one long tussle against intrigues and persecution. It is no wonder she should try to prepare for herself an honourable retreat free from caprice and treachery, and surrounded by the respect and ceremony which the habit of courts made an imperious necessity. Twice already she had been made to feel the insecurity of her position at the Court of Madrid, and on how slender a thread hung her favour at Versailles, and also, notwithstanding her energy and health, she was doubtless feeling the weight of her sixty-nine years and the need of rest. It was these reasons probably as much as ambition which pushed her to abandon the dictatorship of one of the most important monarchies of Europe, to wear the diadem of a little state of scarcely greater importance than the Duchy of Bracciano.

THE SOVEREIGNTY

Here is the famous story of her sovereignty as related by Saint-Simon, her bitter enemy since her quarrel with the Duc d'Orléans :

Accustomed to reign and see everyone at her orders in Spain and France, she found it distasteful to be a private person and aspired to sovereignty. God, who had neither raised her ancestors nor given her any shadow of pretext to raise herself so high, seemed even to have willed the contrary by her sex and childless widowhood. But nothing arrested her, and disposing entirely of the will of the King and Queen of Spain, she dared put it into their heads, when the question of peace came to be discussed, to bestow on her a sovereignty or give her one on their own frontiers. For this the approval and consent of France was necessary, but she flattered herself to succeed through Madame de Maintenon in due course. Her project was to obtain a province which should be desirable to France, to exchange it for one on the banks of the Loire, to retire there and become a sovereign in her own country, perhaps to make it hereditary in her family. However it be, no sooner did she hear of the overtures of peace than she set her irons on the fire, and so little doubt had she of success that she sent her equerry d'Aubigny to France with large sums of money, who bought, without lands or estate, a large piece of ground near Amboise and began to build there a Royal palace. It was there that she had fixed the site of her little throne and she wished to take time by the forelock and find all ready. The conferences of Utrecht beginning to take shape, she had the audacity to send the Baron de Câpres as her envoy, to join her pretensions to those of the Spanish plenipotentiaries, who had orders to demand it in the name of the King their master, and were supported by those of France. The idea of the future sovereign excited nothing but laughter in all the Powers, who would not even hear it mentioned. They thought rightly that if Spain wished so much to give her a sovereignty she might do it at her own expense without importuning the rest of Europe, who owed her no sort of recompense. . . . This vast attempt having failed, the Princess turned her thoughts to Guipuscoa and Roussillon. The King and Queen of Spain desired it with all their hearts, but the King [Louis], more wise, opposed it when he saw that they seriously meant to dismember his grandson's crown which the Emperor had already despoiled of its fairest flowers.[1]

This folly, he adds later, was the first cause of the Princess's ruin, and he shows how:

This sovereignty, which was beyond the reach of Madame de Maintenon herself, offended her and hurt her pride, making her feel the distance of rank and birth which were at the

[1] Saint-Simon, v. 508.

bottom of so high an aspiration. She felt with jealousy that the immeasurable credit which had raised Madame des Ursins so high was nothing but the result of her own protection, and could not tolerate that she should abuse it to the point of raising herself so far above her, and that the sovereignty she should found and enjoy under her own eyes. The King likewise felt the extravagance of the scheme, but he was also vexed to see peace retarded by it, and to be forced to conclude peace without this sovereignty in spite of his grandson, who would not give way and ceded only from the impossibility of holding out against so many enemies if he were abandoned by France, and all for so small and strange a matter. The fury of Madame des Ursins can also be imagined, after having pushed her point with such excessive obstinacy, to have made herself a spectacle in the eyes of all Europe and gained nothing but shame and contempt for so mad an enterprise.[1]

So much for the story according to Saint-Simon, fairly correct in the main points, but vague. Here is the affair made clearer by the documents.

Louis had, as is known, but one serious ally in Europe, the Elector Maximilian of Bavaria, whose support he had promised to reward, as usual not at his own expense, but that of his grandson.

The large Spanish possessions in the Netherlands had been gradually reduced to the four states Luxembourg, Namur, Charleroi and Nieuport—and in 1709 these had been included in the territory claimed by Austria in the negotiations for peace. Louis had done his utmost to extract from Philippe the cession of these four states and had even menaced sending his troops to force him if he refused, but, directed by the Princess, Philippe had refused with a firmness all Louis' efforts failed to shake, and the states remained provisionally in his possession pending the treaty of peace after the victory of Villaviciosa. The Elector of Bavaria having lost his own country during the war claimed as the reward of his alliance these four states in the Netherlands. Louis naturally made no objection, and wrote to his grandson that he must keep faith with their ally, and that any hesitation on his part would be dishonourable.[2] But Philippe, grown less pliant and having already promised the greater part of the states to the Princess, did hesitate and finally even refused, and it was not till January 1712 that, harassed and menaced by Louis with the withdrawal of his troops, he unwillingly

[1] Saint-Simon, xxiv. 213.   [2] Millot, iii. 203 ; letter of Nov. 1710.

THE SOVEREIGNTY

gave in, and even then on one condition only—that out of the ceded territory the Duchy of Limbourg, an ancient feudal state with a history dating from the eleventh century, should be reserved and given as a reward for her services to the Princess des Ursins.

The gift was, as has been seen, extracted by the Queen at the desire of her favourite as early as the autumn of 1709, but the official deed of donation was not signed till two years later.

On this sovereignty of Limbourg the Princess had set her heart, but three things were necessary before it could be in any way assured to her. First, the consent of Louis XIV., since she was still nominally his subject; next, that of the Elector of Bavaria, who, though easy-going enough, might not be willing to sacrifice so large a slice of his promised states; and thirdly, that of the Allies, who would certainly object to a piece of ground so near the frontier being in French hands. She dispatched d'Aubigny to Versailles to plead her cause with Louis, and the Queen on her side wrote to Madame de Maintenon to beg her intercession as follows, obviously at her dictation:

You doubtless know of the King's request to his grandfather when the treaty was concluded by which he ceded the Netherlands to the Elector of Bavaria, to reserve us a little sovereignty of thirty thousand crowns revenue. The King promised it and I think the Elector willingly consented, being so small a thing in comparison with what he receives. We now ask, therefore, the fulfilment of this promise. The King is writing to his grandfather to-day and I implore you to speak to him from me. . . . I think you will do so all the more willingly when you know that we destine this sovereignty to the Princess des Ursins, who merits it in so many ways and deserves that you should interest yourself in her, for I assure you you have no better friend. Would it not be shameful for the King and me, after all we owe her, not to give her some proof of our gratitude? There is no dignity except this that we can give her, since she has them all. Thus I think that no one will consider what we do for her exaggerated. As for you, *ma chère Madame*, I do not doubt the pleasure you will have, and that the King and I shall have your entire approbation. I must add also that this gift belongs to the King and can do no harm to the King his grandfather, who has no share in it, and that it ought to please him that a subject so devoted as the Princess des Ursins has always been to him should make a considerable figure. I confess that I am vain enough to feel pleasure in doing more for my Camarera Mayor than the queens my predecessors have done for theirs. I conclude then that we shall have this satisfaction, but I wish to owe to you and my sister that no difficulties shall be raised in the matter and that it shall be settled immediately, since it depends on the King my grandfather to make Monsieur de Bavière consent to what is so reasonable.[1]

Neither Louis nor Madame de Maintenon seems to have been so horrified at the suggestion as Saint-Simon makes out. On the contrary, the former answered his grandson very amiably:

I praise the gratitude you and the Queen feel towards the Princess des Ursins and your intention to prove it to her. The Elector of Bavaria has been informed of the reserve you wish to make in the Netherlands. . . . I am persuaded you will meet with no difficulty on his part. There will perhaps be more in forming a sovereignty of thirty thousand crowns revenue in two provinces so sterile as those of Luxembourg and Namur. Nevertheless, I will speak to him at once about it.[2]

And Madame de Maintenon, though not enthusiastic, accepted the idea without apparent ill-will: "It seems that your sovereignty is going on very well and that you ought to be pleased with the King," she wrote kindly enough to the Princess.[3]

As for Torcy, he had already promised his adherence and help: "Monsieur d'Aubigny," he wrote on 27 July, "has spoken to me of an affair which concerns you of which the King of Spain has written to the King. I can assure you of my zeal and application in surmounting the difficulties should any arise."[4]

Thus the matter seemed at first to have caused neither anger nor objection at Versailles, and the petty jealousy Saint-Simon attributes to Madame de Maintenon was not at all in her character, her own position besides being so superior in every respect except the mere title. Louis' anger was due only to the opposition of the Allies and Philippe's obstinate refusal to sign any treaty of peace till the sovereignty was guaranteed. But the Elector objected strongly to the sacrifice of so important a portion of his territory. "He represents vividly," Torcy wrote announcing this objection, "the bad state of the two provinces of which he may now take possession and how difficult, not

[1] Millot, iii. 454 ; letter of 7 July, 1711.
[2] Ibid., iii. 482 ; letter of 20 July, 1711.
[3] Bossange, ii. 202 ; letter of 10 Aug. 1711.
[4] Trémoïlle, v. 204 ; letter of 27 July, 1711.

to say impossible, it would be to lop off from them a sovereignty of thirty thousand crowns revenue."[1]

Louis was as good as his word, however, and tried to persuade him, and while the decision was pending Philippe, without awaiting his consent, signed the deed of donation.

The document, evidently composed by the Princess, is of great interest as being a *résumé* of her life at the Spanish Court and showing the high value she placed on her own services there.

It was written at Corella and bears the date 20 September, 1711:

> Philippe, by the grace of God King of Castile, Leon, Aragon, the Two Sicilies, Jerusalem, Navarre, Granada, Toledo, Valentia, Galicia, Majorca, Seville, Sardinia, Cordova, Corsica, Murcia, Gibraltar, the Canary Isles, and the Indies East and West, etc., Archduke of Austria, Duke of Burgundy, Brabant, and Milan, Count of Habsbourg, Flanders, Tyrol, Barcelona, etc., to all present and to come, greeting.
>
> Our very dear and well-loved cousin the Princess des Ursins has rendered us since the beginning of our reign, and continues to render us, so many essential and agreeable services that we have thought fit no longer to defer giving her some signal marks of our gratitude and of the esteem in which we hold her. This Princess, after having quitted the rank and prerogatives which she held at the Court of Rome, to accept the post of Camarera Mayor to our very dearest wife, went to meet her at Nice in Provence. She conducted her to our states of Spain and acquitted herself of all these functions with so much care, exactness and wisdom as to acquire all possible confidence and consideration. When, in order to go and take command of our armies in our kingdom and states of Italy, we left the regency of our kingdoms in Spain to the Queen our dearest wife, the Princess des Ursins redoubled her zeal and assiduity near her person. She has always assisted her with her care and counsels with so much prudence and affection that we have at all times and on all occasions felt the happy effects of conduct so judicious, faithful and estimable. Since it has pleased God to bless our Royal House and assure its succession by a happy posterity, she has again accepted to give the tenderest and most effectual cares to our very dear and well-loved son the Prince of the Asturias, in whom the result and progress are remarkable.
>
> All these services so distinguished and important to the good of our states and the happiness of our reign, the application with which this Princess gives us ever more proofs of her complete attachment to our person and to that of the Queen our very dear wife and of the Prince our child, and the good success

[1] Trémoïlle, v. 208; letter of 17 Aug. 1711.

which has followed the salutary counsels she has given us, have engaged us to seek the means of rewarding her in proportion to so many services, and which may serve in future as a sure token of the greatness of our gratitude as well as of the merit and virtues of the Princess. It is this which has given us the idea to assure to her, not only a considerable revenue, but also a country of which she can enjoy the sovereignty. To which we are all the more inclined that this Princess, belonging to the House of Trémoïlle, one of the most illustrious in the kingdom of France, is allied not only to the princes of the blood of the House of France, but also to many other sovereign Houses of Europe, and that, knowing her enlightened mind and wise conduct in all things, we are convinced that she will govern with justice the people and country subject to her, and that this great grace will always be regarded as an effect of the justice and magnificence of sovereigns towards those who have been happy enough to render them important services.

For which reasons we declare . . . that we have given to our very dear and well-loved cousin Marie-Anne de la Trémoïlle, Princess des Ursins, for herself, her heirs and successors, the duchy, town and castle of Limbourg, forming part of the Spanish Netherlands, with its towns, market towns, villages, castles, houses, lands, etc., and the same rights and powers shall belong successively after her to her nearest heir, *in case she has not otherwise disposed of it*, and that she shall enjoy entirely and without charge the revenues of thirty thousand crowns rent. . . . All which rights and revenues she will begin to enjoy from this day. . . . And in consequence will remain incommutable proprietor of the said Duchy of Limbourg *with power to dispose of it by donation during her lifetime or by testament to such person and with such conditions as she thinks fit, even to effect an exchange or otherwise*.[1]

And since among the divers propositions made to us from time to time to arrive at peace, some tend to a dismemberment of the said Spanish Netherlands and the other States which compose our monarchy, we declare our intention that no attack on this gift shall be made by the treaties of peace, and that all the princes and powers interested shall ratify the gift made by us of the said Duchy of Limbourg . . . and that this be a condition of the treaties which shall be made concerning the Spanish Netherlands.

Given in our town of Corella in the Kingdom of Navarre, the 20th day of the month of September, in the year of grace 1711, and the eleventh of our reign.[2]

Eight days after, probably owing to the Elector's objec-

[1] The italics are my own, the words being important as a proof of the truth of Saint-Simon's statement that she intended exchanging the property with Louis for another in Touraine.
[2] Geffroy, 480.

tions, this donation was considerably reduced. The feudal state of Limbourg no longer figures as the proposed sovereignty, which has dwindled to three of its towns—Fauquemont, Dalheim and Rolduc. The second document of donation, also written from Corella, bears the date 28 September, 1711.[1]

But even these three towns were too much for the Elector to resign out of the barren territory allotted him, and in November he sent an envoy — the Comte de Monasterol, to Versailles to treat the affair with d'Aubigny, who was acting for the Princess, the result being that the donation was again reduced to the single state of Durbuy in Luxembourg.

However, since the Princess's intention was to exchange with Louis the principality in the Netherlands for one in Touraine, one tract of land was as good as another provided it were near enough to the frontier to be desirable to him, and she seems to have made little difficulty in signing the fresh treaty, which runs as follows:

> Treaty passed between Marie-Anne de la Trémoïlle, Princess des Ursins, and the Elector of Bavaria, to whom Philippe V. has ceded the Catholic Netherlands. The Elector gives full powers to Ferdinand Solar, Comte de Monasterol, Madame des Ursins confides hers to Louis-Jean-Baptiste d'Aubigny, equerry, Seigneur de la Rochechargé, counsellor to the King, Grand Master of the Waters and Forests of Touraine, Anjou and Maine, secretary and equerry to their Catholic Majesties. The Elector cedes to the Princess the town, castle and county of Durbuy, and will compensate the Seigneur de Grosbendonk for it. Madame des Ursins accepts this treaty and causes it to be sealed with her seal in red wax.[2]

Thus the Elector's share in the matter was settled, but both Philippe's cession to him and his to the Princess had to be ratified at The Hague before either could enter into possession, and, as will be seen, Austria, supported by Holland claiming the whole of the Spanish Netherlands, the Emperor was naturally violently opposed to the Princess, his worst enemy, having any rights in a position of so much military importance, while the clause as to a possible exchange had also excited their suspicions.

From the first the Princess seems to have had in her mind the idea of exchanging her Flemish principality with Louis

[1] Trémoïlle, v. 214.   [2] Ibid., v. 227; dated 8 Dec. 1711.

for one in Touraine, for as early as the beginning of the preceding year (1710) she had commissioned d'Aubigny, then in France as her envoy to the Peace Conference, to buy the post of Grand Master of the Waters and Forests of Touraine, Anjou and Maine, in order presumably to give a pretext for his construction of the magnificent château near Amboise mentioned by Saint-Simon, with which he was occupied during his long stay in France of the present year.[1]

This affair of the sovereignty lasted for more than six years, and might have lasted for sixteen had not her disgrace put a stop to her insistence.

"This sovereignty changed form and place and finally dissipated in smoke," writes Saint-Simon. But before its final disappearance it was solid enough to occupy the attention of all Europe and retard the general peace for more than three years, since at her direction Philippe obstinately refused to sign any treaty which did not guarantee her rights. In spite of Louis' anger and Madame de Maintenon's rebukes, the refusal of Holland and the indifference of the other allies, she held her own and refused to renounce her claim, and it is probable, judging from previous examples of her tenacity, that had ruin not overwhelmed her in the midst of her efforts, she would have succeeded in placing the diadem of Limbourg or its equivalent on her own head as she had in establishing the crown of Spain on that of Philippe V.

[1] Trémoïlle, v. 49; letter of 2 March, 1710.

CHAPTER XIII

DEATHS OF LOUIS' HEIRS (1712)

MEANWHILE the negotiations for peace were progressing. Under the Tory administration England had engaged to make peace with France and retire from the Coalition on the following terms, reasonable enough and affecting France more than Spain — the recognition of Queen Anne as Sovereign of Great Britain, the demolition of the fortresses and ports of Dunkerque, the cession of Gibraltar, Port-Mahon, Newfoundland and Hudson's Bay and the monopoly of the slave trade in America. This treaty was conducted secretly and unknown to the Dutch, who, faithful to their alliance with Austria, exacted the cession of the whole of the Spanish Netherlands to be held in reserve by them for the Emperor till the conclusion of the war. As for the Emperor Charles himself, he refused absolutely to hear of peace or even to send plenipotentiaries to the Conference unless Philippe consented to cede the whole of his foreign possessions with the exception of the Indies, in which case he would allow him to remain King of Spain. So bent was he on continuing the war that he kept an army of a hundred and sixty thousand men ready for immediate attack as a perpetual menace to France, thus keeping the country in a terrible state of nervous tension.

However, in spite of this peace seemed in the air, for the Emperor could not continue the war alone indefinitely, and Queen Anne was inflexible. At the New Year even Madame de Maintenon grew less pessimistic and in a rare outburst of gaiety wrote to the Princess on 25 January, 1712: "Judging from all appearances we shall have a glorious peace, a peace which will establish a great monarchy in the House of France, a peace which will make the happiness of Their Catholic Majesties. Could we have believed that it would have come to us through Queen Anne!"[1] Thus there were rejoicings at the Court of Versailles, amusement was the order of the day and hunting, dancing, feasting and high play compensated the

[1] Bossange, ii. 260 ; letter of 25 Jan. 1712.

courtiers for the sale of their gold plate and the black bread of the war.

As for the Court of Madrid, it amused itself too in its humbler way. " The Catholic Queen continues to keep well in her *grossesse*," wrote the Chevalier de Bourke, so-called ambassador of the Pretender to Spain.[1] "They try to amuse her with some comedies which they began to act yesterday at the palace. It must be confessed that the amusements of this Court are slight and little suited to the age of a prince born at Versailles and a princess born in Turin. . . . These amusements consist in passing three or four hours listening to a very tiresome Spanish comedy played by very poor actors and actresses. Monsieur de Bonnac and other distinguished people are preparing to act a tragedy of Corneille before their Catholic Majesties. They have already had a rehearsal which pleased them exceedingly."[2]

Even the Princess had given herself up to peaceful pursuits and was having the Royal palace in Madrid refurnished and redecorated under her own eye, and the gardens of Buen Retiro, where the Queen was to be confined, replanted and embellished. Louis at her request had sent one of his own architects and a head-gardener to superintend these alterations and was extremely interested in them as being his own special hobby. All these pastimes and occupations indicated that peace was within view and life beginning to resume its everyday routine.

But suddenly comedies, decorations and gardens all were forgotten, and a series of tragedies, such as Sophocles would have attributed to some outraged Deity, struck France, Madrid and all Europe with horror. One after the other the heirs of Louis XIV. were struck down, and he, whose male progeny was so numerous as to seem to defy Fate, found himself within a fortnight with only one sickly infant to carry on his sovereignty in the direct line.

On 7 February Madame de Maintenon had written to the Princess of the terrible ravages the measles were making in Paris, and after enumerating its victims added that the Dauphine, former Duchess of Burgundy, was ill with an

---

[1] Colonel Bourke, an Irishman who had followed James II. to France and later been named by the Pretender ambassador to Madrid.
[2] Trémoïlle, vi. 3; letters of 18 Jan. and 1 Feb. 1712.

inflammation of the jaw, so painful that she had had convulsions and screamed like a woman in labour. The same evening she opened her letter to say that she was a little better, "having taken four doses of opium and chewed and smoked tobacco."[1]

A week later she was dead.

The Dauphin, Philippe's brother, who had not stirred from her bedside, was next attacked and succumbed a few days later. A fortnight after it was the turn of their two children. The eldest, the little Duc de Bretagne, died on 8 March, and the life of the baby Duc d'Anjou, afterwards Louis XV., hung on a thread. On 17 April Madame de Maintenon announced: "To-day everyone goes to Saint-Denis and will see put in the vault on the same day three corpses, of which the eldest is only twenty-nine."

These deaths, instead of being attributed to the lack of hygiene and ignorance of the doctors, who allowed everyone—even Louis himself—to remain in the sick-rooms, were put down to poison; no great personage at that epoch ever died without. In this case the supposed criminal was naturally the person most interested in the succession, the Duc d'Orléans, who was considered capable of any crime and was known to dabble in chemistry.

He had never recovered favour since the affair of the Spanish Conspiracy, and at this new suspicion his ostracism became more accentuated than ever. Louis and Madame de Maintenon refused to see him, all the Court turned its back on him, and even in Paris he was insulted if he showed himself in public. The suspicions against him were fomented by another accusation which followed close on the deaths of Louis' heirs and was said to have been spread by the Princess des Ursins.

The story, which was in everybody's mouth, was as follows: A young officer, his protégé who had served under him in Spain, since turned monk under the name of Père le Marchand, had returned for no apparent reason to Madrid, where he was accused of having mixed corrosive poisons with the food about to be served to the King. Luckily suspicions had been aroused and the poisoned dish seized, but the poisoner succeeded in making his escape. The Princess, with the deaths of Versailles in her mind, at once

[1] Bossange, ii. 264; letter of 7 Feb. 1712.

connected the affair with the Duc d'Orléans and sent her nephew the Prince de Chalais in pursuit. Le Marchand had managed to cross the frontier and taken refuge in a convent near Poitiers when the Prince came up with him. He was arrested and searched, and various powders and drugs were found on him, and these the Prince ordered to be tried on some dogs, all of which died in agony. Doubt was no longer possible, and he was taken by Chalais himself to Paris, thrown in the Bastille and tortured to discover at whose orders he had acted. For three months he endured in silence the worst tortures, and finally was taken back to Spain and imprisoned in the fortress of Segovia where he remained till his death.

It seems incredible that the Princess should have invented a story capable of being verified by so many witnesses, but whether the would-be assassin was, as she insisted, in the pay of the Duc d'Orléans is open to doubt. In any case the accusation added immensely to the suspicions already excited against him, and he hardly dared show himself either in Paris or Versailles.

The sudden death of Louis' heirs was appalling enough as a tragedy, but its political effect was even more fatal. Louis was seventy-four and at his death only one sickly child was between Philippe and his throne. The Testament of Charles II. had expressly stipulated that at his accession he should renounce all rights to the crown of France, but this Louis had not only refused, but had formally confirmed them. At the time little attention had been paid since, with so many between him and the throne, his chances were slight, but now the old bugbear—France and Spain under one sovereign—was resuscitated. Europe began to murmur, and England, which had been so eager for peace, put a stop to all negotiations till Philippe had signed his renunciation in due form.

At the Court of Madrid this was ill received. The chance of a speedy succession to the greatest monarchy of Europe was too tempting to be lightly renounced. Even Philippe the lethargic was attracted by it. As for the Queen, excited by the Princess, she would not hear of renunciation. Between them they had conceived the project that at the death, which then seemed certain, of the little Duc d'Anjou, Philippe should at once return to France and take his place as Dauphin, leaving the Queen Regent in Spain until

Louis' death—when—with the Princess as counsellor who knows but what France and Spain under one monarch would be capable of triumphing over a combined Europe! With such ambitions in view the exactions of England were received not only with hesitation but hostility.

The alternative, however, was worse than a mere break in the peace conference, it was a prompt renewal of the partially dissolved Coalition and fresh outbreak of war. The three English plenipotentiaries, Lord Oxford, Lord Bolingbroke and the poet Matthew Prior, declared formally that if Philippe refused to renounce immediately all his rights in favour of his brother the Duc de Berry, and the Duc de Berry any future claim on Spain, the war would recommence with more violence than before, and he would be forced to abdicate in favour of the Emperor.[1] Louis, with his country already on the verge of a revolution, was terrified and wrote to Bonnac to force Philippe to choose between renouncing Spain and retaining his rights to the throne of France, or signing immediately the act of renunciation.

Make it clearly understood to the Princess des Ursins, and through her to the King and Queen of Spain [he wrote], that all I could do has been to continue the war until the throne of Spain was assured to them, that it is not just that I should complete the ruin of my country solely to preserve for them the right either of one day uniting the monarchies of France and Spain, or dividing them between their children. The Catholic King must therefore decide immediately whether he will abandon Spain and return to France, to live there awaiting a succession which perhaps neither he nor his children will ever inherit, or remain in Spain and renounce his rights as the English demand. . . . I have difficulty in thinking that a prince who has reigned more than eleven years, who loves his subjects and has received so many proofs of their fidelity, can resolve to abandon them to lead a private life in expectation of a succession (the greatest in Europe it is true) but which is uncertain. If the King is not impressed by these reasonings he must be forced at last to understand that it is impossible for me to continue the war any longer and that . . . I shall be obliged to make a separate peace with conditions obviously disagreeable to him and myself. . . .

Remaining master of Spain and the Indies he should not complain of a treaty which guarantees him their possession. But even should he complain, it would not engage me to sacri-

[1] Trémoïlle, vi, 21 ; letter from Torcy to the Princess of 9 April, 1712.

fice my own kingdom, and peace being absolutely necessary my intention is to make it as quickly as possible, whatever answer I receive from the King of Spain.[1]

The same day Torcy wrote to the Princess declaring that it was impossible to continue the war, that the enemy was menacing Arras and Cambrai, that there were no means of resistance since money was lacking, that the frontier was weak, and that if a battle took place and was lost, a revolution would inevitably follow, finally that Philippe must decide one way or the other, as further discussion was impossible.[2]

Coerced by these menaces, on 22 April Philippe, with an ill grace, consented to renounce his rights to the throne of France, but demanded in return for the sacrifice that Gibraltar and all his Italian states should be restored to him and the Princess's sovereignty assured.

As you have so kindly approved the sovereignty which I have given to the Princess des Ursins [he wrote to his grandfather], I hope that you will contribute that this grace shall have effect. To this end I beg you earnestly to give necessary orders to your plenipotentiaries that, whatever may happen in Flanders, this little corner of ground, so unimportant to whoever will be master of that country, shall be reserved for her . . . or, if that is impossible, that she shall be given a sovereignty elsewhere. Besides the infinite attachment which I have always recognised in the Princess for you, which makes her deserving of your goodness, you could give no greater pleasure to the Queen and me. We hope it therefore from your friendship and shall have all the gratitude possible.[3]

From which it will be seen that in the midst of disputes over the largest sovereignties of Europe the Princess had no idea of letting her own small one be forgotten.

But the Emperor, supported by Holland, insisted that the whole of the Spanish Netherlands should be reserved for himself, and the Princess was forced *bon gré mal gré* to renounce her hopes of an eventual exchange with Louis. But a sovereignty of some kind she would have, and since the Netherlands was impossible she cast her eye on one of the Spanish states in Italy, since according to Philippe's demand he hoped to retain them. "One might turn one's

[1] Baudrillart, i. 479; letter to Bonnac of 18 April, 1712.
[2] Trémoïlle, vi. 25; letter of 18 April, 1712.
[3] Baudrillart, i. 484; letter of 22 April, 1712.

thoughts to some rather pleasant place in Italy," she suggested to Torcy, and asked him to insinuate to the English and Dutch that if they complied she "might in future be of use to them at the Court of Spain." [1]

The pretensions of his grandson to be reinstated in his Italian provinces seemed to Louis ridiculous, but to his surprise England not only took them into consideration but made a fresh proposal by which Philippe should retain his right to the succession of France, on condition that he should cede Spain and the Indies to the Duke of Savoy (a favourite with Queen Anne) and reign meantime over a monarchy composed of Sicily, Naples, and the Duke's own states of Piedmont, Savoy, Montferrat and Nice.

Louis the egoist was enchanted, for it was all clear profit to France which, if Philippe succeeded him, would be the richer by the greater part of Italy. Changing his tactics, therefore, he wrote to Bonnac vaunting the advantages of this new proposal, instructing him to use all efforts to persuade his grandson to accept, and to Philippe himself, holding out all the baits he thought most likely to attract him—the residence at Turin so near France, whence he could visit Versailles from time to time, the probability of the early death of the little Dauphin, and even should he live, the certainty of the regency during his minority. "I should regard it as the greatest happiness of my life," he wrote, once more shamelessly eating his own words of the preceding month, "that you should decide to return to me and retain the rights which you will one day regret in vain if you abandon them." [2]

But the same messenger who brought this paternal letter to Philippe carried another to Bonnac to be given to him only if he refused, a letter harsh and menacing, threatening that in that case Louis would sign the treaty of peace without him.

But Philippe (alias the Princess), who had supported eleven years of hardship and peril, now that at last the loyalty of the Spaniards had been won and all the country except Catalonia had returned to its allegiance, now that for the first time Fortune smiled on him, that his treasury was full and his army in good order, found it monstrous that he should be forced to abandon a kingdom preserved with

---

[1] Trémoïlle, vi. 39; letter of 7 May, 1712.
[2] Baudrillart, i. 490; letter of 18 May, 1712.

so much suffering, for one so insignificant. On 29 May, therefore, a battle royal took place between Bonnac and the Princess, in which in Philippe's name she scouted contemptuously the idea that a King of Spain should deign to become Kinglet of Sicily, represented with much reason that the Duke of Savoy would be a dangerous neighbour for France, and finally declared that Philippe absolutely refused the proposal, and a little later—8 July—Philippe issued a proclamation which enchanted his subjects, announcing in due form his renunciation to the succession of France.

In the midst of all these high doings of the year 1712 we have to record a birth, a marriage and a death.

The birth, which took place on 7 June, was that of another Prince—Don Philippe; this time perfectly well made—"fat and big and even more beautiful than the Prince of the Asturias," the Princess announced.[1] The marriage, that of her niece, daughter of the Duchess Lanti (whom she had sent for and appointed *dame d'honneur* to the Queen), with the Duc d'Havré, one of the richest of the grandees. The death, that of the Duc de Vendôme, late conquerer of Villaviciosa.

The marriage of Mademoiselle Lanti with the Duc d'Havré was celebrated on 5 June with great pomp, in the hall of the Queen's apartment, two days before the birth of her son, and is thus described by Bonnac:

> The Queen was present seated on a sofa, her face entirely uncovered, the glands, which up to now had obliged her to wear a scarf under her chin, being almost entirely dissipated, and the slight swelling which remains causing no deformity and being imperceptible except from very near.
>
> The ceremony took place in this manner. The wives of the grandees and other ladies of condition came to the Queen's apartment and placed themselves on her left; the grandees entering from the King's apartment placing themselves on her right. The bride and bridegroom were then called and appeared simultaneously at the doors of the two antechambers facing each other in the hall. They knelt together before the King and Queen and afterwards the Duc d'Havré went to the side of the grandees and Mademoiselle de Lanti to that of their wives. Whereupon the Cardinal del Giudice, who performed the ceremony, entered in his Cardinal's robes with the Patriarch of the Indies as Grand Almoner, and after having put on a stole he performed the usual ceremonies and gave the benediction.

[1] Trémoïlle, vi. 51 ; letter of 7 June, 1712.

DEATHS OF LOUIS' HEIRS

It is the custom that the brides do not respond to the first nor the second interrogation and give their consent only at the third. Mademoiselle de Lanti did not omit this, and being asked whether she would take the Duc d'Havré for husband, threw herself at the Queen's feet and asked her permission to say yes, and then repeated it with a very good grace. The Queen spoke to all the ladies with her usual grace and wit. The King was seated and uncovered. Afterwards they supped in the apartment of the Princess des Ursins in her quality of Camarera Mayor. The table was served by the officers of the Queen. There were only twelve covers, no one having been invited but the godfathers and godmothers, the Cardinal and the Patriarch. Madame des Ursins did the honours.[1]

So much for the marriage. The death of the Duc de Vendôme calls up images less agreeable.

On 9 April he had left Madrid to superintend the defences of Valencia and from thence, under pretext that matters were not sufficiently advanced, had retired with a few boon companions to Vinaros, a town on the sea-coast famous for its fish. Here, according to d'Argenson, "surrounded by a little circle of flatterers and *débauchés*, he gave himself up at his ease to all kinds of orgy dear to him, gorged fish which he loved to madness, whether fresh or stale, well or ill dressed, drank thick strong wines and finally gained a bad indigestion, or rather a malady consequent on repeated indigestions."[2]

Saint-Simon completes the narrative as follows:

The illness increased so quickly and in so strange a manner that those with him suspected poison and sent for help on every side. But the malady would not wait and increased rapidly with strange symptoms. All who were with him abandoned him and fled, so that he remained in the hands of three or four of his lowest valets, while the others pillaged everything and then left him. He passed thus the two or three last days of his life without a priest or any aid except one surgeon. The three or four valets left with him, seeing him at the last extremity, laid hands on the few things which remained, and for want of better dragged the counterpane from over him and the mattress from under him. He cried piteously to them at least not to let him die naked on the straw. Thus died the most arrogant of men![3]

This must certainly be an exaggeration although it is true that he was neglected, since Alberoni, who was with

---

[1] Trémoïlle, vi. 49; letter of 6 June, 1712.
[2] D'Argenson, *Mémoires*, ed. Jannte, i. 133.
[3] Saint-Simon, xxiii. 81.

him at the time, wrote to his friend Rocca, in Parma, that his illness was treated as though it was a small matter and that he died without a proper doctor.[1] But whatever the circumstances of his death he had a nobler burial than he deserved, for he was interred with Royal pomp in the Escurial, among the princes of the blood of Spain.

In the beginning of September the Princess, suffering from dizziness and swellings of the legs—or so she said, left the King and Queen in Madrid and went to Bagnères for her long-retarded three-months' cure. As Altesse of Spain she travelled with great pomp, escorted by a regiment of Royal guards and with all the state and ceremony due to an Infanta. At each town she passed, the notables, civic and ecclesiastic, came to meet her on the road with complimentary speeches, and crowds of suppliants lined her path. Her nights, however, were passed in less agreeable company, and not all her escort of Royal guards could save her from the onslaught of bugs, as she herself relates.[2]

Was this visit really to drink the waters of Bagnères? The Princess was not one in a political crisis to waste time nursing a trifling illness. It will be remembered that the one person in whom she had confidence (and it must be added, the one person who seemed to merit it) was Jean Orry, Seigneur de Vignory, former Minister of Finance, who had shared her disgrace in 1704, and returned with her to Spain the following year. He had again incurred Louis' anger on Puységur's charges of negligence in provisioning the armies, and had been finally recalled in 1708, since which year he had remained in Paris idle and discontented. The Princess, with whom he was in constant communication, had several times demanded his return, but Louis had maintained his refusal, and now at the zenith of power, feeling the need of someone on whose ability, judgment and loyalty she could rely, she had arranged that he should join her secretly at Bagnères to prepare plans for his return, and it seems probable that her cure was merely a pretext for this meeting, since Orry was forbidden to cross the frontier. He joined her there in October soon after her arrival, and the result of their interview was that, early

[1] Bourgeois, *Lettres d'Alberoni à Rocca*, 178; letter of 11 June, 1712.
[2] Bossange, ii. 322; letter of Madame de Maintenon to the Princess of 9 Oct. 1712.

in the following spring, Philippe wrote to his grandfather begging that he would allow him to come to Madrid for a few months only in order to examine the financial situation and consult with his ministers as to the conditions of peace. To this Louis gave a grudging consent, replying coldly that the high-roads were free to all. As will be seen, he remained in Spain until the Princess's disgrace.

His visit to Bagnères was not known at Versailles, as the following entries made by Dangeau in his *Diary* show, for Orry had played too important a part in Spanish affairs to be ignored. Three times he refers to the visit of the Princess without any mention of him. The first entry is of 17 October: "The Princess des Ursins has arrived at Bagnères escorted by the King of Spain's guards. She writes here that she has already taken the waters during three or four days, that her swellings have diminished, and that she does not mean to return to Madrid till the end of November."

On 8 November: "The Princess des Ursins has left Bagnères to return to Madrid. She will pass through Bidache, where she will see the Queen-Dowager. From thence she will go to Bayonne and will be in Madrid before the end of the month."

And on 19 December: "The Princess des Ursins has arrived in Madrid in very good health, and the King and Queen show her more friendship than ever." [1]

[1] Dangeau, xiv. 241, 260 and 281.

CHAPTER XIV

PEACE WITHOUT HONOUR (1713)

IT is unjust to accuse the Princess, as do Saint-Simon and others, of prolonging the war and preventing Philippe from signing peace with Holland solely because the republic refused her sovereignty in the Netherlands. As has been seen, she had resigned herself to accept one elsewhere, but she considered with justice that the King of Spain could not do otherwise than show resentment at the insolence with which the Dutch had maintained their refusal, which constituted a veritable affront to the nation itself.

So thought the Duc d'Ossone, chief of the Spanish plenipotentiaries, who had no special liking for the Princess nor any interest in her sovereignty, but having an immense pride and tenacity for the honour of his country had refused to accept peace without it, since it had been stipulated by his master as one of the conditions of his signature.

At the beginning of the year 1713 all Europe except Austria was desirous of peace. On 10 April Louis, having with great difficulty extracted free powers from his grandson, signed a separate peace with England, Prussia, Portugal and Savoy on the terms above mentioned, namely the recognition of Queen Anne as Sovereign of Great Britain; the withdrawal of his support of the Pretender, who was to quit his country; the renunciation by Philippe of all claim to the throne of France and of the Duc de Berry and the Duc d'Orléans to that of Spain; the demolition of the fortresses and ports of Dunkerque; the cession of Gibraltar, Minorca, Hudson's Bay and Newfoundland to England, together with the monopoly of the slave-trade; the guardianship of the Spanish Netherlands to be committed to Holland till the Emperor consented to peace; the recognition of the Elector of Brandenbourg (father of Frederic the Great) as King of Prussia; the kingdom of Sicily to be given to the Duke of Savoy, together with the succession to the throne of Spain failing Philippe's descendants. In return for which mutilation of his country Philippe would remain King of Spain and the Indies, the Emperor would evacuate Catalonia, hostilities would be suspended in Italy, and Lille and Bethune restored to France by Holland. Finally a sovereignty with a revenue of thirty thousand crowns would be assured to the Princess des Ursins in Luxembourg.

On 17 April, the day on which he signed this treaty, Louis wrote in the highest spirits to his grandson: "At last your crown is established and you are recognised King even with eagerness by your enemies."[1] And to Bonnac his ambassador: "Tell the Princess des Ursins that the clause in the treaty which gives me most pleasure is that which establishes the sovereignty which the King of Spain has reserved for her in the Netherlands."[2]

The Queen wrote enthusiastic thanks and the Princess, delighted, was all gratitude: "This magnificent gift," she wrote, "has become more precious since I have known it was agreeable to Your Majesty and that Your Majesty has so kindly contributed to my obtaining it."[3] And to Torcy: "I confess ingenuously that I am very sensible to this dazzling proof of the esteem which two kings have given me and I have no false modesty on the subject."[4] It will be seen presently how premature were her thanks.

Louis was charmed at having thus extricated himself from the war of his own making with relatively small losses, but when the details of the treaty reached Madrid and the mutilation of Spain became known, the indignation was intense. Even Philippe, now a man of thirty and presumably less foolish than formerly, bitterly resented the seizure of his provinces at a moment when his military successes gave him the right to expect better terms. "I will maintain my kingdom intact while I have a drop of blood in my veins!" he had declared when victory seemed hopeless, and now that he was victorious the spoliation imposed on him, and so joyfully accepted by Louis, was that of a defeat. Out of all his immense possessions nothing but Spain and the Indies! In Flanders nothing. In Italy nothing. Sicily ceded to his most treacherous enemy with the possible succession to Spain itself. Gibraltar and

[1] Baudrillart, i. 524; letter of 17 April, 1713.
[2] Trémoïlle, vi. 106; letter of 17 April, 1713.
[3] Ibid., vi. 110; letter of 1 May, 1713.
[4] Ibid., vi. 117; letter of 30 May, 1713.

Minorca lost. Catalonia still in the hands of the Emperor and the Emperor himself, in spite of the defection of his allies, bent on continuing the war. From the Spanish point of view there was little cause for rejoicing and the Princess would have been a traitor to the country of her adoption had she counselled Philippe to sign without protest so ignominious a peace.

But she did not. She incurred the wrath of Versailles by forcing him to hesitate, to raise objections, to refuse his signature, to propose amendments—even that Louis himself should compensate him for his losses by the cession of some of his own territory.[1]

It was not long before she discovered that she also had been duped. In August the Elector of Bavaria wrote to her that since the states promised him by France and Spain had been reduced to the small Duchy of Luxembourg, it would be impossible for him to cut off it a sovereignty of thirty thousand crowns revenue, and she could not but admit the justice of his objection. She learnt about the same time also that Louis' plenipotentiaries at The Hague, while feigning to support her claim, had done so with so much indifference that it was hardly mentioned at all, and that the Duc d'Ossone, the only one who had insisted on its being at least discussed, had been severely rebuked by Louis. It was on the discovery of this chicanery that she set her teeth and vowed that, come what might, her sovereignty she would have, and directed the Duc d'Ossone to attack the treaty and insist that she should be put in possession of the original gift of Limbourg or, if Limbourg was impossible, of some province of equal value.[2]

She had already gained the support of Queen Anne who had formally engaged herself to guarantee her sovereignty in return for certain commercial concessions and permission to construct fortresses for the protection of the slave-merchants on the Rio della Plata.[3] This guarantee she now

---

[1] Trémoïlle, vi. 119 ; letter from Torcy to the Princess of 3 June, 1713.
[2] Ibid., vi. 137 ; letter to Torcy of 20 Aug. 1713.
[3] The Queen signed the engagement in June 1713, in the following words : "Ut constaret quanti Sua Sacra Majestas regina Magnæ Britanniæ dominam principessam Ursini faciat, jam articulo vigesimo primo conventionum pacificatoriarum inter marchionem à Bedmar ex parte M. S. Catholicæ et comitem Lexington ex parte dictæ Majistratis Britannæ, matriti die 27 martii proxime elapsi firma-

insisted on Holland observing, and Philippe, indignant at his own humiliation, needed little persuasion to refuse his signature without it. In vain Louis menaced, Torcy scolded and Madame de Maintenon rebuked, "Do not suffer it to be said that you and your sovereignty are the sole cause of the continuance of the war." [1]

Dangeau, faithful echo of Versailles, notes in his *Diary* on 12 August: "The Spanish plenipotentiaries are still at Utrecht, peace not having been signed between Spain and Holland; but it is hoped it will soon be finished, one small difficulty only remaining, the sovereignty in Flanders promised by the King of Spain to Madame des Ursins to which France and England have agreed." To which Saint-Simon adds: "This hitch in the treaty and for such a cause displeased the King infinitely, and this mad ambition may be reckoned as the cause of the Princess's ruin." [2]

Louis was more than displeased, he was furious. And he revenged himself in his usual way. The Emperor, because he needed his troops to attack France rather than from any idea of fulfilling his compact, had at last removed his army from Catalonia, but had succeeded so well in stirring up the people against Philippe that they refused any sort of submission. To gain their favour at the beginning of his occupation he had restored the old privileges which Philippe, from a just idea of equality, had abolished on his accession. Therefore they preferred his rule and declared themselves ready to fight not only Spain but France also, rather than accept Philippe as their sovereign. The Austrian troops evacuated the province in July, but when Philippe's viceroy, the Duc de Popoli, presented himself to take official possession he was greeted with a volley of cannon. There remained nothing, therefore, but to besiege the capital and reduce the rebels by force, and Louis had promised to send troops to help him which were awaited with the greatest anxiety.

turarum D. S. Majestas Regina Magnæ Britanniæ se obligavit et præsenti articulo se obligat promittit et spondet se effecturam et realitur procuraturam ut, statim et nullâ interpositâ morâ domina principissa Ursini mittatur in realem et actualem possessionem ducatiis Limburgi aut aliarum ditionum, quæ, in Belgicis provinciis, ad plenam dictæ dominæ principissæ Ursini satisfactionem subrogabuntur." (See Geffroy, 486.)

[1] Bossange, ii. 429; letter of 3 Sept. 1713.
[2] Dangeau, xiv. 461 and xv. 7.

Refusal for refusal, thought the Egoist of Versailles. Since Philippe would not consent to sign peace with Holland in his interest neither would he consent to help him subdue his rebels. "You will easily understand," Torcy wrote coldly to the Princess, "the difficulty of furnishing what you require for a siege in Catalonia while the war continues in Germany."[1]

On 29 October Dangeau notes in his *Diary*: "The affairs of the Princess des Ursins have hitherto prevented the conclusion of peace between Spain and Holland. The King of Spain desires absolutely that the States-General shall guarantee the sovereignty demanded for her in the Netherlands. The Dutch made proposals approved by Monsieur d'Aubigny, her minister at Utrecht, but the Duc d'Ossone would not consent."[2] And on 22 November: "They write from Holland that the peace between that country and Spain does not advance nor the difficulties diminish. Monsieur d'Aubigny, *chargé-d'ffaires* of Madame des Ursins, has returned to Paris, where he has taken a house."[3]

In October, Louis, still vindictive, ignoring her demand that the new ambassador should be her old friend Tessé, without the usual formalities of Philippe's consent, sent her bitter enemy the Marquis de Brancas, friend and protégé of the Duc d'Orléans, with the special mission to employ all possible means to induce Philippe to sign peace with Holland and force the Princess to renounce her claim to the sovereignty.

The most urgent matter is that which regards the sovereignty of the Princess des Ursins [he himself wrote to Brancas]. This matter alone at present forms an insuperable obstacle to peace between the King of Spain and the Dutch Republic. The Duc d'Ossone, deceived by the counsels of those whose interest it is to retard the conclusion of peace, flatters himself he will obtain the guarantee of the States-General in favour of the Princess, and his representations have been accepted at Madrid against the advice of the Marquis de Montaleone and the Sieur d'Aubigny. They, however, knew better than he the disposition of the Dutch, as you will see by their resolution absolutely to refuse this guarantee.[4]

Louis de Brancas-Cereste, of the Neapolitan family of

---

[1] Trémoïlle, vi. 139; letter of 23 Aug. 1713.
[2] Dangeau, xv. 17.   [3] Ibid., xv. 30.
[4] Trémoïlle, vi. 150; letter of Louis XIV. to Brancas of 19 Oct. 1713.

Brancaccio, was at the date of his embassy forty-one years of age. It was not his first visit to Spain for he had already been sent as envoy-extraordinary on the birth of the Prince of the Asturias and had assisted the preceding year at the conquest of Girone, for which he had been rewarded with the Golden Fleece. According to Saint-Simon he was handsome, well-bred and intelligent, and Madame de Maintenon was never tired of singing his praises as one of the most simple-minded, disinterested and straightforward of men. He had, however, a physical defect which was perhaps symbolic, his right hand was deformed—like a lobster's claw it was said—and he always wore it gloved, even when eating.

His reception at Madrid was anything but cordial. Philippe treated him with the greatest coldness, the Queen hardly deigned to notice him and the Princess did him every ill turn in her power. She prevented his being lodged in the palace like his predecessors, would neither allow him to see the King nor assist at the Council, opened his dispatches, and in fact conducted herself precisely as she had done towards the d'Estrées.

It was a repetition of the same story, a life-and-death struggle for the mastery between the Ambassador representing Louis' interests and the Princess representing those of Spain. This time the result was not doubtful, for aided by her former experience the Princess had prepared her plan of defence, and how could an ambassador fulfil a mission which necessitated constant access to the King and Queen when he never saw either of them?

Brancas would seem to have gone to Spain with the deliberate intention of ruining the Princess, not so much from obedience to Louis as from the rancour he bore her as partisan of the Duc d'Orléans, and there was besides at Madrid another person whom he detested with almost as much virulence—her right hand and counsellor, Orry. As has been seen, the latter had been smuggled into the country on false pretences, but the months passed and a year, and still there was no talk of his departure. On the contrary he had taken root and place under the protection of the Princess and the favour of the King and Queen. On 31 January he received the title of Veedor or Controller-General of Finance, but being a French subject had to ask Louis' consent before he could accept it. This was refused, but so independent of Louis had Spain become that he retained both title and office, to the extreme fury of Brancas, who missed no opportunity of exciting Louis against him. His official dispatches are filled with attacks against him and the Princess, and to read them it would be imagined they were the worst enemies not only of France but also of Spain.

Bonnac, who was the Princess's friend, on his departure had left a memoir full of good advice concerning her for the benefit of his successor. "There is not a single courtier or minister here," he wrote, "who can boast of having the entire confidence of the King and Queen except the Princess des Ursins, but she adapts her wishes and words so well to those of their Catholic Majesties and has so much authority over their minds that they do always what she wants, while letting it appear that she wants always what they do. As long as she is in Spain there is but one way of handling any business with which one may be entrusted—to address oneself to her and gain her confidence."[1]

But Brancas had little interest in gaining her confidence. What he wanted was to obtain her disgrace, and for this he spared himself no pains. At his first interview he attacked her about her sovereignty, thus exciting her animosity and causing her to set in motion all her machinery against him, and from that day war was declared between them.

He began his attacks with relative moderation:

Madame des Ursins [he wrote to Torcy soon after his arrival] has received me with much courtesy and politeness, but I find no more in her the freedom and frankness she had formerly. At first I visited her frequently, but for some time I have seen her more rarely because three times she refused to see me, excusing herself on the pretext that she was with the Queen. I understood that she was not very pleased that I went so often. She is always equally courteous and polite when I see her, but I see clearly that she would have wished someone else in my place.... I see that an ambassador who is not to her taste will never succeed in this country and will not be able to serve the King usefully. It is only through her and by her means that any affair can succeed, and any other path would be useless and damaging. My first step was to speak to her against her interests and engage her to persuade the King and Queen to desist from their demand of the guarantee, which she did with a good grace, or so it seemed to me.... However, it is

[1] Trémoïlle, vi. 134; dated 7 Aug. 1713.

easy to see by her words that she thinks France is opposed to her pretensions and that the King's ministers have thwarted and delayed the establishment of her sovereignty. . . .

You know perhaps that little by little she has acquired a distinction at the Queen's receptions which no Camarera Mayor before her ever had. It is to be seated on a chair, the wives of the grandees being seated only on cushions on the floor. At first, on pretext of not being able to sit so low, they piled several cushions one on the other, and afterwards to avoid so many cushions they gave her a chair. The wives of the grandees were very vexed, but not one of them dared complain.[1]

Not long after he began his attacks on Orry:

The prejudice of the King and Queen and the Princess des Ursins in favour of this man is so great that they think him the cleverest person in the world. I thought it my duty to speak to Madame des Ursins and beg her to engage him to be more exact in keeping his word and in the payments due to the King's troops, and she replied shortly: "I see plainly that you are all furious against Monsieur Orry and want him to leave, but he will remain notwithstanding," and she asserted that France always wished to withdraw those who served Spain, as when Amelot was recalled. I told her she ought to have quite a different idea of France, which had given her sufficient proofs to the contrary. The conversation was rather sharp.[2]

One of his worst grievances of which he made the most was that the Queen had not yet deigned to admit him to her presence, a neglect which he knew would enrage Louis as a lack of respect towards himself.

Alas—if the Queen refused to receive him it was perhaps not so much from lack of courtesy as that the terrible disease which had first manifested itself more than two years before had begun its last ravages.

[1] Trémoïlle, vi. 156; letter of 30 Nov. 1713.
[2] Saint-Simon, xxiv. 431; letter of 16 Jan. 1714.

CHAPTER XV

DEATH OF THE QUEEN (1714)

On 11 November, 1713, the Princess had written in great anxiety to Torcy of a violent fever which had attacked the Queen in this last month of her pregnancy. It abated, however, and a fortnight later—23 November—she was delivered of another son, the third Prince living.[1] The event, which secured another successor to the throne of Spain, was her own death-warrant, for though the confinement had passed off well, and she had even suffered less than usual, she had no force to resist the subsequent exhaustion. The series of disasters and sufferings physical and mental which had been her married life had shattered her health, already undermined by insidious disease. For more than thirteen years she had struggled courageously against treachery, revolt and intrigues of every kind, had supported the fatigues and anxieties of government, the perils and privations of sudden flights, the bitterness of her father's cruelty, above all the exigencies of a selfish and abnormally sensual husband, and it is small wonder that at twenty-five she had no force left to resist the exhaustion of another maternity combined with the inroads of a tuberculosis of long standing.

A fortnight after the birth of the little Prince Ferdinand —" a very strong child with every intention of living," as the Princess wrote to Tessé—she had another violent attack of fever, but as before it passed away and she was proclaimed out of danger and progressing satisfactorily. She had no appetite it is true. Everything disgusted her, and the conditions of her life were not calculated to improve it. The weather was bad, it rained continually so that she could not go out, and as the windows of her room were never opened it is a marvel that she recovered even so far.

On New Year's Day, 1714, Brancas wrote to Torcy that he thought she was very much worse than was supposed. " It seems certain that it is a languorous malady, and that what they call heat is a slow fever which consumes

[1] Ferdinand, later Prince of the Asturias, who mounted the throne as Ferdinand VI. in 1746.

her. They say she is very sad and melancholy, and in truth I do not understand how she can support being shut up, without the windows of her apartment having been opened for more than six months."¹

To his great anger he had not yet been admitted to her presence, although to amuse her comedies had been acted in her room by her pages and the officers of her household, and it was not till two months after his arrival that he was finally presented.

"At last I have had the honour of seeing the Queen," he wrote to Louis on 15 January. "I did not find her so dejected as I feared after so long an illness. She was in an arm-chair near the fire, and I remarked that she rose with a good deal of energy and remained standing for some time without seeming tired." And on the same day to Torcy: "We went together, I and the Ambassador of Sicily.² The Queen had her hair dressed and was rouged a little." Later in the day he opened his letter to announce that she was much worse, so weak that they feared for her life. All the doctors of the city had been sent for, and all had agreed that the sole chance of saving her was—the nourishment given only to the dying—human milk.³ Poor Queen with no appetite reduced to a diet so disgusting!

The same day Philippe, desperate at the fear of losing her, sent a special messenger in hot haste to Versailles to beg his grandfather to send immediately the celebrated physician Helvétius, but there was little hope he could arrive in time to arrest the malady or even to find her living.

"He did not wish to go," Dangeau notes in his *Diary*, "as he is not well and very subject to gout, but the King commanded him and he has left in a post-chaise, with another following in case his own should break down, and five or six men on horseback. They think she will be dead before he arrives."⁴

He travelled incessantly day and night, relays being prepared for him at every posting-town, and sparing himself no fatigue he managed to arrive in Madrid on 11 February. As soon as he had seen her he said that

¹ Saint-Simon, xxiv. 429 ; letter of 1 Jan. 1714.
² The Duke of Savoy had been recognised King of Sicily in Sept. 1713.
³ Saint-Simon, xxiv. 430 ; letters to Louis XIV. and Torcy of 15 Jan. 1714.
⁴ Dangeau, xv. 85.

only a miracle could save her, and three days after—on 14 February—at nine o'clock in the morning, she died.

The day before [Brancas wrote] she seemed a little relieved, but at ten o'clock in the evening she grew worse and continued to grow worse till six in the morning when she lost consciousness. Never has been seen so much courage, firmness, and at the same time resignation. She called the doctors often to ask if she had still much time to live, in order to make the most of her last moments. They forced the King to leave her room at five in the morning, and as soon as she was dead they put him in a coach accompanied by his confessor and the captain of his guard, who conducted him to the house of the Duke of Medina-Cœli which had been prepared for him, where he shut himself up in his room with his confessor without wishing to see anyone. Shortly after the Princess des Ursins conducted the three Princes to the same house.[1]

Helvétius himself added the following details: "This great Princess expired last Wednesday, the fourteenth of the month, at nine in the morning. She preserved a healthy judgment and perfect consciousness up to the last moments of her life and employed them in suffering patiently and praising God—death sad but inevitable."

Details of the autopsy follow. All the organs of the body were healthy except the lungs, which were completely decayed. The tuberculosis from which she died dated from a long time and was incurable. The gland malady, which had caused so much anxiety, hardly existed.

So died this girl of twenty-five, of all the crowned heads of her time the most admirable, one of the few among the Royal princesses who preserved simplicity and dignity. Serious, loyal and sincere in an age of frivolity and intrigue, generous and enthusiastic in her affections, magnificently loyal to the one person she loved and esteemed, conscientious in performing the duties of her position, courageous and uncomplaining in misfortune, she offers a marked contrast to the princesses of Versailles, avid for amusement, incredibly frivolous—even to her own sister, the Duchess of Burgundy. She did more than anyone else to keep the poor-spirited egoist she had married on the throne, and it is doubtful if, with all her genius, the Princess would have succeeded without her in forcing the Spaniards to accept so unpopular and stupid a monarch.

[1] Saint-Simon, xxiv. 434; letters from Brancas to Louis XIV. and Torcy of 14 Feb. 1714.

CHAPTER XVI

ALLEGED SEQUESTRATION OF THE KING (1714)

WE have seen that the moment the breath had left the Queen's body Philippe, like a piece of furniture, had been transported from his palace to the house of the Duke of Medina-Cœli at the other end of the city, not far from his own summer palace of Buen Retiro, where he was joined shortly after by the Princess, who, as *gouvernante* of the princes, had conducted them also away from the house of death.

"The King of Spain was extremely moved," writes Saint-Simon, "but rather *à la royale.*"

So much *à la royale* indeed was his grief that a day or two after he was hunting and shooting, and in less than a month was making inquiries in all the Courts of Europe for a new wife.

"He was out on one of these expeditions," continues Saint-Simon, "when the body of the Queen was transported to the Escurial, and was close to the funeral procession. He looked at it, followed it with his eyes and continued his hunting"—an indifference which extracted even from the prince of snobs the censure: "Are these princes made like other human beings?"[1]

Brancas in his dispatch to Torcy of 19 February confirms this episode:

The King of Spain was persuaded to take exercise yesterday and the day before, a league from Madrid, in order to dissipate his grief, and knowing exercise to be good for his health. It is certain that nothing should be more precious, but it seems to me that he might have walked in the gardens of the house he lives in for a few days more, not to break an etiquette and custom so uniformly observed in Spain as that of remaining at home for nine days after the death of a near relation. The Court and people were very surprised to see their King out walking the same day that the Queen's body was borne to the Escurial.[2]

Brancas, however, was not consistent. His overwhelming

[1] Saint-Simon, xxiv. 181.
[2] Ibid., xxiv. 437; letter of 19 Feb. 1714.

desire to injure the Princess made him, at the same time that he justly finds fault with the King's unconventional promenades, complain bitterly of what he calls his sequestration, and launch a series of innuendoes, hints of a scandal so tremendous as to seem well-nigh incredible, but which ran like wild-fire throughout Europe—namely that the Princess des Ursins had the inconceivable audacity to aspire herself to replace the young Queen on the throne and in the bed of the King of Spain.

Brancas had been recalled. His embassy had proved a failure, a humiliation to himself and useless to Louis. At the beginning of March, Philippe, directed as usual by the Princess, had written to his grandfather insisting on his recall, to which Louis consented without difficulty since, instead of succeeding in his mission, he had proved himself entirely incompetent, the influence of the Princess being stronger than ever and her position more firmly established.

However, he was not one to allow himself beaten. His lobster claw was capable of a rough pinch, and the short time at his disposal he employed in inventing and amassing a series of calumnies against her, of which that of the sequestration was perhaps not the most injurious in the eyes of Louis and his ministers. There was hardly a crime of which he did not accuse her—of suppressing Philippe's authority completely and raising Orry to her side as co-dictator, of allowing no one to approach him but her own creatures, of hatred and abuse of France, of preventing his signing peace with Holland on account of her sovereignty, the loss of which she openly attributed to Louis. Finally, by a series of hints and insinuations, he succeeded in spreading the report that she was employing all efforts to make Philippe marry her and recognise her as Queen of Spain.

This last scandal the Court immediately took up and spread abroad till it reached the ears of Louis himself, to his intense indignation, the anger of Madame de Maintenon, and the terror of the Duc de Noirmoutier and the few friends who remained to her at Versailles.

Saint-Simon gives voice to the gossip of the Court on the subject:

It has been seen with what art the Princess des Ursins had unceasingly isolated the King of Spain, to what point she had

SEQUESTRATION OF THE KING

shut him up with the Queen and rendered him inaccessible, not only to his Court, but to his chief officers, his ministers, even to his most indispensable valets, so that he was served by two or three only who were French and devoted to herself. On pretext of his grief for the Queen's death she continued this seclusion and preferred the retreat of the Palace of Medina-Cœli to that of Buen Retiro because it was more retired and in a place much less extensive than the Royal palace, where all the Court could assemble and where it would have been difficult to prevent people from approaching the King. She herself took the place of the Queen and, to have some sort of pretext to be near him in the same solitude, had herself named *gouvernante* to his children.[1] But in order to be able to remain with him always, and that no one might know when they were together, she caused a wooden corridor to be made, leading from his cabinet to the apartment of his children in which she was lodged, so as to pass without being seen and without having to traverse the long series of rooms between, which were filled with courtiers. Thus no one ever knew if the King was alone or with Madame des Ursins, nor which of the two was with the other, nor when nor for how long they were together. This passage, roofed and glazed, was ordered with so much haste that, in spite of the King's piety, the work continued even on Sundays and feast days.

It was suspected that she had higher ambitions than becoming sole companion of the King. There were several princes. Equivocal words were spread abroad—namely, that with all which it had pleased God to bless him he had no more need of posterity, but only of a wife and one who could govern them. Not content to pass all her days with the King like the late Queen, nor to forbid him to work with his ministers except in her presence, she wished to render it durable by making sure of him continually. He was accustomed to the open air and all the more eager for it that he had remained shut up during the Queen's last days and those following her death. She chose, therefore, four or five men to accompany him and named, in preference to all others, Chalais, Massaran, Robec, and two or three more on whom she could rely, to follow him whenever he went out. They were called " the King's Recreadors "—those charged to amuse him. With all these plans, obsessions and preparatory words carefully spread abroad, everyone suspected that she had formed the project of marrying him, and this suspicion, as well as the dread of it, became general. The King his grandfather was terrified, and Madame de Maintenon, who had never succeeded in being recognised, was wrought up to the last pitch of jealousy.[2]

[1] She had been *gouvernante* of the Prince of the Asturias since his birth in 1707.
[2] Saint-Simon, xxiv. 214, etc.

In his additions to the *Journal* of Dangeau, who makes no allusion to the scandal, he writes:

> For reasons of friendship Dangeau does not mention the strange solitude in which Madame des Ursins kept the King of Spain after the Queen's death. Having no longer the Queen's help, she invoked that of solitude and a house where he could not hold his Court. The Buen Retiro was a Royal palace, superb and vast, and very distant from that in which the Queen died, and where it was most natural the King should go; but there he would have been too accessible. She usurped then the Queen's place, and so completely—almost to the bed —that all Spain and the King's grandfather were for a long time in the most mortal fear of seeing her declared Queen of Spain. The King worked before her and with her, as he did with the Queen. She directed the ministers, who did nothing without her order. The King left her only to take air, when none dared follow him except four or five men chosen by herself, and as the main part of the house where he was lodged and her own apartment were on opposite sides of the court, communicating only by an open terrace, with strange precipitation and in twenty-four hours she caused a gallery to be made, roofed and enclosed on all sides, with a few small windows through which nothing could be seen from outside, to allow herself and the King liberty to pass from each other's cabinet without being seen.[1]

It needed such bitter and unscrupulous enemies as Brancas and Saint-Simon to magnify a matter so trivial, so necessary even, as the building of this corridor into an *affaire d'état*. What was more natural than that a melancholy morose creature like Philippe, after his bereavement should wish to be alone and in a place free from associations with his dead wife, since at Buen Retiro they had spent each summer together? And what more natural than that, having either to pass through rooms crowded with courtiers or traverse an open terrace to reach his children, he should prefer that it should be roofed in, as much to protect him from the weather as from prying eyes?

Here is the source of these scandals, Brancas' official dispatch to Torcy, written three days after the Queen's death:

> It is my duty to tell you that since the Queen's death the King of Spain has seen nobody whatever except his confessor, the Princess des Ursins, Monsieur Orry and Monsieur de Grimaldo. . . . He dresses in private in his room, where he

[1] Saint-Simon, xxiv. 399.

SEQUESTRATION OF THE KING 299

hears mass without anybody entering. Afterwards he goes to see the princes or in the garden, where Madame des Ursins generally walks with him. He dines in private in his room and passes all the rest of the day with the princes and the Princess des Ursins. He even sups in a little room in the princes' apartment, where he is served by their *caméristes*, and none of the officers of his household may enter. There is no likelihood that he can very long support so great a solitude, and people are already murmuring. Everyone remarks the care with which Madame des Ursins prevents as much as she is able that no one whatever shall speak with him except those whom she believes absolutely devoted to herself. Orry seemed very dazed the day the Queen died, but since then he has adopted a higher tone than ever. . . .[1]

Two days later he hints at her project of marriage:

A wooden gallery is being prepared so that the King of Spain can go from his room to the apartment of Madame des Ursins without being seen by anyone. He sups every evening in one of the Princess's rooms, served by the *caméristes* of the princes, and no officers of his household may enter. . . .

The Council was held yesterday in the bureau of Monsieur Orry, a thing which seems most monstrous. It was proposed that the King should go to join his army, or at least to the frontier of Catalonia. It was Orry's opinion, but not that of Madame des Ursins, who will not leave His Catholic Majesty for one moment. . . . People talk already about his state and each one according to his own idea already gives him a wife, for everybody thinks he cannot do without one. I should not dare to write all that is said on the subject.[2]

And again:

I have already told you that no one whatever sees or speaks to the King of Spain except those whom Madame des Ursins permits. I have spoken of a wooden gallery which has been made so that he can pass from his room to the apartment of the princes without being seen. Truly one would not dare to say that the King of Spain condemns himself to this kind of prison. . . .[3]

A little later he attacks her on the matter of her sovereignty:

I told you of the conversation I had three days ago with the Princess des Ursins. Many people have remarked her ill-humour for some days. I attribute it to the bad state of the

[1] Saint-Simon, xxiv. 427; letter to Torcy of 17 Feb. 1714.
[2] Ibid., xxiv. 438; letter to Torcy of 19 Feb. 1714.
[3] Ibid., xxiv. 439; letter to Torcy of 2 March, 1714.

affair of her sovereignty, which she sees is in great danger. She might, however, regard as some slight compensation what she has just inherited from the Queen, namely all the jewels, furniture and plate not belonging to the Crown, and all her wardrobe. They say it amounts to more than two hundred thousand crowns.[1]

And the following week:

Time is a great remedy for grief. Although that of the King of Spain was very keen, it seems now much moderated, and I think it is no longer the motive which keeps him more shut up than ever. The prejudice of Madame des Ursins in favour of Orry is greater than ever, and he more insolent. . . . The King of Spain is so deceived on the subject of this man that he regards him as the restorer of his monarchy, while he is on the contrary its destroyer.[2]

And again:

I have the strongest suspicion that my last letters have been waylaid and opened. . . . I know Orry to be very capable of such a turn, and it is nothing new. . . . I doubt not but that he irritates and excites against me Madame des Ursins, who is not, as you know, prejudiced in my favour, and the bad state in which she sees the affair of her principality vexes her I think a great deal. She continues to lay the blame of it on France. . . . Helvétius will leave in two days. He has been very much courted, apparently in order that on his return to Paris he may sing the praises of Orry, of whom he is an old friend.[3]

Truly if Brancas had not a lobster's claw he had a viper's tongue.

This series of accusations, specially chosen for that purpose, irritated Louis profoundly, and the insinuations concerning her project of marriage drew from Madame de Maintenon the following rebuke:

"It is true that you have just suffered a terrible affliction and will never forget what you have lost," she wrote ironically, "but each day lessens such ideas, above all when one is very occupied. I do not at all understand, neither does anybody here, why the King of Spain does not force himself to return to his palace. Already they begin to say

---

[1] Saint-Simon, xxiv. 440; letter of 5 March, 1714.
[2] Ibid., xxiv. 441; letter of 12 March, 1714.
[3] Ibid., xxiv. 441; letter of 19 March, 1714.

SEQUESTRATION OF THE KING 301

here that you wish to keep him in the country so that he may see no one."[1]

How much truth there was in the insinuations of Brancas and Saint-Simon will probably never be known. Given the ambitious nature of the Princess and her former aspirations, it is possible, probable even, that the project did actually take shape in her mind either of a morganatic marriage such as Madame de Maintenon's, or even, it may be, to be recognised Queen of Spain. She knew, no one better, the feeble character she had to deal with, as well as the temperament, "more ardent than delicate," which made any woman desirable in his eyes so long as the union was blessed by the Church. The Président Hénault, very *au courant* of the Court scandals of that time, puts the case thus:

> When Philippe V. lost his first wife Madame des Ursins was the only person at the Court of Spain in whom he had confidence. He saw only her. She dared aspire to marry him. She had kept near him all the young *caméristes* who served him during the life of the late Queen, for at that time, as he never left her, these *caméristes* served them both; but it was strange that young girls should continue about his person. It was they who gave him his dressing-gown in the morning and assisted at his rising. Madame des Ursins' plan in this was to prevent his being surrounded by the nobles who might, if they were always with him, acquire an influence, and to keep him in a kind of voluptuousness from which she hoped herself to profit. As soon as he was dressed he went to her apartment, which adjoined his own, she having thus arranged the rooms since the Queen's death. He found her in bed, and this woman, nearly sixty years old [she was seventy-two], was so well-preserved, so fresh, and employed so much art, taste and magnificence to appear to advantage, that it was not too bold an enterprise on her part to flatter herself she could please a prince who had more temperament than delicacy, and on whom habit and opportunity had the same effect as the charms of youth she lacked. When he arrived he sat by her bedside. They served him his chocolate, which was the best he ever tasted. He was entertained with all the small news of the town, and above all with that of the Court of France, with which she took great care to be informed, and thus she amused him the greater part of the morning.

Madame des Ursins was not anxious about her present credit but for the future, and she regarded it as a very slight advantage to please the King if she was not sure of its lasting. He was pious. He needed a woman. Madame des Ursins was all that was desirable for that, but it was a strange proposal to

[1] Bossange, iii. 37; letter of 5 March, 1714.

make to the King of Spain to marry a lady of his Court who, though certainly of a good house, was not a Royal princess. The example of Madame de Maintenon supported her vanity and gave her hopes that her pretensions were not chimerical.

Meantime the King amused himself in her society. To amusement succeeded business, in which she had all his confidence. Nothing was done in the kingdom without her consent and counsel. She governed, but she did not reign. From time to time she spoke to the King of marrying again and made him feel that it was absolutely necessary, that a King has no true and reliable confidante except his wife, because she has no other interests than his; that, though a second marriage might bring inconveniences when there were children of the first wife, it was very easy to prevent these by marrying a woman who could give him no others. Arrived at this point, she ran over all who might hope for so august an alliance, passing in review all the elderly princesses from whom he might choose. It was easy to find in each some reason for exclusion, but not so easy when the King began to name such as were young and pretty. A prince sharper-witted than Philippe V. could hardly have suspected that she was thinking of herself and he had not the least suspicion. What was to be done to give him the idea?

One morning, when he entered the room, she pretended to hide some papers which were lying on the bed. The King seemed curious to know what they were, but she refused to say and he did not insist. He asked her what was the news and wanted as usual to talk of France, which was their general subject of conversation. Madame des Ursins pretended to be embarrassed, which appeared to him strange. He pressed her. She refused to answer, but finally, as though unable to resist any longer—"Here!" she said, throwing him the papers which she had gathered together. "See what fine things they are saying in Paris!" He read, and found that the talk was of his marriage with Madame des Ursins. It was a moment very critical and interesting to a woman so ambitious. She watched him; he grew very red and said, returning the papers: "Strange news indeed!" He then rose, left the room, and the next day did not return.[1]

Saint-Simon gives a different version of the matter:

The King of Spain, always eager for news of France, asked it often of his confessor, the only man to whom he could speak who was not a partisan of Madame des Ursins. This confessor, the clever and audacious Robinet, as alarmed as everyone else at the progress of the plot of which no one in the two Courts of France and Spain doubted, allowed himself to be questioned in the embrasure of the window whither the King had led him, and feigned reserve and mystery the more to excite his curiosity. When he saw him at the desired point he replied that since the

[1] Hénault, *Mémoires* (Paris, 1911), pp. 172, etc.

King forced him he would confess that the latest news from France was the same as that of Madrid, where nobody doubted any longer but that he was going to do the Princess des Ursins the honour to marry her. The King grew red and answered curtly: "*Oh, pour cela—non!*" and left him.

Now whether the Princess was informed of this sharp answer or that she had already despaired of success, she stopped short, and judging that this interlude at the Palace of Medina-Cœli could not last for ever, resolved to make sure of the King by a Queen who should owe to herself so great a marriage, and who, having no other support, should throw herself into her arms out of gratitude and necessity. With this in her mind she spoke of her intentions to Alberoni, who since the death of the Duc de Vendôme had remained in Madrid as *chargé-d'affaires* for Parma, and proposed to him the marriage of the Princess, daughter of the Duchess of Parma and of the late Duke, brother of the reigning Duke who had married his widow. Alberoni could scarcely believe his ears. An alliance so disproportionate seemed to him all the more incredible that he dared not hope for the consent of the Court of France, and still less that it could be concluded without. In fact it did not seem possible to make Queen of Spain a person of birth doubly bastard, of a Pope on the father's side and a natural daughter of Charles V. on the mother's, daughter of a petty Duke of Parma and an Austrian mother, sister of the Dowager-Empress and the Dowager-Queen of Spain. . . .

Nothing, however, stopped her. She disposed of the King of Spain's will, she realised how changed towards her were the King [Louis] and Madame de Maintenon, and had no more hope of a return to favour. She even thought it well to resist the authority which had raised and could abase her, and prepared hastily to make a marriage from which she hoped everything, and to make the same use of the new Queen as she had done of her she had just lost. The King of Spain was pious. He had need of a woman. The Princess was at an age when her charms were due to artifice only. In a word she set Alberoni to work, and one may be sure that there was no difficulty in Parma, from the moment they could be persuaded that it was serious and they were not being mocked.[1]

If this vision of a crown did actually dazzle the mind of the Princess it did not last long, for less than a month after the Queen's death she herself wrote to Madame de Maintenon on the subject of his remarriage. Her letter is not forthcoming, but on 19 March Madame de Maintenon replied to it as follows: "I understand very well that the King of Spain will marry again. He is too young and pious to remain in his present state, but one does not find twice

[1] Saint-Simon, xxiv. 217, etc.

in a lifetime two marvels, and the children of different beds cause many difficulties. His Majesty is of so solid and enlightened a piety that he will know how to put himself in God's hands." [1]

We must leave for a moment the question of his marriage, which has carried us beyond the sequence of events, and return to more public matters.

[1] Bossange, iii. 41 ; letter of 19 March, 1714.

CHAPTER XVII

THE PEACE OF RASTADT (1714)

BRANCAS had been recalled and Orry had received permission to remain. These concessions were made by Louis probably because he could do no otherwise with a grandson so rebellious, but at his orders Torcy made an inquiry into the cause of his ambassador's failure, which resulted in the following memoir:

The King of Spain complains of the conduct of the Marquis de Brancas during his short stay in Madrid. He did not cease to listen to and approve the complaints of those who were discontented with the Government. He promised them his support, gave them advice, consulted with them how to draw up seditious memoirs which they spread abroad. His conversation was injurious to the King.[1]

Such were the ostensible reasons for Philippe's demand for his recall, but it is doubtful if they were believed at Versailles. It was another defeat for Louis, his fourth representative ignominiously dismissed, and so irritated was he that he hesitated no longer to execute his oft-repeated threat, and on 6 March signed a separate peace with the Emperor, in which he allowed his grandson to be treated with the greatest ignominy. This was the Treaty of Rastadt, which was signed by the Emperor with all Philippe's titles—King of Spain and the Indies, Catholic Majesty and the rest, and which Louis countersigned without any objection.

When the Princess heard of this fresh outrage she was beside herself with fury and wrote letters *à feu et à sang* to Madame de Maintenon full of abuse and insolent enough to extract the following reproach:

It is easy to see you are not pleased with the peace of Rastadt. Here it is judged differently and is not considered important that the Archduke preserves the title of King of Spain, as the King of England takes that of France. It is difficult to justify you for what is passing at present in Spain. Monsieur de Bergeyck dismissed, Monsieur de Brancas disgraced, Monsieur

[1] Saint-Simon, xxiv. 444; dated April 1714.

de Berwick refused, Monsieur Orry at the head of all affairs, few Spaniards in the Council, the form of government absolutely changed and the King completely secluded.[1]

Berwick refused—it is the first time we have heard that. Berwick, for whom she had been clamouring for so many months, her old friend of more than sixteen years. The letters are not very clear as to the reason, but that she did so refuse him in Philippe's name documents to be cited in place prove, showing also that he had turned against her and was in league with Saint-Simon and the Duc d'Orléans to get her dismissed.

At the beginning of March he had been appointed to bear Louis' official condolences on the death of the Queen. The date of his departure was decided and he had received his instructions which included an order to try to make the Princess more submissive to Louis' will.[2]

Did the Princess, who had spies everywhere, know of this? Or was she aware of the cabal to be spoken of presently in which he took part? Whatever was the reason for her sudden antipathy the fact remains that Philippe at her order immediately wrote two letters within two days of each other telling his grandfather that he would not be a *persona grata* at the Court of Madrid and begging him to send another in his place.[3]

On 31 March Brancas left for France, leaving his secretary Pachau to perform the duties of the embassy. Doubtless in his anger against the Princess he was counting on continuing *a vivâ voce* the calumnies with which his dispatches had been filled and pouring out the tale of his wrongs, the Princess's crimes and Orry's arrogance. So at least thought the Princess, and twenty-four hours before his departure, in the greatest secrecy, she dispatched to Versailles no less a personage than the Cardinal del Giudice, Grand Inquisitor of Spain, ostensibly to discuss the question of Philippe's marriage and beg for troops for the siege of Barcelona, but actually to arrive before Brancas and get first hearing. He had orders to travel with the utmost speed and relays were prepared at every posting-town so that there should be no delay.

[1] Bossange, iii. 52 ; letter of 23 April, 1714.
[2] Trémoïlle, vi. 178.
[3] Saint-Simon, xxiv. 443 ; letter from Louis XIV. to Philippe V. of 9 April, 1714.

MADAME DE MAINTENON
From a portrait by Mignard in the Musée du Louvre.

THE PEACE OF RASTADT

But Brancas had wind of it and determined to outwit her. It was a helter-skelter race between the two, but Brancas, who knew the country well, by a series of short cuts and seizing the relays prepared for the Cardinal, succeeded in reaching Versailles three days before him. We may be sure he made good use of his time, and that the doors of the Royal cabinet were not closed to him.

Echoes of his attacks are apparent in other of Madame de Maintenon's letters besides that quoted above. "We consider that Spain is badly governed," she wrote soon after his arrival, "that decisions are too often changed, that the Spanish are not enough considered and that you ought not to put Orry in the high place he fills." [1] And each letter ends with the same menace—no more troops until peace is signed with Holland.

It was of no consequence to Louis that the Allies had robbed his grandson of all his foreign possessions; that the Emperor refused even to hear his name, and continued to affix to his signature all Philippe's titles; that England insisted on his renunciation of his rights to the throne of France and the possible succession of the Duke of Savoy to that of Spain; that Holland contemptuously refused to keep her word as to the Princess's sovereignty, and that he was slighted and humiliated by all the European Powers. All he desired was to escape with as little damage to himself as possible from the conflagration he had kindled, and Philippe's refusal to sign the peace with Holland which he had guaranteed was a constant menace to himself. Therefore, no signature, no troops.

And a fresh source of difficulties now arose in another sudden catastrophe which overtook his house, causing fresh exactions on the part of the Allies and fresh hesitations on that of his grandson. This was the death, due to a hunting accident, of the fat and healthy Duc de Berry, Philippe's younger brother, which took place on 4 May, after three days' illness, at the age of twenty-eight.

This death of Louis' only remaining descendant in the direct line, excepting the little Dauphin and Philippe, renewed the tension which had somewhat slackened since the latter's renunciation, and England was on the watch, ready at the least sign of his intention to break his word, to withdraw her treaty. As for the Princess, she was

[1] Bossange, iii. 57; letter of 2 May, 1714.

x

furious with herself for having allowed him to sign it, and even Philippe expressed some regret. To have renounced his rights to the most important monarchy of Europe had been bitter enough even when it was in favour of a beloved brother, but now there was nothing but a sickly babe of four between that throne and his worst enemy the Duc d'Orléans, with the certainty in any case of the regency. And what had he received for his immense sacrifice but contemptuous treatment and a kingdom shorn of its possessions?

We may be sure that the Princess spared him none of these arguments. The prospect of playing in France the rôle of dictatress was a dazzling possibility compared with which the crown of Limbourg seemed a mere toy and Spain itself of little importance. Who knows what fresh ambitions surged up in her mind when, at Louis' death, which could not be far off, she might take the same place at the brilliant Court of Versailles as here in melancholy Madrid, relegate Madame de Maintenon to Saint-Cyr, and trample in the dust the d'Estrées, Brancas, and even the Duc d'Orléans! It was no illusive dream like her sovereignty, dependent for its realisation on the goodwill of ill-disposed powers, for, if the throne itself was doubtful, the regency for many years was a certainty.

With so dazzling a prospect in view, a signature and extorted promise, she argued, were not binding, and Philippe, who with all his piety was never above breaking his word, was not deaf to the voice of the serpent which insinuated that his renunciation was not only extremely foolish but a crime—the denial of his birthright, a treachery to his own country and blood.

After much persuasion and menaces on the part of his grandfather, he had finally been forced to yield, and had sent word to his plenipotentiaries to sign peace with Holland, which surrender had delighted Louis, for the first time victor in his duels with the Princess, and he had immediately sent orders to Berwick to proceed to Spain with a large army for the reduction of Barcelona. But the death of his brother had materially altered Philippe's ideas and he lost no time in sending word to the Cardinal del Giudice, now ambassador to Versailles, to give Louis to understand that, justified by these fresh circumstances, he considered himself free to revoke his renunciation, since

THE PEACE OF RASTADT 309

it had been made without his free consent, and at the same time ordered him to withdraw all allusion to it in the treaty with Holland.[1]

Had England and Holland been without suspicions before, this omission would naturally have roused them, and they sent at once to know the reason and delay the signatures. Louis was furious to see all his efforts thus frustrated. The sudden death of Queen Anne had already alarmed him, for his enemies the Whigs were again in power, and there was talk of reinstating Marlborough. Therefore he reprimanded his grandson with the greatest severity, and, as though his own honour were immaculate, reproached him on the grounds of morality for so dishonourable an idea. "I think you would be sorry," he wrote sternly, "to let it be thought that you seek pretexts to retract your renunciation which you have solemnly sworn."[2] And a week later, taking matters into his own hands, he assured England through his ambassador that he should "punctually fulfil all he had promised, and had not dreamt of making the least change in the solemn renunciation made by his grandson, and would maintain exactly the conditions of the treaty."[3]

Philippe dared say no more. The matter was too delicate to insist, since Louis' own death was implicated, and the situation in Catalonia was too perilous for him to risk a fresh withdrawal of troops. He ceded for the moment, but for the moment only. After his grandfather's death he formally retracted his oath, and a tussle took place for the regency between him and the Duc d'Orléans, under an influence equally ambitious and less scrupulous than the Princess's, that of the Abbé Alberoni of whom we have now to speak.

---

[1] Baudrillart, i. 583; letter from Grimaldo to Giudice of 23 May, 1714.
[2] Ibid., i. 588; letter from Louis XIV. to Philippe V., of 14 Aug. 1714.
[3] Baudrillart, i. 589; letter from Louis XIV. to Berville, French ambassador to England, of 22 Aug. 1714.

CHAPTER XVIII

ALBERONI (1714)

THE Abbé Alberoni, who had accompanied Vendôme to Spain as almoner and secretary, had remained in Madrid after his death, ostensibly as agent of the Duke of Parma but actually for his own ends, since he was paid little or nothing by that impoverished little state. Alberoni, vulgar adventurer though he was, whose chief ambition was self-aggrandisement, was at the same time a man of genius and past-master in the art of intrigue, and as the welfare of Italy was inseparable from his own, with a stretch of charity he may even be called a patriot.

For it seems undeniable that the main object of his intrigue against the Princess des Ursins was the aggrandisement of Parma (and consequently of Giulio Alberoni), to wrest Italy from the clutches of the Emperor, reinstate Spain in her possessions signed away at the Peace of Utrecht, and, with Philippe's protection, unite the country under his master the Duke. For this it was necessary to have a free hand, untrammelled by the presence of the dictatress who had shown as little sympathy for Italian domination as for French. Even before Vendôme's death (and presumably supported by him) he had conceived some part at least of his designs and had relied on his military ability to further them. After his death, having no one to rely on but himself, he concentrated all his forces and determined to gain his point single-handed.

One of the salient characteristics of this man of low birth and great talents was his conviction that all men could be won through their stomach and the unconscious cynicism with which he acted on it. As he had gained Vendôme by preparing him succulent Italian dishes, so now he brought his culinary talents into play to win the favour of the Queen and Princess and all whom he thought capable of furthering his interests. The Queen was Italian and loved the food of her country. The Princess, more than half Italian, loved it also. She drank nothing but Italian wines and adored Parmesan cheese and macaroni. Directly after Vendôme's death Alberoni began to play on these tastes, wrote to Parma for sausages, cheeses, truffles and a special wine called Lambruscho much appreciated by the Princess, and sent to the Royal table and that of the Camarera Mayor Italian dishes cooked under his own eye. Besides this he invited to his house all who were in favour and likely to be useful, and his macaroni suppers became the rage. The ministers and grandees were amused by the good-natured Abbé, accepted his cheeses and sausages, laughed at him behind his back and considered him of so little importance that they discussed state matters openly at his table, little suspecting that after their departure he sat down in his cabinet and wrote all he had heard to the Duke his master.

Before the Queen's death his idea had been to gain her as an Italian to work for an alliance between Spain and his new Italy, in which it is possible he might have succeeded. Nothing could have led him to foresee that a young woman of twenty-seven, who had supported fourteen years of hardship, would be carried off at the moment when her life was becoming more tranquil. But her death was a godsend to him and before the breath was out of her body his schemes were already ripe for a marriage with his master's niece. When her illness became serious and people began to whisper of a fatal issue, he had written to the Duke of his project and even spoken of it to his compatriots at the Spanish Court, notably the Duc de Popoli and the Prince of Cellamare, and one and all counselled him to win over the Princess des Ursins—"who is both King and Queen combined."

Alberoni, sharp-eyed and keen-witted, could not have failed at the moment of the retreat to the Palace of Medina-Cœli to suspect the Princess's design of herself replacing the Queen, and when the matter became notorious, aware of her strength, had probably renounced his own plans. It has been seen how quickly these illusions vanished before Philippe's contemptuous *"Pour cela—non !"* and how with her usual promptness she immediately turned her mind to other ways of consolidating her position.

With this eclipse of her hopes those of Alberoni revived and he set to work in good earnest. Without rousing her suspicions by any emphasis, he missed no opportunity carelessly to vaunt the tractable and docile character of his master's niece, according to him a modest simple-minded girl with the sweetest nature imaginable, humble and homely and grateful for every kindness shown her. It needed no more to make the Princess prick up her ears. Such a girl was precisely the wife she sought for Philippe.

On 29 March, therefore, little more than a month after the Queen's death, in the course of conversation she suddenly attacked the Abbé: "*Eh bien*—it seems you want to marry the King of Spain?" He feigned the utmost amazement that he should be thought capable of such audacity, but without more words she led him to the King's apartment and then and there proposed his marriage with the docile and tractable Elisabeth Farnese.[1]

The funeral of the late Queen had not yet taken place when the choice of her successor was decided. All wheels were set in motion, but in secret, for the Princess and Philippe himself, fearing Louis' objection to a granddaughter so insignificant, determined not to announce it till matters had gone too far to draw back. Alberoni was instructed to write to the Duke of Parma and ask whether his niece was free (for there had been some talk of a prior engagement with the Prince of Piedmont, son of the Duke of Savoy now King of Sicily) and informally to propose a marriage with the King of Spain, and the Prince de Chalais was dispatched secretly to Paris to be ready at a moment's notice to announce the engagement as a *fait accompli*, but with the strictest orders to say nothing about it till the moment arrived.

Towards the end of May, Philippe and the Princess left the house of Medina-Cœli, which was to be enlarged and redecorated in honour of the new bride, and took up their abode at the Pardo, a kind of hunting-lodge thirteen kilometres from Madrid.

At this move Alberoni was in despair, for the Pardo was too small to house the Court and so isolated that for miles round there was neither house nor inn, so that he had to go to and from Madrid each day, and Alberoni, though only fifty, was subject to fever and far from strong. However, it was not the moment for weakness, for the Princess must

[1] Bourgeois, E., *Lettres intimes de J. Alberoni, addressées au Comte I. Rocca, Ministre de Finance du Duc de Parma* (Paris, 1893), and *Alberoni, Madame des Ursins et Elisabeth Farnese* (Paris, 1891). The letters from which the above facts are taken were discovered by Bourgeois in the College of San Lazzaro in Piacenza, founded by Alberoni himself.

be gulled and others watched to prevent her learning the truth, and he continued to discourse of the simplicity, the good heart and pliable nature of his master's niece, declaring even that he feared she was too meek and lowly to fill the great position for which the Princess destined her.

It was a dangerous game, possible only from the insignificance of the Parma Court, for everyone who had been there knew that Elisabeth Farnese was exactly the reverse —haughty, self-willed and authoritative, that she had been brought up, or rather had brought herself up, with masculine licence, and that her gun and her ambition were her main considerations.

The Abbé, however, was equal to the task and played his game so well that no shadow of suspicion entered the Princess's mind, and none of the rare visitors from Parma were allowed to approach her. On 10 June, therefore, the Princess sent for him and announced the welcome news that Philippe had written to her nephew the Prince de Chalais to announce the marriage to Louis—a mere form, she took care to add, since, no matter what objection he might make, the marriage was decided and would take place.[1]

Since the Queen's death Philippe had fallen ill of his old malady which he called the vapours. Four months had scarcely elapsed since the Queen's death, but they had been months of complete abstinence, for notwithstanding the pressure put on him to take a mistress for the sake of his health, he had insisted on "living holily," as the Princess called it, but it nearly cost him his life. This being the case a speedy marriage became an absolute necessity, and in June the silence imposed on Chalais was removed, and he was sent to break the news of his marriage to Louis with the following letter from Philippe to be given after:

The Prince de Chalais will have informed Your Majesty of my intentions and the reasons which oblige me to make a second marriage. He will also have explained those which lead me to prefer the Princess of Parma to all other eligible princesses. I hope you will have approved them, but if you have not already given him your answer when you receive this letter, I beg you to do so at once, for time presses, the season advances, and my intention is that this Princess shall be here before the winter. She suits me best for all sorts of reasons. The Infanta of Portugal, eligible by her birth, would not have suited because my subjects would have been dis-

[1] Bourgeois, *Alberoni, Madame des Ursins*, etc., p. 22.

contented and she belongs to a house very cruel and strange. . . . There is also the Princess of Bavaria, but I am assured she is ill-bred and ugly, and besides has been brought up among my enemies. Thus there was left only the Princess of Poland, of whom much good is said, but to whom I prefer without comparison the Princess of Parma. She is accustomed to a Court where there is but little amusement, and having a sweet nature will, I think, be happy in mine, where the Queens have always lived a more retired life than in any other. I hope for all these reasons that Your Majesty will kindly consent to my marriage with this Princess, and I beg you again to give me a prompt answer.[1]

As may be imagined, Louis was shocked and horrified at the independence shown in this letter. As head of the family if not as King he had an indisputable right to have been consulted, and this empty formality of asking his consent for a choice already made seemed to him the height of rebellious arrogance. But his spirit was broken by age and misfortune and nothing was left but to make the best of the inevitable. He gave his consent, therefore, but coldly and curtly:

"The Prince de Chalais has acquitted himself of the secret mission you gave him for me. . . . I approve your idea of the Princess of Parma and the reason you gave to prefer her to the Princess of Portugal."[2]

And since he could not vent his anger on Philippe and the Princess des Ursins, poor Chalais was the scapegoat. "The King has commanded me to write to you confidentially," Torcy wrote the same day to the Princess, "that if the King of Spain desires to confide to somebody his secret commissions for His Majesty, he hopes he will not in future choose the Prince de Chalais."[3] And Madame de Maintenon, in spite of the entreaties of the Princess, refused to receive him.

Alberoni was radiant. The marriage was a triumph of diplomacy, the consecration of his policy. "For me," he wrote to Rocca, Minister of Finance at the Court of Parma, announcing the success—" I have nothing left to wish for and can say with old Simeon: *Nunc dimittis servum tuum!*"[4]

[1] Trémoïlle, vi. 194; letter of 23 June, 1714.
[2] Baudrillart, i. 594; letter of 2 July, 1714.
[3] Trémoïlle, vi. 199; letter of 2 July, 1714.
[4] Bourgeois, *Lettres d'Alberoni*, 323; letter of 16 July, 1714.

And the day that the special envoy was dispatched to the Court of Parma with the official demand for the hand of the Princess Elisabeth Farnese, the fate of the Princess des Ursins was decided in his mind in all its details.

It was not only in Spain that the die was cast against her. Naturally Louis attributed to her not only the choice of the wife, but also the secrecy with which the marriage had been arranged. According to him things had been going from bad to worse since the Queen's death, and he held her responsible for all.

Fresh complications had arisen with England and Holland, for Philippe's ambition for the regency had escaped none of the Powers. At Versailles suspicion of his intention to revoke his renunciation had been confirmed by a series of effusive letters written by the Princess to Torcy, giving him to understand as plainly as though put into words that if he would favour Philippe's claim he would retain his post and enjoy the highest favour and gratitude of the King of Spain. Louis felt bitterly that his authority was ignored as though he were already dead.

Madame de Maintenon, losing all patience at this indifference towards her King, wrote to the Princess more sharply than ever: " Our correspondence would certainly not be insipid if we said all we thought to each other. I should expect little praise for us, and you would hear very much blame for the solitude in which you keep the Catholic King."[1]

Pride goeth before a fall, and a haughty spirit before destruction. Alas, both fall and destruction are not far off. The Princess, arrived at the zenith of power, lost her head to the point of treating Louis XIV. with too little consideration. Her reasons for choosing a princess of Parma, by her birth so unworthy to wear the crown of Spain, were very well understood at Versailles, and Saint-Simon only echoed the general comments when he wrote: " She resolved to assure herself of the King of Spain by a Queen who should owe to her so great a marriage." She had intrigued successfully to prevent Louis' almost certain objection to such an alliance. Little did she think that she herself was to be the victim of her own plot.

For to give the devil his due, the skill with which Alberoni prepared and carried out his difficult task was

[1] Bossange, iii. 84 ; letter of 9 July, 1714.

a masterpiece of diplomacy and foresight, and had he executed his plans for the advancement of his country with the same ability, a united Italy would have taken the lead among the nations with the Duke of Parma as its king, and himself as prime minister.

The plot for the Princess's ruin by means of the new Queen has been attributed to many—to Louis, to Madame de Maintenon, to the Duc d'Orléans, the Cardinal del Giudice working for the Jesuits, to the Queen-Dowager, and to Philippe himself. It is not too much to say that one and all of these had a share in it, but the master-hand which moved the pieces on this formidable chessboard was the hand which had pruned the vines and set the church bells ringing in Piacenza.

Alberoni had thought of and foreseen everything. In the first place that Louis' consent, or at least tacit acquiescence, was absolutely necessary if his heroine, as he calls Elisabeth Farnese, was herself to escape disgrace. For how was it possible that an insignificant princess of Parma on her promotion, accepted unwillingly by Louis, should dare without express permission, the moment she set foot in Spain, to attack and expel the all-powerful dictatress, his own subject and accepted by all Europe as his agent? Some kind of permission it is evident had been obtained, and a series of documents discovered among the papers of Saint-Simon after his death throws considerable light on the matter.[1]

It will be remembered that the deaths in 1712 of Louis' heirs had excited the strongest suspicion of poison against the Duc d'Orléans as most interested in the succession, that these suspicions had been increased by the Princess's discovery, real or supposed, of Père le Marchand's plot to poison the King of Spain, and that in consequence the Duke had been ostracised by all the Court including Louis, and narrowly escaped the disgrace of the public tribunal. Saint-Simon, his sycophant and already counting on his accession to the Regency, had fiercely resented this attack on his patron, and his long and close friendship for the Princess had, in consequence, turned to the bitterest enmity.

[1] The documents were first published by Armand Baschet in 1874 : *Le Duc de Saint-Simon, son Cabinet et l'historique de ses Manuscrits* (Paris, 1874).

At this moment of her semi-disgrace at Versailles, when Philippe's refusal to sign peace on account of her sovereignty, her so-called sequestration of him and ambitious projects of marriage had excited Louis, Madame de Maintenon and all the Royal family against her, he found the occasion good to give her the final *coup de grâce*.

Aware that the Duke, though longing for vengeance, was too indolent himself to undertake it, either to gain his favour or possibly pushed by some agent of Alberoni, Saint-Simon spared no pains to facilitate matters, and composed letters for the Duke to copy and present to Louis, urging her immediate dismissal as fatal to the interests of Spain and France. The letters are immensely long and complicated, but the following extracts are sufficient to show with what acrimony and violence these attacks were to be made.

PROJECT OF A LETTER TO BE WRITTEN BY THE DUC D'ORLÉANS TO LOUIS XIV.

It is Madame des Ursins, Sire, who teaches the King of Spain ingratitude towards Your Majesty and denies him even the acts of nature by the captivity in which she keeps him. It is she who has quarrelled with all whom you have sent to Spain in no matter what capacity, and whose cunning is so fatal to your glory that all Europe puts to your account all that goes on in Spain, her wish being since the peace that the Spanish shall resent it to the point of stoning all the French. . . .

The remedy, Sire, lies in your puissant hands and is conformable to the equity and goodness of your nature, the glory of your name and the justice you owe to yourself and the Spanish, oppressed by a woman who has persecuted all those who had a share in the testament of the late King of Spain, who has admitted to the Council only the one man who opposed it, who has given all the posts to foreigners but not one Frenchman among them, who has changed completely the entire constitution of the Spanish Government, who keeps your grandson in a captivity equally shameful and dangerous, surrounded by a very small number of foreigners devoted to herself and inaccessible to all except them. With her fall would perish also the hatred and despair of the Spanish, all the dangers on both sides of the Pyrenees, the perpetual dread of her cabals, and of a marriage the disadvantages of which Your Majesty has so thoroughly understood, but which are easier to cut at the root than to combat perpetually. With her would disappear all the difficulties internal and external as to peace, the shame concerning the State which she insists shall be given her, and the perpetual irritation of schemes and Court intrigues. Your Majesty would justify yourself in the only suitable way in the eyes of all Europe and would thus regain the heart of all Spain delivered by your generosity, and soon after that, of the King your grandson.

The means, Sire, are easy to arrive at so many desirable ends. You have only to be deaf to the siren, to remain inactive and indifferent to the cunning of an Italian cardinal [Giudice]. But if Your Majesty is bent on delivering your grandson and Spain and liberating France from the evils which menace her, your superiority in all things would disconcert the Cardinal and all the cabal and free her for ever from fatal troubles, if you declared that, as long as Madame des Ursins and all foreigners not connected with the Spanish monarchy are not expelled from Spain and Madame des Ursins sent to Italy, Your Majesty will interfere no more in anything and will let the Catalans do what they please by recalling all your subjects serving in Spain. By making this known in Spain, Madame des Ursins is bound to quit the game or let the country be torn to pieces, which she would not risk. . . .

I should consider myself lacking in fidelity, gratitude and all other duties if, after having for so long given proofs of patience regarding Madame des Ursins, I did not break silence when it is a question of losing all by maintaining it, after such ample experience that to leave her complete mistress serves only to ruin everything, as without contradiction she has done since she has had no one to oppose her.

In God's name, Sire, let your blood, your authority, your glory, the monarchies submitted to your rule, weigh with you more than Madame des Ursins. It is not a question of her ruin, nor of chastising her as she deserves. It is a question only of ridding the world of her sorceries and of sending her to enjoy in Rome the treasures she has amassed, to prevent that, by a longer administration, she should become the scourge of your own family and the destruction of France and Spain.[1]

And as though this tirade was not enough, he adds a memoir even more ferocious which was to aid the Duke's memory in a personal interview with Louis, in which he accuses her of urging Philippe to revoke his renunciation to the throne of France, and assert his rights to the crown and regency, in order that she herself may dominate France as she does Spain; of having caused Philippe to be detested in Spain and exposed him to a revolution; of making Louis' own name blasphemed throughout Europe, and of having systematically opposed his interests during the twelve years of her rule, etc. "This is enough, Sire," he ends, " to

[1] Baschet, 396, etc.

ALBERONI

show you the urgent necessity as well as the facility of the punishment, which you owe to all Europe, of a woman who, always attacking and always unpunished, thinks that all is permitted her. Rome and her immense wealth should not appear a great punishment, but whatever happens to her, I hope that your children and the State, your glory itself, and if I dare say so, your conscience, will determine you to a step so easy to take and so dangerous to renounce or defer."[1]

Whether the Duke made use of these letters is uncertain, but that he actually attacked Louis on the subject of the Princess's expulsion in response to Saint-Simon's urging is proved by the following somewhat cryptic letter written by him to the latter:

> This Thursday evening, April 5.
> I spoke to him [Louis] the day you left. He received me more coldly than the first time, but still not badly. He said that Berwick would not find what I required very convenient. I replied that the only opposition was from the person who always opposed the will of him whose credit alone supported her [the Princess]. The conversation was long and always with anger against the aforesaid lady. Berwick, to whom I spoke the same day, appeared well disposed to act except on the principal point, namely the total expulsion.[2]

Thus we see that Berwick also had turned against her and did not refuse to join with her enemies, at least as regards her disgrace and dismissal.

To affirm that Saint-Simon was an unconscious agent of Alberoni would, in the absence of proof, be too audacious, yet it is significant that these documents date from precisely the time when his own plans for her ruin originated. As secretary to the Duc de Vendôme, Alberoni was well known at Versailles, and a man of his stamp has always agents to work his intrigues. It is possible if not probable that, aware of her disfavour at Versailles and the Duc d'Orléans' desire of vengeance, his first idea was to employ the simplest and least dangerous means to get rid of her, namely that Louis himself should disgrace and recall her. That Louis refused this is evident, but his coldness and the lack of surprise with which he received the news of an event which shocked and

---

[1] Baschet, 404, etc.
[2] Ibid., 389; letter of 5 April, 1714.

amazed all Europe, proves that he was prepared for it, while his indifference at such treatment of one of his own subjects, and a woman of such high rank, shows that his consent, perhaps tacit, had been obtained.

But Louis' was not the only consent necessary. That of Philippe was even more important. Easy enough to extract, but with a man so feeble not so easy to rely upon, so difficult indeed that the only possibility of success lay in the summary expulsion of the Princess while separated from him, for Alberoni knew that, had she the time and opportunity to plead her cause, from habit only, if from no other motive, he would have yielded. Doubtless he gave his consent readily enough, for he was probably dreading a renewal of her influence over the new Queen and was as eager as Alberoni to be rid of her.

And the Abbé's other pieces, the pawns, so to speak, necessary to checkmate the dictatress—Elisabeth Farnese herself, of whom he knew so little after all—would she be equal to the rôle he had assigned her, the *coup d'état* which was to shake Spain to its foundations? Not without much prompting and drilling evidently, for which it was absolutely necessary that he should be allowed to meet her on the way, which a hundred obstacles might prevent. The months which elapsed between the conception and execution of his plot were a terrible strain and resulted in violent attacks of fever, one of which almost prevented his leaving Madrid at the critical moment of her arrival.

He dominated his nerves, however, and continued to play his game with such consummate skill that the Princess remained wholly unsuspicious. He became even a great favourite with her and was constantly invited to dine in her apartment—"a great honour for me since it is accorded only to those of the first rank and dignity," he wrote jubilantly to Rocca.[1]

At the beginning of August all was ready. "This tremendous act (*questo colpo grandissimo*) which is about to take place will result in immense advantages if we know how to play our cards," he wrote. "If *la Heroina* has confidence she will not be ill served, I can assure you!" "God grant that she be sufficiently fortunate to change things very shortly." "Spain to-day awaits her

[1] Bourgeois, *Lettres d'Alberoni*, p. 32; letter of 16 July, 1714.

as its guardian-angel and sole salvation. She is as much desired as the Messiah by the Hebrews." [1]

According to Alberoni it was to be the triumph of good over evil as personified by the Princess des Ursins, but whether the entire country echoed his opinion is questionable. If so it was not long before they discovered their mistake.

[1] Bourgeois, *Lettres*, pp. 329 and 338; letters of 6 Aug. and 10 Sept. 1714.

CHAPTER XIX

D'AUBIGNY THE FAITHLESS (1714)

So well did Alberoni play his cards, that it was not till a month before the marriage ceremony that the Princess discovered she had been fooled, that the character of the Queen she had chosen was exactly the reverse of what he had described and that, instead of being a docile and simple country girl, everyone who had seen her spoke of her intelligence, her cultivation, her haughty pride, strong will and masculine bearing.

According to the Président Hénault it was the Chevalier de Bourke, representing the Pretender at the Court of Madrid, who first enlightened her as to the true character of her protégée. "One day while dining with many others with the Princess des Ursins," he writes, "he made certain remarks which embarrassed her, seeming to criticise the marriage she was planning. She let the conversation drop, but when dinner was over she asked de Bourke what he meant. He answered frankly that she was about to commit the greatest folly in the world as far as she herself was concerned, that the Princess of Parma had a bitter and dangerous mind, that she would not be able to govern her as she imagined, and that it was extremely likely she would deprive her of the King's confidence if she did no worse." [1]

Others affirm with more probability that the news first reached her through d'Aubigny, who had returned to Spain from his long visit to France on 8 August:

> Everyone has remarked [Pachau, acting as ambassador, wrote to Torcy on 20 August] that the Princess des Ursins has been very sad for some days, and everyone reasons according to his lights on this melancholy, of which I think the counsels and remonstrances of d'Aubigny on her conduct are the true cause. It is said that he spoke no less freely to the King of Spain, and that His Majesty listened quietly to all he had to say, but that he did not find so much docility or indifference in Orry, and that the two insulted each other a thousand times in the presence of the Duc de Veraguas and Monsieur de

[1] Hénault, *Mémoires*, p. 179.

Macanez. I heard this from a friend of the Duke who had witnessed the scene. He was in Orry's cabinet when d'Aubigny entered. He wished to retire and Macanez also, but d'Aubigny begged them both to stay and hear what he had to say to Orry.[1]

D'Aubigny, labelled so lightly by Saint-Simon "the faithful" and imitated by all the biographers, had turned against her, and his defection and disloyalty, proved by the documents, have been hitherto so little remarked that a slight digression at this point is necessary.

D'Aubigny, handsome, supple and serviceable, had grown under the Princess's protection to be a very great personage, secretary and equerry to their Catholic Majesties, Seigneur de la Rochechargé, counsellor to the King, Grand Master of the Waters and Forests of Touraine, as he pompously signs himself. He was also in high favour at Versailles, especially with Torcy, of whom, it is not too much to affirm, he had become the spy.

But d'Aubigny though great desired to be greater, and having extracted from the Princess and Spain all they were capable of bestowing, and furiously jealous of the favour enjoyed by his *bête noire* Orry, had made up his mind to quit Madrid and seek service in France, and with this purpose had for some time been paying an obsequious court to all those he thought likely to further his ambitions, especially Torcy.

As long ago as February 1706 one is surprised to find him in regular correspondence, evidently unknown to the Princess, with her enemy the Duc de Gramont, with whom she herself, in his capacity of Governor of Navarre, was in official communication. The Duc de la Trémoïlle publishes many of these letters in which he tries to ingratiate himself by servile flattery, and even by criticising and blaming his mistress, than which nothing could be more acceptable to Gramont, still smarting under his recall and the failure of his embassy.

In one of these we read: "I have seen with mortal grief what has passed between them [the Cardinal d'Estrées and the Princess]. Twenty times I have been tempted to throw myself into the fray. Monsieur le Cardinal from time immemorial has been my hero, and if His Eminence ordered me to do anything compatible with my first duty,

[1] Trémoïlle, vi. 214; letter of 20 Aug. 1714.

he would find me still his faithful and zealous servant."[1] This at the time when the d'Estrées were doing all in their power to ruin the woman to whom he owed everything, and during the whole of the year 1708, as long as Gramont retained the governorship, he kept up a regular correspondence with him, which, with its mysterious allusions and prayers for secrecy, suggests strongly that he was playing the spy.

In 1713, as has been seen, the Princess, as a first step towards her sovereignty, had obtained for him the post of Grand Master of the Waters and Forests of Touraine, in order to give a pretext for the construction of her château near Amboise, in preparation for the exchange she hoped to make with Louis of the Duchy of Limbourg. Of this château he was to superintend the building and furnishing, and at the same time he was commissioned to act as her agent at the Peace Conference to obtain from the Allies their guarantee for her sovereignty.

But during his long stay in France and frequent visits to Paris, d'Aubigny had seen much of the Court and ministers, especially of Torcy, and heard much which made him realise on what a thread hung her favour, and this, added to his jealousy of Orry, made him cold to her interests. Instead of working for her sovereignty at Utrecht, he threw himself on the side of its opponents, reproved the Duc d'Ossone's insistence, and declared openly that, in his opinion, she ought to renounce her claim.[2] According to San Phélipe, the refusal of the Allies was due in great part to his bad diplomacy or indifference, and he offended Queen Anne, who had formally guaranteed the sovereignty, by making more advantageous offers to Holland than to her, which so enraged her that she cancelled her engagement, declaring—always according to San Phélipe: " Since the Princess des Ursins has recourse to others, I abandon her."[3]

But leaving this somewhat apocryphal testimony, it is

[1] Trémoïlle, vi. 66; letter of 27 Feb. 1708.
[2] On 19 Oct. 1713, Louis wrote to Brancas: " The Duc d'Ossone, deceived by the counsel of those whose interest it is to retard the conclusion of peace, flatters himself he will obtain the guarantee of the States-General in favour of the Princess, and his representations have outweighed the counsels of the Marquis de Montaleone and the Sieur d'Aubigny " (Trémoïlle, vi. 150).
[3] Duclos, *Mémoires*, i. 191.

certain that, in order to curry favour at Versailles, he had the disloyalty to act, not only against her claim to the sovereignty, but also against her protégé Orry, permission for whose return she had with so much difficulty extracted from Louis. On 16 February, 1714, he, being then in Paris, wrote to Torcy at Versailles: "It seems to me essential to note that His Catholic Majesty only asked that Orry might come for a few months, solely to compare projects with the Comte de Bergeyck, that it was on this understanding that he was permitted to go to Madrid, and that he would never have received permission had it been possible to guess that he was to be put at the head of all affairs in Spain, and be made, so to speak, governor of the kingdom."[1] Comment on the disloyalty of this letter is superfluous.

Rumours of his indifference, not to say opposition, to her sovereignty, reached the Princess, and in May 1714 she recalled him, and appointed in his place, as her agent at Utrecht, a nephew of the Maréchale de Noailles, Baron de Câpres, former governor of Ghent. Highly offended, d'Aubigny refused to return, left her letters unanswered and remained in Paris sulking, and it was at this time that he decided to leave Spain and accept service in France. His return to Madrid, far from being in obedience to her order, was merely to settle his own affairs in preparation for his final move.

Who knows what post Torcy had promised him to which Louis' death and his own dismissal put a stop? No mean one certainly to compensate him for what he abandoned in Madrid, for d'Aubigny was a clever knave and capable of good work. In any case, his future in France was so well assured that he felt free to burn his ships in Spain, and on his return, as has been seen, treated the Princess, Orry, and even the King himself, with the greatest insolence. That this behaviour was resented the following words of Torcy prove: "He [Louis] is very sorry, both as regards yourself personally and affairs, that you have reason to be discontented with the way you are treated, and I am ordered to tell you that, when your business is ended, nothing on this side should delay your return to France." And after a profusion of compliments, in themselves sufficient proof of his favour at Versailles, he adds: "This letter will be

[1] Trémoïlle, vi. 171 ; letter of 16 Feb. 1714.

given you unsealed, a precaution not to excite suspicions against you in the mind of the curious." And the letter was written in cipher and enclosed in another to Pachau with the following instructions: "The ciphered letter enclosed, which I have left open, is for Monsieur d'Aubigny, and it is the same cipher which was given him last March. It is important that it be given to him secretly."

Enough has been said to prove the disloyalty of the "faithful d'Aubigny." Naturally, enraged against the Princess as he was, he made the worst of what he had heard at Versailles concerning the Princess of Parma, and this (perhaps also his disloyalty towards herself) was most likely the cause of the melancholy remarked by Pachau after his return. It will be seen presently how he received the news of her disgrace, and how in her hour of need he did not hesitate to throw himself on the side of her executioners and try to satisfy his ambitions at her expense. Well might she say that it was impossible to find stability in the human heart.

[1] Trémoïlle, vi. 273 ; letter of 31 Dec. 1714.

CHAPTER XX

ELISABETH FARNESE (1714)

IMMEDIATELY on receipt of the news of the true character of the Princess she had chosen for her docility, the Princess set to work to find out the truth and dispatched messengers and letters in all directions. The answers from Versailles were far from reassuring.

"The Princess you have chosen," Torcy wrote with a touch of irony, "is very capable of rendering the King of Spain the sweet society he has lost, if the descriptions which have arrived from Italy are true. There is no end to the praise of her. She has all the qualities of body and mind, if one may believe the writers, and you will find no perfection lacking and none which may be added to those she has already received from her birth and education."[1]

To Pachau he wrote later: "According to what is written of the Princess of Parma it is unnecessary that anyone should suggest what she should think or do. She will know perfectly how to act as well as her own interests present and future."[2]

Everyone spoke of her accomplishments and learning, no one of the simplicity vaunted by Alberoni. She knew Latin, German and French, had studied history and philosophy, danced to perfection, painted like a master, rode like a boy, shot like a musketeer—nothing was lacking to this prodigy of culture who had been described to her as an unsophisticated country girl. But intelligence, erudition and masculine accomplishments were precisely what the Princess did not want, being generally incompatible with docility and the domestic virtues.

But the negotiations were well under way. The Cardinal Acquaviva had been dispatched already in July formally to demand of the Duke the hand of his niece, which was naturally granted with a profusion of gratitude. As for the Princess Elisabeth herself, according to the Cardinal de la Trémoïlle, she was so overwhelmed by her good fortune

---

[1] Trémoïlle, vi. 215; letter of 20 Aug. 1714.
[2] Baudrillart, i. 604; letter of 5 Nov. 1714.

that she fainted for joy, after which "she painted with her own hand a portrait of the King of Spain which was sent him by a special messenger."[1] History does not record whether the likeness was faithful nor how it was received.

Louis himself, making the best of the inevitable, had sent a special envoy, the Comte Albergotti, to carry his compliments and official consent to the marriage. The following extracts from his instructions are interesting as a proof that, though aware of the existence of the plot against the Princess des Ursins, he had no part in it, but on the contrary did his best to oppose it.

VERSAILLES, 20 *August*, 1714.

The Princess of Parma will doubtless consider that she owes her marriage to the Princess des Ursins. Consequently she should be inclined to show her entire gratitude for her good offices, and for that reason be disposed to follow the example of the late Queen of Spain both in the confidence and treatment which the Princess received.

The King, persuaded of her zeal and good intentions, will be very glad that she should keep with the new Queen the same credit she had with the first. His Majesty desires, therefore, that Count Albergotti's conversation should tend to confirm this credit. He will, however, note carefully if it is well received and if the Princess of Parma, either of her own accord or from the counsels of ill-intentioned people, has not already taken umbrage and jealousy at the power which the Princess des Ursins has acquired over the mind of the King of Spain.

If he observes that these clouds are already formed, he will try to dissipate them by making her understand that the Princess des Ursins, perfectly instructed in the state of Spanish affairs, faithfully attached to the Catholic King, applied to the education of the princes his children, protected besides by the King [Louis], deserves great consideration on her part, and that this will even be the surest means to live happily and please the King her husband.[2]

The marriage by proxy with all papal ceremonial was fixed to take place on 15 September, and it was now August, but the Princess, distracted by fresh political disasters, had been too occupied to give her mind wholly to prevent it or it is probable she would have succeeded. All Europe was again convulsed at the prospect of war. The Duke of Berwick at the head of twenty thousand French had begun the siege of Barcelona, which turned out more difficult than

[1] Saint-Simon, xxv. 423; letter to Louis XIV. of 28 Aug. 1714.
[2] Trémoïlle, vi. 216; dated 20 Aug. 1714.

had been hoped. So desperately indeed did the rebels 'defend their freedom, that it was not till after four months of the most bloody battles ever fought in Spain that they consented to yield.

The Emperor, furious at Philippe's marriage with an Italian Princess, and possibly foreseeing Alberoni's projects, had excited all his Italian partisans against it. In England the death of Queen Anne had had the worst results, for the Whigs, again in power, desired nothing better than to recommence the war. Marlborough was reinstated in his post, the negotiations for peace were arrested and pretexts sought for quarrels with France and Spain. Cardinal del Giudice, now Spanish Ambassador at Versailles, was accused of working for Philippe's ultimate accession to the throne of France; the attack on Catalonia, they asserted, affected the honour of England which had guaranteed an amnesty, and his refusal to sign peace with Portugal was a further offence. "The conflagration seems to increase," Torcy wrote to the Princess on 27 August, "and I know not to what point it will attain if the British Government remains any longer in the hands of people animated against France."[1]

Smaller matters also were assuming an importance menacing to Spain and adding to her distraction. Giudice, in his capacity of Grand Inquisitor, had committed a crime unpardonable in her eyes, since her policy had always been to combat papal interference in the State. The preceding year Macanez her protégé had published a treatise attacking the Inquisition, which he accused of assuming an authority prejudicial to the Crown. The book had a great success in Madrid and was openly protected by Philippe, *alias* the Princess, and the Pope, terrified at this popularity in the country hitherto so obedient to his jurisdiction, sent orders to Giudice as Grand Inquisitor to condemn it as publicly as possible. This, as prince of the Church more interested in keeping well with the Pope than with Philippe, he obeyed, and signed a decree condemning it as "seditious, scandalous, audacious, injurious, degrading to religion, tending to schism and offensive to chastity," and forbidding any person to read or sell it on pain of excommunication and a fine of two hundred ducats. This decree he ordered to be affixed to all the churches of Spain and even to those of Paris, as though his jurisdiction extended to France.

[1] Trémoïlle, vi. 221 ; letter of 27 Aug. 1714.

The Princess, furious at this assumption of authority, ordered his immediate recall, and Philippe was directed to deprive him of his post of Grand Inquisitor and to forbid his return to Spain. Anxious to defend himself, arrived in Bayonne, he sent messengers begging to be received, but in vain, and being pitied and consoled by the Queen-Dowager, who had her Court there, he was quickly taken into favour in their common hatred of the Princess, and was employed by Alberoni, as will be seen, in the plot for her ruin.

To return to the marriage.

The Princess had sent her spies to Italy to discover the true character of the future Queen, and the accounts of her strong will, independence and haughty pride they brought back so terrified her that, in spite of her pre-occupations, she decided to make a desperate effort to prevent the marriage. But time was short. The ceremony by proxy was on the point of being celebrated and there was barely time for the swiftest messenger to reach Parma. However, she dispatched one at fullest speed with orders to Acquaviva, at all costs and by no matter what means, to retard it. According to Duclos the man succeeded and reached Parma the very morning of the marriage, but the Duke and his niece had received a warning and took their part with a promptness worthy of the Princess herself. He was waylaid and arrested before he entered the town, and the alternative of immediate death or a large sum of money was offered him, to gain which he had only to remain hidden till the marriage was over, when he would gallop into the town as though just arrived. Needless to say he did not hesitate. The wedding was celebrated with all pomp and he handed his papers to Acquaviva only when it was irrevocably concluded.[1]

No sooner was the marriage concluded than all tongues were loosened and the truth poured in from every side, to the Princess's despair, for whatever were the differences of opinion as to her personal charms, there was but one verdict as to her authoritative and ambitious character. Here is the description of the Comte d'Albert, sent by the Princess to report on her:

She has a good figure. Her head is well set on her shoulders, her chest is sufficiently developed, her complexion white. She

[1] Duclos, *Mémoires*, ed. Collin, i. 99.

is good-looking enough to make one think she will be much better later, especially if she grows fatter. Eyes sharp and a very assured expression. Her teeth seemed to me rather large, but white. Her face, from the mouth upwards, has suffered very much from the smallpox.[1]

Here is that of the Princess's old friend the Prince of Monaco, through whose states the Queen passed on her way to Madrid:

The Queen is neither tall nor short, but her figure is very good. Her face is long rather than oval. The smallpox has thickened her features—more, she is not only marked, but one sees scars and kinds of cuts. . . . All to my mind is redeemed by the infinite grace with which her head is nobly set on her shoulders—she has no less in her gait and other movements—and by the blue eyes which, without being very large, sparkle like flame and with which she knows how to say all she wants.

The mouth is rather large, which serves when she laughs to show that she has very pretty teeth, and she has always the most amiable smile I have ever seen. And this is not its only charm, for from it issues a delicious voice and speech filled with infinite courtesy.

She loves music passionately, knows it thoroughly and accompanies perfectly on the *claveçin*, but sings very little because, as she herself told me, her voice is too weak. She paints very prettily and seems to be of a gay humour. She loves riding and rides boldly. Hunting is one of her chief pleasures and they say she shoots well on the wing. It is said that, though her temper is very sweet, what she wants she wants very decidedly.[2]

For our own benefit I insert the following criticism of Duclos:

She had natural intelligence but without the least culture. She was ambitious without elevation of soul. Incapable of business because she was ignorant, mistrust and suspicion were all the prudence she possessed. She had the cunning and ways of the lower classes. Violent by nature she restrained herself by interest, using artifice where candour would have been more advantageous and thinking always that people wanted to cheat her because she always wanted to cheat them.[3]

Finally, according to Alberoni's own showing later, she was masculine in all her ways and tastes, ate for two, drank like a trooper, killed her bird at each shot, and

[1] Trémoïlle, vi. 258; letter of 13 Dec. 1714.
[2] De Courcy, *L'Espagne après la Paix d'Utrecht*, p. 296; letter to Torcy of 19 Oct. 1714.
[3] Duclos, *Mémoires*, ii. 281.

accepted and returned the coarsest jokes—all tastes which, though in the fashion of the day, were little in keeping with the meekness and modesty he had represented to the Princess.

Elisabeth Farnese was born 25 October, 1692, and was thus twenty-two at the time of her marriage. She was the daughter of the Duke Odoardo of Parma and Dorothea-Sophia, daughter of the Elector Palatine and sister of the Queen-Dowager of Spain and the Dowager-Empress of Germany. The Farnese owed their fortune to the marriage of the bastard son of Pope Paul III. to the bastard daughter of the Emperor Charles V., when the Duchies of Parma and Piacenza were bestowed. The present Duke, who was childless, had married her mother, his brother's widow, and she became thus by adoption heiress to the Duchies of Parma, Piacenza and Guastalla, to the succession of Tuscany and the Isle of Elba, so that the marriage was not without advantages to Philippe, who had lost all his Italian territory, and justified to a certain extent the policy of Alberoni. As a young girl she had the reputation of being the most beautiful of the Italian princesses till the small-pox ruined her skin and thickened her features. When Saint-Simon saw her seven years later, he expresses himself " terrified at her face, so excessively disfigured was it."

The marriage by proxy was celebrated on 15 September by the Cardinal Gozzadini, representing Clement XI., who arrived with five hundred persons in his train, and the new Queen left Parma a week later for Spain accompanied by her mother in a coach-and-six, escorted by a suite so numerous that she took three days to traverse her uncle's small states. She was followed by the Princess of Piombino (an old friend of the Princess des Ursins and appointed by her to serve as Camarera Mayor till her arrival in Spain), by the Cardinal Acquaviva and the Marquis de los Balbazés, who conducted the cortège. It was arranged that she should embark at Sestri-Levante and proceed by sea to Alicante. On 26 September, therefore, she and her immense suite set sail for Spain, but as with her predecessor, the weather was so stormy and she suffered so much from sea-sickness that after a few hours she insisted on returning to Genoa and continuing her journey by land.

" Man proposes and God disposes," wrote the Princess, rritably announcing this change cf programme to Madame de Maintenon. "Yesterday His Majesty learnt by a messenger sent by the Queen that it was impossible she should continue her journey by sea and that she should go by land. She wrote that she wished to arrive living, and if she went by sea she would arrive dead. . . . You will allow that these things are very vexing."[1]

Vexing is too mild a term. The arrangements for the voyage and her reception at Alicante had cost enormous sums. "All the King's equipages have been there for a long time," Orry wrote to the Intendant of Marine at Toulon, "two months have been spent in levelling the mountains and making the roads easy from Alicante to Madrid. The palaces in the towns where the Queen was to pass the night have been prepared, decorated and handsomely furnished—all of which is now useless."[2] Louis also was put to considerable expense, for during her slow and pompous passage through his states the cost of entertaining her and her suite fell on the governors of the provinces through which she passed, and had to be refunded from the Royal treasury.

Balbazés did his best to remonstrate, representing the huge outlay the change would cost, not to mention the delay, for Louis' permission to pass through France must be accorded before the procession could even start. In vain. The Queen had a will of iron. "She knows very well how to say what she will or will not do!" he excused himself to the Princess for his failure, "and I dared not use force."[3]

It has been said that this change of programme was part of Alberoni's plot in order that she might pass through Bayonne and visit her aunt the Queen-Dowager, with whose aid the finishing touches were to be put, but the Abbé's own letters to Rocca, who was in his confidence, disprove this. On the contrary, he was as great a victim to her caprice as anyone, for on 18 September he had already left Madrid suffering from high fever to go to Alicante to meet her, a week's journey at the risk of his life, only to hear on his arrival of her change of plan. His letters of the three months during which she was lazily amusing herself on her journey through France betray the utmost anxiety, for the success of his intrigue depended entirely on his

[1] Bossange, iv. 495; letter of 14 Oct. 1714.   [2] Courcy, 254.
[3] Trémoïlle, vi. 268; letter of 13 Dec. 1714.

meeting her before her arrival and drilling her in the part she had to play, and he feared not only for his own health, but that the Princess, his enemy since her discovery of his treachery, might find means to put a stop to it.

The Queen herself seemed in no hurry to reach her kingdom and thoroughly enjoyed the pomp and ceremony to which she had been so little accustomed in her uncle's tiny Court. She travelled alone in a magnificent litter, started late, rested often, and enjoyed the good cheer provided for her and the magnificent receptions, harangues and Royal salutes which greeted her at each resting-place.

What a procession! Her Italian suite consisted of a lady-in-waiting, four maids of honour, four pages, an almoner, confessor, physician, surgeon, two equerries, the officers of her guard and gentlemen of her household, each of these with their own retinue of servants, not counting her own chief of the kitchen, three cooks, three butlers, the officers of her wardrobe, valets, grooms, *femmes-de-chambre*, etc. —in all, including the suites of her Camarera Mayor, of the Cardinal Acquaviva and the Marquis de los Balbazés, more than six hundred souls to be fed and lodged by the unfortunate governors of the provinces through which she passed. The Comte de Grignan (Madame de Sévigné's son-in-law, now an old man of eighty-three), as governor of Provence, on her change of programme had to procure at a moment's notice thirty-six coaches, seventy-four saddle-horses, six carriages for the inferior servants, and endless mules and wagons for the baggage—and pay for everything, for the Duke of Parma, who was poor, had provided nothing and the Princess had not a sou in her pocket.

This mighty caravan traversed the country in all its ponderous state, arriving at Antibes on 20 October and five days later at Brignoles, where Louis had sent a master of ceremonies, Desgranges, to arrange the difficult questions of etiquette.[1] At Marseilles the Comte de Grignan entertained her so royally that she insisted on spending three days in his palace and going to the theatre, where *La Malade Imaginaire* was given in her honour.

At Arles, which she reached 2 November, she was entertained by the Archbishop, who prepared her feasts

---

[1] These and the following notes on the Queen's journey through France are taken from Desgranges' official letters to Torcy, published by Courcy, op. cit., 266, etc.

so sumptuous that she had a violent attack of indigestion and was unable to continue her journey for several days.

Meanwhile Philippe, sick and feverish from abstinence, sent messenger after messenger to beg her to travel more quickly. But hurry herself she would not and proceeded on her way, taking no notice of his importunities. In vain Desgranges implored her to leave her litter and travel in the more expeditious coach-and-six, but she refused. "She loves to rise late, and will not dine before leaving because it would be too soon after her chocolate," he wrote in despair to Torcy. She would never start before eleven, would travel for an hour and then stop to dine at midday, and after a long siesta crawl along again till it grew dark, which, considering it was November, left her little more than two hours. It is not surprising that she rarely covered more than a few miles a day and took no less than three weeks to go from Arles to Tarbes.

At Tarbes she had a welcome surprise. Louis, prompted thereto by Desgranges, had sent her by the Duc de Saint-Aignan, brother of the Duc de Beauvillier, an autograph letter of greeting and some costly wedding-gifts, among them a gold watch, a bracelet with his own portrait encrusted with diamonds, and a beautiful mother-of-pearl snuff-box. She was delighted, put on the bracelet immediately, took snuff out of the snuff-box, and admired the handsome young Duke who brought them. She would have been less pleased had she known that he was charged with the mission to follow her to Madrid, to spy upon her and report on her behaviour and the influence she was likely to have over the King.

The route originally fixed for crossing the frontier was by Bayonne, and she was looking forward to a long stay with her aunt the Queen-Dowager, but whether Philippe foresaw this fresh delay or that the Princess des Ursins feared their meeting, on arriving at Bordeaux to her great annoyance she received orders to go instead by Pau and Saint-Jean-Pied-de-Port. However, *ce que femme veut Dieu veut*—aunt and niece had both made up their minds to meet and meet they did, the Queen-Dowager travelling to Pau to join her niece with another procession almost as formidable as her own.

Her cortège consisted of ten coaches, a dozen carriages

for her servants, sixty baggage mules and an infinity of wagons, the whole escorted by a volunteer regiment of the young nobles of Bayonne, with whom she was extremely popular, the two caravans, as may be imagined, blocking up all the mountain passes. The meeting took place on 30 November just outside Pau, and aunt and niece after the most affectionate greeting proceeded together to the château prepared for them.

There was no end to the fêtes and amusements organised by the Queen-Dowager to entertain her niece nor to the gifts and caresses she lavished upon her, for she hoped through her to obtain her liberty and be reinstated in Madrid. The Queen-Dowager, though she never paid her debts, was generous, and on this occasion made the young Queen many magnificent gifts, among them a set of diamonds, another of pearls and a superb coach. The first morning after their arrival she sent for her riding-hat, pretending she wanted to have it copied, and returned it with a splendid clasp of diamonds and emeralds.

The two, dressed in hunting costume, both superb horsewomen and good shots, hunted all day and sang and played the *claveçin* all night. Comedies were acted and balls given in their honour, but neither danced, the Dowager declaring she was too old and the young Queen suffering from a sprained ankle which she had twisted at Toulouse.

The Princess, whose agents reported to her this sudden intimacy, grew more and more suspicious and persuaded Philippe, himself very irritable at the prolonged delay, to send imperious orders that she must make more haste, warning her that winter was near and that the mountains would soon be impassable with snow. These orders like the former had no effect, and for another week the two queens continued to amuse themselves as though no such person as Philippe V. existed.

This indifference was due, it appears, to the Queen's resentment at the order she received at Toulouse that all her Italian household, even her *femmes-de-chambre* and her confessor, must quit her at the Spanish frontier and return to Parma. The order, signed by the Princess and sent to Acquaviva, she attributed to her malevolence, and her fury increased against this woman whom Alberoni had already represented as her chief enemy and rival. She had received it with the greatest indignation, had declared it quite impossible to obey, swore she had no orders to receive from anybody, and in open revolt ordered her people to remain with her, notwithstanding the despair and remonstrances of Balbazés and the Princess of Piombino.

On 6 December, having exhausted all their amusements, the two queens left Pau and pursued their leisurely way to Saint-Jean-Pied-de-Port, which they reached on the 9th. Here the Dowager, officially in exile, was forced to leave her niece, and they parted at the foot of the mountains very tenderly. Desgranges, to whom we are indebted for all these details, his mission ended, returned to Versailles, but before leaving he wrote to Torcy the following description of the Queen:

> I learnt from the Queen's almoner that she is perfectly well brought up and instructed in things suitable to a princess, even in philosophy, that she has made a special study of history, has read books of politics and of the interests of princes, and that her mind is sufficiently cultivated, that she is gentle and accommodating, but maintains always with a noble pride her position of princess, without wishing to be governed by nor have complacence for anybody, nor recourse to flattery to obtain what she wants.[1]

After her aunt's departure she continued her journey, still without haste, to Pampeluna, which she reached on 11 December. Here Alberoni, still suffering from fever but anxious and eager, was awaiting her, and according to his system had prepared for her reception a magnificent banquet of which everything was Italian cooked by Italian cooks—macaroni, mortadella sausage, Parmesan cheese, salad with garlic, and Lombard wines such as her soul loved; nothing was lacking. Homesick and lonely at the idea of losing her Italians, the sight of a compatriot and such a supper filled her with joy, and from that moment Alberoni became her dearest friend, which was precisely what he had hoped for the success of his plot. He succeeded in persuading her to allow her suite to depart, for it was not the moment to risk Philippe's anger by disobedience to his orders, and seized the opportunity when her grief and indignation were at a climax to insinuate that His Majesty would never have dreamt of such an order but for the insistence of the Princess, whose bad influence over him

---

[1] Saint-Simon, xxv. 448; letter of 3 Dec. 1714.

was the cause of this and all the other annoyances she would be made to suffer.

Four days they remained together at Pampeluna in spite of Philippe's impatience and repeated orders to hasten, and the subject of their discourse is easy to guess. Contrary to what is usually asserted that it was the Queen-Dowager who prepared her niece for the part she had to play, from his own showing it was Alberoni himself who instructed her during this stay at Pampeluna and the journey to Jadraque where the Princess was to meet them. Doubtless the Dowager was in the plot, and had her share in exciting her niece against their mutual enemy, but it required no less a mind than that of the arch-intriguer himself to plane down the difficulties and allay the misgivings of the Queen, for the rôle she was called upon to play was fraught with danger both to him and herself.

Every evening for more than three hours, alone "*a quattro occhi*," as he expresses it, he discoursed on the same theme, warned her that as long as the Princess was in Spain she would never be Queen nor sure of her husband, and insisted that the stroke must be dealt immediately while separated from the King, for once in his presence he would fall again under her influence and the favourable moment be irrevocably lost.

It was no easy task, for Elisabeth Farnese, like all the world, was aware of the immense power and prestige of the woman she was called on to attack. It was sending little David armed with his pebble to fight Goliath in full armour, and notwithstanding her audacity she must have trembled at the risk she ran in insulting and expelling from a country in which she herself was a stranger the all-powerful favourite, the woman who was in reality more Queen than herself. A hundred things might happen to turn the tables against her and ruin her in the eyes of Philippe, of Louis and all Europe. She had probably heard of former battles with Louville, Porto-Carrero and the d'Estrées, all of whom had been floored by the redoubtable dictatress, and here was she, young and inexperienced, called on to attack her single-handed. To all these fears and objections Alberoni had to find reassuring answers, to inspire her with confidence and quiet her misgivings, and it is doubtful if he would have succeeded had he not been the bearer of some written encouragement or at least consent from Philippe himself.

It was an anxious moment, for his own fate too was in the balance, and that of his grandiose ideas for the restoration of Italy. Her failure or even refusal meant his own ruin, for the Princess, triumphant and restored to power, with Philippe again enchained, would have but one thought —vengeance on the man who had fooled and cheated her. He was playing with tools of sharpest edge, but he juggled with a master-hand, and before the four days were over had succeeded in exciting his pupil to the point of jealous fury necessary to make her forget her fears and inspire her with recklessness. "The Queen leaves Pampeluna filled with good maxims," he summed up the result of his efforts to Rocca on 14 December.[1]

The most difficult and certainly the most anxious part of his plot was this lesson to the girl to whom he had perforce to confide its execution, but he succeeded, and detest and despise him as one may, one cannot but feel that a man capable of carrying out without a hitch an intrigue so complicated and audacious was also capable of executing his projects of a united Italy.

So filled with good maxims was the Queen that now she had but one idea, at once to attack and fell her adversary. So impatient was she for the fray that she lingered no longer on the road for meals and long siestas, but refused even to stay at the towns decreed by Philippe himself as resting-places, where grand fêtes had been prepared in her honour. But with all her impatience the roads were difficult, and it was eight days before she reached the little town where the Princess was to meet her and escort her in her capacity of Camarera Mayor to Guadalayara, where Philippe himself awaited her.

Eight days, during which she was practically alone with her mentor, during which he never ceased to prompt and drill her, to excite her jealousy and stimulate her courage. "The conferences between us *a quattro occhi* continued without truce from Pampeluna to Jadraque," he wrote to Rocca later.[2]

And, forgetful of nothing, he caused to be spread abroad

[1] Bourgeois, *Alberoni, Madame des Ursins*, etc., p. 39; letter of 14 Dec. 1714.
[2] Ibid., *Lettres d'Alberoni*, p. 352; letter to Rocca of 25 Dec. 1714.

in Madrid rumours that with the coming of the new Queen great changes might be expected, that like an avenging angel she was on her way to deliver the Spaniards from the domination of the French represented by Madame des Ursins and Orry.[1] Similar rumours even reached Versailles, as we learn from Dangeau, who notes in his *Diary* under the date 30 December:

> The Marquis Grillo, grandee of Spain, arrived at Versailles to thank the King for his gifts. Since his arrival it has transpired that the Queen is not pleased with the Princess des Ursins regarding herself and complains of the want of consideration shown her since the day she arrived in France. She attributes these dissatisfactions and causes of complaint to the Princess des Ursins and, as this Queen is sufficiently haughty, it is thought that at her meeting with the King of Spain it is likely there will be some changes at the Court.[2]

[1] Baudrillart, i. 610 ; letter from Pachau to Torcy of 12 Nov. 1714.
[2] Dangeau, xv. 318.

CHAPTER XXI

DISGRACE OF THE PRINCESS (1714)

WE must leave the new Queen at Pampeluna assimilating the instructions of her mentor and return to Madrid, where the Princess, full of misgivings, was unwillingly making preparations to meet her.

Her suspicions increased every day, justified by the independence the Queen had shown during her long journey. Since the marriage ceremony had consolidated her position she had revealed herself self-willed and intractable to a degree which left no doubt as to her real character.

Her insistence on travelling by land instead of sea, her defiance of the King's orders and lack of any sort of deference to his wishes, her long visit to the Queen-Dowager, her refusal to allow the departure of her suite, and last (but probably far from least in the Princess's eyes) her want of respect towards herself in leaving her letters unanswered—all these crimes had irritated her profoundly, and it was with a heart full of resentment and the firm resolve to put her in her place without a moment's delay that she started on her journey to meet her.

It is true she had received letters grateful even to the point of obsequiousness from the Duke and Duchess of Parma, thanking her for her great goodness to the new Queen,[1] and that the day before her departure from Pampeluna the Queen herself (at Alberoni's advice) had finally condescended to acknowledge her existence and sent her a few lines of conventional politeness, signed, even before the second marriage gave her full right, with the Royal "*Moi—la Reine.*"[2] But these conventional courtesies did little to allay her suspicions, which were growing every day stronger, that a trap had been set into which she, with all her experience, had been naïve enough to fall.

Less than a week before d'Aubigny wrote to Torcy: "All that is reported of the new Queen does not please the person to whom she owes her elevation, because it is thought that

[1] Courcy, 322; letter of 8 Dec. 1714.
[2] Ibid., 324; letter of 20 Dec. 1714.

she will want to use her own wings, and as they are preparing here to clip them, I doubt if there will be as much harmony in the Royal palace as might be wished."[1]

Misgivings or no as to the new Queen's character, the Princess could have had none as to the ultimate victory. She who had fought and overthrown statesmen, ambassadors and princes of the blood, who had tilted victoriously with Madame de Maintenon, subjugated the Grand Monarque himself, and made of his grandson an obedient slave, could have had no fear that an ignorant girl bred in an insignificant Court, raised by herself to the throne she was to occupy, could triumph over her immense authority, her long experience and formidable influence. A tussle there would doubtless be before this self-willed Parmesan could be taught her place, and the sooner it was over the better. All she had to do, while preserving all the forms of respect prescribed by etiquette, was to let her know at once that she was her protégée and inferior.

Thus, when Philippe, probably so far acquainted with the plot as to wish the meeting to take place as near the frontier as possible, asked her to go to Pampeluna to meet his bride, she refused, excusing herself on the ground of the health of the little Don Philippe, and consented only to go as far as Jadraque, a day's journey from Madrid. The King himself was to await the Queen at Guadalayara, sixty-three kilometres from the capital, where, in the magnificent palace of the Dukes of Infantada, the marriage was to be celebrated.

Thus these two women set forth towards the fatal encounter, the one exploding with pent-up jealousy, well primed in the part she had to play, seeking a pretext to annihilate her adversary, but fully determined to do so without if none offered. The other haughty and contemptuous, resolved to humiliate the ill-bred rustic whom she had raised from insignificance to the second throne in Europe. The collision promised to be tremendous, the crash formidable, but strange to say, it was the older woman, experienced and war-worn, who was demolished, crushed and mangled by the brutality of a coarse virago to whom the laws of courts were unknown and by whom those of humanity were despised.

Many and detailed are the contemporary accounts of the

[1] Trémoïlle, vi. 260 ; letter of 17 Dec. 1714.

DISGRACE OF THE PRINCESS

famous interview, which remains in spite of them somewhat of a mystery. From these accounts I have selected only those of the writers whose character or official position lend probability to their narrative, placing first that of Saint-Simon, since he had it directly from the lips of the Princess herself, while still smarting under her disgrace.

The Queen of Spain [he writes] advanced towards Madrid with all those who had received her at the frontier, equipages, household, and the King of Spain's guard. The Princess des Ursins, who had accepted the post of Camarera Mayor as to the late Queen, had arranged all her household, filling it with all her own satellites male and female. The journey was arranged on both sides so that the King should only arrive at Guadalayara the night before the Queen. The Princess followed in her coach, and directly on their arrival the King shut himself up alone with her and saw no one any more until he went to bed. This was on 22 December. The next day the Princess left with a very small suite to go seven leagues farther to a little town called Jadraque, where the Queen was to pass the night. The Princess counted on enjoying all her gratitude for the unhoped-for greatness she had procured her, on spending the evening with her and accompanying her the next day in her coach to Guadalaxara.

At Jadraque she found that the Queen had arrived. She got out of her coach at a lodging prepared for her opposite that of the Queen. She had come in full Court dress, which she arranged a little and then went to her at once. The coldness and dryness of her reception surprised her extremely at first, but she attributed it to her embarrassment and tried to break the ice. Meanwhile everyone had retired out of respect and left them alone. She then began her discourse, but the Queen did not let her continue and immediately began to reproach her that she was lacking in respect by her costume and manner. Madame des Ursins, whose costume was correct, and who by her respectful manner and words intended to pacify the Queen and thought herself very far from meriting this attack, was strangely surprised and tried to excuse herself. But at once the Queen began with offensive words to scream and cry out, calling for the officers of the guard and ordering Madame des Ursins with insults to leave her presence. She tried to speak and defend herself from these reproaches, but the Queen, with redoubled fury and threats, shouted orders that this mad woman be removed from her presence and lodging, and turned out by the shoulders. At the same time she called Amezaga, lieutenant of the guard commanding her escort, and the equerry in charge of the equipages, ordered the former to arrest Madame des Ursins and not to leave her till he had put her in a coach with six horses and two or three footmen and forced her to leave immediately for Burgos and Bayonne, stopping nowhere on the way. Amezaga tried to tell her that no one but the King of Spain had the power to give such orders. She asked him haughtily if he had not the King of Spain's order to obey her in everything, without reserve or remonstrance. It is true that he had this order, but no one knew anything about it.[1]

Madame des Ursins then was immediately arrested and put in a coach with one of her *femmes-de-chambre*, without having been allowed time to change her costume or headdress or to take any precaution against the cold, nor fetch money or anything else, neither she nor her *femme-de-chambre*, and without any sort of provisions in the coach, no night-gown nor any change of linen. Thus was she embarked in gala costume as she came from the Queen, with the two officers of the guard—all ready prepared as was also the coach. In this haste and confusion she tried to send to the Queen, who, again furious that she was not yet obeyed, gave orders for her immediate departure. It was then nearly seven on Christmas Eve [an error, it was eleven o'clock at night], the ground was covered with snow and ice, and the cold very piercing and stinging, as it always is in Spain. The night was so dark that they could see only by the light of the snow. . . .[2]

This is the account of her martyrdom according to the victim. That of Alberoni naturally gives it a different aspect. He wrote it immediately after the event to his compatriot the Count Pighetti, minister of the Duke of Parma at the Court of Versailles, with the view, as he himself says, that his version might have first hearing.

MADRID, 30 December, 1714.

I send you, my dear Count, a slight account of what has just happened, written in haste, yet full of public matters of which you will make use in the talks you will hear on the subject, without, however, undertaking to justify a great Queen, since she has justified herself. She has acted like Judith and taken a decision which has already placed her on a pinnacle. . . .

She has just told me that you must not seek opportunities to speak of this affair, but speak of it only should occasion arise, and without much eagerness. You must even show superiority and contempt.

The unheard-of and premeditated extravagance shown by the Princess des Ursins the first moment of her meeting with the Queen our Mistress, forced Her Majesty justly to resent and defend the honour and Royal Majesty outraged in her person. That is why, before coming to the event itself, it is necessary

---

[1] In his addition to the *Journal* of Dangeau, Saint-Simon adds at this point: "A strong sign that the King was in concert" (Dangeau, xv. 337).

[2] Saint-Simon, xxvi. 104, etc.

to make known the sentiments of the lady [the Princess] towards Her Majesty, publicly proclaimed in her disrespectful talk, from which everyone foresaw very bad consequences for the Queen and deplored already her unfortunate position.

The arrival of Monsieur d'Aubigny in Madrid immediately caused her to regret having contributed to this marriage, the said d'Aubigny persuading her that a Princess of twenty-two, of superior intelligence and eminent qualities, could not preserve sentiments of affection and gratitude towards one who thought to make of her a miserable slave and not a Queen. The lady's first care was to persuade the King to keep the Queen in ignorance of all affairs, since she would arrive already disposed by the Court of Parma to favour that of Rome. She passed her time in turning the Queen into ridicule about her journey, affirming that the slight progress she made showed complete indifference, not to say lack of respect, for the King, who desired her so much, and that her travelling by night especially showed a strange and ill-balanced judgment. . . . She did not omit saying to several people that the King had made this marriage solely for the repose of his conscience, and that already she had cause to regret it, knowing well that the qualities of the late Queen would not be found in her. . . .

The lady, not content with having cruelly refused to allow the Queen to bring with her two servants for her inferior service, to whom Her Majesty had been accustomed from childhood, as also her confessor, she accused all the suite which had accompanied her to Pampeluna of a thousand larcenies, and to humiliate her still more caused Orry to write letters at the King's orders to the intendants of France to acquaint them with the said thefts. . . .

The lady went to Jadraque, a day's journey from Guadalayara. The Queen arrived there at eight o'clock in the evening and met the lady in the middle of the stairs, where she was received and greeted by Her Majesty with so much benevolence and distinction that all who were present thought it too exaggerated for a Queen. It was evidently her intention to try by the sweetest and most insinuating manners to win the lady's heart, insensibly lead her towards a good understanding, and show her her fault in surrounding herself with people who deceived her.

But the lady gave her neither time nor occasion to execute her generous and indulgent design. Her first words to Her Majesty were that her clothes were ridiculous and that she must remain for some days at Jadraque to dress according to the etiquette introduced by the late Queen. Next, that it was neither decent nor proper to run after a husband in such haste like a woman of the people. Afterwards she reproached her about the journey which, by her laziness, had lasted three months, and said that if she had to do with another husband than the King he would have condemned her to remain another three months at Guadalayara without seeing him. Other words still less respectful she said, which the Queen, to her honour, has not communicated to the King, but which forced her to call the officer of her guard and tell him to remove a maniac from her Royal presence, to keep her guarded in his quarters, put her in a coach with a sufficient suite and take her across the Pyrenees, which was executed. All this has been approved by the King with satisfaction and by his subjects, who already admire the Queen as their liberator.[1]

Next we have the diplomatic dispatch of the Duc de Saint-Aignan, written a week after the event, which seems more or less impartial and represents the matter as it was known at the Court of Madrid.

Since the last post I have learnt some details of the event of the disgrace of Madame la Princesse des Ursins, of which I think fit to inform you.

In the private conversation she had with the Queen a moment after her arrival, she told her, speaking of the confidence with which the King of Spain had up to now honoured her, that the greatest mark he had given her, which had touched her most, was to have put himself in her hands to choose the Princess he destined to reign with him, that she thought she had perfectly responded in arranging the marriage of Her Majesty, whose personal merit and great qualities would make the King forget his misfortunes, that she hoped the pains she had taken on this occasion would gain her also the confidence of the Queen, of which she would render herself worthy by an inviolable attachment, and that Her Majesty could count upon finding her always between the King and her to maintain things in the state they should be, and procure her all the happiness she might hope for.

The Queen, who had listened to her speech quietly enough up to then, took fire at these last words and answered that she had need of no one between her and the King, that it was impertinent to make her such offers and more than impertinent to dare speak to her in that way after the letters which had been written to her, about which she had kept silence out of kindness. *Some people*, she added, would be very astonished before long. And as Madame des Ursins begged her to repeat this, saying she had not understood, she repeated again that "*some people* would be very astonished, and she among the first." Thereupon the Princess replied that she had nothing to reproach herself and thus knew not what this could mean, and as she continued to talk without restraint, the Queen impatiently told her to stop and leave the room. This caused fresh vivacities on the part of Madame des Ursins, to which the Queen, beside herself with rage, put an end by calling the captain of

[1] Trémoïlle, vi. 271 ; letter of 30 Dec. 1714.

DISGRACE OF THE PRINCESS 347

her guard and telling him to remove this maniac. These were her very words. . . . She wrote on one knee the order of arrest, too impatient to wait till they brought her a table, and I hear that the terms she employed concerning her expulsion and journey out of the kingdom were nearly the same as those used by Madame des Ursins in exiling the Queen-Dowager, whether it was mere chance or that the affair had been concerted between the two Queens, for no one doubts but that the Queen-Dowager has had much to do with it, as also the Cardinal del Giudice, and it is said that the Abbé Alberoni more than anyone has been one of the chief actors in what has taken place. It is certain that he is now very well at Court and is looked upon as one who will have much credit there.

I have been assured on good authority that the Queen would not have taken such violent steps against the Princess but for the assurance she received that the King of Spain would consent to her expulsion. It is said that, displeased at the style of some letters she received from the Princess, vexed also at the change of her domestics which she attributed to her, and encouraged in these ideas by the person I have just named, she made strong instances to His Catholic Majesty to obtain her dismissal, even going so far as to say that if he would not consent he must allow her to return to Parma, because she preferred to be deprived of the happiness awaiting her in Spain than buy it at the price of having every day to support fresh scenes from a person she would never be able to endure, as much for the true interest of His Majesty as for the insurmountable aversion she felt naturally for her. It is said that upon this the King finally resolved to approve the said expulsion, without, however, deciding either the time or manner, that the Abbé Alberoni had carried this message to the Queen during her stay at Pampeluna, and that what passed in the conversation just related hastened the execution of the project and apparently changed the circumstances. The same person told me also that the King of Spain seemed very pleased to find himself free.

The joy in Madrid at the dismissal of Madame des Ursins has been nearly universal. It is very much hoped that the departure of Monsieur Orry will be the result, and no one tries to conceal their thoughts. I have heard that the Queen has spoken of him to the King as a man whose government damages His Majesty's reputation, but it seems necessary to defer things for some time since he only has knowledge of all affairs.[1]

The next narrative, more favourable to the Princess, is that of the Président Hénault, who in his capacity of historian is probably more or less reliable.

The Queen arrived finally at Jadraque. Madame des Ursins met her as she got out of her coach. She made her kindly

[1] Trémoïlle, vi. 277; letter of 7 Jan. 1715.

reproaches that she had kept them waiting, spoke of the King's impatience and tried to entertain her while they mounted the stairs, to give herself countenance in the eyes of the little Court and attract some words from the Queen, who had a cold and severe air, answered her shortly and dryly and did not at all try to reassure her. They arrived at her apartment, the doors were shut as soon as the Queen and Madame des Ursins had entered. Immediately after their voices were heard violently raised, and the Queen reappeared at the door and called for the captain of the guard, to whom she gave the order to arrest Madame des Ursins.

The surprise at this moment may be imagined. A foreign Princess, who had not yet seen the King she was to marry, who gives orders to arrest the Prime Minister, for such was Madame des Ursins! The Queen saw the captain's embarrassment and asked if he were not there to obey her. The officer replied that he did not hesitate to execute her order, but took the liberty to ask that it should be written. She wrote the order to remove Madame des Ursins immediately, to make her travel with the greatest possible speed and conduct her to France. It is to be noted that this was in December.

Madame des Ursins set out. The Princess of Parma began her toilet. She supped and, without seeming at all concerned with what had just passed, she slept with the greatest tranquillity in the world. It was said that the Abbé Alberoni had brought the King's permission to execute all that had just taken place, and that in the letter he wrote that they would never be at peace if this woman remained at the Court.[1]

This latter statement is corroborated by other though less reliable writers. In the *Secret History of the Court of Madrid* of 1714 cited by Combes, it is stated that the Queen had herself written to Philippe to ask his consent to treat the Princess as she chose: " I ask of you but one thing," she wrote, " the dismissal of Madame des Ursins. Give me full power in the matter, for on it depends the happiness of my home." To which Philippe replied that he had given written orders to his captain of the guard to obey her in everything, and even added, " But take good care at least not to miss your shot at first, for if she is with you for only two hours she will enslave you and prevent our sleeping together as with the late Queen." [2]

The following is a contemporary Spanish version, less favourable to the Princess, written the day after the event:

The Queen, having arrived at Jadraque 23 December, Her Highness the Princess des Ursins, who was in the town, did not

[1] Hénault, *Mémoires*, p. 180. [2] Combes, 523, and Duclos, i. 101.

DISGRACE OF THE PRINCESS

go to meet her on the road and was not present at the moment of her arrival, but went to receive her, descending part of the staircase of the house. Her Majesty admitted her to her presence with much affability, pretending not to have remarked this lack of attention. They entered the apartment together and shut the door. The Princess reproached the Queen with having voluntarily retarded her journey, with having started very late from the resting-places and with not wishing to remain at Jadraque to receive her instructions as to how she should govern, criticising her dress which she said was that of a *comédienne*. All this took place alone without witnesses but has been revealed, and it is certain that the Queen threw open the door and cried with a loud voice, " *Qu'on enlève cette folle !* "

Afterwards she ordered the captain of the guards, Amezaga, to put the Princess in prison and send her immediately, at eleven o'clock at night alone with fifty guards, beyond the Pyrenees.

Amezaga, having executed the first order, observed to the Queen that out of pity she should accord her a servant and more comfort as regards food and linen, and the Queen permitted that she should have one servant and a footman.

On receiving the order from Amezaga, Her Highness the Princess rebelled, saying that it could not be executed without the King's order. Amezaga insisted that she must obey, but she replied that she was unwell and could not travel. He begged her not to force him to have her put in the coach by four of his guards. Thus the Queen's order was executed at the hour named. The Princess entered the coach with Don Thomas Ydiaquez and another officer, surrounded by fifty soldiers. The next morning the Queen sent the Count Alberoni to the King at Guadalayara to tell him what had happened, and His Majesty approved her resolution. The fact being made public, the King's confessor begged His Majesty to allow the Prince de Chalais and Don Alessandro Lanti to follow the Princess, with permission that she might rest where they overtook her, and His Majesty consented, thinking that on the Queen's arrival her fault might be found less grave. The two cavaliers left Guadalayara in haste, but the Queen arriving the evening of the same day, he revoked the order. . . .[1]

In the following version, written by a certain Sieur de la Loire to the Comte de Pontchartrain a few days after the tragedy, the details are crushing as regards the coarseness and brutality of the Queen:

MADRID, 31 *December*, 1714.

The circumstances of the event which took place between two persons alone and without witnesses are difficult to penetrate, but the truth may be guessed by some words uttered by

[1] Trémoïlle, vi. 263 ; dated 24 Dec. 1714.

the Queen in a loud voice—" Speak thus to *me*!—to *me*! " It is supposed that the Queen, having reproached the Princess des Ursins very bitterly for having intercepted three letters from the Queen-Dowager and having kept them to prevent the King giving her permission to visit her, she answered disrespectfully and excused herself ill, whereupon the Queen called someone in the ante-room and going to the door cried to the officer of the guard who appeared, " Remove this maniac from my presence! "

The Princess did not understand and asked him, " What did the Queen say ? " To which he replied, " That Your Highness must retire to your apartment." Some time after the Princess, thinking the Queen's anger would have cooled down, sent a message to beg Her Majesty to accept a jewel which it was the custom for the ladies-in-waiting to present to the Queen. The messenger called her "Her Highness," and she replied, " Who is this Highness ? I know of none in Spain except the Prince of the Asturias." And taking the jewel she gave it to the Princess of Piombino, saying, " Here, Madame! Here is a present for your *femme-de-chambre*."

The Queen, who had not recovered from her emotion, called to the officer in the ante-chamber and said, " Go and tell Madame des Ursins to prepare to leave Spain immediately, with one *femme-de-chambre*, one footman, two officers with her in the coach, and an escort of fifty guards." As the officer was going with this order to the Princess, she called him back, saying, " Wait! I will give you the order in writing." Which she did. You must know that Monsieur d'Amezaga, who commanded the detachment of guards, had orders to obey her in everything.

The officer went to announce his order to the Princess, who asked him to show it. He refused on the ground that he had not been told to do so, and went to ask the Queen, who replied, " Give her a copy or the original, no matter which, only make her leave directly." All was prepared beforehand and orders given to guard all the doors so that no one should be allowed to go out.

The Princess, who knew this, told her secretary, the Sieur Hocquat, to get out of the window, which he did, but he was arrested, as well as all her suite of servants. . . .

Meantime all was being prepared for the journey, though it was snowing and such cold as had not been felt in Spain for thirty years. The Princess, seeing there was no means of avoiding it, sent to represent to the Queen that a woman of her age, suffering in the legs, could not leave without some other precautions. To which the Queen replied, " What! Not yet gone! It is not legs she will lack, for I have given her fifty horses who have legs, and sound ones. Give her a mattress for her feet, and send her off at once." [1]

[1] This is quite in keeping with what Alberoni himself writes of the coarse humour of Elisabeth Farnese.

DISGRACE OF THE PRINCESS 351

It was past eleven on the darkest of nights when she got into the coach, and on leaving she said, "I am sorry to have vexed the Queen."[1]

In his work on Elisabeth Farnese, Edward Armstrong cites the following contemporary account of the meeting, evidently inspired by Alberoni, from a manuscript by Bellardi in the Biblioteca Ambrosiana, Milan, which exactly reverses the rôles:

Alberoni reached Jadraque three hours before the Queen. " Well! " cried the Princess, " when will the Queen arrive? She treats us very cavalierly making us wait like this, travelling all night like a prostitute. . . . You represented her to me like a heroine, but it seems to me she is but a poor creature, from her appetite downwards. It is said she eats nothing but garlic and hard-boiled eggs!"

Pretending to suffer from swelled legs, she stood at the top of the stairs without descending a step. She led the Queen into her room while Alberoni listened at the door, and said, "You have treated the King, Madame, very cavalierly, for you have paid little attention to his impatient desire to see you." Then, taking her by the waist and turning her round like a marionette, she said, " My word, Madame! You are very ill-made." Then the Queen, without answering a word, cried out indignantly, " Count Alberoni! Take this mad woman away!" The Princess left the room in astonishment, and Alberoni in silence accompanied her to her chamber and stationed sentinels there.[2]

Lastly we have the Queen's own version as told to her husband and passed on by him to his grandfather in one of his deplorably foolish letters:

MADRID, 29 *December*, 1714.

As I flatter myself that Your Majesty will wish to share my joy in having the Queen, I send this messenger to make known to you that I find in her all that I could desire, and hope we shall be happy together. My joy, however, has been disturbed by what happened at Jadraque, where the Queen was forced to dismiss the Princess des Ursins because of what passed there, which was as follows:

The Queen received the Princess on first meeting her with much kindness, although dissimulating already her annoyance that she had only descended half the staircase to meet her, and had mounted the rest by her side, without making all the demonstrations due to her rank.

Afterwards, having shut the doors in order to talk together,

[1] Saint-Simon, xxvi. 434, etc.
[2] Armstrong, *Elisabeth Farnese*, p. 32.

the Princess began by disapproving the Queen's decision to arrive as I desired the next day at Guadalaxara, where I awaited her with much impatience, because, she said, the Queen's dress was not suitable to the solemnity of such a day, and though it was only a travelling dress the Princess dwelt strongly upon it, saying it was unworthy of a person of her rank. From that she proceeded to give the Queen other lessons regarding her conduct, which, although I believe they were due to her attachment to me, were said in terms which extremely displeased the Queen, going so far that, though she knew how mortified she was at the delay in her journey, she reproached her severely for it, taxing her with lack of respect and friendship for me.

At these words the Queen could no longer restrain herself, and attacked in her tenderest point, was so indignant that she ordered the officer commanding the guards who accompanied her to remove her and sent her out of Spain. . . . The Queen at once sent to tell me what had passed, and having received her letter only a few hours before her arrival at Guadalaxara, considering that, since the Queen was angry with the Princess and mistrusted her as she did, it would be impossible to avoid continual domestic discord, which would disturb the peace and harmony I desired so much, I resolved, although with sorrow, to take the Queen's part for the time. I wrote to the Princess to suspend her journey for the moment till I could be better informed of what had happened and hear what the Queen would say. This Princess confirmed in more detail all I have just said, and explained to me very vividly the pain the Princess's attitude had caused her. What she said touched me very much, and having heard her reasons and being much interested in them as well as in the pain and mortification she had suffered, for which she could not console herself, foreseeing besides how impossible it would be to me and also to the Queen to be tranquil if the Princess des Ursins appeared again in her presence, I decided to make her continue her journey to France. This decision . . . in assuring me the peace and quiet which I doubt not you desire for me in my marriage, I flatter myself you will approve, after having well weighed my reasons for taking it. You can well believe, besides, that the Spaniards look askance on the authority which the Princess des Ursins had in this country in which she was a stranger. . . .[1]

And by the same messenger the Queen herself sent two letters, one to Pighetti, the Duke of Parma's envoy, the other to Louis himself. That to Pighetti is in the handwriting of Alberoni, who probably dictated both.

> The lack of consideration shown by the Princess des Ursins towards me should be regarded with indignation not only by

[1] Trémoïlle, vi. 265 ; letter of 29 Dec. 1714.

myself but also by His Very Christian Majesty. When she met me at Jadraque she lacked every form of respect due to me. Not content with a personal offence which I let pass, she went so far as to insult the King my Master by insolent words and bold reproaches. She obliged me therefore to repress her incredible and scandalous audacity by having her arrested and conducted out of Jadraque, with the intention to expel from Spain so bold a person, whom I considered dangerous in the highest degree to the King my Master, to whom I immediately gave notice of what had happened, submitting myself entirely to his ultimate decision as was my duty. And His Majesty was kind enough fully to approve my resolution, as will also I hope His Very Christian Majesty.[1]

To Louis himself she wrote with more restraint:

"I hope Your Majesty has not been offended at my resolution to repress the too great audacity of the Princess des Ursins, and will not think it was from lack of respect to the King my Lord, but from a real and definite necessity, and knowing how great is your clemency and justice, I flatter myself that what I have done will not lessen the continuance of your goodness, which I shall try to merit." And she signs with her pompous "*Moi—la Reine.*"[2]

From all these different narratives we can make our choice of the most probable, but from one and all it is certain that, whatever provocation the Princess may have given her, the Queen's brutality exceeded all limits and was rather that of a savage than a woman accustomed to Courts. From all we know of the Princess it is quite possible that she did give herself the haughty airs of a protectress, but as for the breaches of etiquette, she was too broken in to the ways of courts to fail in the observance of a ritual which had become to her a second law of Nature.

The letters above quoted reached Versailles on 8 January, as Dangeau records in his *Diary*, and his way of recording it is worthy of remark: "A messenger has arrived from Madrid," he wrote, "having left the 30th. The King and Queen of Spain write that——"

That is all. The phrase is left unfinished, as though the writer, always a sincere friend to the Princess, was too shocked and distressed to transcribe the abominable fact.[3]

Now let us see what Alberoni himself has to say on the subject.

[1] Trémoïlle, vi. 264 ; letter of (the day is omitted) Dec. 1714.
[2] Ibid., vi. 267 ; letter of 29 Dec. 1714.
[3] Dangeau, xv. 331.

On 25 December, two days after the tragedy, jubilant and triumphant he wrote to Rocca from Guadalayara, whither he had gone immediately to prepare Philippe before the Queen's arrival. If any doubt existed as to his authorship of the plot the following letter would dissipate it:

GUADALAYARA, 25 *December*, 1714.

AMICO CARISSIMO,—I behold the entire world stupefied with admiration to find a Queen not yet enthroned take a resolution so bold. Dear friend, the conferences *a quattro occhi* held from Pampeluna to Jadraque have resulted in the happiness with which the Queen to-day finds herself mistress of her husband, which could never have been but for the removal of the obstacle in her path. She is a great soul, who, well guided and served on these principles, will shortly cause to be renewed the most glorious actions of the glorious princes her ancestors.[1]

The latter words are of special interest as referring to his project of the union of Italy by her means.

Two days later he writes still more triumphantly that she has given him the private *entrées* to her presence at all hours—"a thing without precedent." This "strong woman of the Evangelist," so he names her in his bombastic way, "seems consummate in the finest art of reigning. It is magical how passionately this great Heroine has made herself loved by the King."[2]

And a week later:

"Our Heroine is the admiration of everybody and the idol of the Spanish. She cannot go out but all Madrid unites in singing her glory, calling her their Saviour and Restorer. . . . Her act is worthy of Ximenes, Richelieu and Mazarin."[3]

And again:

"Thank God the Gordian knot is cut on which the salvation of the Queen depended. She goes by the name of the Strong Woman of the Evangelist, and is considered a divinity descended on the earth. At the first moment she broke the chains of slavery which would have kept her miserable all her life."[4]

At once as a reward he received the appointment of

---

[1] Bourgeois, *Lettres*, p. 352; letter of 25 Dec. 1714.
[2] Ibid., p. 353; letter of 31 Dec. 1714.
[3] Ibid., p. 354; letter of 7 Jan. 1715.
[4] Ibid., p. 369; letter of 11 Feb. 1715.

DISGRACE OF THE PRINCESS 355

envoy extraordinary from the Duke of Parma, he who had before to be contented with the simple title of agent, and was furnished by the Queen with coaches and liveries conformable to his new dignity. He had nothing left to wish for, he declares, except perhaps the Papacy. "She in Spain and I in Rome, we could hold the world in mockery!" he exclaims in the exuberance of his triumph.[1]

All this to his friend Rocca. To the Duke of Parma himself, now that his intrigue was successful, he avowed himself its sole author and instigator. "Your Highness," he wrote a month after the event, "was not wrong in supposing that the resolution was not only taken with my acquiescence, but at my suggestion," and he proceeds to describe it in detail, telling how he had planned it in the certainty that the Princess des Ursins would, by her insolence and arrogance, give sufficient pretext to the Queen to put a stop once and for all to her tyranny. Thus, at the first opening she would certainly give, the Queen was to reprove her for her insolent message sent by the Comte d'Albert, which reproof the Princess would be sure to resent, and give her a plausible excuse to dismiss her. Meanwhile he himself would remain outside the door, ready to transmit her orders to the captain of the guard. Preparations had been made for her immediate departure, orders given to the post-master to grant no horses to anybody and to guard the roads to Guadalayara so that none of the Princess's suite could pass. The Queen had replied that the plan was bold, but that she believed her salvation to depend on it, and had asked how the King would take it, to which Alberoni had replied that he would most certainly approve it when done, but not if it were previously communicated to him. The Queen thereupon retired for the night, promising to think it over. Early next morning, before starting for Jadraque, he came to her room for her reply. "I have not slept all night," she said, "but I am resolved to execute your plan. Let us both commend ourselves to God that He may assist us in our enterprise."[2]

The documents are sufficiently complete for the authorship of the plot to be no longer a mystery.

[1] Bourgeois, *Lettres*, p. 373; letter of 18 Feb. 1715.
[2] Ibid., p. 373; letter of 18 Feb.; and Armstrong, *Elisabeth Farnese*, p. 29.

CHAPTER XXII

EXPULSION (1715)

WE left the Princess driving over the mountains on the darkest of nights in a cold so bitter that her coachman's hands were frostbitten, guarded like a criminal by two officers and fifty soldiers, a prisoner and exile from the country she had saved—she who twelve hours before had been all-powerful. We continue the painful narrative in the words of Saint-Simon:

It is not easy to represent the state of mind of Madame des Ursins in the coach. Excessive astonishment and stupefaction prevailed at first and suspended all other emotions, but soon grief, vexation, rage and despair replaced them, in their turn succeeded by sad and profound reflections on a proceeding so violent and unheard of, based on so little cause, reason, or the slightest pretext. Finally, on the impression it would make at Guadalaxara, the hope in the King's surprise and anger, in his friendship and confidence, in the group of faithful servitors with whom she had surrounded him and whose interest it would be to excite him in her favour. The long winter night passed thus away with nothing to protect her from the terrible cold—so cold that the coachman lost one of his hands. The morning arrived. It was necessary to stop to feed the horses, but for human beings there is nothing whatever in the Spanish inns, where generally they merely indicate where necessities can be bought. The meat is generally living, the wine thick, flat and strong, the bread sticks to the walls, the water is bad, beds there are none except for mule-drivers, so that everything has to be carried with one, and Madame des Ursins had nothing at all. Eggs, when they could be found, were their only resource during the whole journey, and these only boiled, fresh or stale. Up to now the silence had been profound and uninterrupted. During all this long night the Princess had had leisure to think of what she should say and compose her features. She spoke of her amazement and of the small things that had passed between the Queen and her. Reciprocally the two officers of her guard, accustomed like all Spain to fear and respect her more than their King, replied as they could from the depths of their amazement, from which they had not recovered. Soon they had to harness and depart. Presently, too, the Princess began to perceive that the aid she had hoped from the King was very late in coming. Neither rest nor food nor any change of clothes until Saint-Jean-de-Luz. As the distance increased, the time elapsed, and no news arrived, she understood that hope must be renounced. One can imagine the rage which succeeded in a woman so ambitious, so accustomed to reign publicly, to be thus swiftly and ignominiously precipitated from the summit of complete power by the hand she herself had chosen to be her most solid support in perpetuating her authority. Who could have imagined treatment so strange and unheard of? . . . Her nephews Lanti and Chalais, who had permission to join her, completed her consternation. But she was faithful to her character. Not a tear escaped her, neither regrets, nor reproach, nor the slightest weakness. No complaint even of the excessive cold, nor the complete lack of all necessaries and the fatigue of such a journey. The two officers who guarded her could not get over their admiration. Finally an end was put to her physical sufferings and to the watch over her at Saint-Jean-de-Luz, where she arrived on 14 January and where at last she found a bed and could borrow something for the night and sleep and eat. There she recovered her liberty.[1]

Thus for two weeks this woman of seventy-three, in feeble health, was jolted over the ill-kept roads, galloped up and down the mountain passes in mid-winter in the hardest frost that had been known for thirty years, without food or bed or change of linen, in full court dress as she had come from the Queen, in close contact day and night with two petty officers whose existence she would not have recognised the day before, she whose high rank exacted that she should be alone in her coach like a sovereign. It is a marvel that both mind and body did not collapse under such martyrdom. And meanwhile the brutal virago who had driven her out was triumphing in her vengeance: "The Princess of Parma began her toilet. She supped, and without seeming at all occupied with what had just happened, she slept with the greatest tranquillity in the world."

Besides sleeping and eating, she wrote and dispatched a letter to the King describing the incident in her own way, and the following morning Alberoni himself started off at sunrise to render an account of the affair.

The officer of the guard [continues Saint-Simon] whom the Queen dispatched with a letter for the King of Spain as soon as the Princess had left Jadraque, found him just going to bed. He seemed moved, wrote a short answer to the Queen, but gave no order. The officer departed immediately. The strange thing is that the secret was so well kept that it only transpired

[1] Saint-Simon, xxvi. 107, etc.

at ten o'clock the next morning. The emotion and agitation of all the Court at Guadalaxara can be imagined. No one, however, dared mention it to the King . . . Chalais and Lanti risked asking his permission to go and find Madame des Ursins and accompany her in her abandonment. Not only he allowed it, but charged them with a letter of formal politeness, saying he was very sorry for what had passed but was unable to oppose his authority to the Queen's will, that he maintained her pensions and would see that they were paid. They were also the bearers of two orders, one to liberate all her suite, the other to the captain of the guard commanding that she should be allowed to rest where and for as long as she pleased, but both orders were revoked after the Queen's arrival.[1]

We continue the narrative in the words of Orry in his official dispatch to Torcy, in which he speaks of himself in the third person:

The next morning the Abbé Alberoni came to wait on the King at Guadalaxara. When the King entered the palace, Orry was told that a lackey of Madame des Ursins had something very urgent to tell him, and having learnt what had happened at Jadraque he mounted to the apartment of the King, whom he found sealing a letter alone with the Abbé Alberoni. He drew the Abbé aside while the King was writing the address, and asked him hurriedly what was the news and why he had left the Queen. He answered that it was to bring the King a letter of compliment and that he had no news. The King rose, gave him the letter he had just sealed and dismissed him.

Orry then found himself alone with the King and took the liberty of telling him what he had just heard. The King said it was only too true, that the Queen had told him that Madame des Ursins had been lacking in respect, that he was truly sorry for what had happened, but could not show any resentment because he wished to be well with the Queen he was about to marry, and His Majesty, having ordered Orry to tell him what he thought best to do in such a circumstance, he implored him at least to soften the rigorous treatment with which Madame des Ursins was being conducted to the frontier, declaring that it was to expose her to die on the road to force her to continue travelling thus day and night by roads rendered impassable by the snow, in a terrible cold, without a bed, without equipages or servants, guarded like a criminal, and that at her age it was impossible to support the state to which she was reduced. The King, impressed by these truths, had the goodness to write at once a consoling letter to the Princess and charged the Prince de Chalais with it, permitting him and Monsieur de Lanti to go and join her, with orders to suspend her journey, set her servants at liberty and fetch her equipages. His Majesty

[1] Saint-Simon, xxvi. 111.

EXPULSION

consented that she should wait where most convenient to her until, after having heard the Queen, he might decide otherwise.

The Queen arrived soon after they had left. The rest of the day was spent in the ceremonies of the marriage, and it was known only that the same evening the Queen said to the King that she doubted not but that he had approved her attitude towards the Princess, and His Majesty replied that it would have been desirable that she had done nothing. The next day, the 25th, the Abbé Alberoni informed the Queen of the counter-order sent the evening before, and she pressed the King so urgently that His Majesty, with the same idea of wishing to keep well with her, revoked it, and the messenger charged with this revocation made so much haste that he arrived before the two nephews of Madame des Ursins, so that she was forced to continue her journey until they overtook her, when they obtained that at least she might go by Burgos, the road they were taking being impracticable. Then Madame des Ursins wrote herself to the King and informed him of the sad state she was in, not having enough even to pay her expenses on the road.

This letter and what was said to His Majesty had the effect that he consented that the Princess should leave his kingdom, but that liberty must be allowed her to go where and how she judged proper, and giving the command of her escort to Messieurs de Chalais and Lanti, both exempts of the guard, with liberty to choose such men as they thought fit to accompany her, not as a prisoner but as due to her rank, and he sent her at the same time two thousand pistoles for her expenses on the road. . . .[1]

Here is the King's letter brought her by her nephews. It is doubtful if with all her optimism she was much consoled by it.

GUADALAYARA, 24 *December*, 1714.

I have just heard, Madame, with as much surprise as grief, what has passed between the Queen and you. You ought not to doubt that I feel all the gratitude which I owe to your friendship and attachment to me; thus I pray you to be patient and count on my doing everything in my power to set things right.[2]

And his way of showing his gratitude and setting things right was to approve the Queen's brutality, to aid her in her vengeance, to allow the Princess's friends to be insulted, her servants arrested, and to destroy the deed of gift bestowing on her in reward for her long services the principality of Cardone in Catalonia.

[1] Trémoïlle, vi. 274 ; letter of 5 Jan. 1715.   [2] Ibid., vi. 262.

This principality of Cardone was a new ambition of the Princess. Though she had resigned herself to the loss of her sovereignty in the Netherlands, she had not abandoned her desire of independence, and during her so-called sequestration of Philippe at the palace of Medina-Cœli had extracted from him, subject to the reduction of Barcelona, the promise of the rich province of Cardone, which with its fortified town of Rosas was to be erected into an independent sovereignty for her benefit. The deed of gift had been prepared for some time and needed but his signature, and he had brought it with him to Guadalayara, a fresh proof, if any were needed, that he was aware of the projected expulsion, and sought in a fit of remorse to compensate her for her exile from the capital.

According to the Duc de Saint-Aignan, commissioned by Louis to search into this affair, which had been kept absolutely secret, Philippe had signed the document immediately after her departure for Jadraque, and Orry, when he heard of her disgrace and expulsion, had begged that it might be sent after her to console her in her misfortune. To this Philippe had consented and had even ordered his Secretary of State Grimaldo to carry it to her at her first resting-place. The Queen's arrival, however, had put a stop to any feeling of remorse or generosity he may have had in this decision. One night in her arms and he was thenceforth her humble slave, ready to sacrifice honour and dignity at her demand, and her first act was not only to make him cancel the gift of the principality, but even to revoke his order that she should be permitted to rest before crossing the frontier.[1] Of the document no more is heard. It is probable that the Queen in her malignance forced it from him and destroyed it.

Delighted with her triumph, she had arrived at Guadalayara the day following her exploit as though nothing had happened. "The King," writes Saint-Simon, "received her on the stairs, gave her his hand and led her at once to the chapel where the marriage was celebrated anew; from thence to his room, where immediately they went to bed, before six o'clock in the evening, to rise again for the midnight mass. What was said between them on the event of the preceding day no one knew either then or later. The day after—Christmas Day,—alone in a coach and followed

[1] Trémoïlle, vi. 310 ; letter to Torcy to 4 March, 1715.

EXPULSION

by all the Court, they took the road to Madrid, where there was no more talk of the Princess des Ursins than if the King had never known her." [1]

The Baron de Breteuil, very *répandu* in society, in his Memoirs still in manuscript, giving voice to the general gossip at Versailles, comments thus on the affair with which all Europe was ringing:

> Those who inspired the Queen with the audacity to commit an act so bold, and so dishonourable to the King of Spain, must have given her very positive assurance of his feebleness and the influence which the woman he slept with could take over his mind, to risk so unheard-of an act. She had not yet seen the King. She could not flatter herself, ugly as she was, that her face could strike him sufficiently to obtain at once permission to expel from Spain his favourite, his prime minister, so to speak, the soul of all he had done since he was on the throne. But the good King, exaggeratedly pious and in haste to satisfy the needs of a robust constitution, idle since the death of his first wife, had no sooner slept with her than he ratified all she had done at Jadraque.

And he adds:

> The King was in bed for sixteen hours with the new Queen the first night of their marriage, and it is said that he waked her every hour. The boiling ardour of youth, held in check for so long by the dykes of devotion, became a furious torrent when it found a legitimate outlet.[2]

Though few were aware of the truth, all contemporary writers considered the affair as the result of a plot and most of them accuse Philippe of complicity. Orry, more *au courant* with Alberoni's intrigues, was near the truth when he attributed it to political rather than personal motives, an intrigue, he said, of a cabal of Italians desirous of occupying the chief posts in Spain, who had commissioned Alberoni to make the new Queen their catspaw. Breteuil considered the Queen-Dowager more responsible than the Queen herself, as having excited her to such a pitch of jealous fury that she was no longer mistress of her acts. As for Saint-Simon, who certainly was aware of the truth, anxious to exculpate the Duc d'Orléans from any share in the matter, he asserts and repeats *ad nauseam* that it was due entirely to Louis XIV. and his grandson Philippe V. His remarks

---
[1] Saint-Simon, xxvi. 112.
[2] Ibid., xxvi. 439, appendix iii.

are worth noting in face of the documents already cited which reveal his own complicity in the plot.

Let us now collect such facts as may help us clear the mystery [he writes]. A quarrel à *l'allemand* without any apparent reason, cause, or pretext, made the first instant of their meeting by the Queen to the Princess, and suddenly pushed beyond the last extremities. Is it conceivable that a Parmesan girl, brought up in a garret by an imperious mother, would have dared of herself commit an act so audacious, unheard of, to a person so considerable, in the entire confidence of the King of Spain and reigning publicly, within six leagues of the King whom she had not yet seen ? The mystery is made clearer by the order, so unusual and secret, which Amezaga had from the King to obey the Queen in everything without reserve, which was made known only when she told him to arrest and take her away. The tranquillity with which the King [Louis] and the King of Spain each of them received the first notice of the event and the complete inertia of the King of Spain; the coldness of his letter to Madame des Ursins and his perfect indifference as to what might happen to a person so cherished up to the night before, night and day on the roads covered with snow and ice, deprived of everything without exception. . . . Add to this what I have heard from the Maréchal de Brancas [our old friend the lobster-clawed, made Marshal of France in 1741] that Alberoni had said that, being alone with the Queen one evening during the journey, she had seemed agitated, striding up and down the room and uttering from time to time broken words, till growing more heated the name of Madame des Ursins escaped her, followed by: "I shall get rid of her first!" He exclaimed to the Queen and tried to show her the danger, madness and uselessness of such a proceeding, which petrified him. "Hold your tongue about it all!" she said to him, "and never let what you have heard escape you. Do not speak! I know what I am about." All this throws great light on a catastrophe equally surprising in itself and in the manner of doing, and clearly proves that the King was its author, that the King of Spain was consenting and aiding by the extraordinary order given to Amezaga, and the Queen acting and charged to execute it, no matter in what way, by the two kings.[1]

For the sake of his reputation it is a pity that Saint-Simon did not destroy the papers concerning his own projects for the Princess's disgrace.

Orry, himself expelled soon after the Princess, became convinced later that the plot had its origin in the vengeance

---

[1] Saint-Simon, xxvi. 113.

of the Cardinal del Giudice and summed up his reasons in a memoir to Torcy:

The bad reputation of the Abbé Alberoni, and the share he has had in what has been done at Jadraque to expel the Princess des Ursins from Spain, makes one judge that he had imagined, proposed and executed this enterprise, but what has been since learned at Bayonne reveals that it had a much more dangerous source, for it is positively known that it was hatched by the Cardinal del Giudice, who, displeased since Paris with the journey of the Prince de Chalais, furious at the order he found on his arrival in Bayonne and attributing it to Madame des Ursins, decided her ruin.

For this purpose he insinuated himself into the friendship of a Madame Lucas, who enjoys all the confidence of the Queen-Dowager, and introduced by this means into her closest intimacy, proposed to her that he should warn the Queen, directly after her departure from Parma, of all which could inspire her with mistrust, aversion and even indignation against Madame des Ursins, so as to dispose this young Princess to hate her before knowing her and to get rid of her before there was time for her to be undeceived.

As regards the execution of this project, His Eminence, in order to determine the young Queen, proposed that Her Majesty should immediately on arriving in Spain take measures to render herself mistress of the King's will, that to succeed in this she must expel the Princess from Spain, which she would never achieve once she had been delivered to her inspection, partly because of her influence over the King's mind, partly because she herself would be deceived by her flattery and engaging manners. That therefore she must at their first meeting get rid of her at once and with so much precaution that the King would be unable to prevent it before she arrived to consummate the marriage, and that, exacting his approval at that time, she was certain to obtain it, after which she would find no obstacle of any sort either present or future. That what ought to determine her to this act, violent though it seems, was the necessity of foreseeing the result of her marriage with the King of Spain, who, having three princes by the late Queen, would probably exclude her own children from all hope of the monarchy of Spain and reduce her one day to return to Parma to seek there a retreat wherein nothing would be assured her but what she had been able to amass during her reign in Spain.

That this consideration alone, inspired by the Queen her aunt, should suffice to make her understand the importance of getting rid of the Princess, under whose eyes and those of the present Government it would be impossible for her to amass wealth, while, the Princess being expelled, she could change the ministry and compose it of her own creatures. His Eminence offered to return to Spain expressly for this, to direct the Government and be so much at her orders that she could dispose of everything and arrange the return of the Queen-Dowager to the Court, so that between them and himself measures could be taken to influence the King's will.[1]

From all that has yet transpired it would appear that, though delighted to be rid of the Princess, both Louis and Philippe were shocked and even remorseful at the gross manner of doing it. In the King of Spain this remorse was immediately stifled by the Queen's caresses, but Louis, though unwilling to quarrel with his grandson, took the matter more to heart and even did his best to protect her.

The following curt allusion to the event in his answer to Philippe's letter shows plainly enough his disapproval:

"I confess that, knowing the zeal of the Princess des Ursins for you and your confidence in her, I cannot help pitying the misfortune she has had to displease the Queen so quickly." That is all his comment, and to the Queen herself he wrote even more coldly: "You should not doubt that I am keenly interested in your satisfaction and should be very sorry that it should be disturbed by the misfortune the Princess des Ursins has had to displease you." And he adds ironically: "But the King my grandson seems very far from wishing to protect those who are not agreeable to you."[2]

The following document is a proof that, while others were exulting over her ruin, he did his best to soften her fall and procure her the sovereignty he disapproved, but which alone at this time would have neutralised her disgrace and redeemed her in the eyes of Europe.

In the instructions given to his ambassador the Comte de Luc at the Court of Vienna, sent about this time, appears the following clause:

His Majesty has not desisted in the protection he gave the Princess des Ursins that she should obtain the sovereignty which the King of Spain reserved for her in the Netherlands. . . . But His Majesty leaves to the prudence of the Comte de Luc to speak of this affair at the appropriate time so that it shall appear that he is really interested in its success, that he desires it for his own satisfaction and that his intervention must not be regarded as merely the effect of the King of Spain's recommendation.[3]

[1] Trémoïlle, vi. 308; letter of (day omitted) March, 1715.
[2] Ibid., vi. 282 and 283; letters of 11 Jan. 1715.
[3] Courcy, *L'Espagne après la Paix d'Utrecht*, p. 360.

CHAPTER XXIII

HOPES AND FEARS (1715)

WE must now return to Saint-Jean-de-Luz and follow step by step by means of the documents the dolorous Calvary which the Princess bore with so much courage and dignity as to extract the unwilling homage even of her enemies.

She arrived at Saint-Jean-de-Luz [writes Saint-Simon] on 14 January. There she recovered her liberty. The guards, their officers and the coach which had brought her returned, and she remained with her *femme-de-chambre* and her nephews. She had leisure to think of what awaited her at Versailles. In spite of the folly of her sovereignty pursued for so long, and her audacity at having made the King of Spain's marriage without the King's participation, she flattered herself that she would again find help at a Court which she had dominated so long. From Saint-Jean-de-Luz she dispatched a messenger with letters for the King, Madame de Maintenon and her friends, in which she related briefly the thunderbolt which had fallen on her and asked permission to come to the Court to relate it more in detail. The return of her messenger she awaited at this her first resting-place of liberty and repose, which in itself was agreeable.[1]

Here are her letters, written from Tolosa near the frontier four days before her arrival at Saint-Jean-de-Luz.

To Louis she wrote with restraint since etiquette forbade the slightest abuse of one sovereign to another:

SIRE,—What happened to me when I had the honour to see the Queen of Spain at Jadraque is so astonishing that Your Majesty would have difficulty in believing it if I did not flatter myself that you believe in my truthfulness. This Princess, Sire, to whom I had the honour of presenting a letter from the King your grandson, filled with a thousand obliging things concerning me and his impatience to see her arrive at Guadalayara where the marriage ceremony was to take place, received it so badly that it drew upon me treatment quite new to me and little in keeping with the respect I showed her. After reproaching me for things she pretended I had written, which had much displeased her, but which touched only on

[1] Saint-Simon, xxvi. 110.

His Catholic Majesty's eagerness for her arrival and my own to present her my homage, I answered that the King of Spain had read them and been so pleased that he had even deigned to thank me. The Queen then, unable to continue her disapproval of these letters, told me I was insolent and impertinent, and calling with a loud voice to the officer commanding her guards, ordered him to conduct me to my room and not to let me speak or write to anyone whatsoever. I assured her that it was not necessary to surround my apartment with guards, since I should obey her orders without resistance. Her Majesty, Sire, not content with this, which I certainly did not merit, ordered a coach to be prepared and fifty guards to conduct me to the French frontier, with only one woman to serve me, for which she made great difficulties. Her orders were punctually obeyed. I left at eleven o'clock at night in a tempest of snow and wind and frightful cold, every moment nearly dashed over a precipice, so that the coachman who drove me lost one of his hands. They continued afterwards to treat me with the same rigour, forcing me to sleep on straw, to eat nothing but bread and eggs, and would not even permit me to attend mass on Christmas Day. God, who knows my respectful attachment to Your Majesty and the King your grandson, has preserved me, and I have the honour to write to Your Majesty from Toulousete and count on arriving in three days at Saint-Jean-de-Luz to await Your Majesty's orders.[1]

To Madame de Maintenon she wrote with less restraint:

You must have been very astonished, Madame, if you have heard of the treatment I have received from the Queen of Spain, when I might have expected something so different. Her Majesty has expelled me shamefully with insults at Jadraque, where the King of Spain had ordered me to go to tell her of his impatience to see her. . . . I know not how I have been able to support all the fatigues of the journey. I have been made to sleep on straw and fast in a way very different to the meals I am accustomed to . . . I have not forgotten, in the details I have taken the liberty to write to the King, to tell him that I ate only two stale eggs a day. I thought that this circumstance would excite him to have pity on a faithful subject who merits in no sort of way treatment so contemptuous. I am going to Saint-Jean-de-Luz to rest a little and hear what it will please the King I should do.[2]

To Torcy on the same day she wrote as follows:

As I am uncertain whether you have heard of the surprising adventure which has happened to me, I send you the letter I have written to the King unsealed so that you may read what

[1] Trémoïlle, vi. 280; letter of 10 Jan. 1715.
[2] Collin, *Lettres de la Princesse des Ursins au Maréchal de Villeroy* (Paris, 1806); letter of 10 Jan. 1715.

I have taken the liberty to tell him. Perhaps I have told it too much in detail, but I thought he would be good enough to pardon it. Never, I think, has such a thing happened to a person like me, who might have hoped for marks of consideration and goodwill from a Queen who ought to be content with what I have done. It is, I assure you, a miracle that my health has been able to resist the fatigues I have been made to suffer. I attribute it a little, between ourselves, to my own courage which, thank God, never forsakes me on any occasion whatever. I know not what to do. I have neither goods nor residences, and I can protest to you with some vanity that I owe more than I am worth. It is this which made me regard as a refuge agreeable and glorious under any circumstances, the sovereignty with which His Catholic Majesty had honoured me. He has written me a letter of which I send you a copy and has commanded that part of the guards whom the Queen ordered to conduct me like a criminal should return, and has placed the rest at my orders from Aranda de Duevo to the frontier. I thought Saint-Jean-de-Luz would be a suitable place to wait, as the messengers of France and Spain passing there would bring me news. I beg you therefore to let me know what is to become of me. I have need of some rest, for certainly my fatigues have been cruel and I think there is no precedent of anyone having been so harshly treated as I have been in every way.[1]

These letters reached Versailles on 19 January as Dangeau notes in his *Diary*:

Letters have arrived from Madame des Ursins. . . . She ought to reach Saint-Jean-de-Luz on the 14th, where she will await the King's reply. She asks permission to put herself at his feet to justify herself on what is imputed to her. She writes that her innocence has sustained her in her misfortune and the rigours of a journey from which she has suffered much. Messieurs de Chalais and Lanti, her nephews, are with her. The King permits her to come, and she will receive letters from people of consideration assuring her of a good reception.[2]

On 14 January Pachau, still in charge of the embassy at Madrid, wrote to Torcy in his turn:

Madame des Ursins left Burgos the 4th. She has had some attacks of fever, but got better and ought to arrive to-day at Saint-Jean-de-Luz, where she will stop to rest and await news from the Court of France. Her secretary and steward are busy here arranging her private and domestic affairs in order to join her as soon as possible.[3]

---

[1] Trémoïlle, vi. 279 ; letter of 10 Jan. 1715.
[2] Dangeau, xv. 344.
[3] Trémoïlle, vi. 286 ; letter of 14 Jan. 1715.

But her martyrdom was only begun. To be publicly disgraced and insulted by the woman who owed her everything was terrible enough, but to learn that she had acted in full concert with the King of France was a tragedy still more painful. This was Alberoni's trump-card, played, it must be owned, with an assurance which proves it to have been not altogether an invention, a master-stroke carefully prepared to serve two ends, first to shield himself and the Queen in the eyes of Europe, and next to overwhelm his victim and complete her ruin.

Thus on her arrival at Saint-Jean-de-Luz, where she had been hoping for a little tranquillity, she was greeted by the news, sent from Madrid to Bayonne and from thence spread throughout Europe by the care of the Queen-Dowager, that in insulting and expelling her with so much ignominy the Queen of Spain had acted, not on her own responsibility, but in full concert with the King of France.

Stung to the quick and incredulous of such treachery, she immediately dispatched Lanti to Versailles to demand if it were true, and he carried three fresh letters announcing the scandal and praying that it might be contradicted.

To Louis she wrote:

SIRE,—Since I took the liberty of writing to Your Majesty from Tolosette to inform you of the most extraordinary event which could ever happen to a subject of Your Majesty, honoured with so many marks of his goodness and that of the King of Spain, I have heard rumours so extraordinary, spread abroad in Madrid and carefully published in Bayonne and all the frontiers, that I have thought it not only to my own interest but to that of Your Majesty and His Catholic Majesty to inform you of it in pure truth, foreseeing that it might have terrible consequences if Your Majesty is not thoroughly acquainted with it. It is this which forces me to send my nephew Don Alessandro Lanti to Your Majesty's Court, so that you may do him the honour to hear him.[1]

To Madame de Maintenon she was more explicit:

Conceive, Madame, the situation I am in, treated in the eyes of all Europe with more contempt by the Queen of Spain than if I were the worst of criminals. I am, however, among the first of the King's subjects, sent to the Court of Spain to occupy one of the most important posts, honoured by the confidence of the two greatest monarchs in the world. And now they try to persuade me that the King [Louis] has acted in concert with

[1] Trémoïlle, vi. 289; letter of 20 Jan. 1715.

the Princess who has treated me with such cruelty. I regard these rumours as a proof of the blackness of the infamous cabal which has caused my ruin, and for this reason I have begged Monsieur de Lanti my nephew to go to your Court to let the King know all the mystery of this amazing affair, the results of which might be dangerous if His Majesty does not at once cut it at the roots. He will tell you all the details, for I have too high an opinion of you to suppose you will follow the established custom of all Courts and turn your back on the unfortunate, and besides your great heart would oppose it. I shall await the King's orders at Saint-Jean-de-Luz, where I am living in a little house by the sea-shore. I see the sea often agitated and sometimes calm like the Courts. . . . I agree with you that one should not seek stability except in God. Certainly it is not to be found in the human heart, for who was surer than I of the heart of the King of Spain? [1]

To Torcy she wrote as follows:

There exists, I believe, no precedent that a person like myself, subject of so great a King, servant of His Catholic Majesty, honoured by their favour, has been treated with so much indignity and cruelty as I have been when I had the right to expect all sorts of kindness. In truth the King must be very astonished that I have been expelled from a Court where he placed me and where he knew I remained only in obedience to his will and without the King his grandson having any knowledge of it. . . . Everyone is told that the King [Louis] consented to all which has happened to me, and the Abbé Alberoni, the Queen's favourite, who has the honour to amuse her four or five hours every day, says the same thing.[2]

And again two days later:

Here is a second letter to the King left open, where you will see the object of Don Alessandro Lanti's journey. . . . If I wished to believe the rumours spread in Madrid and Bayonne I should fear that he might be ill-received at your Court, since it is said that the King was in agreement with the Queen of Spain in the shameful and unheard-of way in which she dismissed me; but this can be nothing but artifice, for I know too well the magnanimity and humanity of the King to let myself be deceived by such enormities. Thus I am very sure that he will have the goodness to let all Europe know that he had no share in the terrible event.[3]

No answers to these letters are in existence and it is doubtful if any were written, for by the time they reached

[1] Collin, *Lettres à Villeroy*, p. 225; letter of 20 Jan. 1715.
[2] Trémoïlle, vi. 287; letter of 21 Jan. 1715.
[3] Ibid., vi. 288; letter of 20 Jan. 1715.

Versailles, thanks to the Queen's brutality, Louis' friendly and consolatory attitude had completely changed, and not only were Madame de Maintenon's doors shut to Lanti, but eventually even to herself as well.

Meanwhile, however, answers to her first announcement of the tragedy arrived, that of Louis cautious and conventionally worded but not unkind:

I have heard with sorrow the event related by you in your letter of the 10th of this month. I am still more pained to learn the circumstances of all you have suffered, and I must think how to make you forget them, knowing your zeal and attachment to my interests, as you also know the sentiments of esteem and affection which I have for you.[1]

That of Madame de Maintenon is colder:

I know not which I feel most keenly, grief at your state or astonishment at what has happened. For a long while you have prepared me for your retirement, but I confess I should never have thought that you would have quitted Spain like a criminal.[2]

A week later, her old dread of her rival's presence at Versailles reviving, she wrote again:

Certainly I have been very astonished at the treatment you have received, of which no more must be said out of the respect we owe our masters. . . . I am very impatient to know your plans for the future from the sincere interest I take in it. This is all I have to say.[3]

Madame de Maintenon was not alone in dreading her presence at Court. On 10 January, Madame, Princess Palatine, mother of the Duc d'Orléans, wrote as follows to her sister in Bavaria:

The day before yesterday arrived the great news about the Princess des Ursins, she who has for so long governed Spain, and who had gone to meet the new Queen of whom she was to be the *gouvernante*. Her pride has ruined her. She had written some letters against the young Queen which had been shown to her and when she went to meet her she only descended half the staircase. She criticised her clothes, blamed her for having been so long on the road, and told her that had she been the King she would have sent her back. Upon this the Queen

---

[1] Trémoïlle, vi. 291; letter of 21 Jan. 1715.
[2] Bossange, iii. 163; letter of 21 Jan. 1715. The date is misprinted 12 instead of 21. On the 12th Madame de Maintenon had not yet received the Princess's letter announcing her disgrace.
[3] Ibid., iii. 165; letter of 28 Jan. 1715.

ordered an officer of her bodyguard to remove this mad woman from her presence and to arrest her. At the same time she sent a messenger to the King with strong complaints on the subject. The King replied that she could do as she judged proper. So at eleven o'clock at night the Princess was put in a coach with only one *femme-de-chambre*, some lackeys and the guards, and orders were given to drive her immediately to France, which was done.

I cannot pity her for she has always persecuted my son in a horrible manner. She persuaded the King and the late Queen that he wanted to dethrone them, and that he conspired against their life, which is so false that however much she has tried she has never been able to justify her accusation the least in the world. For this reason I care very little about the misfortune which has happened to her, and this is very natural. I am anxious to know if this wicked devil (*méchante diable*) will come here, for she will not fail to spit out all her venom against my son and me, from which may God preserve us![1]

To prevent which Madame took the initiative and spat out her own venom to such good effect that the doors of Versailles were closed to her enemy.

Meanwhile Torcy's answer, written naturally at Louis' order, was very encouraging, for not only did he transmit his permission to come to Versailles, but even pressed it urgently.

As you will have had time to rest from the fatigues of your unfortunate journey when you receive this [he wrote on 21 January], allow me to tell you that you ought not to lose a moment in coming to see the King. Since it was he who sent you to Spain you ought to inform him yourself of the way you have left it, and your honour as much as your duty obliges you to take this decision. Any other course would make people think and say that you fear to appear before His Majesty, and give your enemies cause to interpret falsely the sentiments he has for you, if you do not yourself come and give an account of your conduct. You have entire liberty to do so, and you will see by the letter he has written you and which I send that his sentiments towards you have not changed.[2]

Madame de Maintenon also had echoed this advice. "Come and speak to the King, that is all I see to be done at present," she wrote, doubtless at Louis' order, the following week.[3]

[1] Brunet, *Nouvelles Lettres de la Duchesse d'Orléans*, p. 75; letter of 10 Jan. 1715.
[2] Trémoïlle, vi. 290; letter of 21 Jan. 1715.
[3] Bossange, iii. 167; letter of 28 Jan. 1715.

From all these documents it will be seen that Louis' first movement toward her was friendly and sympathetic and that Versailles, with the exception of the Orléans family, was disposed to receive her rather as a victim than a criminal. And this also the vigilant Alberoni had foreseen and frustrated.

The amazing optimism which, coupled with her ambition, is the dominant characteristic of the Princess, even in this hour of supreme defeat, did not forsake her. It needed no more than this encouragement to fill her heart with fresh hopes, perhaps of a similar triumph to that which had followed her first disgrace. On receipt of these messages she plucked up heart and in a letter surprisingly cheerful considering the circumstances, she wrote to Orry, who was still in Madrid and who had offered her his country-house at Gournay as a temporary home, that she had received an autograph letter from Louis " the most obliging and consoling in the world," that Torcy had urged her in his name to go at once to Versailles, "to receive marks of his favour," and that she intended obeying without a moment's delay. " I have only one coach drawn by four mules," she ended, " the others are all broken, but I shall travel as well as I can to Bordeaux where I shall find my friend the Maréchal de Montrevel [Governor of Guyenne], whose kindness will furnish me with all the help I need. That of the Maréchal de Villeroy will be beyond all expression, he writes me . . . Monsieur de Noirmoutier [her brother] insists absolutely that I shall stay with him on arriving in Paris. I might well make use of your country-house after some days. You offer it with too much goodwill to be refused." [1]

It is pleasant to think that she retained at least some friends in her hour of adversity.

Foremost among these was her brother the blind Duc de Noirmoutier, who immediately sent her such things as she might need and, indignant at her treatment, made a formal complaint to Torcy. "His Majesty," he wrote, "is too clear-sighted not to judge that my sister's disgrace was already prepared and decided by the Queen of Spain. It has been accompanied by circumstances which cause me the greatest anxiety for her health, both mind and body having certainly suffered equally from a journey so long and hard in so bad a season." And he demands that an

[1] Trémoïlle, vi. 293 ; letter of 25 Jan. 1715.

explanation shall immediately be sent her and that if Louis has expressed compassion and sorrow for her treatment Torcy should let her know, "as the best remedy for the affront and her affliction." [1]

The Cardinal de la Trémoïlle also took up the cudgels on her behalf, but evidently more for the outrage to his own name than from any love of his sister. He awaits with impatience, he wrote to Torcy, to know if the "incredible news" he has heard is true, for if so, "what has been done is unheard of and I am bold enough to say that the King, Master of Madame des Ursins and myself, should not remain silent." [2]

To Louis himself he wrote with hardly less arrogance:

SIRE,—The treatment which Madame des Ursins has just received in Spain is so very far removed from the ordinary laws of humanity which great princes are kind enough to observe towards the least of their subjects and domestics, that I think it is also allowed, without wanting in respect, to show that one is not indifferent. We can do this only under the protection of Your Majesty. The few which remain of our family are dispersed in different parts of Europe, but we are all by the goodness of Your Majesty honoured with employments or dignities which exact from us a public account of our conduct, and to make it known that we have given no cause for the contempt with which Madame des Ursins has been treated. The King of Spain is one of the greatest princes in the world. He is master of his acts and we have nothing to do but to submit, but I must assert that the Queen was not yet the mistress when she treated Madame des Ursins as she did, like a State criminal. It is too important to us that the public should know she did not merit that treatment, which can only be done by the special protection of Your Majesty and the knowledge that you will not abandon a person who has been honoured by your confidence and bounty to the discretion of a Princess who desired, before having seen her husband, to mark the beginning of her reign by an act shameful to herself.[3]

And that the Papal Court echoed his disgust at the grossness of her treatment we learn from a letter from Amelot, now in Rome on a mission to the Pope, and guest of the Cardinal de la Trémoïlle in the Princess's palace of the Piazza Navone.

Here it is generally agreed [he wrote to Torcy] that though it would not have been surprising that the advent of the new

[1] Trémoïlle, vi. 282 ; letter of 11 Jan. 1715.
[2] Ibid., vi. 291 ; letter of 22 Jan. 1715.
[3] Ibid., vi. 303 ; letter of 5 Feb. 1715.

Queen should diminish the Princess's credit and have resulted in an honourable though perhaps involuntary retirement, yet the treatment employed on this occasion to a lady of her birth and rank, of her merit and age, based on a pretended lack of respect, appears to everyone unheard of.[1]

However, the blame of the College of Cardinals probably left the Queen of Spain as indifferent as the reproaches of the Princess's relatives. She knew herself to be too well supported by her husband and the Orléans family to fear them, and she continued her attacks with insatiable fury.

Not content with having insulted and ignominiously expelled the woman to whom she owed her throne, she thought fit on her arrival in Madrid to persecute all her friends and arrest and expel her domestics. Her niece the Duchesse d'Havré she dismissed from her post of *Dame du Palais* and her husband from his colonelcy of the Gardes Wallonnes and sent both into exile. All the other ladies who were guilty of having been protected by the Princess she also dismissed, declaring with characteristic coarseness that "she could dispense with all these married women who are always either with child or brought to bed."[2] Her secretary Hocquart and her steward, occupied with winding up her affairs, received orders to decamp immediately, and Chalais and Lanti, the latter only just married, were told never to return. All these orders were signed by Philippe himself, for she had learnt during the sixteen hours of her bridal-night how to make him obey her without question. Orry was allowed to remain long enough to explain to his successor the state of affairs and was then suddenly and ignominiously dismissed. Only d'Aubigny remained unmolested, probably because his treachery towards his mistress was known and approved.

"Le Sieur d'Aubigny," wrote the Sieur de la Loire to the Comte de Pontchartrain, "who has remained in Madrid suffering from the gout, having learnt the disgrace of his mistress, exclaimed with an oath that he had told her a hundred times she was digging her own grave, but she would listen to nothing but her own obstinacy and now she found herself the reproach of all nations."[3]

On learning the catastrophe, with no generous impulse

---

[1] Trémoïlle, vi. 304; letter of 12 Feb. 1715.
[2] Saint-Simon, xxvi. 436.
[3] Ibid., xxvi. 436; letter of 31 Dec. 1714.

like her two nephews to follow his benefactress and console her in her abandonment, or like Orry to plead her cause with the King, while she was being hunted across Europe this disloyal servitor thought only of his own safety, and without losing a moment wrote to Torcy begging him to tell him how her disgrace had been received at Versailles that he might conform his own behaviour to that of his new patrons. "My lack of curiosity," he wrote, "added to certain reflections as to my state (?) happily prevented me from being present at this scene, which would have been more approved if the manner of its execution had been different. Since then nothing but graciousness from the King to me, Monsieur de Grimaldo having repeated to me only this morning by his order that he desired that all which had to do with the Princess should pass between him and me."[1]

To which Torcy answered by return of post: "Accept, I pray you, my compliments on what has passed, and on your state since the event of Jadraque. I am very glad the King of Spain does you justice. I do not think, however, it will engage you to remain in Madrid longer than you intended. Meanwhile, your reflections on the present and future would give me much pleasure, and I beg you therefore to communicate them to me."[2]

This invitation was soon complied with. In an immensely long letter, which might be the official dispatch of an ambassador, he criticises the new Court and Government. The following extracts are of interest:

> Those who have the least penetration see clearly that the King of Spain, abandoned entirely to the Queen, . . . will give his confidence to the Italians who will abuse it; that the Spanish, less pleased to be governed by them even than by the French, will think themselves the most unfortunate people on earth; that the princes, abandoned to a stepmother bold and ill-bred, will run the risk of having neither suitable care nor education, and that France is on the eve of seeing less union than ever between the two Crowns. The King of Spain, too mistrustful of his own lights, . . . will decide scarcely anything without consulting the Queen. . . . The Abbé Alberoni, to whom the doors are always open, hardly quits Their Majesties. . . .
> The Queen is not beautiful. Everyone praises her figure, but

[1] Trémoïlle, vi. 272; letter of 31 Dec. 1714.
[2] Ibid., vi. 286; letter of 14 Jan. 1715.

nevertheless she walks badly and her head is hardly ever still. She has not a contented face. Nature has so made her that she will be contradicted in nothing, and it is even said it is sufficient to propose something for her to do the contrary. Her Majesty appeared thus during the journey, and since she is here her vivacity is the same in her acts, though she feigns to consult the will and tastes of the King in the smallest things. Neither the Secretaries of State who work in her presence with the King, nor those who by their posts approach her more closely, have been able to say if she has as much intelligence as they wrote from Italy, nobody up to now having heard her sustain a conversation or talk seriously of anything. I know not if this is because no one understands the bad Italian which is all she speaks, or that she is ignorant of the other languages spoken at Court. The King says, however, that she expresses herself well enough in French. Her Majesty pays no attention whatever to her toilet. Provided it is done quickly she is satisfied. Her *femmes-de-chambre* appear accustomed to her harsh manners. The other servants tremble when they serve her. As to the courtiers, men and women all say that they have not yet heard her say one gracious word. In a word, they say she has been badly brought up, that she has a very violent temper capable of great outbursts, and that, instructed by the Abbé Alberoni, she works successfully to influence the King's mind.

Alberoni himself he abuses with even more acidity, insisting that Louis shall order the Duke of Parma to recall him, "as author of the outrage to the Princess and lack of respect of the Queen towards the King her husband in striking on her own authority a blow so audacious in all its circumstances. The public," he adds, " await certainly some satisfaction on the subject, the honour of the King of Spain exacts it, and this Abbé, too ignoble in every way, does not merit to have access to the King, nor be as he is, the adviser of Their Majesties"[1]—a post which d'Aubigny probably coveted for himself.

We must leave him in Madrid paving his way dishonourably to future favour, and return to the Princess hastily preparing her long and painful journey towards Paris, where, instead of the triumph or at least compensation she had hoped for, the worst of all catastrophes awaited her.

[1] Trémoïlle, vi. 300 ; letter to Torcy of 5 Feb. 1715.

MADAME, DUCHESSE D'ORLÉANS, PRINCESSE PALATINE
From a portrait by Largillière in the Musée de Chantilly.

CHAPTER XXIV

DISGRACE AT VERSAILLES (1715)

BEFORE leaving Saint-Jean-de-Luz the Princess had sent a messenger to Bayonne, which was to be her first resting-place, to ask permission of the Queen-Dowager to pay her a visit.

What was her motive for desiring this meeting? To attack and accuse the woman whom at last, in spite of former blindness, she must have realised to have aided in her disgrace, and reproach her with the hypocrisy which had made her flatter and fawn upon her in her triumph? Probably the Queen thought so, for she refused curtly to receive her, the first in the series of rebuffs which were in future to be her portion. She remained, however, for several days in the neighbourhood of the town, in a château lent her by one of her friends.

On 4 February early in the morning she arrived at Bordeaux, where she was received with all honour by the Maréchal de Montrevel, who sent coaches to meet her on the road and entertained her royally in his own palace. But she was in too much haste to reach Versailles to linger and on the 7th was already on her way, Montrevel insisting on her accepting his own equipage and enough money to proceed with dignity and comfort.

On 13 February she reached Poitiers, still travelling in his coach. From here she wrote to Orry in Madrid that Torcy had written to tell her that Louis had received her nephew Lanti, had spoken " very obligingly " about her, but had refused to answer anything concerning his complicity in her disgrace, saying he would do so only to herself.[1] This her optimism construed into a favourable sign, and she redoubled her speed to reach Versailles.

From this letter it would appear that Louis had not yet changed his intention to receive her with kindness and distinction. On the contrary, there was talk of his giving her an apartment in his palace of Saint-Germain, a rumour which her enemies at once reported to Madrid.

[1] Trémoïlle, vi. 306 ; letter of 15 Feb. 1715.

It needed no more to redouble the Queen's fury and excite her to fresh brutalities. Aware that such a mark of friendship and protection would be considered by everyone as a reproach to herself and that all sympathies would be diverted to her victim, she sent for Giudice and ordered him to tell the French Ambassador Saint-Aignan to remonstrate with Louis, and at the same time, probably through the Queen-Dowager, stirred up the Duc d'Orléans and all his family to oppose any sort of favourable reception.

Here is Saint-Aignan's letter, dated 20 February:

> The Queen has manifested some anxiety concerning the journey of Madame des Ursins to Your Majesty's Court. . . . She fears that the reception Your Majesty has seen fit to accord her is a kind of disavowal of the vivacity with which she accompanied her dismissal, that in this uncertainty she was not sufficiently reassured by the letter Your Majesty wrote to her immediately after the event at Jadraque, and that fresh assurances would contribute to the good intelligence so much desired by the two countries.[1]

This veiled menace displeased Louis, who answered his ambassador with sufficient coldness, but it had nevertheless the desired effect and, combined with the other forces set in motion, caused him to withdraw his protection.

For now the Duc d'Orléans and his wife the Duchesse, his mother the Princess Palatine and his daughter the Duchesse de Berry, surged up and, strong in numbers and Louis' failing health, offered a formal and violent opposition to his reception of her at Versailles, probably incited thereto by the Queen of Spain herself.

On 23 February Dangeau notes in his *Diary*: "Madame la Princesse des Ursins will arrive to-morrow in Paris. Monsieur le Duc d'Orléans has begged the King to order her when she comes to Versailles not to show herself where may be found the Duchesse de Berry, Madame la Duchesse d'Orléans or himself." [2]

Such an order was practically to forbid her appearance at Court and cause the doors of all France, and indeed of all Europe, to be shut in her face.

So much for the vaunted good-nature of Philippe d'Orléans, prince of *roués*. He was in high favour at Court since the death of the Duc de Berry, for now nothing stood between him and the Regency, and only one sickly babe

---

[1] Trémoïlle, vi. 308 ; letter of 20 Feb. 1715.   [2] Dangeau, xv. 368.

DISGRACE AT VERSAILLES

between him and the throne of France. Louis was ageing fast, already in the grip of the malady which was to carry him off six months later and had no spirit left to oppose the will of so many important members of his family. So, let us hope with something of remorse, perhaps of shame, he ceded to force and gave the order exacted by his nephew so that the doors of Versailles, where the Princess had hoped to find refuge and protection, were closed in her face and she, who had hurried across France in mid-winter at a few encouraging words from her sovereign, was to find herself on her arrival condemned to the most complete ostracism.

In his additions to Dangeau's *Journal* Saint-Simon thus comments on the matter, seeking as usual to justify his patron:

Madame de Maintenon's protection was entirely withdrawn from Madame des Ursins. Thus the King willingly accorded this mortification, which the Duke himself perhaps would not have asked but for the three princesses, his mother, wife and daughter, who made a point of it. That done, they all three forbade their households to receive her, and the Duke exacted it of his private servants. He permitted only that I [Saint-Simon writes of himself here in the third person], who like my mother had been her intimate friend, should see her once on her arrival and once again when she left for Italy. This I caused to be told to her, and although we lodged next door to each other I kept my word, but the visit I made her was with closed doors and lasted from two o'clock in the afternoon till ten o'clock at night. . . . The Memoirs will note presently her short and dry visit to Versailles, very different to those of the past and promising nothing better for the future. At first she had numerous visits, her friends made a point of it, most of them from curiosity, but this soon died out, and even in Paris she was made to feel all the weight of her double disgrace. But she bore it all with the same grandeur, without humility as without insolence.[1]

These few words of involuntary praise from the man who had done his best to injure her are more eloquent than all his former eulogies.

Much later again he refers to the subject:

At last the Princess arrived in Paris and lodged with her brother the Duc de Noirmoutier in a small house he occupied in the Rue Saint-Dominique next door to my own. The journey must have seemed to her very different to the last she had made to France, when she appeared as Queen of the Court. Few people except her old friends came to see her, a few, however,

[1] Dangeau, xv. 369; addition of Saint-Simon.

from curiosity, which made a sufficient crowd the first few days, after which the visits grew rarer, and solitude reigned as soon as the result of her visit to Versailles was known. The Duc d'Orléans felt that it was materially to his interest and not from feeble vengeance, to show by some scandal that it was only to her hatred and intrigues that he owed the Spanish affair which had so nearly brought his head to the scaffold. Madame de Maintenon had turned her back on her and so, freed as regards this latter enemy, he did not think it necessary to spare her. To this he was urged by the Duchess and still more by Madame, so that he begged the King to forbid her to show herself in any place, even in the town, where the Duchesse de Berry, Madame, himself and the Duchess might meet her, and at the same time they strictly forbade any of their households to see her and demanded the same of those specially attached to them. This caused a great scandal as showing plainly Madame de Maintenon's abandonment and the King's indifference and greatly embarrassed the Princess.[1]

Thus the ranks of her Royal persecutors had been importantly swelled. The Duchesse d'Orléans, Louis' haughty and arrogant bastard (Madame Lucifer, her husband called her), the brutal and vindictive Princess Palatine his mother, and the drunken harlot at once his daughter and mistress, had it in their power to condemn her to complete ostracism.

Madame de Maintenon, though no friend to the Orléans family, had supported too much from the insolence of her rival during the later years of the war to care now to renew her protection. On the contrary she seems to have been as anxious as they to keep her at a distance and prevent her approaching Louis. In a letter to one of her protégés, the Curé of Saint-Sulpice, she writes: "Monsieur le Duc d'Orléans is in despair at the return of Madame des Ursins. He wants to go to Paris, fearing that if he finds her in his path he would not be able to prevent himself insulting her, which would be terrible in the King's house. . . . He thinks that it is I who have obtained her permission to come here. However, I worked hard to prevent her sleeping at Versailles and to make her leave Paris as soon as possible."[2]

The worst tragedy of the Princess's disgrace began only on her arrival in Paris. She had probably never seriously considered that Versailles also could condemn her and this hope was justified by the letters she had received on her journey. But it was not long before she was undeceived.

[1] Saint-Simon, xxvi. 178.
[2] Geffroy, *Madame de Maintenon*, ii. 362 ; letter of 24 Feb. 1715.

Immediately after her arrival in Paris she had sent a messenger to Versailles to know when Louis would receive her. But already the cabal had done its work. The Queen of Spain's objections, the Orléans' attack and Madame de Maintenon's coldness had dried up whatever pity or sympathy he might have had for her, and he sent word coldly that she might come the following week, but must return to Paris directly the interview was over.

Outraged at this injustice, she acted with dignity and courage and on the day fixed for the visit sent word that she was suffering from an inflammation of the eyes and would be unable to come, and it was not till nearly a month later that she deigned to accept the humiliating interview.

On 1 March Dangeau notes baldly as usual in his *Diary*: "Madame des Ursins was to have come here to-morrow. The King would have received her at two o'clock, she would then have gone to see Madame de Maintenon and after have returned to Paris, but she has a fluxion of the eyes which prevents her coming." [1]

And on 27 March: "After dinner the King heard the sermon and then gave audience in his cabinet to Madame des Ursins. The audience lasted two hours. Afterwards Madame des Ursins went to Madame de Maintenon where she remained till the King came there. She had arrived in the morning and had dined with the Duchesse de Lude and slept in the town in the house of Madame Adam, wife of one of Torcy's chief clerks. To-morrow she will dine with Madame de Ventadour and then return to Paris." And he adds significantly: "In the evening there was a grand concert in the apartment of Madame de Maintenon." [2]

What passed during that two hours' visit is not recorded. It is probable that the talk was more of Spanish affairs in general than of the Princess's wrongs and that Louis avoided as far as possible any hint of reproach to his grandson and his wife, for there is solidarity among kings as among workmen. She herself says nothing either of her interview with Louis or Madame de Maintenon, from which it may be gathered that she had nothing pleasant to relate.

What a change from her last visit ten years before when she had been the idol of the Court, the most honoured of Louis' guests, when a glance of recognition from her was a social success, when all the princes and princesses of the

---

[1] Dangeau, xv. 372.   [2] Ibid., xv. 390.

blood flocked to her apartment to pay their court to the new favourite, when the sycophant Saint-Simon thought himself honoured by her nod. Now officers guard the Royal cabinet to warn the Orléans family that the enemy is there. Chamberlains conduct her by private corridors and secret stairs to the back doors and at her exit she, with the right as Altesse of Spain to an escort of Royal guards, must slink by bypaths to the streets of Versailles and the house of one of Torcy's clerks in which to sup and pass the night, while Madame de Maintenon gives a grand concert in her apartment at which she may not assist.

Saint-Simon thus describes his own interview with her at her brother's house in the Rue de Grenelle:

> Some days after she went to Versailles I went to see her at two o'clock in the afternoon. At once she shut her doors to everybody and I was alone with her till ten o'clock in the evening. It can be imagined how many things can be passed in review in so long an interview. I found in her the same friendship and frankness, very reasonable about the Duc d'Orléans and his family, very frank as to the rest. She related her catastrophe without once dragging in the King [Louis] or the King of Spain, whom she praised all the time and, without expressing her sentiments on the Queen, she foretold what has since taken place.[1] She hid from me nothing of her amazement, her bad treatment, nor even of the gross insults deliberately prepared, of her departure, her journey, her state of mind, of all which she had suffered. She spoke also very naturally about her visit to Versailles, her disagreeable position in Paris, of the late Queen, the King of Spain and various persons who had figured in the Government in her time, lastly of her indecision and uncertainty as to an honourable retreat, the site of which was undecided in her mind. This eight hours' conversation with a person who had so many extraordinary things to say seemed to me no more than eight minutes.[2]

To his credit be it said that in financial matters Louis behaved with a certain grandeur. At the prayer of the Duc de Noirmoutier he had already on her arrival sent her twenty thousand francs in payment of her yearly pension and this pension he now converted into an annuity of forty thousand which doubled her income from this source, a piece of generosity criticised by Madame to her sister in Bavaria as follows:

[1] Written after Cellamare's conspiracy to set Philippe in the Regency.
[2] Saint-Simon, xxvi. 178, etc.

"I am to-day, as they say in our dear Germany, as angry as a bug. . . . The King, wishing to reward the Princess des Ursins who behaved so horribly to my son and tried to make him pass for a poisoner, has given her forty thousand francs pension."[1]

Besides this increase of pension he risked the ferocity of the Queen of Spain by proposing to his grandson that he should also come to her rescue.

I consider it in the interest of my honour as well as your own [he wrote on 30 April] to remedy the state of the Princess des Ursins' fortune, and that it is neither desirable for me nor for Your Majesty that strangers should see in indigence a person whom I called from Rome to Spain and whom you have honoured with your confidence during so many years. It is on these grounds that I have given her contracts of forty thousand francs annuity, and as I know your heart and sentiments I am persuaded that not only will you be very glad at what I have done but will even follow my example in the way you may think most appropriate. Remember that formerly you would have accorded her all she might have asked, and that her present state seems to exact that you should remedy a prejudice due to her disinterestedness.[2]

It is easy to imagine the fury which this letter excited in the Parmesan virago and the pressure she put on her husband to refuse a request so reasonable and made with so much dignity. Philippe, who had kept all Europe at war while he haggled over the Princess's sovereignty, was base enough under her influence to refuse her the pension she might have exacted as her due.

As regards the Princess des Ursins [he answered his grandfather], I think that on reflection you will find that after the cause she has given the Queen to act towards her as she did, I have done no small thing in coming to her aid with the five thousand pistoles and more which I have sent her, that it is not suitable that I should show her more favour, and that you will not find it amiss that I refuse what you demand for a person who has had the misfortune to displease the Queen, to satisfy whom is one of my principal occupations and who merits so strongly the extreme tenderness I have for her. I beg you also to observe that the Princess des Ursins has already a pension of six thousand crowns in Sicily which I have given her.[3]

[1] Brunet, *Nouvelles Lettres de la Duchesse d'Orléans*, p. 79 ; letter of 19 April, 1715.
[2] Trémoïlle, vi. 315 ; letter of 30 April, 1715.
[3] Ibid., vi. 319 ; letter of 19 May, 1715.

This foolish and cruel letter irritated Louis profoundly, but the time was over when he could express his sentiments with freedom and call his grandson what he must have considered him, a cowardly imbecile. He wrote to his Ambassador, however, severely enough to show his disapproval:

The King of Spain has answered me decisively as to my recommendation in favour of the Princess des Ursins. He refuses absolutely to show her any favour, thinking that the Queen of Spain would have reason to be offended by it. I had judged differently and thought that this Princess, having cause to be satisfied with having expelled the Princess from Spain, would have considered it beneath her to push her resentment farther, that she might even think there was more grandeur in procuring her the means to live comfortably in the place she may choose for her retreat.[1]

At the same time he instructed his Ambassador to inquire into the real state of the Princess's finances and whether the Orléans' stories of her fabulous wealth and the riches she had amassed through the late Queen's generosity were true. After careful examination the Duke wrote to Torcy in reply a letter which may be accepted as an absolute refutation of the charge so often brought against her by her enemies that she had enriched herself by dishonest means.

The Princess [wrote Saint-Aignan], during the lifetime of the late Queen, enjoyed the appointments of Camarera Mayor, which at most are not more than seven or eight thousand francs, besides which the King of Spain accorded her a pension of sixteen thousand francs on the confiscated property of the kingdom of Sicily, which the new King [the Duke of Savoy] has since promised to continue. The Cardinal del Giudice told me that she had besides ten thousand crowns for the payment of some costumes which etiquette formerly obliged the queens to wear on certain feast-days, and which Madame des Ursins appropriated at the wish of the Queen, who always dressed very simply, but I am positively assured that this was never more than about one thousand pistoles. This was all she had fixed, for she received nothing for her charge of *gouvernante* of the princes.[2]

She was deeply wounded when she heard of Philippe's ignoble refusal and expressed her disgust to Madame de Maintenon: "I do not recognise His Catholic Majesty in this refusal and I see clearly by the way he explains himself, so contrary to his generosity, that his answer has been

[1] Trémoïlle, vi. 320; letter of 3 June, 1715.
[2] Ibid., vi. 327; letter of 19 Aug. 1715.

inspired by those whose souls are very far from knowing true glory. Thus I abstain from attributing to him sentiments so base." [1]

In truth her cup of bitterness was filled to overflowing, for she began now also to feel the effects of her reception at Versailles, Madame de Maintenon's coldness and the public withdrawal of Louis' protection.

" The ferocity here against Madame des Ursins is carried beyond all that can be imagined," her old friend Madame de Caylus, niece of Madame de Maintenon, wrote to her aunt. "All has been done to corrupt me, for I call it infamous corruption to seize this opportunity. However it be, she is unhappy, she is my old friend, and I pity her infinitely." [2]

I say nothing of Madame des Ursins nor of the celebrated Monsieur Orry [wrote in a lighter vein a certain Abbé Mascara from Paris to the Minister Grimaldo in Madrid]. Last year they were great personages, at present they are effaced from the calendar. Without exaggeration there is no more talk of them than if they had been dead and buried for eighteen centuries. They are as far away as Cæsar and Pompey. Madame de Maintenon herself looked askance at the Princess. . . . She is like one abandoned, which causes her much suffering, for the good lady is accustomed to be adored. Only Villeroy at first paid her some attention, but the Duc d'Orléans was displeased and very soon everyone showed that the friendship of a disgraced person is avoided like a contagious disease. [3]

And since troubles never come singly, her sight also seemed on the point of giving out and leaving her totally blind. Although her general health by a miracle does not appear to have suffered, as might have been expected, from the shock of her expulsion and the terrible drive over the mountains, yet the cataract in her eyes grew worse and added to her anxieties. "I have put my eyes under the care of Monsieur de Saint-Yves," she wrote to Madame de Maintenon at this time. "To lose my sight as well as my favour would be too much misfortune at the same time." [4]

Happily this last horror was spared her, and such sight as she had she retained up to her death.

[1] Collin, *Lettres à Villeroy*, p. 231 ; letter of 6 June, 1715.
[2] Caylus, *Souvenirs*, ed. Raunié (Paris, 1881), 255. Date omitted.
[3] Baudrillart, i. 646 ; letter of 29 June, 1715. The Abbé Mascara was Canon of La Scala, Milan. Half spy, half courtier, he wrote all the scandals of Versailles to Madrid to amuse Philippe.
[4] Collin, *Lettres à Villeroy*, p. 231 ; letter of 6 June, 1715.

CHAPTER XXV

UPHEAVALS IN MADRID (1715)

MEANWHILE all who had been her friends in Spain were being expelled with all possible insult and ignominy, and all her enemies recalled and rewarded with the highest posts. Orry, who had been retained long enough to put the affairs connected with his different posts in order, on the completion of his task was dismissed at two days' notice, and during these two days was guarded like a criminal and insulted by the officers appointed to watch him. Of his demands for a farewell interview no notice was taken and he was conducted to the frontier like a prisoner. In spite of this treatment, however, he managed to make his exit with some show of dignity, accompanied by a goodly retinue of servants, among them what remained of the Princess's own household.[1]

Lanti and Chalais, who had escorted the Princess to Paris, received orders not to return. Both were grandees, both had been among the closest and most favoured of the King's Recreadors during his so-called sequestration; Lanti's bride of three months had been left behind in Madrid; their only crime was their fidelity to their aunt and benefactress, yet they were immolated to the Queen's insatiable fury, and it was not till four years later, when the entire aspect of Spanish affairs was changed and their aid was needed, that they received permission to return.

In spite of her vaunted intelligence and study of Machiavelli, Elisabeth Farnese was completely ignorant of politics, and having dominated Philippe through his senses and being dominated in her turn by Alberoni, she became a mere tool in his hands, her own idea of government consisting in a systematic reversal of the work of the Princess. Thus in less than a month after her advent the Inquisition was re-established in all its privileges, the Queen-Dowager was authorised to settle in Germany, a reconciliation was

[1] Saint-Simon, xxvi. 500; letter of Saint-Aignan to Torcy of 16 Feb. 1715.

UPHEAVALS IN MADRID 387

demanded of the Duc d'Orléans, the Cardinal del Giudice was reinstated in all his offices and the old-fashioned etiquette resuscitated with all its antiquated customs.

Not only was Giudice reinstated in his post of Grand Inquisitor but appointed Prime Minister, and one of his first acts was to insult the Princess by writing to inform her brother the Duc de Noirmoutier of his return to favour.

"The Spanish post brings many letters from the Cardinal del Giudice," wrote Dangeau in his *Diary* on 3 March. "He sends word to many courtiers and ladies of his happy return to Madrid, and it is even thought very extraordinary that he has written it to Monsieur de Noirmoutier, brother of Madame des Ursins. The King of Spain has put him at the head of affairs political, judicial and religious."[1]

His nephew the Prince of Cellamare was sent as ambassador to Versailles with special orders to "combat the malicious representations" of Orry and the Princess. Here is an extract from his instructions signed by Philippe himself:

May 14, 1715. Although I doubt not that when you arrive in Paris the talk excited by the expulsion of the Princess des Ursins and Orry will have calmed down, it is necessary still to be very much on your guard in order to confound the impressions which remain from their malicious representations against my justification and that of the Queen. . . . Suspecting that the Princess and Orry, to conceal false and misleading designs, have tried to influence the mind of my grandfather as also of his ministers by suggesting that the French have been turned out of Spain, thus fomenting their aversion to an Italian Queen by declaring her a violent partisan of her compatriots, you must make known the true motives which have decided me to expel those above mentioned.[2]

One of Alberoni's first acts was to reconcile Philippe to his fellow-conspirator the Duc d'Orléans by the liberation of Flotte and Regnault, which was effected amid a volley of family congratulations, Louis thanking Philippe, Philippe thanking the Duc d'Orléans, the Queen expressing her delight and the Duke his gratitude, all with more or less malignant allusions to the diabolic influence which had separated them. It will be seen presently how long this friendship was to last.

[1] Dangeau, xv. 373.   [2] Trémoïlle, vi. 318.

2 C

Here is one of the Duke's letters to Alberoni:

You have taken so efficacious a part in what I had so much reason to desire [he wrote, evidently with more reference to the Princess's expulsion than the reconciliation] that I can take no course more agreeable than to charge you with my very humble thanks to the Queen. . . . The Marquis Monti has given me a faithful account of all your zeal for me and I beg you to rely on my gratitude. The general deliverance produced by the change of government on the Queen's arrival unites in me the keenest gratitude to the sincerest admiration for so accomplished a Princess, and I cannot sufficiently recommend you to show her to what a point I feel these sentiments.[1]

Meantime d'Aubigny arrived in Paris, having tranquilly and systematically arranged his own affairs to his satisfaction, but done nothing for those of his benefactress. On 15 March, two days before his departure from Madrid, he wrote one of his most fulsome letters to Torcy, which he ended thus: " I leave the day after to-morrow without having been able to do anything for Madame la Princesse. All that concerns me I have finished very satisfactorily, but have failed shamefully each time I tried to speak in her interest. The harshness here goes so far as to refuse to pay her what they acknowledge to be her due."[2]

Whether he was also received in the house of the Duc de Noirmoutier is not recorded, but that there was no open rupture between him and the Princess is evident since she employed him in certain money affairs with Torcy, and it is doubtful if she ever learnt the full extent of his treachery. Their separation was, however, complete, and there was no question of his following her into exile. She allowed him to retain, or perhaps to buy, the magnificent château of Chanteloup in Touraine, which he had acquired and furnished at her order in prevision of her sovereignty.

The complete ruin of this ambitious woman [writes Saint-Simon] did not permit her to inhabit this beautiful residence. It remained the property of d'Aubigny, who received there very well the neighbours, the curious, and travellers of distinction, to whom he did not conceal that it was neither for himself nor with his own wealth that he had built and furnished it. He settled down there, made himself liked and esteemed, lost his wife there, who left him only one daughter very young, and this daughter, very rich, married the Marquis d'Armentières.[3]

[1] Saint-Simon, xxvi. 515 ; letter of 20 May, 1715.
[2] Ibid., xxvi. 508 ; letter of 15 March, 1715.
[3] Ibid., xxii. 141. From the editor's note we learn that his

Elsewhere he writes:

D'Aubigny, despised at Utrecht, where he had gone to negotiate the sovereignty of the Princess, and where he had never been able to pass beyond the antechambers, had returned to Paris and Touraine and worked hard at this magnificent building. It was carried on so rapidly that it was almost finished when the thread snapped as to the sovereignty, and d'Aubigny, seeing that it could no longer serve for what his mistress proposed, put a stop to all as far as possible and bought little by little some fiefs in order that such a beautiful building should not be absolutely without grounds. Madame des Ursins, ashamed of this folly, left it all to him, who, though not well born enough to suit the place, was sufficiently rich to receive there the neighbours and travellers. He passed there the rest of his days, liked and considered in the country, with enough intelligence to leave behind him in Spain his grand airs and high aspirations. This place is called Chanteloup and was inherited by Madame d'Armentières his daughter. It is one of the handsomest and most singular places in France and the most superbly furnished.[1]

Thus while the Princess, after fifteen years of unlimited authority, during which she could without blame have amassed immense wealth, left Spain in comparative poverty, and, as will be seen presently, was forced to sell her titles and property in order to live with dignity,[2] her secretary had been able to amass sufficient wealth to live *en grand seigneur* in a semi-royal palace. The death of Louis XIV. a few months after his arrival in France, and the consequent change of ministry, put an end to whatever ambitions he may have had of advance under Torcy, but, already middle-aged, he probably consoled himself with the comfortable life and pursuits of a country gentleman.

wife was noble—Marie-Françoise de Rennemoulin—and that his daughter was born in 1717, so that he must have married soon after his return to France.

[1] Saint-Simon, xxiv. 212. The château, situated near a small village, four kilometres east of Amboise, was bought in 1761 by the Duc de Choiseul, who retired there after his disgrace. Confiscated during the Revolution, it was utilised as a factory for beetroot sugar and was demolished in 1825. Nothing now remains of it except the park.

[2] In August of this year 1715 she sold to the Duke of Gravina the right to the Soglio which belonged to her, and the Duchy of San Gemini, one of the estates she inherited from the Duke of Bracciano (*see* Trémoïlle, vi. 328; letter from La Chaussé to Torcy from Rome of 20 Aug. 1715).

CHAPTER XXVI

FAREWELL TO FRANCE (1715)

WHERE to go, what to do, when all the world is against you—when your enemies are the most puissant sovereigns of Europe with the power to close to you all their frontiers? This was the problem which posed itself night and day to the woman before whom all Europe only two months before had bowed respectfully. In Versailles she dared not show herself. Paris also was closed to her, for the fiat had gone forth that "she must leave France as soon as possible." From the country of her birth she was expelled, as surely, if less brutally, as from that of her adoption.

Her choice of a retreat in itself proves the desperate and disordered state of mind to which she was reduced—Holland, of all imaginable or unimaginable places.

"She has not yet made up her mind," Torcy wrote to the Cardinal her brother, "where she should live, but seems to have a leaning towards Holland, foreseeing much annoyance in living in Rome." [1]

This fear of annoyance was due to the Cardinal himself, who probably either dreaded the presence in Rome of a disgraced sister or wished to remain sole inmate of her palace in the Piazza Navone which she allowed him to occupy.

"Taking everything into consideration," he had written to Torcy, only too ready to put obstacles in her way, "she is right in considering a residence here in Rome impracticable, for she would receive even more disagreeables than she thinks." [2]

Spain, France, Italy, Austria, Germany—all Europe, in fact, shut to her. In her despair she fixed on Holland—Holland where she was detested, the scene of the disaster of her sovereignty. Perhaps she still nourished hopes of winning over the States-General to her cause by her personal influence and eloquent tongue, otherwise the choice is unaccountable.

[1] Trémoïlle, vi. 313 ; letter of 15 April, 1715.
[2] Ibid., vi. 316 ; letter of 7 May, 1715.

But Holland, too, rejected her—at least from The Hague and Amsterdam. "The Princess des Ursins' project up to now," Dangeau notes in his *Diary*, "was to go to Holland, but as messieurs of the States-General do not desire that she shall settle either at The Hague or Amsterdam it is thought she will choose the town of Utrecht to reside in." [1]

"The Princess has begged the Maréchal de Villeroy to tell His Majesty and Madame de Maintenon," the Duc de Noirmoutier wrote to Torcy about the same time, "that she is quite ready to go and settle in Utrecht, since her unhappy destiny forces her to take so extreme a step to try to end her life in repose and tranquillity, in obeying the King's wishes, which will always be the rule of her conduct." [2]

Happily Utrecht was abandoned, and in spite of her brother the Cardinal, it was in her own Roman palace that she finally decided to fix her home.

On 7 May Dangeau notes: "The Princess des Ursins had resolved to retire to Utrecht, but she has changed her mind and made a decision which her family and friends find more noble and reasonable. She will go to Rome where she has a beautiful palace, but before leaving will wait till she has received a passport from the Emperor, which is necessary since she must pass through the Milanese province." [3]

Annoyed at this decision, so contrary to his personal interests, her unworthy brother again wrote to Torcy to dissuade her: "I cannot help saying that it is grievous for her, being in France, where the King has been good enough to give her effective marks of his protection, to be forced to seek a retreat in a place where she foresees rightly she will have to suffer many disagreeables." [4]

This time his words had their intended effect, and once again discouraged she changed her plans and sought a home elsewhere. It was the little papal state of Avignon to which she sadly resigned herself, at least for the moment.

On 20 July Dangeau notes: "Madame des Ursins has

---

[1] Dangeau, xv. 408.
[2] Trémoïlle, vi. 314; letter of 29 April, 1715.
[3] Dangeau, xv. 455.
[4] Trémoïlle, vi. 321; letter of 11 June, 1715.

received the money she demanded for her journey. She is preparing to leave but will not go to Rome yet. She will make a fairly long stay at Avignon till the season is fit to go to Rome. Many even think she will remain in Avignon and not go at all to Rome, where her presence would embarrass the Pope." [1]

The tragedy was not yet ended, for even this dreary little town was shut to her. At the last moment, when all was prepared for her departure, the nuncio arrived in haste with the order from the Pope to defer her journey till he had heard whether the King and Queen of Spain would be annoyed if he allowed her to settle in any part of his states.[2]

What do you think [she wrote to Madame de Maintenon, in revolt at this persistent cruelty] of the difficulty made by the Pope about receiving me in Rome—the fatherland common to all Christians, and which I may regard as my second country since I have my residence there ? This is what is called the cup filled to overflowing. Hunted from Spain with indignity, received kindly by the King whose subject I am, yet deprived of the consolation of paying him my homage, urged by my best friends to leave the kingdom, as though my presence embarrassed them—all this in truth appears to me incredible, and I know not how I have strength to support so cruel a state. . . . Would you have believed, when you counselled me not to leave Madrid, that I should find no place for the sole of my foot? [3]

To which Madame de Maintenon coldly replied: "I did not think the Pope would have refused you a refuge in Rome, but I feared that your enemies would have time to thwart your intention and that is one of the reasons I had for so urgently pressing your departure." [4]

But here Louis, eager to be rid of her, or perhaps touched by the extremity of her misfortune—intervened, and without awaiting his grandson's permission, sent word to the Pope that he would himself guarantee his consent to her residence, either in Rome or Avignon, as she thought fit, and told the Princess she could leave whenever she chose.

[1] Dangeau, xv. 455.
[2] Trémoïlle, vi. 325 ; letter from Torcy to Saint-Aignan of 15 July, 1715.
[3] Collin, *Lettres à Villeroy*, p. 231 ; letter of 6 June, 1715.
[4] Geffroy, *Madame de Maintenon*, ii. 370 ; letter of 14 July, 1715.

To Philippe he wrote dryly enough:

> The Pope, informed of the departure of the Princess des Ursins for Rome, has sent to ask me if this journey would displease you. I have taken on myself to give him your consent and that of the Queen, because I am persuaded that the Princess's intentions should not be suspected by you, and that even should they be so, Rome is the place where she could least damage your interests and where you would be best informed of her conduct. Thus Your Majesty will do me the favour to confirm what I have said to the Pope.[1]

The severity of this letter did not fail to make an impression at Madrid, and the Queen thought fit to abate a little of her ferocity in consequence. "You have judged very well of the sentiments of the Queen and myself as to the journey of the Princess des Ursins to Rome," she permitted Philippe to reply. "We shall not oppose her making her home there and the Pope may be assured of it."[2]

Thus it seemed finally settled that Rome was to be her home, Rome which she had left fifteen years before full of ambition and aspirations, realised, it is true, beyond her wildest dreams, only like dreams to vanish at the supreme moment. It will be seen that as she drew nearer to the scene of her first triumphs, the idea of returning thus, disgraced and repudiated on all sides, hurt her too profoundly to allow her to proceed, and that it needed four years of the esteem and honour shown her by the Genoese Republic before she found sufficient courage to make it for the second time her home.

One final interview with Louis was accorded her—the last which in any case she would have had, for Louis too was summoned to make a journey longer and even more tragic than her own. The farewell visit took place at Marly on 6 August, and she left, according to the Abbé Mascara, with tears in her eyes and a sword in her heart.[3]

Saint-Simon gives some interesting details of this farewell visit:

> She arrived at Marly from Paris on Tuesday, 6 August, timed to arrive at the hour when the King came out from dinner, that is to say, at two o'clock. She was at once admitted to his

---

[1] Trémoïlle, vi. 326 ; letter of 15 July, 1715.
[2] Ibid., vi. 326 ; letter of 29 July, 1715.
[3] Baudrillart, i. 647.

cabinet and remained more than half an hour alone with him.
She went at once to that of Madame de Maintenon, with whom
she remained an hour, and from there got into her coach to
return to Paris. I knew she was bidding farewell only on her
arrival at Marly, where I had difficulty in meeting her. It
happened that I had just thought of seeking her coach so as
to ask her people what had become of her, when, as I was
speaking to them, she appeared in a chair. She seemed very
pleased to see me and made me get into her coach, where we
remained little less than an hour talking very freely. She did
not hide her fears, the coldness of the King and Madame de
Maintenon towards her in her two audiences, in spite of the
politeness they had shown her, the solitude in which she found
herself at the Court and even in Paris, and finally the uncertainty she was still in as to the choice of an abode; all this in
detail and nevertheless without complaint, regret or weakness,
always measured, always as though she were speaking of
another person and was superior to any event. She spoke
a little of Spain, the credit — ascendant even — which the
Queen had over the King, giving me to understand that it
could not be otherwise, alluding lightly and modestly to the
Queen, praising always the goodness of the King of Spain.
The fear of passers-by seeing us made her put an end to our
conversation.[1]

Dangeau writes of this last interview: "The King gave
audience in his cabinet to Madame des Ursins who took
leave of him. She stayed three-quarters of an hour with
him and then went to Madame de Maintenon, where she
remained much longer."[2] And again, on 14 August:
"The Princess des Ursins has left Paris. She has taken
leave of all her friends as one who does not count on seeing
them again. Her two nephews accompany her to her
first resting-place, which will be Essonne" (Essonne near
Corbeil on the high-road to Lyons).[3]

This was her final farewell to the monarch and country
which had so cruelly dismissed and abandoned her.

But she was not one to parade her wrongs in public,
and she left her brother's house in some state, one is glad
to learn, escorted by her two nephews who remained
faithful up to the last, and followed by her household in
seven chaises and by eight mounted guards.[4] At least in
her misfortune she bore herself with dignity and avoided
any appeal for pity. So much courage did she show,

[1] Saint-Simon, xxvi. 258, etc.   [2] Dangeau, xvi. 5.
[3] Dangeau, xvi. 95.   [4] Saint-Simon, xxvii. 180, note 5.

indeed, that Madame de Caylus who saw her just before her departure, wrote to Madame de Maintenon: "Rely upon it, this woman counts still on making a great place for herself, I do not well know where nor how, but the sentiment is in her heart." [1]

[1] Caylus, *Souvenirs*, p. 262.

CHAPTER XXVII

DEATH OF LOUIS XIV. (1715)

THE Princess left Paris on 14 August and a fortnight later Louis XIV. also bade farewell to France and started on his last journey. He was seventy-seven, and his health had been failing for several months. He had grown thin and his huge Bourbon appetite had forsaken him. Two months before, the English gazettes had been full of his approaching end, publishing that bets were being made that he would not live till September. Torcy, whose duty it was to read him these, one morning stopped suddenly and grew very red. Questioned as to his embarrassment he remained silent, but Louis insisting, was forced to tell him of these bets. Louis said nothing, but seemed deeply moved, and at dinner, which he still took in public, tried to appear gay and eat with good appetite, though everyone could see that the food stuck in his throat.

On 1 September Dangeau notes: "The King died this morning at a quarter-past eight, and gave up his soul without effort like a candle which has burnt down."[1]

"I have seen the King die like a saint and a hero," wrote Madame de Maintenon ten days later in answer to the Princess's condolences.[2]

Louis had been capricious towards her, had been harsh and unjust in her prosperity, indifferent in her misfortune, treacherous when she was in his way, but in a sense he had protected her. With all his egoism he remained always *grand seigneur* and had never lowered himself to the hypocrisies and petty meanness of his grandson. It is probable that she regretted him bitterly when the news reached her, all the more that she had the worst to fear from the brutality of Philippe d'Orléans, now Regent, who had already pursued her with so much cruelty.

The preparations for her departure were already completed when the news of his illness reached her. She had probably seen death in his face at their last meeting and

---

[1] Dangeau, xvi. 136.
[2] Bossange, iii. 179 ; letter of 11 Sept. 1715.

DEATH OF LOUIS XIV 397

was anxious to leave France as soon as possible. Saint-Simon with his usual malignity accuses her of flying with indecent haste at the first announcement of his illness.

Madame des Ursins, well aware of the King's state [he writes], hastened to leave France with a precipitation little decent and which showed all the terror she had at finding herself in the power of the Duc d'Orléans, whom she had so cruelly offended. Up to then, undecided as to the place of her retreat, amused by a remnant of friends and acquaintances and those of her brother who had many, occupied in withdrawing her possessions from Spain and arranging her affairs for so great a change of condition, she had let time go by in uncertainty, but the fear of losing the King, or rather of finding herself in the Duke's hands, left her not an instant to lose. She had been so struck during her last visit at the change in the King since she had seen him on her arrival from Spain that, thinking herself lost, she hastened her departure and the speed of her post-chaise till she reached Lyons. Once near the frontier she took breath and rested, still uncertain as to the place of her retreat. She had abandoned the project of Holland, to which the idea of liberty had attracted her, but the equality and absence of rank of a republic disgusted her. She could not make up her mind to return to Rome where she had formerly reigned, without position, with a faded face and the fear of being ill received after what had passed in Spain, as one proscribed to demand asylum where she had reigned so brilliantly. Turin was a theatre unworthy of her. The King of Sardinia [1] had not always been pleased with her, and besides they both knew too much of each other. In Venice she would not have known what to do. She let time go by thus with one foot in the stirrup and on the alert as to what was said of the King's illness, but when she heard he was dying she again took to flight with the same precipitation and fled to Chambéry as the place safest and nearest, and arrived there breathless. This refuge was her first resting-place and here she took her time to choose a fixed abode and make arrangements to settle in it.[2]

All this talk of indecent haste and breathless flight is disproved by the documents. It was not her fault, but that of her enemies, that she had not already left for Rome two months before. Nevertheless, the above details of her journey are fairly correct.

She left Paris with the intention of remaining at least for a short time at Avignon, but hearing at Lyons of the King's death she changed her plans, fearing, as well she

[1] The Duke of Savoy, now King of Sicily, later King of Sardinia.
[2] Dangeau, xvi. 5 ; additions of Saint-Simon.

might after her recent experience, that the vengeance of the Duc d'Orléans, now Regent of France, would cause her to be arrested on the road. Instead, therefore, of proceeding to Avignon she took the road to Chambéry, at that time belonging to the Duchy of Savoy, who knows with what hope of obtaining the King of Sicily's protection.

This journey across a hostile France was perhaps the culminating point in the tragedy of her disgrace. On arriving at Pont-Beauvoisin, she sent a messenger to ask the King of Sicily, then in residence at Chambéry, to receive her on her way to Aix, where she intended taking the waters, and to allow her to pass the winter at Chambéry. But the gates even of Chambéry were shut to her. The King returned answer that her visit would be ill-timed, and that she could very well continue her journey to Aix without stopping at Chambéry. Here is the letter from the French *chargé-d'affaires* at Chambéry recounting this fresh brutality:

Madame des Ursins is at Pont-Beauvoisin since some days. She has sent a gentleman to the King of Sicily to ask to be allowed to come and pay him her homage at Chambéry on her way to take the waters at Aix two leagues distant. She asked permission at the same time to pass the winter at Chambéry. The King of Sicily has sent answer that he is here without the Queen and in a manner without a Court, that thus the time was unsuitable to see either him or the Queen, and that she could pass on her way to Aix without stopping at Chambéry. As regards her proposal to remain here this winter, the King replied that he did not think the air was good for her health, and that the season was still very suitable to continue her journey to Rome.[1]

And a week later:

Madame des Ursins is still at Pont-Beauvoisin. It is not known where she will go nor when. The King of Sicily told Monsieur Amelot and me that the reason why he does not wish to see her is on account of Monsieur le Duc d'Orléans. Since then he told me that he had besides little wish to see her and that the consideration he owes the Duc d'Orléans had quite decided him.[2]

After this last rebuff she thought no more of Aix. In proposing a winter at Chambéry she had probably hoped that in memory of the dead Queen she might find a welcome

---

[1] Trémoïlle, vi. 328 ; letter of 15 Sept. 1715.
[2] Ibid., vi. 329 ; letter of 22 Sept. 1715.

and temporary home at the little Turin Court. Now again she was at a loose end and her Calvary recommenced.

Already on hearing of Louis' death she had written to condole with Madame de Maintenon who, in mortal terror of the Duc d'Orléans, had retired immediately to Saint-Cyr as to a sanctuary. Now again from Pont-Beauvoisin the Princess wrote to her, giving way for the first time to depression. "You are going to live among the holy maidens who owe you their perfection," she wrote, "and I know not yet where I may die!"[1]

Her melancholy, however, did not last long and she soon regained her splendid temperamental optimism. She was a woman of action above all and her next move was extremely practical. Her enemy the Duc d'Orléans being now all-powerful, she bowed her head to the inevitable, and wrote to her friends at Versailles to beg for his protection, become a necessity, since as a French subject she could not move without it. Happily we have not to record that he refused though, as will be seen, he did not hurry himself in granting it.

The idea of Rome under her present circumstances was distasteful to her, but she was Italian by taste and predilection and it was to Italy and the little aristocratic Republic of Genoa that she turned in her extremity. The climate was soft and agreeable, the surroundings beautiful. As will be seen, she had not lost hope of a return to favour in Madrid, and Genoa was a convenient half-way house between Spain and Rome.

All things taken into consideration [writes Saint-Simon] she preferred Genoa. The liberty pleased her. The society of a rich and numerous nobility, the beauty of the place and climate, a kind of centre between Paris, Madrid, and Rome—all this decided her. She had kept up her relations with the three capitals. She was keenly interested in all that passed and the overthrow of so many great realities and still greater dreams had not destroyed her hopes, much less her desires.[2]

On 5 November Coutlet, French envoy to the Genoese Republic, wrote to the Maréchal d'Huxelles, who, under the Regent, had replaced Torcy as Foreign Minister:

Madame des Ursins has written to me from Pont de Beauvoisin the 22nd of last month that she intended to leave the

[1] Collin, *Lettres à Villeroy*, p. 236; letter of 27 Sept. 1715.
[2] Saint-Simon, xxvi. 262 and 412.

26th or 27th to come to Genoa to pass the winter. She supposes that before her letter reached me I should have received one from Your Excellency telling me that the Duc d'Orléans had accorded her his protection, so that I could have instructed the Republic, but up to now you have given me no such order. I think I shall risk nothing in rendering her as a private person all the little services at my command. For that it suffices that she is French and the sister of the Cardinal de la Trémoïlle. But as the King's *chargé-d'affaires* I shall be careful not to take the least step in her favour without an express order from Your Excellency.¹

Thus the Princess des Ursins, former dictatress of Spain, who had held her own against all the crowned heads of Europe, was now protected by the *chargé d'affaires* to the little Republic of Genoa only because she was sister to the insignificant Abbé she had herself raised to the dignity of cardinal.

To its honour, however, be it recorded that the Genoese Republic was the first state which gave refuge to the outcast, and this even before the Regent's protection was made known. On 19 November Coutlet announced her arrival:

She is lodged at Sestri in the house of Monsieur Ambrogio Imperiali, Genoese gentleman. She has hired one in the town where it is said she will pass the winter. It appears that the nobility of this country will not trouble her much on account of the treatment of Altesse which she pretends to exact. I have heard that Monsieur Alexandrino Grimaldi, former envoy of the Republic to Rome, went some days ago to Sestri to offer a kind of compliment to her and tell her of the regret of his superiors not to be able, under the present circumstances, to have the same attentions for her as in the past, nor give her, at least in public, all the marks of distinction she merits, but that she was mistress to remain in their states as long and in what manner she thought fit, assuring her that she would certainly be disturbed by no one.²

Finally the Regent deigned to accord her somewhat grudgingly his protection. On 19 November the Maréchal d'Huxelles wrote to Coutlet: "You can make known, should occasion arise during the sojourn of the Princess des Ursins in Genoa, that Monsieur le Duc d'Orléans will not disapprove the marks of attention which the Republic or private persons wish to show her, and for your own part

¹ Trémoïlle, vi. 229; letter of 5 Nov. 1715.
² Ibid., vi. 330; letter of 19 Nov. 1715.

will conduct yourself in such a way as to deserve her praise."[1]

This is the last notice we have of her in this eventful year. We will leave her to rest in Genoa, tranquil at least that she will not have to spend the rest of her life on the high-roads, and give a last glance at the Court from which she had been expelled.

[1] Trémoïlle, vi. 330; letter of 19 Nov. 1715.

CHAPTER XXVIII

LEX TALIONIS (1715-21)

WHAT was happening in Madrid under the reign of the new Queen? Precisely what happened under that of the first. Before the bridal-night was over the lamentable puppet whose crown she shared had collapsed at her feet, ready to sign away such honour and dignity as he had at a word or sign from her "who made his only joy," as she on her side was ready in her ignorance and arrogance to sign away the welfare of the country at a word from Alberoni.

"The Court is always the same," jeered one officer to another, " except that every morning there is a masquerade in which Orry is disguised as a cardinal and the Princess des Ursins as an abbé! "[1]

In the hands of Alberoni everything was practically left. All the Queen's energies were directed to gaining entire mastery over her feeble husband, and to this she sacrificed her own comfort and even her formidable will. She allowed herself to be his toy. At all hours that his morbid sensuality desired her she was at hand to satisfy it. Night and day they were never apart. She sacrificed her indolence and lazy habits. She, who detested to rise before midday and never dined before five nor slept till midnight, now rose betimes to accompany him to the chase, dined with him at two and went to bed at half-past ten. Her complacence bid fair to ruin the health of both, and to such an extent did Philippe abuse it that his physician warned him it was at the risk of his life—whereupon he was immediately dismissed by the Queen.

But if towards her husband she curbed her will for her own interest, towards everyone else she remained hard and cruel, haughty and despotic, violent and unjust. Her people trembled in serving her, the nobles were treated like servants, and her servants like dogs. Her husband adored her as the female necessary to his well-being, but everyone else, and especially the Spaniards, soon learnt

[1] Trémoïlle, vi. 326 ; letter of Saint-Aignan to Torcy of 6 Aug. 1715.

to detest her and regret their *Savoyarde*. As for the little Prince of the Asturias, so healthy and promising under the Princess's guidance, he became sickly, morose and of an incredible timidity, so completely changed and in so short a time that the Spanish accused her of having poisoned him.

Everyone whom Philippe seemed to like or esteem she chased from the country as she had chased the Princess and Orry, even his confessor the Père Robinet. Only one adviser she allowed him—Alberoni—who occupied the same place under her as the Princess under the first Queen. He was her chief favourite, counsellor and friend, for to him she owed her crown and, if the plans he unfolded to her should succeed, would owe him one day that of an empress. Versailles, become aware what these ambitions were, hinted the danger of Italian influence and the advisability of his dismissal, but in a furious outburst of temper she declared to the ambassador that she would keep him in spite of everybody.

As before the advent of the Princess under Louville's influence Spain ran the risk of becoming a mere province of France, so now under Elisabeth Farnese and Alberoni it was in the hands of a clique of Italians, and the Spaniards complained bitterly that since Philippe's accession they had always been the slaves of foreigners.

As for Alberoni himself, his arrogance and insolence passed all bounds. He knew himself omnipotent and gave Versailles to understand by veiled hints and menaces that he was a force to be reckoned with. Louis at first tried to repress his insolence with a high hand and ordered Saint-Aignan to hint that the same punishment might overtake him which he had meted out to others. But very soon his power had perforce to be recognised and flattery succeeded to threats. The pension he already received from France was increased, but it was not enough. Nothing would satisfy him but the cardinal's hat.

Nominally Giudice was Prime Minister but actually he was a nullity. It was Alberoni who directed everything, and Giudice played the Porto-Carrero to his Princess des Ursins. The ambassadors addressed themselves not to him, but to the Abbé. The Queen treated him with open contempt. At the Despacho he sat silent, or if he dared open his lips it was to be flatly contradicted by Alberoni. It did not take him long to realise that the Abbé coveted his post, and he protested to Louis against all the humiliations he had daily to support. But Versailles was powerless to protect him against the Parmesan fury and her favourite.

His fall was imminent. One day without any warning he received a curt note from Grimaldo announcing that the Duke of Popoli had been appointed governor of the princes in his place. Broken in health and spirits he had no force to struggle, and sent in his resignation as Grand Inquisitor, which was accepted without a word. He still continued, however, to assist at the Despacho, but presently another note forbade even this, and shortly after he received the order, signed by Philippe, to quit Spain, without a word of explanation, and, as with Orry, permission to take leave was refused him. If really he had taken an active share in the Princess's expulsion the *lex talionis* had been swift in overtaking him.

At his dismissal Alberoni immediately stepped into his place as Prime Minister, and in August of the same year received the grandeeship and the cardinal's hat, although the Pope declared that in giving it he prostituted his dignity. Nothing now stood between him and the realisation of his ambitions, personal and patriotic. To restore Spain to her former greatness by reconquering all that Philippe had signed away at the Peace of Utrecht, make an alliance with the Turks against the Emperor, gain Holland by concessions to remain neutral, cripple England by arming the Pretender to a fresh attack on the Crown, stir up civil war in France, deprive the Duc d'Orléans of the Regency and set Philippe in his place, and finally hand over the whole of Europe thus conquered to the Duke of Parma with himself for Prime Minister — such were his immeasurable ambitions. It must be owned they were grandiose, and had he had the force or good fortune to carry them out, no doubt his name would have been handed down to posterity as one of the greatest statesmen the world has ever seen. But the country he dominated had neither the means nor the energies to accomplish such vast designs and the only result was to set Europe again ablaze with war and unite all the Powers against Spain.

He began his projects by attacking Sardinia, which the treaty of peace had assigned to Austria, and invaded Sicily, which had been finally ceded to the Duke of Savoy, which breach of faith resulted in the dishonouring of Philippe's name, and the forming of a new alliance against him, this time with the addition of France—a formidable coalition. Immediately he was abandoned by the Turks, Holland joined the Quadruple Alliance, the English sent their fleet which destroyed a Spanish squadron off Syracuse, the Pretender was driven by a tempest from the coast of England, Cellamare's conspiracy against the Regent was discovered, and an army sent by the Duc d'Orléans successfully invaded Spain. Philippe, conquered and humiliated, was reduced to implore peace, which was granted only on condition of the immediate dismissal of Alberoni.

In 1719 the vulgar clever adventurer, who had opened himself a path to fortune by an abominable intrigue, was in his turn disgraced and expelled, and the woman to whom he had given her crown turned her back on him cruelly and pitilessly, refusing to see him or even to break the seal of the letter he wrote imploring her protection. Like the Princess, he found all the frontiers of Europe shut to him, and step by step followed the same dolorous path to which he had condemned her, with this difference that, while she had retained her dignity and the esteem of all who knew her, he, given up to his vices, ended his days in enforced retirement, condemned by the ecclesiastical tribunal in Rome for the scandals of his private life.

And since we have advanced so far beyond the chronological sequence of events, before returning to the admirable heroine of these pages, we will give a last glance at the brutal, implacable woman, dubbed by Carlyle the she-dragon or termagant of Europe, who by her ignorance and arrogance had made possible these acts which had armed all Europe against the miserable weakling of whom she was at once the master and the slave.

In 1721 Saint-Simon, sent as ambassador to the Court of Madrid, was himself witness to the terrible fate she had prepared herself, fettered eternally to an unclean lunatic whose life was passed between outbursts of violent passion and fits of sordid melancholy.

Of Philippe at this date he gives the following hideous portrait:

> The first glance I had of the King of Spain amazed me so much that I had to use all efforts to recover myself. . . . He was very bent and shrunk, his chin protruded far beyond his

chest, his feet quite straight and overlapping each other as he walked, though he walked rapidly, and his knees more than twelve inches apart. What he said was well said, but his words dragged so and his expression was so foolish that I was confounded.

To such a monkey-like being at the age of thirty-eight had degenerated the grandson of the handsome Louis XIV.

Of the Queen he gives a more favourable portrait, but says that he was "terrified by her face, so marked, cut and excessively disfigured was it by the smallpox."[1]

And here is the Dantesque picture he gives of their married life:

The Queen and Alberoni . . . shut the King up between them and rendered him inaccessible to all the rest of nature. Alberoni expelled, the Queen, tired of having been so long a prisoner, victim of her own ambitions and those of Alberoni, tried many times to free herself from her slavery without ever being able to succeed. The King's habits were too deeply rooted . . . and soon she despaired of loosening her fetters. Here is their life in all places, at all times, and in all seasons—

They had but one and the same apartment and one bed—and in fevers, sickness, even in childbirth, never a single night apart—and the bedroom was very small.

He goes on to describe their day, but at too much length to quote. Mass, dinner, audiences, work with the ministers, hunting, driving, walking, supper, always together, even at their prayers, and he ends his description of this terrible solitude *à deux* with the following words: "Finally, their Catholic Majesties had but one wardrobe and their two *chaises-percées* were side by side in all their palaces."[2]

To finish with these crowned sovereigns, both in their different ways among the basest of humanity, here is the description of the last years of Philippe V.:

Without any apparent illness he was sometimes six months without leaving his bed, without shaving, cutting his nails or changing his linen. When his shirt rotted to pieces he would put on only what the Queen brought him, fearing, he said, to be poisoned in any other. He ate and slept at any hour that the fancy took him, sometimes going to bed at ten in the morning and rising at night. He let his toe-nails grow so long and sharp

[1] Saint-Simon, ed. Delloye, xxxv. 110. The later volumes of the *Mémoires* have not yet been published in the edition of De Bois lisle hitherto cited.
[2] Ibid., xxxvi. 273, etc.

that they tore his flesh at night, and seeing these wounds he declared that assassins had wounded him in his sleep, at other times that scorpions were all round him stinging him. Sometimes he thought himself to be dead and asked why he was not buried. He would keep a gloomy silence for several days and often emerged from it in furious passions, when he would strike and scratch the Queen, his confessor, and doctor, and all within his reach, biting his own arms, with frightful shrieks. Asked what was the matter: "Nothing," he would say, and a moment after would sing or fall again into his reverie. Sometimes he would rise in the night and want to go out in his shirt with bare feet. The Queen would run to prevent him, and he would strike her so hard that she was often bruised. After passing whole months in bed in the most horrible filth he would remain for months without going to bed at all, sleeping in an arm-chair, so that his legs were swelled with always hanging down.[1]

As he grew older, what, since he was a king, was called his "ardent temperament," and in ordinary mortals would be diagnosed as satyriasis, calmed down, and the Queen, finding that her hold over him was gone, did not hesitate to poison him with aphrodisiacs, to which the increase of insanity of his later years is probably due.

It is with relief that we turn from these sinister beings to the healthier atmosphere of their victim in the beautiful Italian retreat she has chosen.

[1] Duclos, *Mémoires secrètes*, 1808, ii. 274.

CHAPTER XXIX

"I HAVE FOUGHT A GOOD FIGHT, I HAVE FINISHED MY COURSE" (1716-22)

WE left the Princess in Genoa, protected if not welcomed by the Republic, safe, for the moment at least, from the vengeance of her persecutors, so contented with the peace she had conquered with so much suffering that all her worldly interests and vanities — if indeed she had ever abandoned them — returned, and, reaching the ears of Madame de Maintenon in her conventual retreat of Saint-Cyr, excited her reprobation. "Let us confess," she wrote to Villeroy at the beginning of the year 1716, "after having entirely fulfilled our duties towards the Princess des Ursins, that she is too frivolous for her position and her age."[1] A condemnation which we read with pleasure since it shows that she was neither moping nor melancholy.

On 21 April of this year Coutlet, French *chargé-d'affaires*, wrote to the Maréchal d'Huxelles:

It seems that the Princess des Ursins is resolved to fix her residence here, at least for some considerable time. She has just hired a house larger and more convenient than the one she occupied. Some ladies of the country have begun to visit her, and if she will relax her exactions as to ceremony she will receive all sorts of politeness and marks of attention from the nobility.[2]

And four months later:

Madame des Ursins is still here in perfect health. She is living at present in a magnificent palace where it seems she is sufficiently happy. She has furnished it anew and arranged it so as to make one think she has no wish to leave for some time, although many are of opinion that she flatters herself still that she will return one day to Spain.[3]

Undoubtedly she did so flatter herself. The few documents which exist of these years in Genoa show clearly enough why she remained within relatively easy distance

---
[1] Geffroy, *Madame de Maintenon*, ii. 380; letter of 5 Jan. 1716.
[2] Trémoïlle, vi. 330; letter of 21 April, 1716.
[3] Ibid., vi. 331; letter of 18 Aug. 1716.

of Madrid, ready to embark when the moment arrived on the Royal galley sent for her by a repentant King. During the whole of this year she was in frequent correspondence with the Secretary of State Grimaldo, ostensibly about the payment of her pension, but everyone in Madrid, reading between the lines, affirmed that she was working for a reconciliation with the Queen.[1] It seems that her astonishing optimism stirred her not only to visions of a return to Madrid but to fresh power, visions of puppets again, pliant and placid, of Philippe dominated afresh and even the brutal Parmesan tamed by judicious flattery.

Nothing in her character gives the right to suppose that she had the petty vice of enjoying the downfall of her enemies as Saint-Simon asserts, but if so, this was also allowed her. On 6 April of the following year—1717— Coutlet wrote to d'Huxelles:

It seems that we shall soon have here the Cardinal del Giudice, whose house has been prepared for some time. The Princess des Ursins, hearing that various people were curious to know how she would act towards him, and if they would have any relations with each other, she judged it advisable to declare beforehand that she would not see him, being unsuitable both for him and her in their present position to have any relation with each other, above all in a country like this where people would not fail to interpret badly any reciprocal politeness between them.[2]

Thus when on his arrival in his native city, furious and humiliated, the Cardinal sent to ask her permission to visit her, hoping for her sympathy against their mutual enemy, she refused.

In this decision, with the possibility growing every day more certain of a reconciliation with Spain, she acted wisely, for Giudice was far from showing the same moderation and reserve as herself, and his conversation consisted of nothing but violent abuse of Philippe, the Queen and the whole Court of Spain and its ministers. Philippe he accused of robbing the gold of the country for the benefit of Parma and Alberoni of selling State secrets to Austria.

A great difference is observable both of judgment and courtesy between the Cardinal and the Princess des Ursins [Coutlet

[1] Baudrillart, ii. 247; letter from Saint-Aignan to the Regent of 25 Nov. 1716.
[2] Trémoïlle, vi. 331; letter of 6 April, 1717.

wrote to d'Huxelles on 15 June]. She has as little reason as he to speak well of the Court of Spain, yet no one has ever heard her speak otherwise than well of it, and she is on the contrary as careful to praise their Catholic Majesties as if she were in the greatest favour with them. It is true, however, that the King of Spain, who still preserves his esteem for her, writes to her from time to time, but very secretly and without the Queen's knowledge.[1]

During the two months that the Cardinal remained in Genoa she maintained her resolution, though he did his utmost to be received by her, and he had to leave for Rome without having seen her. There he continued to attack and accuse the Court of Spain, and ended by throwing himself completely on the side of Austria. The Emperor named him *chargé-d'affaires* to the Pope, but dismissed him after a few months, and so ended ignominiously the career of the man who, having held the highest posts civil and ecclesiastic and enjoyed the favour and friendship of Louis XIV., was ruined like the Princess herself by the adventurer Alberoni.

It is pleasant to think that the tranquillity of these last years in Genoa, so different from the storm and stress of her political life, was at least not distasteful to her. She kept up a correspondence with Madame de Maintenon, who wrote to Villeroy at the beginning of this year (1717) that she seemed happy enough in her retreat,[2] and she herself confirms this in a letter to her old friend, the Maréchal de Tessé: "I ask nothing but tranquillity of mind," she wrote, "and to repose myself from the fatigues I had when I dwelt in courts. Thank God I conform myself to my state, and if the sea air were not so detestable for my eyes I should find myself passing a happy life" (*une vie douce*). An assertion which, however, she qualifies by adding: "as much as is possible when one is far from one's relations and those one loves."[3]

It could hardly be the Cardinal her unworthy brother, nor even the Duc de Noirmoutier, for whom she was pining, and the relations she most loved and appreciated were those with the Court of Spain.

To this hope of a return to favour she was prepared to sacrifice not only her eyes, but even the dignity she had

[1] Trémoïlle, vi. 332; letter of 15 June, 1717.
[2] Geffroy, *Madame de Maintenon*, ii. 387; letter of 20 Feb. 1717.
[3] Trémoïlle, vi. 336; letter of 24 Nov. 1717.

"I HAVE FINISHED MY COURSE" 411

preserved so admirably up to now, and for the first time we have to record her guilty of an act unworthy of her, though at the same time perfectly comprehensible to one who had not yet renounced the world. In July of this year Alberoni, at the zenith of his power, received the cardinal's hat, and she seized the occasion to pay court to and flatter the man who had so cruelly betrayed her.

"Madame des Ursins," Coutlet wrote, announcing the event to d'Huxelles, "always attentive to what might give pleasure to the King and Queen of Spain, has sent her confessor to congratulate the Marquis de Saint-Philippe" (San Phélipe, now Minister to the Genoese Republic) " on this promotion, saying that she would have written herself to express her pleasure to their Catholic Majesties if she had dared." And he adds pertinently: " By her behaviour it would seem that she still retains some hope of being one day able to return to Madrid." [1]

She had other reasons for supposing the Court of Madrid to be veering round in her direction, for at this time both Lanti and Chalais received permission to return to Spain, the latter being begged to accept employment in the army. On 20 August Dangeau notes in his *Diary*: " The Prince of Cellamare " (now Spanish Ambassador at Versailles) " took to the Prince de Chalais a letter from the Cardinal Alberoni telling him that the King and Queen of Spain desire his return, and that he should go straight to Barcelona, where he will receive orders of what he has to do. It seems that they wish to make use of him in the projected expedition " [2] (the expedition against Sardinia, Alberoni's first move in his project of reconquering Philippe's lost Italian territory).

And a month later: " Monsieur le Prince de Chalais, whom the King of Spain has recalled, had orders to go straight to Barcelona, where he would receive instructions as to what he would have to do. The Cardinal Alberoni has sent him word that he has only to come straight to Madrid where he will be well received by their Catholic Majesties and that he would have reason to be content." [3]

The Princess, however, was not so fortunate as her nephews, and the months rolled by without the hoped-for invitation. The cataract in her eyes grew worse, but she

[1] Trémoïlle, vi. 335; letter of 20 July, 1717.
[2] Dangeau, xvii. 150.   [3] Ibid., xvii. 164.

still lingered in spite of the fatal salt air. She was seventy-six years old and with this exception still in good health and with all her faculties of body and mind intact. All her energies, aspirations and ambitions were as keen as ever, and these energies she was restless to utilise. Impatient at her inactivity, probably bored at the restricted society of the little republic, like a racehorse all her nerves were quivering to be up and doing, and there is little doubt that, had she at this time been received at the Court of Madrid, she would have taken an active share in the mesh of intrigues woven by Alberoni.

After a long silence Orry had resumed his correspondence with her, and in reply to one of his letters she wrote with evident irritability: " As no one can enjoy complete happiness, mine is very much obstructed by anxiety about my sight obscured by clouds, which the salt sea-air has very much increased. Except for that I should be well enough in this town, where I seem forced to remain, not knowing what to do." [1]

And three weeks later to Tessé: " This detestable sea clouds my sight, which causes me anxiety. It will oblige me to go in the spring to a casino four or five miles distant to find softer air, breathing nothing in this place but one piercing and salt which kills me." [2]

It is evident that her long suspense was getting on her nerves.

Ten days later it was partially rewarded, and her hopes received fresh stimulus. The King of Spain sent his minister San Phélipe in ambassadorial pomp publicly to recognise her in his name, certain preliminary to the invitation to return.

I defy you to have reached such a state of indifference [she wrote rapturously to Tessé, all her optimism bubbling up in pleasurable anticipation] as not to share my joy at the signs of the return of the King of Spain's kindness for which I have always hoped. This very happy moment has arrived. His Majesty wished that they should be made public by ordering his envoy, the Marquis de Saint-Philippe, to come in his name to assure me that he honours me with the continuation of his esteem and Royal protection. This is not all. Monsieur de Saint-Philippe has given me a letter from the Cardinal Alberoni, very polite and gracious, in which His Eminence informs me

[1] Trémoïlle, vi. 336 ; letter of 25 Jan. 1718.
[2] Ibid., vi. 337 ; letter of 15 Feb. 1718.

"I HAVE FINISHED MY COURSE" 413

that he has written to the Cardinal Acquaviva at His Catholic Majesty's order to explain to him his favourable intentions concerning me, of which, if I go to Rome, he desires that no one shall be ignorant. You will readily judge, knowing my very respectful and faithful attachment which nothing is capable of diminishing, to what point I am sensible of all his goodness.[1]

That the French Court was well aware of this sudden turn in her favour the following extract from a letter from Madame to her sister in Bavaria proves—written on 18 September of this year: " Many people think that Alberoni poisoned his benefactor the poor Duc de Vendôme in order to please Madame des Ursins whom later he caused to be expelled. . . . Now he has caused this wicked old hag (*cette méchante vieille sorcière*) to be reinstated in favour at the Court of Madrid." [2]

And again three days after the discovery of Cellamare's conspiracy, apparently attributing to her some complicity in the plot: " This incarnate devil the Princess des Ursins will hunt my poor son to his death, and the sole motive of her hatred is that he found her too old to wish to be her lover." [3]

What was the reason of this sudden change of attitude towards her who had been so cruelly dismissed three years before, a change emanating obviously not from the half-demented King, but from Alberoni himself? Precisely the same which made him recall and offer employment in the army to her exiled nephew. The die was cast in Spain, and a new war of larger extent was on the eve of being declared, a war in which France itself was to be included in the enemy. Cellamare was already in receipt of his instructions for the plot by which the Duc d'Orléans was to be kidnapped and replaced in the Regency by Philippe, with the tempting probability of the throne of France in the background, for Alberoni would certainly not have hesitated, had it succeeded, in making away with the little King, and according to his calculations the Princess would have been only too eager to have her share in these ambitious prospects.

[1] Trémoïlle, vi. 337; letter of 26 April, 1718.
[2] Brunet, *Nouvelles Lettres de la Duchesse d'Orléans*, p. 174; letter of 18 Sept. 1718.
[3] Ibid., p. 184; letter of 11 Dec. 1718.

And so perhaps she would have been had matters continued to go as favourably for Spain as the first campaign in Italy. But Fate ruled otherwise. On 9 December Cellamare's plot was discovered, and thenceforth it was open rupture between the two countries and a new alliance was formed between England, Holland, France and Italy. At the very moment of realising her dearest wish the Princess was put in the awkward position of having to throw in her lot with Spain or declare herself openly on the side of the Regent.

It must be owned that the situation was difficult to a woman of her ambition, and exceedingly disappointing after three years of effort and hope. In France she had few friends, and no prospect of filling any sort of rôle, while in Spain, with Alberoni as a friend, she might well enjoy another epoch of power. However, her political acumen came to the rescue and forced her to recognise that Alberoni's projects were bound by their very extravagance to fail, and that Spain would have no chance against a coalition composed of England, France, Italy and Holland. It did not take her very long, therefore, to decide to throw in her lot with France and the Quadruple Alliance.

On 7 February, 1719, Coutlet wrote to the Abbé Dubois, now Minister of Foreign Affairs:

> The Princess des Ursins appears since the declaration of war much less zealous for the advantage of the King of Spain. The ministers of His Catholic Majesty have not yet ceased to go from time to time to her house where they often meet by chance the envoy of England, but it is said that she receives them rather out of politeness than inclination, having announced that she is too good a patriot and incapable of cutting herself off from her country and His Royal Highness [the Regent]. . . . The Prince de Chalais her nephew, who is at present in Rome, has quitted the service of Spain.[1]

And a month later:

"The Prince de Chalais arrived here the day before yesterday. He is lodging with the Princess des Ursins, who it is said intends to keep him for some time, not being at all of opinion that he should fight against his country."[2]

To Dubois, in high favour after his success in allying

---

[1] Trémoïlle, vi. 339; letter of 7 Feb. 1719.
[2] Ibid., vi. 339; letter of 7 March, 1719.

England to France, she now paid her court and seized the occasion of a small commission from her brother the Cardinal to write him flattering compliments:

"I have thought, this occasion presenting itself, that you would permit me to assure you that I render all due justice to your merit, which it would be impossible to reward too highly after the great service you have rendered the State." [1]

So strongly indeed was she assured of the peril of Spain that she hesitated no longer to throw herself completely on the opposite side, going so far as to offer services which can be qualified only as espionage.

Thus a certain Chavigny, Dubois' secret envoy to the Court of Hanover, being in Genoa, she went out of her way to offer him civilities and compliments, to such a point indeed as to excite his suspicions. She gave him to understand that she was in constant communication with the Court of Madrid, and knew all that went on there, that a Spanish Jesuit of her acquaintance in Genoa had been chosen as the Queen's confessor, and that through him she would have much influence over her. In a word she offered her services to His Royal Highness the Regent, "having always, as she said, retained the zeal she owes to France and him, however inexorable he has been towards her." [2]

In April of this year Madame de Maintenon died, but we have no record of how she was affected by it, the relations between the two being of the coldest.[3] Dangeau notes in his *Diary* on 15 April: "Madame de Maintenon died at Saint-Cyr this evening after a prolonged fever which lasted a month. She was eighty-three years old." To which brief notice Saint-Simon adds with his usual acrimony where she is concerned: "This fatal woman did great evil to France and, having nothing more important to govern than a private house, exercised at Saint-Cyr all her bitter and narrow humour. Her death was a great relief there, and outside was scarcely remarked." [4]

[1] Trémoïlle, vi. 340 ; letter of 24 Sept. 1719.
[2] Ibid., vi. 340 ; letters from Chavigny to Dubois of 3 Oct. and 26 Dec. 1719.
[3] On 8 January, 1717, Madame de Maintenon wrote to her niece Madame de Caylus: "I have received a letter from Madame des Ursins for the New Year. Our relations are completely ended" (Haussonville, *Souvenirs de Madame de Maintenon*, iii. 192).
[4] Dangeau, xviii. 32.

Students of the memoirs and letters of the epoch will appreciate this perversion of facts as it merits. Madame de Maintenon, loyal, disinterested and charitable, so far from having been fatal to France had a more beneficial effect both on Court and country than any other woman of her time. The aid and sympathy she gave to the poor were immense, half her income being expended in helping those in need, but she hid her bounty from all except her friends of Saint-Cyr. Her influence over Louis XIV. was for good and the relative decency of the Court after he installed her there was due entirely to her. Her death, so far from being regarded as a relief, was the cause of the most intense and heartfelt grief to her friends and protégés, by all of whom without exception she was adored as a saint. The popular ideas concerning her are due chiefly to the bitter abuse and false charges of Saint-Simon, based only on his sycophantic prejudice in favour of Philippe d'Orléans, who as prince of the blood detested her for her co-operation with Louis in his legitimation of the children of Madame de Montespan.

To return to the Princess.

The failure of her hopes of a return to power in Madrid rendered further stay in Genoa useless and she decided to return to Rome, but, notwithstanding Saint-Simon's repeated assertions of her " prodigious opulence," it appears that she had not even sufficient money for the expenses of the move nor to keep her palace in the Piazza Navone, since, in May of this year, she hired that of the Cardinal Dada. Her brother the Cardinal, who had looked forward with so much misgiving to her presence in Rome, was spared such disagreeables as he feared, for at the beginning of the following year he died, leaving her and the Duc de Noirmoutier heirs of all he possessed, but since that consisted entirely of debts neither were the richer by their inheritance.

This spendthrift, who but for his sister would probably have remained a mere abbé all his life, had been endowed with the archbishopric of Cambrai and the two rich abbeys of Saint-Amand and Saint-Etienne-de-Caen, besides other benefices, yet all the wealth he drew from them did not suffice for the extravagant pomp he thought necessary to his dignity as a prince of the Church.

The Cardinal de Rohan-Chabot, commissioned by Dubois

to look into his affairs, wrote later: "He was personally an honest man but of infinite weakness and terrible disorder. His valets were his masters. He borrowed money of the Pope, who seemed to like him but esteemed him very little."[1]

The Princess did not leave Genoa till August, six months after his death, it would seem because she lacked the necessary money, since in April we find her, together with her brother the Duc de Noirmoutier, selling to the Regent the Isle of Noirmoutier on the coast of Brittany, from which he took his title, for the sum of a million francs.

On 26 April, 1720, Dangeau notes:

> The Princess des Ursins, who is in Genoa, has sold to Monsieur le Duc d'Orléans the Isle of Noirmoutier, for which he gives a million, and of this million the Duc de Noirmoutier her brother will receive one hundred thousand crowns which she owed him and one hundred and fifty thousand francs for the moors and fens which were his portion. The five hundred and fifty thousand francs which remain will be sent to Madame des Ursins, who is leaving Genoa because the air there is very unhealthy and she will go to Rome.[2]

According to Saint-Simon she left Genoa for no other reason than that she was tired of it.

> Finally she grew bored (*l'ennui la gagna*) [he writes], perhaps disappointed not to be sufficiently considered. She could not live without meddling with affairs, and how can that be done in Genoa when one is a woman and superannuated? She turned therefore all her thoughts to Rome, sounded the Court, revived what remained of her old friendships, linked on again to those which were possible, felt the ground everywhere, and above all took care to assure herself of the treatment she would receive from those connected with France and Spain. Thus she left Genoa and returned to her nest.[3]

Of her journey from Genoa to Rome we have no record. We know only that it took place in August and that she paused at the Villa of Bagnaia near Viterbo belonging to her nephew the Duke of Lanti, which we remember for its association with her sister the Duchess Angélique. Here she intended to remain till the great heats were passed and the danger of Roman fever over.

On 14 September one of Dubois' correspondents in Rome, the Cardinal Gualtiero, sent him word of her arrival:

[1] Trémoïlle, vi. 346; letter of 31 July, 1721.
[2] Dangeau, xviii. 274.   [3] Saint-Simon, xxvi. 262.

"The Princess des Ursins has arrived at Bagnaia, forty miles distant from here. She is lodged in a country-house of the Duke of Lanti her nephew and will remain there till the end of November, at which date all fear of the air for returning to Rome ceases." [1]

In January of the following year (1721) she sold her palace in the Piazza Navone, as we learn from the following letter from the French consul in Rome written to Dubois: "The rumour goes that the palace formerly Orsini, which belonged to the Princess of that name, has been sold for ninety-two thousand Roman crowns to a certain Sieur Angelini of Parma, who having gained immense sums at Law's Bank and found the means to pass it out of the kingdom, is come to settle in this city." [2]

The end of our history is approaching and the documents are well-nigh exhausted. On 4 November we have a final letter to her old friend the Duchesse de Noailles which betrays a certain sadness. "I think that if I returned to France," she wrote, "I should come back as from another world and scarcely anyone but you would recognise me." [3]

But even now the amazing vitality which had made her force reasserted itself. Far from abandoning herself to futile regrets and sighing over her vanished greatness she threw herself with all her energy into the new life and interests which awaited her in Rome.

James Stuart, known as the Old Pretender, recently married to the granddaughter of Sobieski, King of Poland, had been invited by the Pope Clement XI., in whose eyes he was always legitimate King of England, to take up his residence in Rome. As he had no money the Pope had presented him with a villa at Albano and a palace in the city, as well as a detachment of his own guards to lend a semblance of royalty to his miniature Court. He had known the Princess at Saint-Germain during the lifetime of his father, and to him and his young wife she now attached herself and soon gained over them the same ascendancy as over the King and Queen of Spain—two fresh puppets to replace the old. [4]

[1] Trémoïlle, vi. 345; letter of 14 Sept. 1720.
[2] Ibid., vi. 346; letter of 21 Jan. 1721.
[3] Ibid., vi. 350; letter of 4 Nov. 1721.
[4] The Pretender retired to Rome as James III. 1718; married Marie-Clementine Sobieska in Rome, 3 Sept. 1719.

"I HAVE FINISHED MY COURSE" 419

Saint-Simon, supremely scornful of what he calls "this deplorable little Court," thus describes her new friendship:

It was not long before she attached herself to the King and Queen of England, nor attached herself long before she governed them, and soon publicly. A sad resource. But, however, it was the semblance of a Court and a little suggestion of affairs to one who could not do without. She ended her life thus in great health of body and mind and in prodigious opulence, which was not without its use at this deplorable little Court. For the rest, moderately considered in Rome, of no sort of importance, deserted by those whose interests were in Spain, visited little by the French, but without suffering anything on the part of the Regent, well paid by France and Spain, always occupied with the world, with what she had been and was no longer, but without pettiness, with courage and grandeur. The loss in January 1720 of the Cardinal de la Trémoïlle, though without friendship on either side, left a void. She survived him three years, preserved her health, strength and intelligence up to her death, and was carried off at over eighty by a very short illness in Rome, the 5th of December, 1722. She had the pleasure to see Madame de Maintenon forgotten and reduced to nothing at Saint-Cyr and to survive her, and the joy to see arrive in Rome one after the other her two enemies, as completely disgraced as herself—of whom one precipitated from such a height—the Cardinals Giudice and Alberoni—and to enjoy the perfect negligence, not to say contempt, in which both were fallen. Her death, which some years before would have resounded all over Europe, made not the slightest sensation. The little Court of England regretted her, as well as some private friends, of whom I was one, and did not conceal it, although not in relations with her on account of the Duc d'Orléans. For the rest no one seemed to perceive that she had disappeared. Nevertheless she was a person so extraordinary during the course of her long life, and she had figured everywhere with so much importance and singularity, her intelligence, courage, energy and resources were so rare, finally her reign was so absolute and public in Spain, her character so sustained and unique, that her life merits to be written and would take a place among the most curious pieces of the history of the time in which she lived.[1]

In the short but exhaustive biography he wrote of her in his *Duchés verifiés sans pairie*, published in de Boislisle's edition of his works, he writes:

In Rome she ended her days in a state very opulent and honourable, even much considered, but very much below the brilliance of her earlier years and which had no sort of resemblance to her least days in Spain. But as she had to govern

[1] Saint-Simon, xxvi. 262, etc.

somewhere and somebody she attached herself to the King of England and to the Queen his wife, who had taken refuge in Rome, and became all-powerful at their Court. This did not make much noise in the world nor even in Rome, where people wondered how, after having reigned so long and absolutely in Spain, she could decide to belittle herself rather than remain quiet. Her faithful d'Aubigny, enriched in Spain and well established in France, did not follow her in her retirement, where she finally died at an age extremely advanced, but intact in body, mind, humour and graces, regretted by a very small number of people, and the death of the woman who had for so long made such a prodigious figure and filled Europe with her name and authority was scarcely remarked anywhere.[1]

And finally in his latest *Mémoires*:

At last the celebrated Princess des Ursins died in Rome, where she had finally retired and been settled for more than six years [eighteen months only], liking better to govern the little Court of England than not to govern at all. She was eighty-five [she was only eighty], still fresh and upright, with grace and charm and perfect health up to the short illness of which she died, her mind and intelligence as at fifty, and very honoured in Rome.[2]

On 1 December, 1722, a journal in Rome published the following notice:

"The Princess des Ursins has been for three days in bed with the nephritic pains which attack her from time to time. The Princess Sobieska visited her yesterday evening. This evening she is very depressed."

And four days later:

"Madame des Ursins died yesterday."[3]

Our final notice is from the pen of the Abbé, afterwards Cardinal de Tencin, at that time French *chargé-d'affaires* in Rome:

Madame la Princesse des Ursins is dead. She leaves Monsieur de Noirmoutier heir of her furniture, her jewels, and all which she possesses outside Italy. She gives to Monsieur le Duc de Lanti her rights and actions against the House of Orsini. She leaves several private legacies, among them to the Chevalier de Saint-George [the Pretender] a gold snuff-box encrusted with diamonds, and to the Princess his wife a toilet-set of gilt enamel which belonged to the late Queen of Spain.[4]

I cannot do better than close this history with the words

[1] Saint-Simon, v. 514. [2] Ibid., ed. Delloye, xxxviii. 111.
[3] Trémoïlle, vi. 150. [4] Ibid., vi. 351.

"I HAVE FINISHED MY COURSE"

of the Marquis de Courcy from the appreciative notice he gives of her in his work *L'Espagne après la Paix d'Utrecht*:

The destiny of the Princess des Ursins was strange and grand in the varied adventures which led her through the dolorous valleys of exile and abandonment to the summits of the highest position possible to one whose head is uncircled by a crown—grand in the vastness of the horizon where for so long she played the leading part and the predominating influence she exercised there, grand in the confidence with which she was honoured by the greatest personages of her time, grand also in the immensity of the services she rendered to France and Spain, in the clamour excited by her first disgrace, the enthusiasm which greeted her return, grand finally in the very excess of the faults of her authoritative and imperious nature, in the valiant resignation she opposed to the brutal strokes of fortune and in the dignity of her last exile.[1]

[1] Courcy, *L'Espagne après la Paix d'Utrecht*, p. 22.

THE END

BIBLIOGRAPHY

BAUDRILLART, A., *Philippe V. et la Cour de France.* Paris, 1890–1901. 4 vols.

BERWICK, Duke of, *Mémoires.* Paris, 1820.

BOSSANGE, *Lettres inédites de Madame de Maintenon et la Princesse des Ursins.* Paris, 1826. 4 vols.

BOURGEOIS, E., *Alberoni, Madame des Ursins et la Reine Elisabeth Farnese.* Paris, 1891.

BOURGEOIS, E., *Lettres intimes de J. M. Alberoni au Comte I. Rocca.* Paris, 1893.

COLLIN, *Lettres de Madame de Maintenon.* Paris, 1806. 6 vols.

COLLIN, *Lettres inédites de la Princesse des Ursins au Maréchal de Villeroy.* Paris, 1806.

COMBES, François, *La Princesse des Ursins. Essai sur sa Vie et son Caractère politique.* Paris, 1806.

COURCY, Marquis de, *L'Espagne après la Paix d'Utrecht, 1713–15.* Paris, 1891.

COURCY, Marquis de, *Renonciation des Bourbons au Trône de France.* Paris, 1889.

DANGEAU, Marquis de, *Journal, avec les additions inédites du Duc de Saint-Simon.* Ed. Soulié et Dussieux. Paris, 1860. 19 vols.

DUCLOS, ed. Collin, *Mémoires secrètes sur la Règne de Louis XIV.* Paris, 1808. 2 vols.

GEFFROY, A., *Lettres inédites de la Princesse des Ursins.* Paris, 1859.

GEFFROY, A., *Madame de Maintenon d'après sa Correspondance authentique.* Paris, 1887. 2 vols.

GEFFROY, A., *Fragments d'une Notice sur la Vie et le rôle politique de Madame des Ursins.* Paris, 1858.

HÉNAULT, Le Président, *Mémoires.* Paris, 1911.

HILL, Constance, *Story of the Princesse des Ursins in Spain.* London, 1899.

BIBLIOGRAPHY

HIPPEAU, C., *Lettres inédites de la Princesse des Ursins.* Paris, 1862.

LAVALLÉE, *Correspondance générale de Madame de Maintenon.* Paris, 1865. 4 vols.

LOUVILLE, *Mémoires secrètes sur l'établissement de la Maison de Bourbon en Espagne. Extraits de la Correspondance du Marquis de Louville.* Paris, 1818. 2 vols.

MASSON, G., *Lettres inédites de la Princesse des Ursins au Maréchal de Tessé.* Paris, 1879.

MILLOT, L'Abbé, *Mémoires politiques et militaires pour servir à l'Histoire de Louis XIV. (Mémoires du Duc de Noailles).* Maestricht, 1777. 4 vols.

SAINT-SIMON, Duc de, *Mémoires,* ed. Boislisle (" Les Grands Ecrivains de France "). Paris, 1889. 34 vols. (Not yet completed.)

SAINT-SIMON, Duc de, ed. Delloye. Paris, 1840. 40 vols.

SAN PHÉLIPE, *Mémoires du Marquis de San Phélipe pour servir à l'Histoire d'Espagne sous la Règne de Philippe V.* Traduits par le Chevalier de Maudave.

TAILLANDIER, *Madame Saint-René, la Princesse des Ursins.* Paris, 1926.

TRÉMOÏLLE, Duc de la, *Madame des Ursins et la Succession d'Espagne.* Nantes, 1902. 6 vols.

APPENDIX

CHRONOLOGICAL TABLE OF EVENTS IN THE LIFE OF THE PRINCESS DES URSINS

THE following table has no pretension to be complete as regards public events concerning the War of Succession which are incorporated as forming the background to the life of the Princess.

1642. Birth of the Princess.
1659. Marries Adrien-Blaise de Talleyrand, Prince de Chalais.
1663. The Prince de Chalais, menaced with the Bastille for fighting a duel, flies to Spain. The Princess follows him.
1670. The Prince and Princesse de Chalais leave Madrid for Rome. The Prince dies at Mestre near Venice.
1673. *Sept. and Oct.* Through Cardinal Nidhardt the Princess offers her services to the Emperor of Germany and demands to be made Princess of the Empire. The outbreak of hostilities between France and Germany puts a stop to her pretensions.
    At the recommendation of Cardinal d'Estrées, Louis XIV. appoints her secret agent at the Papal Court to further the Bourbon succession to the Spanish throne.
1675. *March.* Marries the Duke of Bracciano.
1676. Is in Rome working for the Bourbon succession.
1677. Is separated from her husband and living in the Convent of the Holy Sacrament at Montmartre.
1682. 11 *Nov.* Is in Paris where she marries by proxy her younger sister Louise-Angélique to the Duke Antonio Lanti delle Rovere.
1683. *Feb.* Returns to Rome with her sister the Duchess Lanti.
1685. Is living in Rome with her husband.
1687. 28 *Jan.* Creditors seize her husband's property and she leaves for Paris, where she remains till 1695.
1688. *Aug.* The Duke of Bracciano goes over to Austria and returns to Louis XIV. the Order of the Saint-Esprit. Louis transfers his pension of ten thousand francs to his wife.
1689. The Abbé de la Trémoïlle joins his sister in Rome in the autumn.
1690. Is in Paris but through her agents working in Rome to obtain a pension from the wreckage of her husband's fortune.
1691. Is present at a banquet given by Louis at Versailles.

TABLE OF EVENTS 425

1692. *Feb.* Applies for the post of *dame d'honneur* to the Duchesse de Chartres which she later refuses.

April. Is at Versailles with the Court and accompanies it to Marly.

June. Is at Saint-Germain assisting at the confinement of the Queen, Mary of Modena, wife of James II. of England.

1693. *Jan.* Is in semi-disgrace at Court for having refused the post of *dame d'honneur* to the Duchesse de Chartres and retires to Paris where she takes to live with her two nieces, Mademoiselle de Royan and Mademoiselle de Cosnac.

1695. *Dec.* The Duke of Bracciano adopts Don Livio Odescalchi as heir and she goes to Rome to oppose it.

Don Livio buys Bracciano and the Duke takes the title of Prince Orsini or des Ursins.

The Princess begins a lawsuit against Don Livio for having extorted his adoption. Begins a lawsuit against the Jesuits concerning her husband's property.

1696. *April to Oct.* Is in Rome with her husband.

1697. *March.* Gains her lawsuit against Don Livio.

Aug. Quarrels with Cardinal de Bouillon, now French Ambassador at the Papal Court.

Helps to arrange the marriage of the Duke of Burgundy with the Princess of Savoy.

7 *Dec.* Marriage of the Duke of Burgundy with the Princess Marie-Adelaide of Savoy.

1698. *April.* Death of the Duke of Bracciano.

25 *Nov.* The Duchess Lanti dies of cancer in Paris.

1700. *May.* Cardinal de Bouillon is recalled and exiled.

1 *Nov.* Charles II., King of Spain, dies, leaving a testament in favour of Philippe d'Anjou, grandson of Louis XIV.

16 *Nov.* Louis accepts the crown of Spain for his grandson.

5 *Dec.* Philippe V. leaves France for Spain.

27 *Dec.* The Princess demands to be appointed to conduct the Princess Marie-Louise-Gabrielle of Savoy, proposed as his wife, from Turin to Madrid.

The War of Spanish Succession begins with the Declaration of War by Austria, on France and Spain, in January 1701

1701. *Jan.* Declaration of war by Austria, on France and Spain.

March. Louis XIV. excites the suspicions of England and Holland by replacing the Spanish garrisons in the fortresses of the Spanish Netherlands with French.

20 *June.* The Princess receives the official appointment to conduct the Queen of Spain to Madrid.

4 *Sept.* Prince Eugène of Savoy-Carignan invades Lombardy and defeats the French and Spanish armies at Carpi and Chiari.

1701. 7 *Sept.* England, Holland and Austria sign a treaty of alliance against France and Spain.
11 *Sept.* Marriage by proxy at Turin of Philippe V. to the Princess of Savoy. The Court takes up its residence at Barcelona.

1702. 8 *April.* Philippe V. leaves for Italy to take command of his troops and appoints the Queen Regent.
April. The Queen and Princess leave for Saragossa.
17 *April.* Philippe arrives in Naples.
April. The Princess is officially appointed Camarera Mayor.
25 *April.* The Queen as Regent opens the Cortes at Saragossa.
June. Philippe V. joins the Duc de Vendôme in Lombardy.
30 *June.* Official entry of the Queen and Princess into Madrid.
15 *Aug.* Battle of Luzzara in which both sides claim the victory.
22 *Oct.* The English and Dutch destroy the Franco-Spanish fleet in the Bay of Vigo, laden with gold from the Indies.

1703. 17 *Jan.* Philippe returns to Madrid accompanied by the new ambassador, the Cardinal d'Estrées, and his nephew the Abbé d'Estrées.
Jan. Cardinal Porto-Carrero resigns his post as Prime Minister.
Jan. Quarrels begin between the Princess and the d'Estrées.
21 *Jan.* The Princess resigns her post of Camarera Mayor.
9 *Feb.* Louis accepts her resignation.
8 *March.* The Queen begs Louis to allow her to remain.
18 *March.* Louis consents on condition that she is reconciled to the d'Estrées.
March. Official reconciliation between her and the d'Estrées.
April. Quarrels again break out between her and the d'Estrées.
July. Cardinal d'Estrées is recalled and his nephew the Abbé appointed ambassador in his place.
20 *Sept.* The Elector of Bavaria defeats the Allies at Hochstadt.
10 *Oct.* Cardinal d'Estrées leaves Spain for France.
Oct. The Duke of Savoy allies himself definitely with Austria.
The Archduke Charles, son of the Emperor Leopold of Germany, marches on Spain at the head of Austrian troops.
Quarrels recommence between the Princess and the Abbé d'Estrées.
Dec. The Princess opens the Abbé's official letters and sends copy with annotations to her brother, the Marquis de Noirmoutier, to give to Torcy. Louis is furious and decides her recall.

1704. *Jan.* Louis, emboldened by a year of comparative success, sends an army to join that of the Elector of Bavaria with the intention of marching on Vienna.

TABLE OF EVENTS 427

1704. 4 *March.* Philippe joins his army in Aragon.
19 *March.* The Princess is recalled as well as the Abbé d'Estrées.
11 *April.* The Princess leaves Madrid for Alcala where she remains for five weeks.
May. The Duc de Gramont is appointed ambassador in Spain.
18 *July.* The Princess leaves Pau for Toulouse.
24 *July.* Gibraltar taken by the English.
Aug. The Princess arrives in Toulouse where she has permission to remain.
13 *Aug.* Marlborough and Prince Eugène defeat the French and Bavarians at Blenheim with a loss of 30,000 men. Hochstadt is retaken and the Elector loses his states.
Aug. Orry is recalled.
Oct. The Queen begs Madame de Maintenon to intercede with Louis for the Princess's return.
18 *Nov.* Louis consents to her return.
Dec. The Maréchal de Tessé, appointed generalissimo of the French troops in Spain, goes to Toulouse to announce her return.
8 *Dec.* She leaves for Paris.

1705. 4 *Jan.* The Princess arrives in Paris.
11 *Jan.* She is received by Louis and Madame de Maintenon at Versailles.
12 *Jan.* Is received by Madame de Maintenon.
13 *Jan.* Is again received by Louis and Madame de Maintenon.
14 *Jan.* Louis decides her return to Spain.
5 *Feb.* The King of Spain sends an envoy officially to thank Louis for her return.
19 *Feb to* 29 *April.* Is at Marly with the Court.
21 *March.* Gramont is recalled.
30 *March.* Amelot is appointed ambassador in his place. Orry is reinstated as Minister of Finance.
5 *May.* Death of the Emperor Leopold who is succeeded by his son Joseph.
15 *June.* The Princess takes leave of Louis and Madame de Maintenon at Versailles.
16 *June.* Louis increases her pension by ten thousand francs and creates her brother, the Marquis de Noirmoutier, duke.
She leaves Paris for Madrid.
5 *July.* Reaches Bordeaux.
4 *Aug.* Arrives in Madrid.
Oct. Catalonia acknowledges the Archduke Charles as King of Spain, and he takes up his residence in Barcelona.

1706. 10 *April.* The Duc de Vendôme defeats the Imperialists at Calcinato near Brescia.
May. The Archduke marches on Madrid.

1706. *May.* The Abbé de la Trémoïlle is made Cardinal.
May. The Pope recognises the Archduke as King of Spain.
23 *May.* Marlborough defeats the French at Ramillies.
June. Flight of the Queen and Princess to Burgos.
2 *July.* The Archduke is proclaimed King as Charles III.
5 *July.* The Queen and Princess arrive in Burgos.
7 *Sept.* Prince Eugène defeats the French under La Feuillade, Marsin and the Duc d'Orléans at Turin and they are forced to evacuate Italy.
Oct. Philippe returns to Madrid.
25 *Oct.* The Queen and Princess return to Madrid.
Oct. The Queen-Dowager is exiled to Bayonne.

1707. 18 *April.* The Duc d'Orléans, appointed generalissimo of the combined French and Spanish armies, arrives in Madrid.
25 *April.* The Duke of Berwick defeats the Portuguese at Almanza.
Aug. The Duke of Savoy at the head of Austrian troops besieges Toulon but is forced to retreat by the Maréchal de Tessé.
25 *Aug.* Birth of the Prince of the Asturias, to whom the Princess is appointed *gouvernante*.
13 *Oct.* The Duc d'Orléans takes Lerida.
8 *Dec.* Baptism of the Prince of the Asturias.
Dec. The Duc d'Orléans returns to France.

1708. *Feb.* The Duc d'Orléans returns to Spain for his second campaign.
May. The French under Vendôme take Ghent and Bruges.
July. The Duc d'Orléans takes Tortosa.
11 *July.* Marlborough and Prince Eugène defeat the French at Oudenarde.
Aug. Louis urges Philippe to abdicate. He refuses.
Nov. Louis renews his efforts to make Philippe abdicate. He refuses.
Nov. The Duc d'Orléans returns to France.
8 *Dec.* Lille surrenders to the Allies and Ghent and Bruges are retaken.

1709. Hardest winter on record.
April. The Princess expels all French from posts in Court and Government.
April. Louis again urges Philippe to abdicate. He refuses.
April. Oath of fealty to the Prince of the Asturias.
30 *April.* In consequence of Louis' reproaches the Princess resigns her post.
June. Discovery of the Duc d'Orléans' conspiracy against Philippe, and arrest of Regnault and Flotte.
27 *June.* Tournai is besieged by the Allies.

TABLE OF EVENTS 429

1709. *June.* Louis makes overtures of peace to the Allies but their exactions are too excessive to be acceptable.
June. He menaces to withdraw his troops from Spain if Philippe will not abdicate.
2 *July.* Premature birth of another prince who dies a week later (9 July).
July. Amelot is recalled and replaced in the embassy by Blécourt.
18 *July.* The Princess insists on resigning her post.
Aug. Disgrace of the Duc d'Orléans for his conspiracy in Spain.
Aug. Bergeyck begins his attacks to force the Princess to leave Spain.
Aug. Bezons abandons Fort Balaguer to the enemy.
2 *Sept.* Philippe leaves for Balaguer and appoints the Queen Regent.
3 *Sept.* Tournai capitulates.
9 *Sept.* At the Queen's prayer the Princess consents to remain on condition that she retires from affairs.
11 *Sept.* Marlborough and Prince Eugène defeat the French at Malplaquet.
Sept. Bergeyck renews his attacks and she again insists on leaving.
The Queen begs Louis to forbid her.
14 *Sept.* Death of Cardinal Porto-Carrero.
15 *Sept.* Philippe makes secret overtures to England and Holland for a separate peace.
Oct. At the Queen's request Philippe bestows on the Princess the Duchy of Limbourg in the Netherlands.

1710. *Jan.* The Allies prepare for a fresh campaign.
2 *March.* The Princess again insists on leaving Spain.
March. She sends d'Aubigny to The Hague as her agent to obtain the Allies' guarantee to her sovereignty and to buy and furnish the Château of Chanteloup near Amboise.
17 *March.* Louis sends her an official order to remain in Spain.
April. Philippe joins the armies in Aragon and appoints the Queen Regent.
14 *April.* Mysterious arrest of the Duc de Medina-Cœli who is imprisoned for life in the fortress of Segovia.
April and May. Louis makes fresh overtures for peace, but the Allies' exactions force him to withdraw his plenipotentiaries.
26 *June.* Marlborough captures Douai.
27 *July.* Defeat of the Spanish at Saragossa.
1 *Aug.* The Queen as Regent begs Louis to send the Duc de Vendôme as generalissimo, to which he consents.
26 *Aug.* Marlborough takes Béthune.
Sept. Vendôme, accompanied by Alberoni, arrives in Spain.

1710. 9 *Sept.* Flight of the Queen and Princess to Valladolid.
Sept. Entry of the Archduke Charles into Madrid as Charles III.
Sept. Through the Duc de Noailles Louis again urges Philippe to abdicate. He refuses.
20 *Sept.* Vendôme takes command of the armies.
Oct. The Queen and Princess retire to Vittoria for safety.
3 *Dec.* Vendôme, having cleared Toledo of the enemy, escorts Philippe to Madrid where they make a triumphal entry.
9 *Dec.* Accompanied by Philippe, Vendôme marches in pursuit of the Archduke and defeats the English at Brihuega in Castile.
10 *Dec.* Vendôme defeats the Allies at Villaviciosa.
Dec. Vendôme and the Princess receive the title of Altesse of Spain.

1711. 3 *Jan.* Saragossa retaken by Vendôme.
Jan. Girone retaken by Noailles.
Feb. Balaguer retaken.
Feb. The Queen and Princess join Philippe at Saragossa.
Feb. Vendôme begins preparations for the siege of Barcelona.
March. The Coalition shows signs of breaking up.
April. The Queen falls ill.
15 *April.* The Dauphin, Philippe's father, dies of smallpox.
17 *April.* The Emperor Joseph dies of the smallpox and is succeeded by the Archduke Charles.
April. England withdraws from the Coalition.
June. The Queen, partially recovered, goes with the Princess for change of air to Corella.
22 *June.* Louis urges Philippe to make peace by ceding his foreign possessions.
7 *July.* Philippe and the Queen ask Louis to demand of the Elector of Bavaria the Duchy of Limbourg for the Princess.
Aug. The Elector objects.
5 *Aug.* Louis sends as ambassador to Madrid the Marquis de Bonnac with the mission to force Philippe to sign peace with Holland.
4 *Sept.* Bonnac arrives at Corella.
20 *Sept.* Philippe signs the deed of donation of the Duchy of Limbourg to the Princess.
28 *Sept.* In consequence of the Elector's objections he signs another deed bestowing on her the towns of Fauquemont, Dalheim and Rolduc instead of Limbourg.
Oct. The Archduke Charles is elected emperor.
Dec. The Elector of Bavaria and the Princess sign a treaty in which the former promises to cede her the Comté of Durbuy in the Netherlands.
Dec. Disgrace of the Duke of Marlborough.

1712. 12 *Feb.* Death of the Dauphine, sister of the Queen.
18 *Feb.* Death of the Dauphin, Philippe's brother.

TABLE OF EVENTS 431

1712. 8 *March.* Death of the Duc de Bretagne, their son.

9 *April.* In consequence of these deaths the Allies exact Philippe's renunciation of his rights to the throne of France and threaten a renewal of the war in case of refusal.

18 *April.* Louis insists on his choosing between France and Spain under penalty of signing a separate peace with the Allies.

22 *April.* Philippe consents to renounce his rights to the throne of France on condition that Gibraltar and his Italian states be restored to him and Limbourg assured to the Princess.

7 *May.* Austria claiming the whole of the Spanish Netherlands, Limbourg is refused.

May. England proposes that he retain his rights to the throne of France, cede Spain and the Indies to the Duke of Savoy, and reign as King of Sicily over his restored Italian states and those of the Duke of Savoy.

18 *May.* Louis, delighted, instructs Bonnac to force Philippe to accept this proposal.

29 *May.* Philippe refuses.

June. The British under the Duke of Ormond withdraw their troops from the Netherlands.

5 *June.* The Princess marries her niece, Mademoiselle Lanti, to the Duc d'Havré.

7 *June.* Birth of a prince, Don Philippe.

10 *June.* Death of the Duc de Vendôme at Vinaros.

8 *July.* Philippe officially renounces his rights to the throne of France.

24 *July.* Villars defeats the Allies at Denain and retakes Douai and Bouchain.

Sept. The Princess leaves for Bagnères for a three months' cure.

Oct. Orry visits her at Bagnères.

Dec. The Princess returns to Madrid.

1713. 31 *Jan.* Orry returns to Spain under pretext of a short visit. Is appointed Veedor or Minister of Finance.

April. Philippe, pressed and menaced by Louis, authorises him to act in his name with the Allies.

17 *April.* Louis signs peace with England, Prussia, Portugal, and Holland, and exacts Philippe's signature which he has guaranteed. Philippe refuses.

April. The Elector of Bavaria, having received only Luxembourg, refuses to cede to the Princess the Comté of Durbuy.

June. Queen Anne guarantees the Princess's sovereignty.

22 *July.* Villars captures Landau.

July. Catalonia, evacuated by the Austrians, refuses to acknowledge Philippe as king. The siege of Barcelona is decided and Louis promises to send troops on condition that peace is signed with Holland.

1713. *Aug.* Philippe refuses to sign peace with Holland till the Princess's sovereignty is assured and Louis refuses his troops.
Sept. The Duke of Savoy is recognised King of Sicily.
Oct. Louis sends as ambassador to Madrid the Marquis de Brancas with instructions to force Philippe to sign peace with Holland and the Princess to renounce her claim to the sovereignty.
11 *Nov.* The Queen falls dangerously ill.
21 *Nov.* Villars captures Freibourg.
23 *Nov.* The Queen is delivered of another son, Don Ferdinand, afterwards Ferdinand VI.

1714. 1 *Jan.* The Queen grows worse.
15 *Jan.* Philippe begs Louis to send the physician Helvétius.
11 *Feb.* Helvétius arrives and declares her state hopeless.
14 *Feb.* At nine o'clock a.m. the Queen dies. The King is taken to the Palace of Medina-Cœli and the Princess follows with the three princes.
7 *March.* Louis signs a treaty of peace with Austria at Rastadt.
March. At Philippe's request Brancas is recalled.
29 *March.* The Princess proposes the marriage of Philippe with the Princess of Parma.
31 *March.* Brancas leaves for France.
March. The Cardinal del Giudice is sent as ambassador to Versailles.
4 *May.* Death of the Duc de Berry.
17 *May.* Philippe finally consents to sign peace with Holland, and Louis dispatches Berwick at the head of an army for the siege of Barcelona.
May. Philippe bestows on the Princess, subject to the reduction of Barcelona, the principality of Cardone in Catalonia.
May. Philippe and the Princess leave the Palace of Medina-Cœli, which is to be prepared for the new Queen, and go to the Pardo.
May. The Princess recalls d'Aubigny from the Peace Conference and sends the Baron de Câpres in his place.
23 *June.* The Prince de Chalais announces to Louis, Philippe's decision to marry the Princess of Parma.
July. The Cardinal Acquaviva demands the hand of the Princess of Parma for the King of Spain.
1 *Aug.* Death of Queen Anne.
20 *Aug.* Louis gives his consent to the marriage to the Duke of Parma.
Aug. D'Aubigny returns to Spain.
15 *Sept.* Marriage by proxy of Philippe V. with the Princess of Parma.
22 *Sept.* The new Queen leaves Parma for Spain.
30 *Nov.* Meeting of the new Queen and the Queen-Dowager at Pau.

TABLE OF EVENTS 433

1714. 11 *Dec.* The new Queen arrives at Pampeluna, where Alberoni is awaiting her.

23 *Dec.* Meeting of the Queen and Princess at Jadraque. The Queen expels her with insults and forces her to depart, guarded, at eleven o'clock at night.

24 *Dec.* Second marriage of Philippe V. with Elisabeth Farnese.

25 *Dec.* The King and Queen of Spain return to Madrid.

1715. 14 *Jan.* The Princess, expelled from Spain, arrives at Saint-Jean-de-Luz where she awaits permission to go to Versailles.

21 *Jan.* Louis and Madame de Maintenon express their condolences. Torcy in Louis' name summons her to Versailles.

4 *Feb.* She arrives in Bordeaux.

13 *Feb.* She arrives at Poitiers.

24 *Feb.* She arrives in Paris at the house of her brother the Duc de Noirmoutier and sends to Versailles to know when she will be received.

Feb. Orry is expelled from Spain.

March. The Cardinal del Giudice is made First Minister and governor of the princes.

27 *March.* Louis and Madame de Maintenon receive the Princess.

19 *April.* Louis increases her pension by twenty thousand francs.

April. D'Aubigny returns to France.

April. The Princess decides to settle in Holland.

May. Holland objecting she decides to settle in Rome.

May. The Prince of Cellamare is appointed ambassador to Versailles.

May. Reconciliation between Philippe and the Duc d'Orléans. Regnault and Flotte are set at liberty.

June. The Cardinal de la Trémoïlle dissuades the Princess from settling in Rome and she decides to go to Avignon.

6 *Aug.* She bids farewell to Louis and Madame de Maintenon at Versailles.

14 *Aug.* Leaves Paris accompanied by her nephews Chalais and Lanti on her way to Avignon.

1 *Sept.* Death of Louis XIV.

Sept. The Princess receives the news of his death while at Lyons, and instead of continuing her journey to Avignon takes the road to Chambéry. She sends to ask the King of Sicily for permission to pass the winter at Chambéry which he refuses.

Sept. She demands the official protection of the Duc d'Orléans, now Regent of France.

22 *Oct.* Announces her decision to settle in Genoa.

19 *Nov.* The Regent accords her his protection.

Nov. Is settled at Sestri near Genoa.

1716. *April.* Hires a palace in Genoa and settles there temporarily.
1717. *April.* Cardinal del Giudice, expelled from Spain, arrives in Genoa and asks permission to visit the Princess. She refuses.

July. Alberoni receives the cardinal's hat.

Aug. The Prince de Chalais receives permission to return to Spain.

1718. *April.* Philippe sends his ambassador to accord the Princess his protection preparatory to her return to favour.

Sept. Alberoni shows signs of desiring her recall to Spain.

Dec. Discovery of Cellamare's conspiracy against the Regent and consequent rupture of relations between France and Spain.

Dec. Forced to choose between France and Spain the Princess throws in her lot with France.

1719. 5 *March.* The Prince de Chalais returns from Rome and the Princess refuses to allow him to return to Spain.

15 *April.* Death of Madame de Maintenon at Saint-Cyr.

30 *May.* The Princess hires the Palazzo Daddi in Rome.

1720. *Jan.* Death of the Cardinal de la Trémoïlle in Rome.

April. The Princess together with her brother the Duc de Noirmoutier sells the Island of Noirmoutier to the Regent for one million francs.

Aug. The Princess leaves Genoa for Rome and remains at Bagnaia till the great heats are over.

1721. *Jan.* The Princess sells her palace in the Piazza Navone to the Sieur Angelini of Parma.

She settles in Rome and attaches herself to the Court of the Pretender.

1722. 1 *Dec.* The Princess is taken ill with nephritic pains.

5 *Dec.* Death of the Princess des Ursins at the age of eighty.

INDEX

Acquaviva, Cardinal, 327, 330, 334, 336
Albergotti, 328
Alberoni, Giulio, 250-2, 281, 303, 309, 310-14, 315-16, 319-21, 322, 327, 330, 333, 337-40, 344-6, 347, 351, 353-5, 357, 358-9, 361, 362, 363, 368, 372, 376, 387, 402-3, 406, 411, 419
Albert, Comte d', 330
Almanza, Battle of, 207
Amelot, 165, 177, 187, 188, 193, 213, 219, 220, 222, 223, 231, 249, 261, 373
Anjou, Duc d', afterwards Dauphin and Louis XV., 275, 276, 279, 307
Archduke Charles, afterwards Emperor, 44, 186, 187, 191, 192, 210, 223, 253, 254, 256, 260, 273, 278, 287, 305, 307, 329
Armstrong, Edward, 351
Asturias, Prince of the, 202, 203, 253, 263, 403
Aubigny, d', 27, 32, 111, 121, 123, 125, 130-1, 132, 133, 137, 245, 265, 267, 272, 288, 322-6, 341, 374-6, 388-9

Balaguer, Battle of, 233, 259
Balbazés, Marquis de los, 332, 333, 334, 337
Barcelona, Siege of, 260, 328
Bavaria, Elector of, 266-8, 271, 286
Beaumelle, La, 8, note 1
Beauvillier, Duc de, 47, 66, 103
Bergeyck, Comte de, 224, 231-2, 236, 238, 240, 244, 245, 246, 305, 325
Berry, Duc de, 52, 277, 284, 307
Berry, Duchesse de, 378, 380

Berwick, Duke of, 37, 40, 141-2, 191, 207, 306, 319, 328
Bezons, Comte de, 214, 217, 218, 228, 233, 234
Blécourt, Marquis de, 60, 92, 93, 231, 235
Blenheim, Battle of, 186
Boislisle, vii
Bonnac, Marquis de, 261-3, 274, 277, 279, 290
Bouillon, Cardinal de, 12, 17, 19-20, 21, 36-41
Bourgeois, 312, note 1
Bourke, Colonel or Chevalier de, 274, 322
Bracciano, Duchess of. *See* Ursins
Bracciano, Duke of, 20-22, 24, 28, 29, 34, 35, 36
Brancas, Marquis de, 288-91, 292, 294, 295, 296, 298-300, 305, 306-7, 362
Bretagne, Duc de, 275
Breteuil, Baron de, 361
Burgundy, Duchess of, 36, 52, 67, 68, 69, 101, 155, 228, 230, 274-5, 294
Burgundy, Duke of, 52, 210, 275

Camarera Mayor, 56-7
Câpres, Baron de, 265, 325
Cardone, 360
Caylus, Comtesse de, 7, 385, 395
Cellamare, Prince of, 311, 387, 405, 411, 413
Chalais, Prince de (husband of Princess), 6, 7, 8, 9
Chalais, Prince de (nephew of Princess), 276, 297, 312, 313, 314, 349, 357, 358, 359, 367, 374, 386, 394, 411, 414
Chalais, Princesse de. *See* Ursins
Charles II., King of Spain, 18, 44

Combes, vii
Cosnac, Mlle. de, 32, 33, 158
Coulanges, Marquis de, 26
Courcy, Marquis de, 204, 421
Coutlet, 399, 408, 409, 411, 414

Dangeau, Marquis de, 29, note 1, 71, 72, 151, 157, 163, 164, 178, 283, 287, 288, 293, 298, 340, 353, 378, 381, 387, 391, 394, 411, 415
Dauphin, 47, 59, 220, 228, 230, 260
Desgranges, 334, 335, 327
Dubois, Cardinal, 414, 415
Duclos, 331, 406

Elisabeth Farnese, Queen of Spain, 252, 303, 311–16, 320, 322, 327–40, 341–55, 357–64, 374, 375, 378, 383, 386, 402–7
Emperor Charles. *See* Archduke Charles
Emperor Joseph, 260
Estrées, Abbé d': coadjutor with Cardinal in embassy, 106; character, 106; intrigues with Louville against Princess, 107, 108; insolence to Princess, 109; quarrels with her, 111–13; reconciliation, 119; appointed Ambassador, 127; fresh intrigues against Princess, 131–7; Princess opens his letter, 134; is recalled by Louis, 140; recapitulation of quarrel, 141, 145
Estrées, Cardinal d': proposes Princess to Louis as secret agent, 14; portrait and character, 17, 18; intrigues for her marriage with Duke of Bracciano, 21; helps to marry her sister, 25; amours with her sister, 26; appointed Ambassador to Spain, 105–7; arrogance towards Princess, 109, 110, 112, 113; reconciliation, 119; insolence to Princess, 123; letter of abuse to Louis, 124; is recalled by Louis, 126, 127; cordial reception by Louis, 139; recapitulation of quarrel with Princess, 145; calumniates her to Louis, 150
Eugène, Prince, 83, 99, 191, 210, 225, 237, 248

Fenélon, 38
Flotte, 214, 217–20, 387

Geffroy, vii, viii, 20, 27, note 1
Girone, Battle of, 259
Giudice, Cardinal, 306, 307, 318, 329–30, 363, 387, 403–4, 409–10, 419
Gramont, Duc de, 105, 147–9, 156, 157, 165, 169–76, 239, 324
Grignan, Comte de, 334
Grimaldo, 360, 404, 409

Harcourt, Duc d', 50, 58, 105, 131
Helvétius, 293–4, 300
Hénault, Président, 301–2, 322, 347–8
Hocquart, 350, 374
Huxelles, Maréchal d', 399, 400

James Stuart, the Pretender, 418
Janson, Cardinal de, 35

Lanti, Don Alessandro, 349, 357, 358, 359, 367, 368, 369, 374, 377, 386, 394, 411, 417, 418
Lanti, Duchess Angélique, 25–8, 32, 40, note 2
Lanti, Mlle. (Duchesse d'Havré), 280–1, 374
Leopold II. of Germany, 8, 12, 18, 44
Lerida, Battle of, 208
Livio, Don (Odescalchi), 34, 35, 36, 40, 41, 42
Loire, Sieur de la, 349, 374
Louis XIV.: claim to throne of Spain, 18; approves Princess's marriage, 21; etiquette at Versailles, 25; quarrel with Innocent XI., 28; kindness to Princess, 29, 30; her attraction for him, 31, 32; mission to Bouillon concerning Fenélon, 38; anger against Bouillon, 39; intrigues for crown of

INDEX

Louis XIV.—*continued*
Spain, 44–6; hesitation to accept, 47; accepts for Duc d'Anjou, 48; instructions to Philippe V., 49–51; tyranny towards Duke of Savoy, 54; hesitates to appoint Princess Camarera Mayor, 58; letter to Blécourt, 60; regulates Queen's journey to Spain, 71, 73; approval of Princess, 79, 80; arrogant attitude towards Europe, 82–3; orders Queen to remain in Spain, 84; objects to her Regency, 86, 87; orders her to go to Madrid, 91; orders her to dress à l'espagnole, 93; approval of Princess, 97; severity towards Philippe, 102; appoints Cardinal d'Estrées Ambassador, 165; anger at Princess's quarrel with d'Estrées, 113; dismisses her, 113; letter to Philippe, 114; withdraws dismissal, 118; letter to Princess, 120; recalls Cardinal d'Estrées, 126; decides to recall Princess, 139; recalls Abbé d'Estrées, 140; recalls Princess, 140; letter to Philippe, 140; letter to Queen, 141; refuses to hear Princess's justification, 144; favour to Gramont, 148; anger against Princess and Orry, 150, 151; letter to Philippe, 150; letter to Queen (not sent), 151; allows Princess to come to Versailles, 152; secret correspondence with Gramont, 152–4, 158, 159, 171, 173; sends Tessé to Toulouse, 157; sends Torcy to welcome Princess, 158; cordiality to Princess, 160–4; renews her appointment, 165; letter to Philippe, 165; attracted by Princess, 167, 168; anger at Philippe's duplicity, 172; touched by his feeble letter, 173; recalls Gramont, 173; despotism towards Spain, 185, 186; treachery to Philippe, 188; failure of policy regarding Spain, 189, 190; desires peace, 205; decides to abandon Spain, 212; urges Philippe to abdicate, 212; makes overtures of peace, 217; accused of share in d'Orléans' conspiracy to depose Philippe, 218; letter to Philippe on the subject, 219; anger against Duc d'Orléans, 220, 221; rupture with Philippe, 224; fresh overtures of peace, 225; closes negotiations, 225; anger of his subjects, 226; the "Pater" of 1709, 226; allows troops to remain in Spain, 228; insists on Philippe's abdication, 229; accepts Princess's resignation, 230; recalls Amelot and sends Blécourt, 231; orders Princess to remain, 244; renews overtures for peace, 248; sends Noailles to urge Philippe to abdicate, 252–3, 255; sends Bonnac to urge Philippe to sign peace with Austria, 261–2; death of his heirs, 275; orders Philippe to renounce rights to French succession, 277; urges him to accept Sicily and the French succession and renounce Spain, 279; signs separate peace with England and Holland, 284–5; tells Princess that her sovereignty is assured, 285; refuses troops for siege of Barcelona, 288; signs Peace of Rastadt, 305; anger at Philippe's marriage with Princess of Parma, 314; official consent, 328; instructions to envoy, 328; receives news of Princess's disgrace, 364; cold reception of Princess, 381; increases her pension, 382; protects her against Spain, 383–4, 393; last reception of her, 343; death, 396

Louville, Marquis de, 14, 52, 53, 65, 66–7, 68, 69, 73, 75, 76, 77, 79, 87, 99, 100–4, 105, 107, 110–11, 113, 117–19, 121, 123, 124–7, 129, 131, 132, 137

Luzzara, Battle of, 208

Macanez, 323, 329
Madame (Princess Palatine), 63, 72, 205, 221, 370–1, 378, 380, 383, 413
Maintenon, Madame de: guest at Hôtel d'Albret, 7; arranges marriage of Duchesse de Chartres, 30; attributed jealousy of Princess, 31, 32, 59, 166, 168; hesitation for acceptance of Spanish crown, 47, 48; proposes Princess to conduct Queen of Spain, 58; relations with Princess, 59; criticism of Philippe V., 64; her solid judgment, 82; reproves Queen of Spain, 152; intercedes for Princess, 152, 155; receives Princess, 160, 161, 164; cordiality to Princess, 162; weekly correspondence organised, 162; policy towards Spain, 163; desires Princess's return to Spain, 167; objects to send troops, 186, 195, 196, 211, 216; coldness to Princess, 187; touched at sale of Crown jewels, 194, note 2; reproves Princess, 211; her unpopularity in France, 226; hostility to Princess, 227, 239, 240; recriminations, 234; dread of Princess's return, 236, 239, 242; desire for peace, 239; letters to Villeroy, 239, 241, 242, 243; persuades Louis to withdraw Princess's recall, 243; letter to Princess, 244, 245; rebukes Princess, 256; kind letter to Princess, 259; letter to her about sovereignty, 268; joy at prospects of peace, 273; rebukes Princess for refusing peace, 287, 305, 307, 315; coldness at her disgrace, 370, 380, 381, 382, 392, 394; sharp criticism of Princess, 408; death, 415; appreciation, 416
Malplaquet, Battle of, 237
Marchand, Père le, 275–6, 316
Marlborough, Duke of, 186, 191, 210, 225, 237, 248, 260, 309, 329
Marsin, Comte de, 60, 80, 84, 85, 87, 99, 105, 107

Mascara, Abbé, 385, 393
Medina-Cœli, Duc de, 175, 223, 246
Monaco, Prince of, 41, 72, 331
Montrevel, Maréchal de, 372, 377

Nidhardt, Cardinal, 8, 11, 13, 14
Noailles, Duc de (Comte d'Ayen), 191, 250, 252–3, 255, 256, 259
Noailles, Maréchal de, 55
Noailles, Maréchale de, 55, 58, 59, 134, 135, 144, 146, 157
Noirmoutier, Duc de, 4, 134, 164, 168, 296, 372–3, 379, 387, 391, 417

Orléans, Duc d', 191, 205–9, 213–16, 217, 230, 246, 275–6, 306, 309, 316–19, 361–2, 378–9, 380, 387, 388, 398, 399, 400, 413, 417
Orléans, Duchesse d', 378, 380
Orry, 93, 128–30, 132, 139, 150, 165, 187, 282–3, 289, 291, 298, 299, 300, 305, 306, 307, 322, 323, 324, 325, 333, 358–9, 361, 362–4, 372, 386, 387, 412
Ossone, Duc d', 284, 286, 288, 324
Oudenarde, Battle of, 210

Pachau, 322, 367
Palma, Comtesse de, 85, 92, 93, 94
Parma, Duke of, 310, 312, 327, 330, 332, 334, 355
Philippe V.: Louis accepts for him the crown of Spain, 48; arrival in Spain, 52–3; his depression, 53; character, 63–7; meeting with Queen, 74; marriage, 75; quarrel with Queen, 76–8; leaves Spain for Italy, 87; arrival in Naples, 99; meeting with Duke of Savoy, 100 – 3; courage at Luzzara, 104–5; his idleness, 113; reproved by Louis, 114; replies sharply, 115; is defended by Queen, 117; dependence on Queen, 122, 125; severely reproved by Louis, 140; despair at Princess's return,

INDEX 439

Philippe V.—*continued*
169; treachery towards her, 171–3; described by Gramont, 174; meeting with Princess, 181; takes command of army in Aragon, 188; his indifference, 189; flight before Austrians, 193; return to Madrid, 197; jealousy of Philippe d'Orléans, 206; feebleness and flaccidity, 212, 224, 226; refuses to abdicate, 212; accuses Duc d'Orléans, 219; letter to Louis, 220; overtures to Holland, 224; with his army in Aragon, 249; defeat at Saragossa, 253; refuses to abdicate, 255; brilliant reception in Madrid, 256; his bed of flags, 257; gives Limbourg to Princess, 267; aspires to succession of France, 276; consents to renounce rights, 278; refuses to renounce Spain for Sicily, 279, 280; refuses to sign peace with Holland, 287; retires to Palace of Medina - Cœli, 295; projects marriage with Princess of Parma, 313; anger at her delay, 335, 336, 338; awaits her at Guadalayara, 342; receives news of Princess's expulsion, 357; marriage, 359; letter to Princess, 359, 360; refuses to protect Princess, 383; abuses her to Cellamare, 387; summary of later life, 402–7

Pighetti, 352
Piombino, Princesse de, 332, 337
Popoli, Duc de, 287, 311, 404
Porto - Carrero, Cardinal, 12; pressure on Charles II., 45; character and portrait, 45–6; friendship for Princess, 56; intercedes with Louis in her favour, 58; official adviser to the Queen, 87; Princess's coldness, 92; ignored by Queen and Princess, 97, 98; jealousy of d'Estrées, 107, 111; resigns presidency of *despacho*, 112; Louis writes excuses, 114; intrigues to force him to resign, 121; Gramont's praise of him, 175; takes part with Portuguese against Philippe, 192, 193; return to Madrid, 197; death, 197, 198; officiates at baptism of Prince of the Asturias, 224

Préhac, 144
Puységur, 139

Queen Anne, 235, 260, 273, 284, 286, 309, 324, 329
Queen of Spain: marriage arranged between her and Philippe V., 54; character and education, 67–70; marriage by proxy with Philippe V., 71; journey to Spain, 72–80; second marriage and bridal supper, 75; scandal of bridal night, 76–8; growing confidence in Princess, 78–9; popularity in Barcelona, 80; Louis orders her to remain in Spain, 84; affection for Princess, 86; appointed Regent, 87; arrival in Madrid, 88; life in Madrid, 90; presides at *despacho*, 95–6; letter to Philippe, 105; meeting with Philippe, 109; defends Princess against d'Estrées, 113, 116, 140; refutes d'Estrées' accusations of Philippe, 115, 117; Philippe's dependence on her, 122; Louville's hatred of her, 125, 132, 133; demands d'Estrées' recall, 126; anger against the d'Estrées, 142; kindness to Princess, 143; protests against her recall, 147; anger with Gramont, 148; defends Princess energetically, 149; insists on her return, 151–4; joy at her return, 169; Gramont's abuse of her, 174; meeting with Princess, 181; appointed regent, 188; flight to Burgos, 193; letter to Madame de Maintenon, 194; letter to Amelot, 195; meets Philippe at Segovia, 196; pregnancy officially declared, 199; birth of Prince of the Asturias,

Queen of Spain—*continued*
202; sorrow at father's treachery, 211; letter to him, 211; refuses to allow Philippe to abdicate, 226; is again *enceinte*, 228; begs Louis to leave troops, 228; birth of deformed child, 229; refuses to allow Princess to leave, 232; appointed regent, 234; occupations of her day, 235; begs Madame de Maintenon to force Princess to remain, 238; demands sovereignty for Princess, 239; letter to Louis asking him to send Vendôme, 249; flight to Valladolid, 253; refuses to abdicate, 255; takes refuge in Vittoria, 255; joins Philippe at Saragossa, 259; falls ill and goes to Corella, 261; letter to Madame de Maintenon about Princess's sovereignty, 267; is again *enceinte*, 274; birth of Don Philippe, 280; birth of Don Ferdinand and subsequent illness, 292; death, 294

Queen-Dowager (Marie-Anne of Bavaria - Neubourg), 44, 45, 50, 180, 192-3, 197, 207, 252, 283, 330, 335-7, 338, 361, 363, 368, 377, 378, 386

Queen-Regent (wife of Charles II.), 8, 11, 13, 18

Ramillies, Battle of, 191
Rastadt, Peace of, 305
Regnault, 214, 217-20, 387
Robinet, Le Père, 302, 403

Saint-Aignan, Duc de, 335, 346-7, 360, 378, 384
Saint-Simon, Duc de, vii, 6, 15, 31, 33, 59, 65, 136-8, 159, 161, 166, 213, 221, 245, 265, 281, 287, 296-8, 302-3, 306, 316-19, 343-4, 361-2, 379-80, 382, 393-4, 397, 405-6, 416, 417, 419
San Phélipe, 192, 233, 254, 411, 412
Saragossa, Battle of, 253

Savoy, Duke of, 54, 58, 67, 100-3, 133, 191, 204, 211, 212, 216, 279, 284, 293, note 2, 307, 397, 398
Secret correspondence with Gramont, 152-4, 158, 159, 169-70, 173
Spanish Court, 89-90
Stahrembourg, 259
Stanhope, General, 214, 218
Succession, War of Spanish, 18, 82-3, 99, 186-7, 191, 204

Taillandier, 27, note 1
Tessé, Maréchal de, 131, 149, 155-6, 187, 212
Torcy, Marquis de, 47, 55, 60, 77, 80, 93, 103, 114, 122, 124, 133, 134, 158, 225, 248, 261, 268, 278, 288, 323, 325, 327, 329, 371, 375, 390, 396, 399
Tortosa, Battle of, 214
Tournai, Siege of, 237
Trémoïlle, Abbé de la (afterwards Cardinal), 5, 30, 40, 373, 390-1, 400, 416, 417

Ursins, Princess des: birth, ancestry and relatives, 3-4; marriage with Chalais, 6; follows husband to Spain, 8; success in Spain, 8; leaves for Italy, 8; widowhood in Rome, 9; Princess of the Empire, 9-14; secret agent of Louis XIV., 14, 19; Saint-Simon's description, 15-16; existing portraits, 15, note 1; d'Estrées and Bouillon her lovers, 19; their intrigue to marry her to Duke of Bracciano, 20; marriage with him, 21; life in Rome, 22; disagreement with husband, 24; goes to Paris, 24; returns to Rome, 27; goes again to Paris, 28; solicits post of *dame d'honneur* to Duchesse de Chartres, 30; refuses it, 30; takes house in Paris, 32; returns to Rome, 34; Duke sells Bracciano and takes name of Orsini, 35; quarrels with Bouillon, 37-41; death of Duke,

INDEX 441

Ursins, Princess des—*continued*
36; her poverty, 42; demands to accompany Queen of Spain, 55; relations with Madame de Maintenon, 59; appointed to accompany Queen, 60; influence over Queen, 68; journey with Queen, 72–5; intrigues for Queen's Regency, 85; leaves Barcelona for Saragossa, 88; receives title of Camarera Mayor, 88; war on etiquette, 89–93; entry with Queen into Madrid, 93; difficulties of government, 94; Louville's antagonism, 103, 104; counterplot against d'Estrées, 107, 112, 113; quarrels with d'Estrées, 109; Louville's abuse, 110, 111; resigns post, 113–15; pseudo-reconciliation with d'Estrées, 118, 119; preparations for departure, 120, 121; quarrels recommence, 122–4; independence of Versailles, 128; quarrels with Abbé d'Estrées, 131–7; recalled by Louis, 140; leaves Madrid, 143; journey to France, 143–6; Louis' anger, 150–2; receives permission to go to Versailles, 155; arrival in Paris, 157; cordial reception by Louis, 159; triumph at Marly and Versailles, 160–2; relations with Madame de Maintenon, 162, 164; reinstated in post, 165; hesitates to return, 165; leaves for Madrid, 178; journey to Spain, 179; triumphant reception, 181; political outlook, 185–7; assumes government, 187; attacks Louis, 188–90; discouragement, 192; flight to Burgos, 193; letter to Madame de Maintenon, 195; raises funds for campaign, 196; return to Madrid, 197; drastic measures, 197; renewed optimism, 199; preparations for birth of Prince, 201–2; stands sponsor for Prince, 203; appreciation by Marquis de Courcy, 204; suspicions of Duc d'Orléans, 206; conflict with him, 208; refuses to allow Philippe to abdicate, 212, 217; intrigue against d'Orléans, 213, 214; suspicions of d'Orléans increased, 217; arrests his agents, 218; culminating point of power, 222; expels French from posts, 223; anger with Philippe, 226; opposition to Madame de Maintenon, 227, 229; resigns post, 229–32; retires to Aranjuez, 232; attacks Louis and Madame de Maintenon, 233; decides to remain in Spain, but in retirement, 235; insolent letter to Madame de Maintenon, 237; intrigues to force her to resign, 238; her sovereignty, 239; accuses Louis of duplicity, 240; demands money due, 240; insists on leaving Spain, 244; letters to Villeroy, 244, 246; consents to remain, 245; orders arrest of Medina-Cœli, 246, 247; demands Vendôme as generalissimo, 249; flight to Valladolid, 253; goes to Vittoria, 255; is made Altesse of Spain, 257; goes to Saragossa, 259; goes to Corella, 261; sovereignty in the Netherlands, 264–72, 278; superintends decoration of Buen Retiro, 274; accuses d'Orléans of attempt to poison Philippe, 275; goes to Bagnères, 282; refuses to allow Philippe to sign peace, 286; retires with Philippe to Palace of Medina-Cœli, 295; her so-called sequestration of Philippe and project of marriage, 296–304; sends Giudice to Versailles, 306; persuades Philippe to revoke renunciation of rights to France, 308; plans marriage of Philippe with Princess of Parma, 312; intrigues of Saint-Simon and d'Orléans to eject her from Spain, 316–19; recalls d'Aubigny, 325; recalls Giudice, 330; misgivings as to

Ursins, Princess des—*continued*
Princess of Parma, 330, 341; goes to meet her at Jadraque, 342; her expulsion, 343–53; tragic journey to the frontier, 356–8, 365; letters to Versailles, 365–7; favourable answers, 370; journey to Paris, 377; cold reception at Versailles, 381–5; expulsion from France, 390; indecision as to retreat, 390–3; leaves Paris, 396; indecision continues, 397–9; demands Regent's protection, 399; settles in Genoa, 408; hopes of renewed favour in Spain, 410–12; her hopes realised, 412; forced to choose between France and Spain, decides on France, 414; returns to Rome, 417; attaches herself to Court of Pretender, 418–20; death, 420; appreciation by Marquis de Courcy, 421

Vendôme, Duc de, 83, 99, 104, 191, 210, 249–53, 255–7, 260, 280–2, 310
Villars, Maréchal de, 237
Villaviciosa, Battle of, 257, 259
Villeroy, Maréchal de, 191, 239, 241, 242, 243, 244, 246, 372

www.ingramcontent.com/pod-product-compliance
Lightning Source LLC
Chambersburg PA
CBHW031305150426
43191CB00005B/90